THE AMERICAN ECONOMY

INCOME, WEALTH,
AND WANT

STANLEY LEBERGOTT

THE AMERICAN ECONOMY

INCOME, WEALTH,

AND WANT

PRINCETON UNIVERSITY PRESS

Copyright © 1976 by Princeton University Press

Published by Princeton University Press, Princeton, New Jersey
In the United Kingdom: Princeton University Press, Guildford, Surrey

ALL RIGHTS RESERVED

Library of Congress Cataloging in Publication data will be found on
the last printed page of this book

This book has been composed in Linotype Janson

Printed in the United States of America
by Princeton University Press, Princeton, New Jersey

PREFACE

I

The essays in Part I look at public policy aspects of how income and wealth are distributed in the U.S. They accept one fundamental fact: Herbert Hoover is dead. So are Friedrich Engels, Lloyd George, Franklin Roosevelt, and George Humphrey. Each did his bit to shape today's U.S. economy. But that economy is not Manchester in 1844 nor Ohio in 1910. It is not even the U.S. of the 1950's. Policies that were joyfully proposed to shape the distribution of income in the 1930's, or belligerently resisted in the 1950's, deserve reconsideration rather than habitual applause.

Some essays in Part I puzzle over the philosophical-ethical premises that underlie key public policies. Others inquire into the logic of our usual ways for analyzing poverty and its correlates. Nearly all pull together new facts. (Technical detail, however, has been banished to footnotes and appendices.)

Economies create wealth to satiate want. But want has many mouths. Want is that specter of starvation which has menaced mankind since Eden. Want is also desire—for joy without limit, for satisfaction without sure origin. And want is "wont" as well: tradition combined with covetousness and advertising to create what Marx labeled "the fetishism of commodities."

What economic system has succeeded in satiating this endless catalog of wants? The resulting tension between goal and result leads to the questions addressed in Part I. "Can American capitalism end poverty?" reviews facts heralded by conservatives—which, however, point to a conclusion urged by radicals. "On confiscation" and "The concentration of wealth" review policies urged by liberals—which turn out to imply conclusions dear to conservatives. "Are the rich getting richer?" is discussed on the basis of new data, which involve sex as much as economics. Propo-

v

sals to end poverty now frequently invoke "per capita income" and "scientific minimum budget standards." Yet inquiry reveals that such measures rest on hidden premises that should appall those who urge such programs. Finally, new data are arrayed, and a more realistic judgment sought, on such stormy topics as: how much "upward mobility"? what links "poverty and starvation" "discrimination and poverty"?

II

Part II provides new data for analysis by radical and reactionary alike. To these data one may apply Saki's remark: "The story has no moral. If it points out an evil, at any rate it suggests no remedy." Five data sets are newly estimated: (1) Wealth distribution in 1970. (Hitherto we have had only one complete wealth distribution, for 1962. Moreover, that was inconsistent with the income distributions customarily used in the study of poverty.) (2) Income distribution in 1900. (We lack an adequate income distribution for any year prior to the Great Depression, or for any high employment peacetime year, 1900–1945.) (3) White and non-white income distributions, 1900–1970. (We have lacked separate distributions for any year prior to 1945.) New estimates are provided (4) for key items that advanced the standard of living since 1900; plus (5) detail for spending since 1900 on 33 categories of those varied services which dominate the "post-industrial world."

I am agreeably indebted to Wesleyan University for its effective faculty research program, permitting Steven Leinwand to labor long and astutely over the numbers in Part II; and to Carl Kaysen and the Institute for Advanced Study for a generous continuum of space and time to work on these essays. My thanks also go to Simon Kuznets, who commented on the manuscript with his usual acuity; and to gracious library staffs at Wesleyan, Princeton, and the Institute for Advanced Study. Acknowledgment to many who helped with data appears at appropriate points in the text.

S.L.

CONTENTS

WEALTH AND WANT

CAN AMERICAN CAPITALISM
END POVERTY?

*"I am as poor as Job, My Lord, but not so
patient"*
—Sir John Falstaff

There exist eight reliable ways to increase poverty. The
United States now pursues seven of them. Should it continue
to do so, poverty in America will continue. Now it is
true that since 1936 the percent of American families below
the official OEO poverty line has been cut, from 56 percent
to less than 10 percent.[1] And with our trillion-dollar GNP
we have the wherewithal to cut that down to 1 percent
by next Sunday. But it may be impossible to end poverty
permanently without changing course on these seven ways.
Yet doing so could change American capitalism beyond
recognition.

We must begin from a truism: few Americans really
want to end poverty. Is that truism contradicted by the
strong speech of the young? by the Kennedy-Johnson poverty programs? or by the Nixon welfare program? Consider
the following. America could immediately end the blinding
poverty of India and Pakistan, if only it chose to do so.
How? Rather simply, by dividing up the incomes of the
three countries, share and share alike. By that single decisive
action we could guarantee those nations against starvation.
Naturally, U.S. incomes would have to fall, from about
$4,000 a person to $600.[2] How many Americans are prepared to take this step?

[1] Taking the official poverty line of $4,275 in 1972 prices as equiva-
lent to $1,250 in 1935–1936, and utilizing data from National Resources
Planning Board *Family Expenditures in the United States*, p. 1, one
can estimate 56% of American families below that figure in 1935–1936.

[2] The U.S., of course, cannot lay sole claim to such bias. Kuwait's
per capita income is more than 10 times as great as Jordan's. Japan's

There is an even easier tack. Thousands of Mexicans now drag out their lives in abysmal poverty. The U.S. could change that, and without giving away a single cent, merely by letting the poorest Mexicans enter the U.S. and earn higher incomes. How many Americans are ready to do so? In 1959 a major church synod called on its "members to pray and work . . . (to) eliminate blighting poverty."[3] One particular prayer they proposed was for an "annual reduction of the number of Mexican nationals imported for agricultural labor." Michael Harrington, champion of The Other America, has quoted approvingly the fierce opposition by a Mexican-American trade unionist to taking any such anti-poverty step.[4] Yet our 19th-century experience strongly suggests that conditions for many immigrants could be improved, with little or no unemployment, at the price of slowing the rise in U.S. wage rates.

I suggest, therefore, that most Americans are not interested in abolishing poverty, particularly the coarse and untidy kind that leads to agony, to starvation, and to death. Their concern is instead: Can poverty in America be abolished? Now what is "poverty in America"? Few of those who exhort on that subject can mean by poverty too small an income for a family to buy enough calories and vitamins, plus a place to live, heat and water, some clothing and medical care. If that were their criterion, then only the poor would be discussing the problem. For the typical *poverty* family today can buy as much food as the *average*

---

is almost 20 times as great as Indonesia's. A combined average for Kuwait and Jordan would cut Kuwait's $3,137 down to $935, raising Jordan's from $254. Indonesia's $89 would rise to $795, cutting Japan's $1,658 to the same figure. Data from United Nations, *Statistical Yearbook, 1972*, Tables 19 and 187. Results would be still more striking for post-boycott years.

[3] 87th Congress, 1st Sess., *Extension of the Mexican Farm Labor Program*, p. 154

[4] Michael Harrington, *The Other America* (1969), p. 50.

U.S. worker could buy in our grandparents' time—plus better housing, more clothing, furniture, heat, and medical care.[5]

Sensitive Americans are therefore exercised about something quite beyond ending starvation, providing a place to live, medical care, etc. They are measuring not by any absolute standard, but by a relative one. Poverty is what afflicts Americans who fall behind today's here-and-now standard of living. As Harrington puts it: "The American poor are not poor . . . in the sixteenth century; they are poor here and now in the United States. They are dispossessed in terms of what the rest of the nation enjoys. . . . They watch the movies and read the magazines of affluent Americans, and these tell them that they are internal exiles. . . ."[6] In an economy that bursts with productivity, that produces so fantastic a volume and variety of goods,

[5] The 1971 low income (poverty) line for a 4-person family was $3,968 (*1972 Statistical Abstract*, p. 329). In 1971 the average income of all families with income below $4,000 was $2,443, and for 4-person (husband, wife) families was $2,400. (Census, *Current Population Reports*, P-60, No. 85, using data from Tables A–4, 1, and 19). The retail price index for 1971 relative to 1900 was 488. (Using 1900–1960 data from Lebergott, *Manpower in Economic Growth* [1964], Table A-17 linked to *U.S. Statistical Abstract, 1972*, p. 348, the resultant $492 figure for 1900 is far above the $375 annual earnings of all employees in 1900, as well as the $441 for non-farm employees. For 1900 data see *Manpower in Economic Growth*, pp. 523–524.

[6] *Op.cit*, p. 178. We should not imply that the concept of relative poverty waited for discovery by sensitive souls in the 20th century. The founder of the dismal aspects of economics wrote: "Almost all poverty is relative" (T. R. Malthus, *An Essay on the Principle of Population* [1803], Bk. III, Ch. v). And Frank Knight argued with great cogency, some decades ago, that men's wants involve "power, prestige, relative status, and winning versus losing in any form of contest." (Cf. his *On the History and Method of Economics* [1956], pp. 241, 261.) He adds: "the goods and services produced, traded and consumed do not correspond to final or real wants. These are largely not individual, as the theory requires, but inhere in social relations, such as 'keeping up with the Joneses,' and 'getting ahead of the Joneses'; or they are symbolic, even deliberately set up, as

poverty comes to be defined as relative to what the typical American enjoys.

I

The first way to increase poverty in the United States follows fairly obviously from that definition—namely, to increase the standard of living. Raise the consumption level of the typical American and you create poverty. Raise it again and you create more poverty. When Ford invented the auto he created poverty. When Zworykin invented TV he created more poverty. Raise the standard decade after decade and you create more and more (relative) poverty even while you are wiping out the old-fashioned (starvation) kind of poverty. "Solely as a result of growing affluence, a society will elevate its notions of what constitutes poverty." (So reports the President's Commission on Income Maintenance.)[7]

Try as hard as it can, a nation cannot succeed in creating relative poverty unless it does three things.

(1) It must use its workers more and more productively. And we know that American capitalism has become more productive with every passing decade.

(2) It must pay those workers more and more. And we know the real wage of American workers has tripled since 1900.[8]

(3) Finally, it must prevent its workers from relapsing into the expenditure pattern of St. Simeon Stylites, or even of Thoreau. If American workers had devoted their increased incomes to the worship of God and nature, the "relative deprivation" kind of poverty could not have arisen.

---

in play, to make action interesting and yield the feeling of success, thus reversing the means-end relation assumed in economics" (p. 261).

[7] President's Commission on Income Maintenance, *Report* (1964), p. 523.

[8] *Manpower in Economic Growth* (1964), p. 523. Real wages more than tripled from 1900 to 1960, and rose still further by 1973.

But when higher wages are earned, and then devoted to raising the workers' standard of living, more poverty is produced. The narrow-visioned worker of 1900 might have been satisfied to ride a trolley to work. But his grandson—even his hippie grandson—requires a car or motorcycle. (Indeed 41 percent of our officially "poor" families own automobiles. Half a million own more than one car.)[9] The 1900 housewife used a tin washboard. The 1975 housewife requires an electric washing machine and dryer (in the local laundromat or at home).

In 1900 15 percent of U.S. families had flush toilets; today 86 percent of our poor families do. In 1900 3 percent had electricity; today 99 percent of our poor do. In 1900 1 percent had central heating; today 62 percent of the poor do. In 1900 18 percent of our families had refrigeration, ice refrigeration; today 99 percent of our poor have refrigerators, virtually all mechanical. (Table 1.)[10]

[9] Bureau of the Census, *Current Population Reports*, Series, P-65, No. 33, p. 5, indicates that as of July 1970 38% of those in the $0 to $3,000 income category had 1 car, 3.8% had 2, and 0.7% had 3 or more. With 11.1 million families in that category, the figures indicate that about ½ million had 2 or more cars.

"Ownership of an automobile, which previously had made New Mexico families ineligible for welfare, will no longer be considered one of the factors in determining qualification for financial assistance, the state Health and Services Board ruled this week. . . . The state's welfare policy had been that possession of a car with a book value of $750 or more made families ineligible, except when the head of the family was disabled, or used the vehicle for transportation to work." (*New York Times*, November 5, 1972.)

[10] Estimates for 1900 based on the author's *The American Economy*, Ch. 15. Estimates for poor families in 1970 come from: for running water, the 1970 Census of Housing, *Structural Characteristics of the Housing Inventory*, HC (7)–4, Table a-10. Fewer than 4% of these family units had more than 1.01 persons per room (using data for those with incomes under $4,000). 1970 Census of Population, *Family Composition*, PC (2)–4A, Table 23, indicates that 1.8% of families with incomes under $4,000 had lodgers, compared to 23% for all families in 1900. Flush toilet and heating data from PC–2 (9A), *Low-Income Population*, Table 36.

TABLE 1

LEVEL OF LIVING

ALL FAMILIES (1900) AND POOR FAMILIES (1970)

	All Families in 1900[a]	Poor Families in 1970[b]
Percent of Families Having		
Flush toilet	15%	99+%
Running water	24 Δ	92
Central heating	1	58
One (or fewer) persons per room	48	96
Electricity	3	99
Refrigeration	18 (ice)	99 (mechanical)
Automobiles	1*	41

[a] Data marked * are for 1910; and Δ, for 1890.

[b] Family incomes under $4,000.

The average American today works a third fewer hours than did his 1900 peer.[11] Yet beyond food, rent, and clothing, his family spends ten times as much on all the other comforts and necessities of life as did the 1900 family (allowing for price change).[12]

These spectacular increases could not, I would argue, have been achieved without heroic contributions by Madison Avenue. Keeping up with the Joneses—as they keep up with the TV ads—has become our normal way of life. Spirit and salesmanship, greed plus gab, produces a distinctive, an American, perspective. It was, after all, two American Marxists, Baran and Sweezy, who classified as poor

[11] Lebergott, *The American Economy*, Ch. 15.

[12] Commissioner of Labor Statistics, *Eighteenth Annual Report, 1903, Cost of Living and Retail Prices of Food* (1904), p. 592, indicates that the survey families averaged $124 a year for "sundries"—all items but food, rent, clothing, fuel, and light. In 1970 the comparable items in personal consumption expenditures aggregated $330.5 billions, or $5,256 per household. (*1972 Statistical Abstract*, pp. 39, 315). Deflating this figure by the implicit PCE deflator–Kendrick–BEA (BEA, *Long Term Economic Growth, 1860–1970* [1973], pp. 222–223)–gives $1,121.

those American families who could not regularly buy cans of "room air freshener."[13] What homage to the advertising profession! What testimony to its success in expanding the American standard of necessity! Another American Marxist has written a text on *Radical Political Economy*, which devotes several pages to the $11-billion-yearly "waste" in "useless automobile model changes," excoriating such "fraudulent and trivial newness."[14] But just as we nod in agreement, he goes on to define poverty. And he stipulates $5,900 a year as a "low absolute level of income"—in part because workers with such an income must "run a used car or use public transport."[15] How terribly vulgar the used car! And how unfortunate those $10,000-income families who do not drive cars just off the show-room floor!

All this is not meant to ignore the ancient, decisive, and ubiquitous presence of envy. Long before the U.S.A. even existed, La Bruyere observed of another culture: "Life is brief and monotonous. It passes away in desire."

But surely one inference follows. If (a) American industry speeds productivity, and pays higher wages, and if (b) advertising helps persuade American workers, to buy new, more elegant products, then American capitalism must continue to generate poverty.

The upward trend in the reference standard makes the end of poverty an ever-retreating goal, and an unachievable one. Such a trend is assumed by the major radical thinkers

---

[13] Paul Baran and Paul Sweezy, *Monopoly Capital* (1966), pp. 288-289. They define poverty "as the condition in which those members of a society live whose incomes are insufficient to cover what is for that society and at that time the subsistence minimum." All, therefore, turns on the definition of the subsistence minimum. They equate it with the BLS "modest but adequate" budget (p. 289). Examination of the BLS budget indicates that it includes the air freshener, replacement of a car at frequent intervals, and a variety of other items of interest, since they are not incorporated in the standard of living of many persons with considerably higher money incomes.

[14] Howard Sherman, *Radical Political Economy* (1972), p. 119.

[15] *Ibid.*, p. 50.

as well as by the liberal ones. Thus Lasalle's "iron and inexorable law" of wages, when read closely, proves to be a complete tautology: "the iron and inexorable law, according to which, under the domination of supply and demand, the average wages of labour remain always reduced to the bare subsistence which, according to the standard of living of a nation, is necessary for the maintenance of life and the reproduction of the species."[16] "Iron and inexorable law," "bare subsistence"—these clamorous and menacing phrases all push into insignificance the proviso: "according to the standard of living of a nation." But that tiny proviso renders meaningless the fearful threat of life on bread and water. For what determines that "standard of living"? Lasalle offers us no system for determining which forces are at work, nor how important any of them may be. That is equally true of official Marxism-Leninism.[17] They give the game away by admitting that "the standard" rises during the course of development.[18]

If we were discussing an economy where productivity and incomes never advanced, no such conclusion would follow. But the income of the American common man promises to continue advancing. Or if we imagined the unimaginable—a whole society rejecting the rising consumption of goods as a goal of life—no such conclusions would follow. But can we imagine this society agreeing

[16] His *Offene Antwortschreiben*, quoted by Edward Bernstein, *Ferdinand Lasalle* (1893), p. 123. The translation into English was by Eleanor Marx Aveling.

[17] O. S. Kuusinen, et al., *Fundamentals of Marxism-Leninism* (Moscow, 1961), p. 274. "The magnitude of wages comprises two elements: (a) . . . the means of subsistence that are absolutely necessary for the worker's existence, the maintenance of his ability to work and support his family and (b) historical, or social, which depends on the development of the vital needs and cultural requirements of the working class in a given country."

[18] Bernstein *op.cit.*, p. 135. Kuusinen, *op.cit.*, pp. 274–275, finds that "the movement of wages depends essentially on the class struggle" and that such struggle" can make its position easier."

with Thomas à Kempis that "Whatever . . . is essential to my peace cannot be the production of the world"?[19] Those who have seen America's poor families go from 0 percent with television to nearly 90 percent in two decades, the non-materialistic young go from 2 percent (?) consuming moderately expensive marijuana cigarettes to 30 percent (?) in two decades, or from buying 50 million phonograph records a year to 200 million, plus stereo sets, airplane rides, etc., would hardly anticipate any such unbelievable turnabout.[20] "The poor ye have always with you," therefore, seems a continuing description of American capitalism.

II

A second way to increase poverty is to allow older people to live apart from their children. Perhaps young people today enjoy such close rapport with their parents that they wish to spend their entire lives with them. But an older generation had no such aspiration. The passage of the Social Security Act in 1936 began the process by which the state gave older people pensions which they could spend as they chose. Many of them promptly decided to live apart from their children: they valued their privacy and comfort. (So did their children and grandchildren.) But this move automatically increased the number of poverty families. And as we continue to allow old people to use their social security checks for living in homes of their own, we continue

[19] Thomas à Kempis, *The Imitation of Christ*, XLVI.
[20] TV ownership data appear in *U.S. Statistical Abstract, 1971*, p. 487. The guesses for marijuana consumption are based on its apparent spread among jazz musicians beginning in the mid 1930's. Phonograph records: 1967 Census of Manufactures, Volume II, Part 3, P. 36D-27, shows about 375 million units produced in 1967. The *Annual Survey of Manufactures, 1951*, p. 92, records a 1947 value of manufacturers shipments figure of $105 million. Assuming a $2 manufacturers average price leads to a 50-million unit total. It is hardly likely that the 15–25-year-olds bought more than 20 of the 100 million records produced in 1947, or less than 200 of the 375 million in 1967.

to increase the number of poor families. Because when the old folks live with their children they are not in the poverty count (assuming they contribute a mere $601 dollars a year to family income).[21] But when they decide to live alone they join the poverty count—unless social security gives them three times as much money. The usual discussions of poverty set a zero value on the convenience that older people get from living their own lives (or from grandchildren living with only one set of overbearing oldsters). Hence the poverty estimators treat such expanded horizons and greater independence as increasing poverty.

But even that is not all. Pensions are pegged to the productivity of the economy in the years just before retirement. Suppose a man has been earning $3,000 a year. Over the next ten years the economy's productivity will probably advance by 30 percent—our long-run trend rate—and average incomes will do much the same. Hence even if a retiree continues to enjoy *exactly* the same goods and services as today, he will automatically drop below the relative poverty standard—merely because the economy has become more productive.

III

There is a third force: the Men's Liberation Front. The male attitude has been tellingly caricatured by V. S.

---

[21] The official poverty minima appear in *Current Population Reports*, P-60, No. 68, p. 11. The minimum rises by $636 (from $3,555 for a 4-person family to $4,191 for a 5-person family)—as would be true if a grandparent came to live with parents and two children. On the other hand, the minimum for a male one person non-farm family is set at $1,827.

Needless to add, not all Americans set high value on the chance for older people to live where they choose. Indeed a recent view of "poverty elimination" in China reports pensions, old people's homes, and adds: "The traditional Chinese family system, under which . . . old people remain within the family unit is also helpful in solving the familiar problem of the isolated, impoverished, individual." Cf. Lloyd Reynolds, "China as a Less Developed Economy," *American Economic Review* (June 1975), p. 427.

Naipaul: "On this island I was telling you about . . . they had this woman, pretty but malevolent. She make two-three children for me, and bam, you know what, she want to rush me into marriage."[22] Our national moral code includes the right of men to propagate children—and desert them. By doing so, of course, they increase poverty: mothers find it difficult to earn any income when they have young children. If they get a job, they must drop their work whenever the children fall ill. They therefore end up with less responsible jobs, at lower wage rates—and are paid for fewer hours. Is it surprising that the percent of families in poverty rises from 8 percent when the husband is present, to 32 percent when he is absent? For white families the rise is from 7 percent to 26 percent. For black families the rise is more than 30 percentage points, from 17 percent to 53 percent.[23] (Table 2 indicates how the sharp decline of low-income families with male heads has been seriously offset by the rise in Negro families with female heads.)[24a]

It is unclear why Women's Lib. has not proposed that men be required to assure, in advance, financial support for any children they may propagate. (That was, of course, one of the reasons for marriage in olden times.) Perhaps the genes of altruism are sex-linked. Or perhaps self-expression is a higher goal than child care. In any event, men remain free to abandon the emotional responsibility of children to the women, and financial responsibility to the taxpayers. Nearly 40 percent of all poor families with heads under 65 years would be removed from poverty if Men's Lib. were ended.[24]

[22] *A Flag on the Island* (1968), p. 175.

[23] 1970 Census of Population, *Low-Income Population*, Table 11.

[24a] The word "Negro" is used throughout (instead of Black) when we refer to reports, Census and other, using the former term.

[24] Of families with male heads aged under 64 years of age, 6.46% were in poverty. Substituting that rate for the 34.4% for female head families in that age interval gives a reduction of 1,547,000 families, or 38% of the 4,106,000 actually reported. Data are from *ibid.*, Table 10.

TABLE 2
Number of Low Income Families: 1959–1972
(000)

	NEGRO AND OTHER RACES		WHITE	
	Male Head	Female Head	Male Head	Female Head
1959	1,452	683	4,952	1,233
1960	1,425	703	4,863	1,252
1961	1,440	746	4,997	1,208
1962	1,368	804	4,657	1,230
1963	1,307	781	4,275	1,191
1964	1,205	697	4,133	1,125
1965	1,177	720	3,628	1,196
1966	993	685	3,070	1,036
1967	874	737	3,019	1,037
1968	697	734	2,595	1,021
1969	674	758	2,506	1,069
1970	703	851	2,606	1,102
1971	644	908	2,560	1,191
1972	611	1,023	2,306	1,135
1973	607	1,002	2,029	1,190
1974	573	1,054	2,185	1,297

Source: Census, Current Population Reports, P-60 series No. 81, Table 1; No. 99, Table 15.

IV

Paying old people not to work. Before Social Security old people simply had to work. In 1939 40 percent of men over 65 worked.[25] But by 1973 only 24 percent were at work, though jobs were easier to locate and real wages far more attractive.[26] Why so? It seems likely that the typical worker is quite ready to quit work after forty years of arduous and monotonous labor, and retire on social secur-

[25] 1940 Census of Population, *The Labor Force*, Vol. III, p. 19.
[26] Bureau of Labor Statistics, Special Labor Force Report, No. 152, "Changes in the Employment Situation in 1972," Table A-2.

ity. He sets a real value on leisure. But Harrington includes every older worker when he refers to "a misery that extends to 40 or 50 million people in the U.S. . . . that have remained impoverished in spite of increasing productivity and the welfare state."[27] Indeed, those over 65 make up the largest single age group in his figure—as they do in most estimates of poverty. But suppose Barry Goldwater had succeeded in abolishing social security. Many older people would still be at work instead of in retirement. Given their years of seniority and skill, they would almost certainly be earning incomes above the poverty level. Hence because social security induced them to stop working, and live on a lower money income, it induced them to join—indeed, to lead—the ranks of "those who have remained impoverished." But they are not impoverished "in spite of" the American capitalist "welfare state." They are in poverty because of it.

V

Raising our social standards. In the past many families kept out of poverty by sending their children to work. Senator Ralph Flanders has described how his father was "bound out" to work without pay.[28] He got only board and room. And his family, of course, received no income. But by reducing the mouths at the table, his work helped to keep the family out of poverty. Our moral standards have advanced mightily since then. In 1900 some 18 percent of all children (aged 10–15) worked.[29] Today very few do. We forbid families to use this method of getting out of

[27] Harrington, op.cit., p. 12.
[28] Ralph Flanders, Senator from Vermont (1961), p. 11.
[29] At the end of the 19th century, eight-year-old children ("brickies") worked in brickyards from 5 a.m. until 8 p.m. (Memorials of Alfred Marshall, p. 107). The poverty studies would count the loss of this group as a social loss—because they count the decline in incomes but do not allow in any way for the reduction in child labor. The 18% worker rate for U.S. children is from Manpower in Economic Growth, p. 53.

15

poverty. We find the moral advance worth the resultant increase in poverty.

Likewise, it used to be possible for a family to increase its income by taking lodgers. As recently as 1910 some 30 percent of the millions of foreign-born Americans crowded 3 (or more) persons into each sleeping room. Some 47 percent of all Polish immigrants lived under such conditions. And 39 percent of all Italians.[30] Today's housing codes forbid families to earn incomes by such crowding and doubling up. Indeed, ever stricter enforcement of such codes is urged by every housing and civil rights organization. Both these codes, and their stricter enforcement, prevent a decline in the number of American families in poverty. Is there an American alive who would want to reduce poverty by challenging these social standards?

VI

A sixth method for increasing poverty is to keep the children of the poor alive. Every major advance in public health work and medical care has cut our death rates. Of 100 babies born in 1850 only 64 percent lived to age 25 and went on to form their own families.[31] Today 94 percent live that long. But the rich already received relatively good care. Hence that tremendous advance surely benefited poor families far more than the rich. Now the poor had their turn. Hence more babies from poor families survived—to be heads of poor families in their turn. Americans rejected, and continue to reject, the older reality design in which the death rate kept down the poverty problem.

VII

A final force for increasing poverty is fecundity. "Alas," wrote England's Reverend Sydney Smith, of himself, "alas

[30] 61st Cong., 2nd Sess. S.D. 338, Report of the Immigration Commission, *Immigrants in Cities* (1911), Vol. I, p. 54.

[31] Ansley Coale and Marvin Zelnik, *New Estimates of Fertility and Population in the United States* (1963), pp. 170, 184.

16

how easily a priest begets children, and with what difficulty he provides for them."[32] If a $5,000 income is divided among a husband, wife, and two children, they escape the poverty count—either by official government standards or those of the National Welfare Rights Organization. But divide the same income among six children, and they cannot escape.

The faster Americans multiply their family size, and thereby divide their family income, the faster they create poverty. As the number of children per family increases from 2 to 9 or more, the proportion of families in poverty rises from 9 percent to 40 percent.[33] (Excluding aid to dependent children would make that rise still greater.) If parents objected to poverty as much as some publicists do, they would never have more than two children per family. There would then be about a million fewer American families in poverty. If Americans adopted the Irish solution after the great famine, they would marry later, expect that each of their fewer children would then be better off. But, as Diderot remarked, "Another child does not concern them: charity will take care of it. And then it is the only pleasure that costs nothing; one consoles oneself during the night for the costs and the calamities of the day."[34]

Our moral and religious principles—Catholic, Socialist, black militant—all declare that a man and wife may have any number of children. Hence anyone is free to move his family into the "poverty" group: by adding children.

[32] Nowell Smith, ed., *The Letters of Sydney Smith* (1953), I:413.

[33] 1970 Census, *Low Income Population* (PC 2-9A), Table 11, shows a rise from 8.6% for 2 children to 39.8% for 9+ children (no detail above 9+ is available). Applying the 8.6% rate for 2 child families to the total of 29,486,417 families with children gives us a family poverty count 940,000 smaller than the actual count.

In 1960 the rise from the 4-person to the 14-person family meant a rise from 17% to 74% in poverty. Cf. Office of Economic Opportunity, *Dimensions of Poverty* study. This unpublished study was based on a tabulation of 1960 census data, and provides estimates of the numbers "below the poverty cut off" in each state.

[34] Diderot, *Oeuvres*, ed. A. Billy (Pleiade), p. 490.

Our value system declares it desirable for the poor to have as many children as they please, however distraught some people may be by the resultant impact on the national poverty totals. Hence, even if every American worker were paid $10,000 a year we would still have poverty—among the families with five, six, or ten children.

WHAT may we say in conclusion? That most Americans do not want to abolish poverty because they accept certain moral values. These include the desirability of not sharing equally with foreigners; the freedom of men to desert their families and of older people to live apart from their children; and the coercive wisdom of the state to forbid persons to double up in their housing, and to forbid children to work.

But even if these attitudes disappeared we could not expect that poverty in America would vanish. For poverty, as defined by either Harrington, or by President Nixon's Income Maintenance Commission, is measured by a changing consumption standard. And the central drive of American capitalism involves changing that standard. Our oligopolies make their way by differentiating products: the poptop can replaces the now ancient Coke bottle, the refrigerator with ice-cube maker supersedes the one without, the fifth edition of the textbook replaces the fourth. *Rolling Stone* and the *New York Review of Books* replace *Colliers* and *Life*. *The New York Times* supersedes the *New York Tribune*. In competitive markets suppliers similarly jostle for the consumers' dollar. Organic rice and marijuana cigarettes struggle against the conventional kinds, and TV sets against movies. Supermarket variety overcomes small-store affability. Internists and psychoanalysts replace the general practitioner. The ebullient capitalist market process in the U.S. continues to cast up products perceived as more succulent. "If," in Milton's phrase, "all the world should in a pet of temperance feed on pulse, drink the clear stream and nothing wear but frieze," then demand would fail to match this supply. But in the U.S. even Zen Buddhists are capital-intensive meditators and require million-dollar airplanes to transport them to a suitable locus for thought.

Hence, so long as Americans harken to the songs that Madison Avenue sings, judging their well-being by the expenditure of others, and so long as American workers are paid enough so that they can buy more and more "goods," the inevitable awaits us: the more successfully American capitalism operates, the more surely will poverty remain among us. It is only fair to add that Communist workers seem as efficient, as productive, and as greedy, as capitalist workers. A Soviet economist recently reported "higher requirements" as more and more Russians discovered a "need to attend movies and theatres, listen to the radio."[35] More-

[35] The average wage in Moscow was 99 rubles when the price of a radio was 75 rubles. (*Problems of Economics*, December 1969, p. 71.) With this ratio the radio is limited in its spread, does not enter the "minimum standard of living," and therefore poverty is kept down. As the Soviet economy advances in productivity, however, the price of the radio can decline relative to the average wage; it then becomes a standard consumption item, and those families who do not have it then become "poor."

Soviet budget studies establish that total family outlays should average 205–210 rubles a month for "minimum material comfort." (*Problems of Economics*, July 1969, p. 54.) Family income required to achieve this is 150–160 rubles (*idem*), while the "social consumption fund" provides the difference. (In 1967 it amounted to 37 rubles (*Problems of Economics*, November 1969, p. 62.)

But by comparing the minimum budget of 206 rubles with the average wage of 103 rubles, and by adding 37 rubles for the social consumption fund, we find it clear that the *average* Soviet worker must be below the minimum budget line. (*Problems of Economics*, November 1969, p. 62.) Since it is unlikely that the official Russian poverty line would be set where the average worker would be in poverty, the solution appears in the statement that as a rule the "first worker" in the family is expected to provide 60% of family income and the second, 40% (PE, July 1969, p. 54). Bluntly put, this means that every wife is expected to be in the labor force as well as raising children. When Harrington "computes the social cost of progress," he notes that working wives mean "more money, and presumably, less poverty. Yet a tremendous growth in the number of working wives is an expensive way to increase income. It will be paid for

over, the Soviets have adopted advertising in recent years.[36] The same fate may therefore await Russian communism as well.

---

in terms of the impoverishment of home life, of children who receive less care, love and supervision. . . . It could mean that we have made an improvement in income statistics at the cost of hurting thousands and hundreds of thousands of children. If a person has more money but achieves this through mortgaging the future, who is to say that he or she is no longer poor? (*op.cit.*, p. 179.)

[33] Marshall Goldman, "Product Differentiation and Advertising," *Journal of Political Economy* (1960) 68:346–58. Cf. the extended discussion of the growth of advertising in Russia in Philip Hanson, *Advertising and Socialism* (1974).

ON CONFISCATION

Man's concern with inequality began in the Garden of Eden. According to our source (which may be biased), Eve first, and then Adam, became troubled by the unequal distribution of knowledge. As the years passed, however, man expressed sharper concern over inequalities in the distribution of income than in that of knowledge. A forceful attempt to cut down such inequality in the United States began with the 1913 income tax law. Tax rates have increased twenty-fold since then. But most Americans surely still believe that too many other Americans enjoy unconscionably high incomes. And both the ancient utilitarian theory and the important new maximin criterion (focussed on benefiting society's least advantaged members) seem to urge taxing the rich until the gap between them and poor is well down toward zero.[1]

It is worth speculating on the gains from simply confiscating the excess income of the rich. How much would be made available for redistribution? The question does not raise the rationale for progressive taxation. Nor does it deal with the complex issue of whether higher taxes could so halt the dynamic of capitalism that the poor as well as the rich might be worse off. The question is one of simple expediency for the first populist Secretary of the Treasury: how much could be gotten for the poor by confiscating the incomes of the rich?

[1] Cf. J. Rawls, "Some Reasons for the Maximin Criterion," *American Economic Review* (May 1974), p. 142. Other than incentive effects, as Arrow suggests, this would lead toward taxation to the point of equalization. K. Arrow, "Some Ordinalist Utilitarian Notes on Rawls Theory of Justice," *The Journal of Philosophy* (May 10, 1973), p. 259. Reference should also be made to Peter Wiles' fascinating lecture, "Revolution, Confiscation . . ." in his *Distribution of Income: East and West* (1974).

To tackle that question, we must first define "the rich." Existing studies—scientific, radical, or reactionary—usually fail to do so. We define a $25,000-a-year income as the limit, with the rich appearing in the lofty regions above that. That figure is chosen for two reasons. First is Roosevelt's statement, when he sought to limit incomes in World War II, that no man needed an income greater than $25,000. As a millionaire himself, and a leader of many with populist sympathies, he should have been able to strike a suitable mean. Secondly, "the rich" can hardly include more than a small percentage of the population. We have neither a scientific basis, nor a political determination, to decide how small that should be. But adopting a $25,000 cut-off would include only 4 percent of American family units, surely a small enough percentage.[2]

There might be an argument for a cut-off at $42,500. Unquestionably few Congressmen would believe that the taxpayer had made them rich by virtue of their $42,500 salary. But a $42,500 cut-off would include only 1 percent of the population. Putting the cut-off still higher—at $100,000 or $1 million—would, of course, include a still tinier percent of the population. Either of these higher cut-offs would provide far less for redistribution. We therefore carry through the discussion below on the basis of a $25,000+ figure for the rich.

I

How much, then, would confiscating the incomes of the rich provide in resources to assist the poor? The main conclusions can be set out very simply.[3]

---

[2] We use the phrase "family units" to describe what the census terms "families and unrelated individuals." Income data for these appear in Census, Current Population Reports, Series P-60, No. 85, *Money Income in 1971 of Families and Persons in the United States,* p. 28.

[3] Data derived from Appendix A, Table 1.

ON CONFISCATION

Confiscation: Net Returns for 1970

	billions
The rich (i.e. those with incomes $25,000 and over) receive	$90
If the state confiscated all their income above $25,000, they would then receive	53
The rich now pay taxes amounting to	42
After confiscation their lower income would only yield taxes amounting to	12
Confiscation would therefore net (90–53)–(42–12)	7

How would the rich react to a policy of confiscation? Would they, in the second year, continue to keep their assets in a form where they generated taxable incomes over $25,000? Let us suppose that they ceased to be able to buy ingenious legal and tax advice. Let us assume they placed no asset where it would cease to provide feathers to be plucked for the social purpose. If so $7 billion could be expected every year. (This $7 billion equals 1 percent of the annual income flow in the U.S.)[4]

II

Would such confiscation provide $7 billion a year *for the poor?* It obviously would—unless there were prior claimants. One remembers that the "peace dividend" (to be available for so many admirable purposes when intervention in Viet Nam ended) somehow disappeared. Would prior claimants also seize the confiscation dividend? History gives us two clues.

---

[4] To get on to the next point, dynamic impacts on the economy are ignored—such as the inevitable reduction in stock prices, the probable decline in new investment, etc. The 1970 AGI total ($632 billion) is rounded up to $700 for non-filers.

(1) The government of the United States spends over $300 billion a year.[5] Virtually every single one of those public dollars is devoted to social purposes defined as higher priority than adding to the incomes of the poor. Is there reason to believe that when confiscation increased that $300 billion by a further $7 billion an advance in altruism would occur? Government expenditures have increased almost twice as much (by $12½ billion a year) over the last two decades.[6] Yet, there have been few resonant claims that a shift in the altruism function has followed.

(2) When federal income tax rates began their climb, in 1931, tax rates for those with $25,000+ incomes ranged from 1 percent to 16 percent. That group now pays from 17 percent to 45 percent. As a result, the rich pay $16 billion dollars a year more now than they would at 1931 rates[7]. For what has that $16 billion been used? (a) One answer would be that it simply goes into the general coffers of the Treasury, and is disbursed proportionately among all federal spending. If so 3 percent—or ½ billion—of the $16 billion taken from the rich by increased taxation has gone to the poor.[8] (b) An alternative estimate would make the increase in federal spending on low income families since 1931 depend wholly on the increased taxation of the rich.[9] If so, $7 of the $16 billion taken from the rich was

[5] *1971 Statistical Abstract*, p. 398, gives these figures for 1969. More recent state and local data are not available, but Federal expenditures are obviously higher.

[6] *1971 Statistical Abstract*, p. 399.

[7] Rates from IRS, *Statistics of Income, 1946*, p. 211, *1970*, p. 7.

[8] Of $194 billions in federal expenditures for 1970, about $7 billions went in public assistance, social services, low and moderate income housing aids. The expenditures on health, education, and farming, whatever their goals, are chiefly spent on other than low-income families, and very little because they specifically aid low income families.

[9] Federal expenditures were $4 billion in 1931, of which $1 billion went for war-related purposes and almost none were specifically for the poor. (U.S. Department of Commerce, *The National Income*

used for the poor—and $9 billion went for other purposes. However, to accept assumption (b) is to accept its corollary: if whatever is given to the poor comes only from taxation of the rich, then most Americans give nothing at all in aid of the poor.

If the proceeds from confiscation were utilized as in (a), then poor families would get $12 apiece.[10] If according to assumption (b), they would get $350 apiece. That the gains to the poor from actually confiscating the incomes of the rich would be so remarkably trivial is the consequence of two facts:

(1) The rich are already taxed at above average rates. Hence confiscating their incomes also reduces the tax flow into the Treasury.

(2) Increased government taxation of the rich since 1931 has largely been diverted to purposes other than helping the poor. Over half a century's experience with income taxation can hardly be ignored in projecting what any mild further increase in federal taxes would be used for.

III

Why has so little of the sharply increased taxation of the rich been diverted to the poor? To answer that question we need one further income cut-off. To get it we take the $7,000 income figure of the National Welfare Rights Organization, used in various campaign proposals of Senator McGovern, to mark the poverty line.[11] Now if the rich

---

and Product Accounts of the United States, 1929–1965, Tables 3.1 and 3.9.) In fiscal 1970 they totalled $197 billion, of which $7 billion went for the poor and $106 billion for national defense, veterans and interest. (1970 data from *1971 Statistical Abstract*, p. 376.)

[10] For the estimate of the number of poor families, see section III below.

[11] The NWRO figure of $6,500 for 1971 is increased to $7,000 to allow for inflation since then. For the NWRO figure, cf. Bradley Schiller, *The Economics of Poverty and Discrimination* (1973).

get over $25,000 a year, and the poor less than $7,000, then about two-thirds of America's families fall into the interval between.[12]

If money is to be found for the poor (beyond the limited amount that could be confiscated from the rich), it must be taken from this great middle group. Who makes it up?

  54 percent of all laborers are in it
  76 percent of factory operatives and truck drivers
  84 percent of craftsmen
  76 percent of clerical
  84 percent of salaried professionals[13]

In this interval are to be found most liberal college teachers (and reactionary ones). So are most social workers, editorial writers, reporters, and union business agents.

Simmel once described the Tertius Gaudens: while two people are struggling over a valuable object, the third comes along and makes off with it.[14] The analogy is close. While the poor are hurling epithets at the rich, and occasionally trying to liberate their excess property, a middle-income group comes along and walks away with that excess. Their accomplishment—carried off in full view, legally, and calmly—seems hardly to have been noted by the two contestants.

IV

Confiscation of the rich would be a moral policy in the U.S. today, but not an expedient one. It is surely moral: we now take 32 percent of incomes over $25,000, while confiscation would demand 56 percent. It is hard to see 32 percent as a moral figure, and 56 percent an immoral one. But it does not appear particularly expedient. The rich

[12] Census, P-60, No. 85, Table 33, indicates that 64.9% of American families in 1971 had incomes in the range.

[13] *Idem.*

[14] Kurt Wolff, ed., *The Sociology of Georg Simmel* (1950), p. 154.

now have the nation in a bind—or vice versa: in acquiring their excessive incomes, the rich have been brought perilously close to providing $1 in taxes for every $1 in income they get. Sequestering their riches would, therefore, cancel that tax flow, give the Treasury little net advantage. We have estimated in Table 1 that they pay about 45 percent of their income in taxes. But that is merely the direct impact. A wise confiscation policy must consider indirect effects. As the rich dumped their corporate stocks, stock prices would fall. With $4 billion in capital gains now realized by the *non*-rich—mostly from corporate stock—a drop in share values would bring a consequent drop in taxes on such income.

V

This review of the returns from confiscating the incomes of the rich points up the empirical aspects of a social policy choice. Two quite different goals have been proposed for reshaping the U.S. income distribution. One goal is to minimize the income spread between rich and poor, or, in the older phrase, to "soak the rich." The other goal is to help the poor.

To reduce the spread between high and low incomes, the continued rise in income tax rates is an appropriate and effective route. The outer limit to such a rise would appear to be, e.g., total confiscation of all incomes above $25,000 a year. Now several Americans receive at least $5 million a year.[15] We may assume them sufficiently canny to survive on $25,000. The confiscatory tax could assuredly cut down by 99+ percent the income range from $0 to $5 million+—either by taxing the rich or by getting them to forsake their U.S. domicile.

If the goal were to help the poor, however, such action

---

[15] Internal Revenue Service, *Statistics of Income, Individuals 1970*, p. 271. Four individuals are reported as receiving $18.7 millions. These state data appear to be the most detailed published for the $1-million-plus income group.

27

would offer small advantage. It would provide a mere $12 a year in additional income to the poor (as estimated above). That estimate rests on the assumption that taxes simply flow into the general funds of the Treasury: taxes paid by the rich have never been earmarked for the poor. But even if they were so earmarked, they would provide only $350 a year to the poor. The rise in the cost of living during 1973 alone reduced a poverty-line income of $3,500 by that amount. It is, therefore, clear that a redistribution policy to benefit the poor significantly must dip far further into the income distribution. Actually confiscating the incomes of the rich would generate only $7 billion, while the incomes of the middle group amount to about $360 billions (after taxes).[16]

It does not appear obvious that this vast middle group is prepared to contribute much to the poor. At most they have, in the past, passed along to the poor the flow from increases in the taxation of the rich. They have therefore added little on their own. The middle class apparently has honored its father, its mother, and its checking account just as fervently as have the rich. In feudal days the tithe was contributed by all to the church, with the clergy then disbursing a suitable share to the poor. Today not a tithe but 37 percent of our national output is contributed to government, with less than 2 percent then passed along to the poor.[17]

---

[16] The gross income figure is derived from *Statistics of Income, Individual, 1970*, Table 4, as is that for the income of the rich used above. The tax rate applied is that estimated by Joseph Pechman and Benjamin Okner, *loc.cit.*

[17] The figures, not wholly comparable, are enough to ·fix the orders of magnitude. The *1971 Statistical Abstract*, pp. 309, 396, 399, indicates a net national product of $852 billions in 1969, government revenue of $308 billions, and government expenditure on public welfare of $15 billions. We arbitrarily double the latter figure to cover obscure contributions to the poor masked under other expenditure categories. Confiscation of great wealth would provide far more for the poor—unless the middle class, once again, took most of the proceeds.

Confiscating the incomes of the rich, then, will prove of trivial assistance in helping the poor in today's economy. Such confiscation may be desirable for many other reasons. But the apparent battle between the rich and poor should be observed in saturnine fashion by the enormous middle class. Income redistribution enough to make a real difference in the income of the poor requires a heavy increase in the tax burden paid upon the middle class, those with incomes between $7,000 and $25,000. What is there in American experience since income taxes began, or in the theory of class interest, to suggest that they will leap forward to assume that burden?

APPENDIX

The estimates in Table 1 were derived in three parts. Since the task is to estimate the impact of confiscation, the usual incidence problem is simplified. Thus, if the rich do not receive high incomes they will cease to be liable for taxes associated with high incomes—whatever ultimate "incidence" may be. (1) The distribution of individual income tax by adjusted gross income level is taken from U.S. Internal Revenue Service, *Statistics of Income, Individuals, 1970,*

TABLE 1

INDIVIDUAL INCOME TAX RETURNS IN 1970 WITH INCOMES OF $25,000
AND OVER (MONEY FIGURES IN $00,000)

Number		2,114,000	
Income (AGI)			
Present		$89,810	
After confiscation		52,850	
(2,114,000 × $25,000)			
Confiscation gain			$36,960
(89,810–52,850)			
Taxes			
Present		41,581	
Federal income:	$22,281		
State & local:	6,358		
Estate & gift:	3,680		
Corporate:	9,262		
After confiscation		11,864	
New effective rate	22.45		
(for incomes $20,000–25,000)			
New tax base	52,850		
New tax: (52,850 × 22.45)			
Tax loss		29,717	
(41,581–11,864)			
Net from confiscation		7,243	
Confiscation gain ($36,960)			
Minus tax loss ($29,717)			

Source: Computed from *Statistics of Income, 1970, Individual Income Tax Returns,* pp. 14, 113, 117, 123, and *1971 Statistical Abstract,* p. 379.

pp. 113, 117. (2) The distribution of all state and local taxes, inclusive of property, etc., is based on one decisive assumption: namely, that the rich, in itemizing their deductions, will list every tax to which they were liable. And 96.4 percent of the rich itemized their deductions (pp. 14, 121). The tax-income ratios for itemizers, therefore, should provide highly reliable estimates for the entire rich group. (3) Estate and gift taxes for 1970 are from the *1971 Statistical Abstract*, p. 379, and are all assumed to be paid by those with $25,000 or more AGI. (4) Corporate tax totals, from *idem*, are distributed among AGI income classes by the distribution of domestic and foreign dividends received (*Statistics of Income*, p. 56). This allocation is similar to the Okner-Pechman IA allocation. Our assumption here is that someone else would have to bear the proportionate share of corporate income taxes if the rich were limited in their incomes. We assume, as can be seen, that the income ceiling would induce them to shift out of corporate stock and into less risky assets.

Table 2 compares (a) the effective tax rates we estimate for 1970 AGI intervals by these procedures with (b) those that Benjamin Okner and Joseph Pechman have estimated for 1966, by "family adjusted income level." (Cf. their "Who Paid the Taxes in 1966?" *American Economic Re-*

TABLE 2
Effective Tax Rates

Income Level ($000)	1966 (Okner-Pechman) IC	1970 (Present)
20–25	24.0%	22.4%
25–30	25.1	24.7
30–50	26.4	27.8
50–100	31.5	35.6
100–500	41.8	45.4
500–1,000	48.0	50.5
$1 million and over	49.3	48.1

view, Papers & Proceedings, May 1974. For comparability in Table 2 we exclude, as they do, estate and gift taxes. But these are, of course, included in Table 1 estimates.

The results are strikingly similar despite the temporal difference; such conceptual differences as the use of tax return versus family, AGI versus family adjusted income; and such estimating differences as our use of major state and local taxes itemized in IRS returns versus the allocation principles used by Okner and Pechman for these items.

PER CAPITA INCOME AND THE
ANGEL OF THE LORD

Let us honor if we can
The vertical man
Though we value none
But the horizontal one
—W. H. Auden

That death will increase the welfare of a family or a nation has probably occurred to no one but specialists in the cause and cure of poverty. It might, indeed, never have occurred to them but for a heady combination of Latin and long division.

Those specialists usually agree that a nation's welfare is to be measured by per capita income—i.e., total income divided by population.[1] But long division tells us that dividing a rupee (or a dollar) by 2 is going to yield a higher per capita income than dividing by 3. How, then, does per capita income measure welfare, if not by assuming that death increases welfare? When a baby dies, its family's "per capita income" promptly rises. So does the nation's. And when a baby is born, its parents' "per capita income" falls abruptly. (However, if it then dies, their per capita income will go back up to its previous level.) Death is thereby calculated to reduce "poverty" and to increase "per capita welfare."[2] The miserably low "per capita" income figures

[1] Cf. the influential study by Gunnar Myrdal, *Economic Theory and Underdeveloped Regions* (1957). His proof of deleterious "backwash effects" rests on the widening gap between national per capita incomes. Barbara Ward, *The Rich Nations and the Poor Nations* (1962), p. 37, asks: "How are we to define the 'poor' nations?" Her answer is "perhaps the most satisfactory method of defining poverty at this stage is . . . in terms of per capita income."

[2] The widely held position that links income and welfare was accurately, succinctly, summarized in Paul Samuelson, *Economics* (1961), p. 801, by a graph of rising per capita income, labeled "Advanced Nations Expect Rising Per Capita Welfare." Other typical statements:

for underdeveloped countries immediately reflect this treatment of life and death.

Would anyone who was inexpert in these arcane matters think that a family became "better off," in any way, if one of its children died? Or that a nation's welfare must fall whenever a baby is born? Such curious conclusions do not, in fact, rest on a chain of logic competent to explain "economic welfare." Neither Latin, nor long division, warrants the universal belief that "per capita income" marks welfare or changes in welfare. We ought to find out how anyone arrived at the unlikely belief that it does. To analyze that long-division view of human welfare we consider, in turn, the two major cultural perspectives on children.

I

"Be fruitful and multiply" is a position anciently held by the world's major religions. It has been accepted by the most diverse cultures. "We have a title," wrote Bishop Jeremy Taylor, "to be provided for as we are God's creatures . . . and therefore it is a huge folly and infidelity to be troubled and full of care because we have many children. Every child we feed is a new revenue, a new title to God's care and providence; so that many children are a great wealth."[3] "Every child we feed is a new revenue"—

"The growth of GNP per capita is . . . probably the best single indicator of growth in living standards, since it takes into account the rise in population. . . ." (Daniel Fusfeld, *Economics* (1972), p. 102.) "Per capita figures . . . indicate how well each individual fared. . . ." (Royall Brandis, *Principles of Economics* (1972), p. 130.)

[3] And, Taylor continues, "if it be said they are chargeable, it is not more than all wealth and great revenues are. For what difference is it? Titius keeps ten ploughs, Cornelia hath ten children; he hath land enough to employ and feed all his hinds; she, blessings and promises, and provisions and the truth of God, to maintain all her children. His hinds and horses eat up all his corn, and her children are sufficiently maintained with her little." Jeremy Taylor, *The Rules and Exercises of Holy Living and of Holy Dying*, Ch. 11, Sect. VI.

a phrase which surely means that its mere existence must increase the well-being of its parents. By that ancient religious criterion the nation's welfare must increase when children are born. Certainly it should not decrease as the "per capita income" calculation insists.

The value of children is held by most members of the U.N. The political desirability of having children has not gone unnoticed. Thus one political leader has urged India's untouchables to reject birth control: They "are a minority in the villages, without land, without homes, in bondage to caste Hindus. To advance they must be in the majority."[4]

Rachel de Queiroz, one of Brazil's "most respected citizens" has declared: "from a national and human point of view . . . international pressures . . . put on us to limit the birth of Brazilians is not only impertinent but also suspect. . . . Would Red China have the force and power to confront a coalition of almost the whole world, if it were not for the tremendous capital represented by her immense population? . . . Let our people grow. . . . And do not preach national suicide for fear of lack of food."[5] And the leader of one of the world's major religions has reaffirmed his church's traditional opposition to "forbidding the poor to be born."[6]

[4] Mrs. Satyavani Muthu, *New York Times* (September 22, 1974).

[5] Quoted by Herman Daly, "The Population Question in Northeast Brazil: its economic and ideological dimensions," *Economic Development and Cultural Change* (July 1970), p. 557. Domingos Susmao de Lima writes: "While recognizing the financial anguish in which the proletariat vegetates . . . I believe it immoral to advise a creature of that type to practice birth control" (p. 566).

[6] "It is inadmissible that those who have control of the wealth and resources of mankind should try to resolve the problems of hunger by forbidding the poor to be born." (Pope Paul, quoted in *New York Times*, November 10, 1974.) Cf. the encyclical Humanae Vitae (1968), which condemns "every action which . . . renders procreation impossible" (reviewed in John Marshall, "Population Policies in the Light of the Papel Encyclical, Humanae Vitae," in International Union for the Scientific Study of the Population, *International Population Conference, London 1969* (1971), Vol. ii.)

35

Among many modern nations, as in the most ancient religions, there is a vital and growing belief that religion, morals, and the national interest alike urge having children. Such values more often than not lead to Sir William Petty's belief: "fewness of people is real poverty; and a Nation wherein are Eight Millions of people, is more than twice as rich as the same scope of land wherein are but Four."[7]

Given that such values dominate these societies, to use GNP per capita for measuring changes in their welfare can lead only to grotesque conclusions. Suppose the Angel of Death destroyed thousands of their babies. Their national GNP per capita would then rise, and their "welfare" improve. Poverty would, just as inevitably, decline. Moreover, GNP per capita would announce tidings of equal joy if an earthquake destroyed thousands of old people. Or if disease carried off thousands of women. (Indeed every death will increase GNP per capita except deaths of middle-aged males who produce more goods valued into the GNP than they consume.)[8]

Political advantage may accrue to some, and masochistic advantage to others, from using GNP per capita to measure welfare despite such grotesqueries. But one may doubt that

---

[7] Quoted N. Georgescu-Roegen, *The Entropy Law and the Economic Process* (1971), p. 301. Cf. *New York Times* (April 9, 1975): "The airlift of children from South Vietnam . . . has left in its wake bitter argument over whether taking children from their homeland is an appropriate or necessary way to deal with a crisis.

Those who have always opposed foreign adoption because they see it depleting nations of their children are angrier than ever."

The expressed concern revolves around "depleting" a nation's population resources.

[8] Even deaths among middle-aged males would also increase GNP per capita—but in the following period the GNP aggregate would decline and, eventually, GNP per capita. Such consequences would not follow for deaths of women (most of whose output is not included in the GNP), of children or of older persons (whose contribution to current output is measured at zero, or less than average per capita).

most users seek to misapprehend the values of such societies. Unless a stronger warrant is found, there seems little basis for allowing figures on GNP per capita to continue to distort our understanding of welfare trends in such societies, comprehending as they do the fairest portion of the visible earth.

II

What of the industrialized nations? In few of them is the decision to have children dictated by ancient cultural or religious imperatives. Nor is it enforced by pro-natalist policies of military leaders and governments.[9] And only rarely do its members emphasize the political advantages of having children.[10] The decision to have children is made by the family itself, as the widespread use of birth control strongly suggests. Over 85 percent of all U.S. couples practice birth control; over 80 percent of American Catholic couples do so.[11] Direct inquiry of a national sample of parents indicates

[9] Perhaps the obvious exception emphasizes the point: Rumania ended legalized abortion in 1966, and initiated premia for births. The pro-natalist position taken by the Third Republic, Facist Italy, and Nazi Germany clearly contrasts with present European policies, except for France.

[10] And then only in response to perceived threats, rather than directly commended. Thus the Reverend Jesse Jackson has stated: "We are clamoring for birth control in this nation when population has in fact declined since the 1950's. . . . Birth control as a national policy will simply marshal sophisticated methods to remove (and control when not removed) the weak, the poor—quite likely the black and other minorities whose relative increase in population threatens the white caste in this nation." Eugene Callender, president of the New York Urban Coalition, has stated that "minority groups in this country view any push toward national birth-rate controls or population constriction as a move towards genocide." (Cf. The Commission on Population Growth and the American Future, *Statements at Public Hearings* (1972), Vol. 7, pp. 165, 228.)

[11] Charles Westoff and Norman Ryder, "Family Limitation in the United States," In International Population Union, *op.cit.*, Vol. II, p. 1311.

that 85 percent of all births are wanted.[12] We infer that parents of the nearly 4 million babies born each year expect to derive as much "welfare" from their children as it will cost to raise them. (Even "unwanted" children are usually treated by their parents as though they were worth a good deal more than the stream of costs they impose.) That they have such value can be tested by a hypothetical choice posed to any U.S. parent: "Would you be willing to have one of your children die in return for a sum equal to the total cost of raising that child?" Surely few parents would take the money.[13] We infer that children do increase family and national well being, even in industrialized societies—and by at least as much as they cost to raise.[13a]

III

Suppose we move down from the grand level of national aggregates and national per capita figures, for it is individuals who alone experience welfare. Consider three stages in the life of a worker. For simplicity we assume that person

[12] Westoff and Ryder, *ibid.*, p. 1312, report that 30% of white women and 52% of non-white women stated that their last pregnancy was "unwanted." The group included married women "ever-pregnant under 45 who intend no more children." Allowing for prior births, these figures are consistent with Westoff's statement that about 15% of all births 1966–1970 were unwanted. (Cf. Westoff in Commission in Population Growth, *Demographic and Social Aspects of Population Growth* [1972], pp. 13, 474.)

[13] We assume only a majority response to the hypothetical question. There might be exceptions. Thus the *New York Times* in 1853 argued that "he who insures his life or health must be indeed a victim of his own folly or others' knavery." Its premise was that poor mothers would murder their infants for insurance benefits—as reputedly had occurred in the U.K. Cf. Frederick L. Hoffman, *History of the Prudential Insurance Company of America* (1900), p. 10.

[13a] "Some more souls, some more joy" is a proverb from one of the oldest industrialized nations—Holland. Cf. Tjalling Koopmans, "Objectives, Constraints and Outcomes in Optimal Growth Models," *Econometrica* (January 1967), p. 13.

is a man who produces a constant level of output and spends his entire income in each stage.[14]

In Stage I, married but childless, he buys football and airline tickets, doilies and dresses, insurance. In Stage II, he and his wife adopt a child. They then substitute for such expenditures ones for milk, toys, and pediatric care. When the experts observe these shifts in expenditure pattern, they discern no corresponding change in the GNP total.[14a] The aggregate of resources required to produce his demands are roughly identical in each of these stages. They therefore report no change in national welfare per capita. His income per capita remains invariant through it all, as does the nation's.

But suppose he and his wife have a child of their own (Stage III) instead of adopting one (as in Stage II). Their "welfare" will drop immediately: their contribution to GNP per capita declines by one-third.

	Income (Output Produced)	Expenditure (Output Consumed)	Per Capita GNP
Stage I	$X	$X	$X
Stage II	X	X	X
Stage III	X	X	$\frac{2}{3}X$

Can it really be true that parents will not change their welfare by adopting a child but that they reduce it by having one of their own? Does that wild conclusion pop out of the principles of national economic accounting? Or welfare economics? How can economics assert that adopting a child *must* create more welfare than having a child of

[14] Obviously the analysis applied equally well to females who do not leave the labor force in any of the four periods. Allowance for periods out of the labor force, as for saving, complicates the exposition, but does not change the conclusions reached.

[14a] For the rare case in which children of other nations are adopted—e.g., Vietnam in 1975—this conclusion does not hold.

one's own? How can it decide to whom that hypothetical increment of welfare will accrue?

The contradictory results that arise as between adopting and begetting a child mark the source of the confusion. Per capita income comparisons must assume no change of tastes if they are to indicate changes in welfare. But every great demographic event in human existence—birth, marriage, death—reflects a massive change in tastes. Parents inevitably decide that their newborn child must be fed, kept suitably warm, etc.[15] And they do so rather than continue spending in accord with their prior preferences. (That they move on to a completely new indifference curve is almost invariably demonstrated by their expenditure behavior.)[16] Can such substitution from veterinary bills to pediatric charges demonstrate that their welfare has declined?

In this clearcut example, per capita economic welfare declines when a child is born. But just whose welfare declines? There are only two choices—parent or child.

Can it be assumed that the parents' economic welfare declines though their income has not changed? Only if one assumes that they really preferred the budget of goods they consumed prior to the child's birth. No such implications of declining welfare are drawn, however, when small cars cut into big car sales, or TV into movie expenditures, or other shifts occur in expenditure patterns. Hence the per capita calculation must be assuming that parents were coerced into consuming an inferior set of goods. Is this a reasonable tacit premise? Behavior testifies quite the contrary.

There are, in effect, long lines waiting to enter maternity wards and short ones waiting in foster-home offices. And,

[15] There appears to be at least as great conformity to this "law" as, say to "the law of demand."

[16] Market behavior, of course, empirically demonstrates a prior change in tastes. One might argue that the couple's tastes had shifted toward a different set of goods before they were actually married, before their child was actually born.

however great the number of adopted children might be were supply unlimited, most U.S. parents prefer to raise children they beget rather than ones they can adopt. Casual but persistent observation indicates that even adoptions are often made only when parents find they cannot have children of their own. That behavior suggests that own-children are not viewed as inferior to adopted ones. The birth of a child does not produce a decline in welfare if the adoption of a child does not.

But we have another set of behavioral information. Given the prevalence of birth control, one must assume that most births are in fact desired by parents. Can it be that parents act to have children, hoping to *decrease* their utility? Or is it more reasonable to assume that they expect to derive satisfactions from children?[17] Market behavior actually indicates a substantial positive measure of the minimum amount of satisfactions in terms relevant to GNP analysis. Foster parents were paid $902 in 1969 for every child they raised.[18] Since own-children are preferred to foster children the utilities from own-children must at least equal that sum. Estimates of Seneca and Taussig suggest that a 3-person family spends 42 percent more than a 2-person family at the $10,000 income level, roughly the median family income in 1969.[19] Since foster children are raised by families whose

---

[17] It should be unnecessary to note that GNP figures uniformly relate only to goods and services from which consumers expect satisfactions. The catalogue of disappointing movies, cars that turn out to be lemons, etc., is long and ever changing. No harsher rule can be applied to expected satisfactions from children.

[18] National Center for Social Statistics, *Child Welfare Statistics,* 1961, pp. 13, 41.

[19] J. J. Seneca and M. K. Taussig, "Family Equivalence Scales . . ." *Review of Economics and Statistics* (August 1971), p. 259. Cf. *Monthly Labor Review* (November 1960), p. 1199, which provides ratios of equivalent income scales for a married couple with no children versus a couple with one child. Estimates are derived from 1950 expenditure survey data, the WPA maintenance budget prices in 1946, as well as 1935–1936, 1941, and 1944 survey data. They show little

incomes are below average, one may not assume that $4,200 for raising own-children and $902 for foster children are wholly comparable. Yet the data are sufficient to establish the inequality: own-children must provide at least as much utility to their parents as the $902 market transaction figure for the cost of raising foster children. What follows? The birth of a child must raise parents' utility, not reduce it as the per capita income calculation implies.

But there remains the alternative. If parents' welfare is not reduced by the birth of a child, is the child's? But can the staid users of data on GNP per capita really wish to imply that the newborn child is worse off because he was born? For if the parents are not made worse off in their "economic welfare" by his birth, the decline in welfare reported by GNP per capita must be his. Such a premise is, of course, not unknown to the most ancient, to the most melancholy, philosophers: "The best of all things for earthly men is not to be born, and not to see the beams of the bright sun" (Theognis, 5th century). But what an odd premise on which to build a measure of "economic welfare," which can deal only with the ephemeral things of this world, and which does nothing but attribute value to such things. Can that premise possibly warrant using per capita income figures to urge aid-to-dependent children, aid to developing nations, etc., etc.?

Consider incomes in different nations—plutocratic in Abu Dhabi and the U.S., miserably low in Pakistan and Jordan. Of nations identical in all other respects, those which typically have larger families must have lower per capita incomes. Now lesser incomes imply lesser command over those goods which "come within reach of the measuring rod of money." Such goods do not, in most societies, include

---

change in ratios between these sources—ranging from 27% to 32% additional. Since the criteria used are different from those of Seneca and Taussig, we refer to them to suggest that the estimates of the latter probably would not be much different had they used data from BLS surveys antecedent to the 1960 one.

children. Children are not monetized. Neither are they delivered to unsuspecting parents by storks, to be raised by elves. Many husbands and wives choose children (rather than abortions), and divert income for these children (rather than directly for themselves). So doing, they cross that invisible line between "economic welfare" and other sources of welfare. They may, thereby, increase their total welfare. But the per capita income calculus firmly, tacitly, declares that they must thereby decrease their welfare. What is the interest of those who compare per capita incomes of nations or of families? Presumably income as an index of welfare. It is time for them to cease relying on so biassed an index.

The simple move from using GNP as a measure of economic welfare to using GNP per capita tacitly implies that the birth of children reduces human economic welfare, and that death increases it. Publicists may well continue to accept that assumption implicitly by continuing to refer to differences in national incomes per capita or ethnic differences in income per capita. But economists would do well to consider the fastidious counsel of the founder of modern economics: "It is also a question outside my subject whether it is better to have a great multitude of Inhabitants, poor and badly provided, than a smaller number, much more at their ease; a million who consume the produce of 6 acres per head or 4 million who live on the produce of an acre and a half."[20]

[20] Richard Cantillon, *Essai sur la nature du commerce en general,* (ed. H. Higgs, 1931), p. 85.

43

THE SUBMERGED TENTH:
COLOR AND ETHNIC GROUP
INCOMES, 1900–1970

"While there is a lower class, I am in it," Eugene Debs once declared. His feeling of affiliation has been shared by many who believe that society fails its essential moral purpose whenever particular groups—religious, ethnic, color—remain mired in a lower class. What has been the U.S. experience from 1900 to 1970? We assume that the income reference standard for the chief minority ethnic and color groups is a simple but a relative one.

It is not "How well did these groups do economically?" It is rather, "How well did these groups do when compared with the great majority—i.e., native whites?"

The exigencies of the real world are always varying the income distribution. And families in every generation will inevitably fall into the lower tenth of the income distribution. The special issue for religious, ethnic, and color minorities, however, is: Are minorities locked in, from decade to decade, more than native whites? If they are, the issue of continuing discrimination looms large. If they are not, then concern about "low income" really stems from other forces—from (1) the overall performance of the economy, and from (2) differentials in market incentive and personal motivation.

We propose to consider the lowest tenth of native white families as setting an income standard for families of different ethnic and color groups. For example, in 1900 the lowest tenth of native white families had less than $285 income a year. What proportion of Irish immigrants, or German, or Negroes, fell below that standard? In 1970 the lowest tenth of native whites had $4,000 a year or less. What proportion of Americans of Irish stock, or Japanese, or Negroes, fell below that standard?

I

Table 1 reports such percentages for families at three dates.[1] As expected, in 1900–1910 far more than 10 percent of foreign-born and Negro families fell below the native white cut-off level. True, foreign-born Irish and German families had about the same 10 percent as native whites. But North Italians had almost 3 times that proportion. So did most foreign born groups (i.e., "all other"). Indeed, about 40 percent of South Italians, Russians, and Negroes fell below the standard for the native whites.

What happened over the decades? Did the relative disadvantage of these groups persist? Did the grandchildren inherit poverty from their parents and grandparents in these groups? If so, their relative position by 1970 would not have changed significantly. Their absolute income would have moved up, but the contribution of a malign inheritance would nonetheless have put them disproportionately into the submerged tenth as of 1970. The columns for 1900 and 1910 in Table 1 relate to the grandparents, while 1970 data relate to the grandchildren.[2]

[1] The 1900 and 1910 surveys included only husband-wife families with children. For comparability we use similar data in Table 1 for 1970—but not in Table 2.

The percent of native white, husband-wife, families with incomes below $4,000 in 1969 was 10.7%, rather than the 10% shown in Table 1. However, Census data for individual foreign stocks are only given for wide income intervals—e.g., $3,000 to $4,999. To approximate the precision available for native whites, it would be necessary to interpolate quite speculatively for a substantial number of foreign-stock groups, in that wide interval. Doing so would add more inaccuracy to the figures than does our procedure, albeit the latter slightly overstates the extent of poverty among Negroes and foreign-stock groups.

[2] The median age of married males, of foreign-born males, and Negro males in the 1910 study was about 37. Cf. Immigration Commission, *Immigrants in Industries*, Part 23, Vol. 1, Table 21. This table comes from the Commission study of employees. Their study of households, which provided the income data we used, was based on a sub sample of the employee sample. The median age of families

INCOME

TABLE 1

THE LOWER TENTH: 1900–1970
PERCENT OF HUSBAND-WIFE FAMILIES IN EACH COLOR
OR ETHNIC GROUP IN THE LOWER TENTH

	1900 (Under $285)	1910 (Under $440)	1970 (Under $4,000)
Native stock			
White	10%	10%	10%
Negro	40	40	14
Foreign Stock			
		Foreign Born	*Native Born*
Irish		9%	9%
German		11	17
Italian-North		28 ⎱ 36	6
Italian-South		40 ⎰	
Russian		43	5
All other		26	9
Total		26	9

Source: Appendix I.

Two main contrasts between the third generation and the first stand out:

(1) The percentage of Negro families in the bottom tenth diminished markedly—from 40 percent to 14 percent.

(2) Marked declines also occurred for the foreign stock as a whole; for South Italian and Russian families in particular. (No change took place for the Irish, while the relative standing of the Germans actually worsened slightly.)

Comparisons for families in other immigrant groups, as well as detail for orientals, cannot be made from the 1970 Census publications. To extend our view to such groups in recent years we show Table 2, which relates to persons rather than families. This table shows the same marked de-

in these groups in 1970 was over 45 years. Cf. 1970 Census, *Family Composition*, Tables 2, 30.

TABLE 2

DETAILED ETHNIC GROUPS:
PERCENT IN THE LOWER TENTH, 1910, 1970

	1910: Percent of Families in Bottom Tenth	1970: Percent of Persons Below Poverty Line
Native white	10%	10%
White-Foreign stock	26	10
Swedish	5	10
Canadian French	8	—
English	9	9
Irish	9	9
German	11	13
Bohemian	17	—
French	20	11
Portuguese	20	9
Lithuanian	25	—
Hebrew	26	—
Italian (North)	28	6
Slovenian	28	{5
Croatian	29	
Magyar	32	6
Polish	34	6
Slovak	34	8
Syrian	38	6
Italian (South)	40	6
Negro	40	35
American Indian ⎫		40
Japanese ⎪		8
Chinese ⎬	40+	12
Filipino ⎪		14
Hawaiian ⎪		14
Korean ⎭		30

Source: Appendix II.

clines for most foreign stock groups. Marked differences separated ethnic and color groups from native whites in the grandparents' generation (1900–1910). But the differences dwindled by the grandchildren's generation. And they did so for virtually every ethnic and color group. The Japa-

47

nese and South Italians experienced the most spectacular declines. But the declines for Syrians, Chinese, and Slovaks were almost as marked. There was, however, great stability for the primary foreign stock groups in U.S. history—English, Irish, German. (About 10 percent of their members were in low-income groups at both dates.)

Two generations of economic and social change, then, had cut the proportion of major ethnic and color groups that fell into the submerged tenth. Economic advance and personal endeavor among most groups had driven down their excess proportions by the third generation, leaving them with rates much like those for native whites.

There is, however, one major exception. Table 1 showed that the proportion of Negro (husband-wife) families in the submerged tenth had decreased from 1900 to 1970 along with other ethnic groups—specifically, from 40 percent to 14 percent. That decline was not quite as great as for South Italians, or Russians, but it was among the steepest declines in the poverty percentage. However, the decline from 1910 to 1970 in Table 2 is only from 40 percent to 35 percent. Here is the single instance in which Table 1 and 2 indicate largely different rates of decline. What accounts for this different view?

A major factor proves to be the increasing proportion of all Negro families headed by females: from 18 percent in 1890 that group had risen to 28 percent by 1970.[3] The number of families, and percent in the submerged tenth,[4] was as shown on page 49.

Female-headed families descend to the lowest income groups largely because of the number of young children in them, requiring that the mother either remain home or work irregularly because of home demands. Nearly half (46 percent) of the Negro families with female heads had

[3] The 1890 estimate is derived from data in the 1890 Census, *Farms and Homes,* pp. 571, 576. The 1970 figure is from 1970 Census, *Negro Population,* Table 8.

[4] Data from *Sources* . . . , Table 3.

TABLE 3

	Percent of Families below $4,000	Number of Families (000)
Negro		
Husband-wife	14%	3,299
Female head	58	1,334
White		
Husband-wife	11	40,257
Female head	35	4,115

at least one child under 10.[5] Thus it was that the proportion of Negro husband-wife families in the bottom tenth decreased from 1910 to 1970 almost as much as any foreign-stock group. Indeed it diminished more than the foreign stock as a whole. Yet all Negro families reported a far smaller decline, for increases in the number of Negro families with female heads had effectively offset much of the decline in poverty among Negro husband-wife families.

We conclude that from grandparents to grandchildren, from 1910 to 1970, economic and social changes sharply reduced the difference between poverty rates of (a) native white Americans, and (b) foreign-born and non-white Americans. Given that 10 percent of native husband-wife white families fell below a $285 annual income in 1910, the percentages for foreign-born Americans were far greater: up to 40 percent for Russian born and South Italian, 40 percent for native Negroes. In 1970, 10 percent of native white husband-wife families fell below an annual income of $1,000, but the percentage for Americans with immigrant grandparents was also about 10 percent. Inded almost every ethnic group for which we have data had about 10 percent. Moreover, the proportion for American Negroes was 14 percent. (The 35 percent rate for all Negro families in 1970 reflects the increased proportion of Negro families

[5] 1970 Census, *Family Composition*, Table 18. The ratio of white female-headed families was 29%.

with female heads.) What made for the convergence between ethnic groups? Why did the typical husband-wife family among foreign-born groups and Negroes cease to appear in the lower income depths so frequently? Surely a thousand separate factors were at work. But among the most potent were advancing U.S. productivity, rising real wages, and the compelling efforts of those groups to train and to work in ways that increased their income.

APPENDIX

I

The data in Table 1 relate to families. Since 97 percent of the families in the 1900 income distribution were husband-wife families, the 1970 data used as comparable were also those for husband-wife families. (It should be noted, however, that 14 percent of the families enumerated in the 1970 Census were not husband-wife families.[6]

For 1900 the data for separating out the native white stock are inadequate—chiefly because the lower end of the distribution for whites is dominated by farm operators and farm laborers. And for these the Census does not distinguish between native and all whites. However, study of the distribution of low income farms, and low wage farm laborers, immediately indicates that the bulk of these were located in the South—a region where the proportion of immigrants outside cities was trivial. We therefore take the distribution of white farm families as equivalent to that for native white farm families.

The distribution of non-farm white families was first adjusted by applying the percentage, at each income level, that was foreign-born.[7] The resultant lower decile level is $262. However, given the sequence of assumptions required to separate out the native whites, it seemed preferable to take the value based on broader data, for total whites. The

[6] Data for 1900 are from "The Distribution of Income in 1900," Section 2, Table D. The 1970 data are computed from 1970 Census, *Sources and Structure of Family Income,* Table 3, and *Family Composition,* Table 30. The 1910 data are from Reports of the Immigra- These data relate to a "family composed of husband, wife and chil- tion Commission, *Immigrants in Industries,* Part 23, Vol. I, p. 331. dren. Groups of persons among whom none of these relations exist are not considered families." (Immigration Commission, *Immigrants in Cities,* Vol. II, p. 4.)

[7] These percentages were computed for normal families from nativity by income data as reported in the Commissioner of Labor, 1903 *Report,* pp. 560-564.

level computed directly from the overall distribution for all white families was $285.

II

1910 data in Table 2 are from the same sources as those in Table 1: *Immigrants in Industries*, Part 23, Vol. I, p. 331. The 1910 estimate for Orientals is based on limited information for Japanese on the West Coast. (Immigration Commission, *Reports*, Part 25, Vol. III and the occupational concentration of Chinese in low wage occupations.)

1970 data are from the 1970 Census, *Low-Income Population*, Table 5. The 1970 groups used to approximate the (1910) groups were U.K. (English); Italy (North Italian, South Italian); Czechoslovak (Slovak); Yugoslavia (Slovenian, Croatian).

For Orientals in 1910 (composed almost solely of Japanese and Chinese) we estimate the same rate as for Negroes, 40 percent, on the basis of survey data for the distribution of daily wages paid each group. The average for male Negroes, $1.77, was virtually identical with the Japanese average of $1.80. (Cf. Immigration Commission, *ibid*, Part 23, Vol. I, Table 13.) Averages for virtually every other ethnic group were higher. There seems no reason to believe that the Chinese proportion in the lower tenth would have been less, and we therefore take the 40 percent rate for Negroes as applicable to Orientals.

A CENTURY OF GUARANTEED
INCOME IN THE U.S.

---

*"It were well if every City were to main-
tain its own Poor, . . . (except) Vagabonds,
and sturdy Beggars, who want Work rather
than Money. . . . To whom is it then that
we would give? How much? And to what
purposes exactly? . . . . 'Tis hard to answer
all these points exactly . . . for the Choice
of the men, I would be satisfied that they
are Poor, and Honest. . . ."*
—Erasmus, *Select Colloquies* (1522)

For more than a century American governments have guaranteed incomes to those in poverty. Little attention has been
paid to that record by recent discussants of poverty and
the guaranteed income. Yet it tells us much about how
American values operate through the political process. And
it reveals that the values of those who legislated in 1850
were surprisingly consistent with those who dominated the
era of La Follette and Mellon, as well as the later days
of McGovern and Nixon. Few polemics on the guaranteed
income define it as necessarily being only one specific dol-
lar-and-cents figure. And few have claimed that the state
should pay a guaranteed income to anyone—rich and poor,
child and parent, foreign student and American citizen.
Therefore the record of how American cities and states
have provided support to their poverty-stricken residents,
and how much, deserves a look. What working standards
did legislators use? Why did so striking a consistency in
criteria for income levels persist over the decades? These
are the questions addressed below.

I

For many decades the United States has had a minimum
guaranteed income, clearly defined and implemented by

the political process. It was the amount that individual states were willing to pay for maintaining "paupers." That pejorative term was eventually superseded by "those in need," by "the poor," and by "the disadvantaged." Maintenance in the form of "outdoor relief" and "almshouses" was superseded by "public assistance." But these changes of terminology and technique do not change the fact that for more than a century public authorities have guaranteed incomes to those in need.

It is obvious that the level of such guarantee is far less than the poor desired, than many people believe was warranted, or that the country could afford. It is no less obvious that the qualifications for receipt have also changed. The ancient criterion of "poor and honest," to which Erasmus referred, are applied decreasingly: increasing numbers of persons either reject a means test or would suppress the terminology. But such changes can hardly controvert the fact of incomes guaranteed to the poor, any more than does heated disagreement about level and impact change the fact that we have minimum wages, old age assistance, unemployment insurance, etc.

The level of assistance that legislators, set over the past century is estimated in Table 1.[1] From an unbelievably low figure for 1850, it has advanced twentyfold—to a figure that still seems unwarrantably inadequate for so rich a nation. How is it that these particular figures were arrived at? A twentyfold increase is far more than the cost-of-living change. It is therefore not consistent with the theory that legislators were prepared to starve the poor to death, which required no such increase, or that they recklessly handed out the taxpayer's money.

Public assistance, wrote Georg Simmel, is given "so that

[1] The 1850–1870 figures are for "pauper assistance" (Appendix A, Table 2). The 1903 figure is for the cost of support to persons in benevolent institutions, and is derived in Appendix A. The 1929ff. figures (Appendix A and Table 3) measure general assistance per case (not aid to dependent children, which is higher).

TABLE 1

POOR RELIEF: 1850–1970

	Per Person per Year
1850	$59
1860	87
1870	119
1903	125
1929	269
1940	287
1950	568
1960	826
1970	1,344

Source: State estimates in App. A.

the poor will not become active and dangerous enemies of society, so as to make their reduced energies more productive, and . . . prevent the degeneration of their progeny. . . . If assistance were to be based on the interests of the poor persons, there would, in principle, be no limit whatsoever on the transmission of property in favor of the poor . . . (and lead) to the equality of all."[2] That observation is, of course, similar to ones brought to mind by Rawls' recent presentation of the maximin principle. U.S. legislators, it may be presumed, manifested little desire, and less warrant, for transferring all the resources of their constituents to the poor. But how could they draw the line between leaving the poor just where they were and total equalization?

II

We hypothesize that legislators picked pauper support levels not from perversity but with respect to the world in which

[2] Donald Levine, ed. George Simmel, *On Individuality and Social Forms* (1971), pp. 154–155. The lack of any objective limit was likewise noted by Dr. Johnson, from a wildly different premise, and to a vastly different inference: "Charity . . . is not definable by limits. It is a duty to give to the poor; but no man can say how much another should give to the poor, or when a man has given too little to save his soul." Boswell's *Life* (Modern Library edition), p. 462.

they function. Their public assistance function has had two elements in it. The first defines the share of their constituents' earnings that they are prepared to take away, both to enhance social stability and to evidence moral worth by redistributing to the poor. Now few legislators have been prepared to take away all of their constituents' earnings, even if the poor starved to death as a result. That share must, therefore, always be less than 100 percent. But there are few societies in which it has been zero, and certainly the U.S. is not one. The rich have always paid their respects to the poor, demonstrated their status, and tossed a douceur to social order, by charity. And the middling classes—above the poor but below the very rich—have been accustomed to tithing, with the church then redistributing to charity. Legislators then pick a level for assistance that is always above zero, but always one suitable by comparison with the income level of their constituents. If the difference between income and charity levels is "too small," then their constituents will discover that they have been working for not "enough" more than they could collect without the drama of boss, subordination, and routine. If the difference is "too great," then they fail to meet the empathy level of the most insistent members of their constituency. (That is a live concern even if there is no danger to the social order.)

As a heroic simplification we take the Table 1 trend in levels of payments to the poor, and compute it as a function of average earnings of common labor. (The latter is used as a proxy for the trend in incomes of legislators constituents.) The result of the comparisons suggests that for the past century legislators were prepared to offer the poor 30¢ more in public assistance for every dollar increase in the wages of common labor.[3] As between states in any year surveyed, $1 more a day in common labor earnings meant 30¢ more in daily public assistance rates. Moreover, as Table

[3] Derivation in Appendix B.

TABLE 2

POOR RELIEF

	As a Percentage of the Earnings of Common Labor
1850	22%
1860	26
1870	24
1903	23
1929	31
1940	28
1950	29
1960	28
1970	29

2 shows, assistance rates ran from 22 percent at the beginning to about 29 percent a century later.

Now the 25–30 percent ratio between the income guaranteed to public assistance recipients and the earnings of common labor is an abstract number. But it may, in fact, relate to other parts of the politico-economic process. What of the Social Security system? Since its founding in 1936 that system has forced individual workers to provide for their own declines in income (a) should they become unemployed, and (b) when they become aged. The net contribution of the federal taxpayer has been very limited. The philosophy of the system has been persistently one of insurance—in which participants simply shared the risks.

Congress could establish any ratio it chose between the worker's current income and that to be received when he becomes unemployed or aged. By skimming enough off in taxation now, it could level the worker's income. He would then receive the same income after retirement as he earned before—giving a 100 percent ratio. Or, if current income were preferred so much that little would be skimmed off during his working years, his retirement income would be say only 1 percent of his current income. Preferences between current and future social security income are not

TABLE 3

	Ratio of	
	Unemployment Benefit to Weekly Wage	OASI Benefit to Earnings
1936	39%	
1945	42	
1950	34	
1951		
2		38%
3		42
4		41
5	32	44
6	33	43
7	34	42
8	35	41
9	33	43
1960	35	41
1	35	40
2	35	39
3	35	38
4	34	37
5	34	38
6	35	37
7	35	36
8	35	35
9	34	38
1970	36	43

determined in heaven, nor by any abstract criterion, but by the actual time preference of the American people expressed through the political process. What exchange ratio has that political process actually worked out? Table 3 gives the ratios.[4]

They indicate that the average weekly benefit for total unemployment has run about 33 percent of the average

[4] *Social Security Yearbook, 1944*, p. 109; *1948*, p. 28. *Social Security Bulletin*, September issues: 1950, p. 44; 1951, p. 29; 1952, p. 33; 1953, p. 29; 1954, p. 41; 1955, p. 35; *Social Security Bulletin, Annual Statistical Supplement*, 1960, p. 14; 1965, p. 12; 1966, p. 14, 1969, p. 34; 1970, p. 38. Henle in *Monthly Labor Review* (June 1972), p. 15.

weekly wage since the end of World War II, down from the 40 percent level during the years of mass unemployment and World War II. And OASI beneficiaries in recent decades received incomes from 37 percent to 43 percent of their prior earnings.

The duration of the unemployment benefits is abruptly cut off after fixed period regardless of the worker's "need." But the duration of old age benefits, and of assistance to the poor, are not so cut off. Presumably the difference in treatment reflects the difference in "moral hazard." Old age benefits are policed at the entry point by an age qualification, and, at the exit, by a higher power. Assistance to the poor is policed by systematic state investigation to determine qualification.

For the income guaranteed to the poor, as that guaranteed to unemployed workers, the ratio to the relevant income standard runs about 33 percent. The gap is obviously intended to deter anyone from readily adopting a status in which he collects income from a public fund. Given a different economy, and different time preferences, the ratios would have been different.[5]

Common labor earnings prior to 1950 are daily rates; the more recent figures are actual earnings. Hence for precise comparison with later figures the earlier figures should be lowered to allow for the average unemployment of common labor. This adjustment would probably be a significant one for 1850–1903, when the labor market was less tightly knit and common labor could expect more frequent intervals of unemployment between jobs. It would also be significant for 1940, when mass unemployment still prevailed. It is, therefore, possible that the approximate 30 percent ratio

[5] No comment is intended about the wisdom of the output of the political process, nor where it may go in the future. There are undoubtedly Americans who consider 33% immorally low for a rich nation, as there are Americans who consider it hardly low enough to achieve their goal of protecting contributions made by other Americans to the pool of funds for redistribution.

for 1950–1970 prevailed back to 1850—once the earlier data had been adjusted for unemployment comparability. (For detailed State estimates 1850–1960 see Appendix A.)

One politico-arithmetic consideration should be added. The common labor figure is an average. At any time some common laborers, and those in related unskilled occupations, would earn less than that average, even though they were in the labor force (or ill) most of the year. Even in the full employment year of 1970 one-sixth of all common laborers earned less than the public assistance level for that year. One-half of those with jobs in personal service industries did so.[6] Some legislators may find it easy, and pleasant, to tax the rich. Many will find it moral, and humane, to transfer income from their constituents to the poor. But few will find it politic to provide gift incomes to the poor that exceed the income that "too many" of their constituents earn by working at dull, laborious, and distasteful jobs.

We may conclude that a guaranteed income has long prevailed in the United States. That income was once provided to qualifying "paupers" and is now provided to qualifying "public assistance cases." The level of that income appears to have run from 25 percent to 30 percent of a common laborer's earnings. And it has done so for more than a century. In a democratic society that persistence suggests the ratio is consistent with the actual preferences of a majority of Americans, whatever their expressed ideals or self-image.

[6] 1970 Census, *Occupational Characteristics*, Table 24.

APPENDIX A

I. Relief Payments

1850–1870. The Census query on the subject of pauperism has received one of General Walker's usual scathing remarks in the Census reports. However his comments relate largely to the inclusion under the category "number of persons supported during the year"—not merely persons "entering a work or alms house" but "every person receiving so much as a half ton of coal in a hard winter, or a dozen soup tickets" (U.S. Census Office, *A Compendium of the Ninth Census*, 1872, pp. 533–534). This difficulty is moderated, however, because we use the number "receiving support on June 1" of each Census year (see infra). On a June date the figure would include the hard core of the poor regularly supported by the state. Since that count is divided into the "cost of annual support," the result would tend to make the average cost figure somewhat high by virtue of the inclusion of costs for coal, soup tickets, etc., given to persons receiving transient help. It is not believed that the bias is great, nor would particularly differentiate one state from the others.

The estimates in Table 1 were computed from the Census data (*Compendium, ibid,* pp. 530–535) by dividing the count of paupers as of June 1 into the "annual cost of support" for an entire year. The June 1 count is probably below a yearly average so far as seasonality is concerned. But the peak of immigrant flows in the spring would tend to bring it above average. Because 40 percent of the June 1 count was in New York, Pennsylvania, and Massachusetts—centers for immigrant arrival—the importance of this latter factor is probably substantial. We therefore accept the June 1 count as a fair annual average.

1903. In order to provide a ratio between the 1850–1870 period and 1929ff. we approximate a figure for 1903. For that year, 753 homes, under public, private, and ecclesiastical sponsorship, reported their activities to the Census (Bureau of the Census, Special Reports, *Benevolent Institutions, 1904*, 1905). The average cost of maintenance per inmate proved to be $125 (pp. 38–39). Reports for 449 temporary homes averaged $118 (pp. 44–45). For those temporary homes reporting charges, the average was about $2.60, or an annual rate of $135 (p. 48). The ratio of $125 maintenance cost to the wage received by common labor was 23.4 percent.[7] (Allowing for the unemployment, sickness and other absence of common labor would increase that ratio to 28.8 percent.)[8]

1929. The U.S. Census, *Special Report, Relief Expenditures by Governmental and Private Organizations, 1929 and 1931* (1932), provides data in Tables I and II on "expenditures for relief to families and to homeless men" and on the "number of families" (outside of institutions) to which such aid was given. The aggregates for private relief, and for the number of families receiving such relief, were deducted from these totals. The averages thus computed were too high because some expenditures were in fact made for homeless men. However, examination of the numbers of "lodgings" given and "meals served" to such men suggests that the costs involved were small, and hence could not have produced much of a bias. The "expenditures for the first three months of 1929" would hardly have included depreciation on buildings and furniture. Hence most of the cost would have gone for the 167,000 meals provided homeless man by public agencies. But an overly generous estimate

[7] *Manpower in Economic Growth*, p. 276, gives a $1.53 rate for common labor in 1900. Earnings of non-farm employees rose 10.5%, 1900–1903 (*ibid.*, p. 524).

[8] 18th Annual Report of the Commissioner of Labor, 1903, *Cost of Living and Retail Prices of Food* (1904), p. 291. These data relate only to male heads of families—the relevant part of the labor force—and include, both unemployment and time lost through sickness, vacation, drunkenness, etc. To infer an alternative common labor income, it seems desirable to include both unemployment and expected usual time out of the labor force.

of 25¢ per meal would account for less than 1 percent of the $14 million in public relief during that quarter year.

1940. Federal Emergency Relief Administration, *Final Report*, pp. 386–400, provides data on the average number of cases by state and the total amount of relief funds extended. We divide one by the other to derive state averages.

1950–1960. Data on the number of cases receiving general assistance, and the aggregate expenditures on such assistance, are given by state for 1950 in the *Social Security Bulletin* (September 1951, pp. 47, 51) and for 1960 in the 1960 *Statistical Supplement* to the *Social Security Bulletin* (pp. 94, 95, 100).

II. Average Earnings of Common Labor

1850–1970. Data for daily wages of common labor are taken from Lebergott, *Manpower in Economic Growth* (1964), p. 541, and multiplied by 311 to give an annual rate. (For comparability with the relief data they were divided by 12 or 52 as necessary.)

1929. Regional hourly wage rate averages for common labor were taken from Lebergott, *idem.* A regression was computed between these wage rates and annual earnings in 1929 of wage earners engaged in lumber and timber manufacturing—a category dominated by common labor employment (1929 Census of Manufacturers, Vol. II, p. 443). The intercept and coefficient from the equation was then applied to estimates for such lumber earnings for each individual state to give state figures for common labor hourly wage rates. These, multiplied by 2,000 hours, gave an annual earnings figure.

For half a dozen states it was not possible to compute such lumber and timber averages. What was done for these states, and a comparable adjoining state, was to compute averages for planing-mill products factories. The ratio of one of these averages to the other (e.g., New Jersey to New York) was then applied to the available (New York) lumber average to give the desired (New Jersey) lumber average.

1950, 1960. From each individual state volume in these Censuses the average earnings of "laborers, except farm and mines" in the Census year were computed. (Table 78 in the 1950 volumes, Table 68 in Vol. 1 for each state in 1960.)

1970. Median earnings of non-farm laborers are from 1970 Census, *Occupational Characteristics* (PC2-7A), p. 487. Average December payment per general assistance case is from *1971 Statistical Abstract*, p. 294. That figure is likely to be slightly off the annual average.

TABLE 4
Pauper Support: 1850–1870

	YEARLY AVERAGE			AS A RATIO TO INCOME OF COMMON LABORER		
	1850	*1860*	*1870*	*1850*	*1860*	*1870*
U.S.	$59	$87	$119	21.6%	26.4%	24.0%
N.E.						
Maine	43	49	101	18.2	15.0	21.1
N.H.	72	67	110	36.7	22.9	27.2
Vt.	64	65	100	28.6	20.1	22.3
Mass.	71	89	194	27.2	28.1	39.0
R.I.	66	70	154	29.5	21.4	33.0
Conn.	55	56	111	23.3	17.1	22.0
M. Atl.						
N.Y.	64	75	189	30.8	23.7	40.5
N.J.	59	71	119	29.2	21.3	23.3
Pa.	61	86	143	38.4	24.9	27.9
E.N. Cent.						
Ohio	57	a	154	32.8	a	30.9
Ind.	99	96	110	57.9	31.5	22.7
Ill.	104	106	235	53.9	32.4	47.2
Mich.	66	80	132	32.2	24.8	27.0
Wisc.	62	64	134	28.1	19.6	28.0
W.N. Cent.						
Minn.	—	—	69	—	46.1	12.7
Iowa	122	123	205	47.3	39.9	39.0
Mo.	105	90	103	45.1	29.5	22.4
N.D.	—	—	—	—	—	—
S.D.	—	—	—	—	—	—
Neb.	—	*	121	—	*	18.3
Kan.	—	20	138	—	5.3	23.7

TABLE 4
PAUPER SUPPORT: 1850–1870

	YEARLY AVERAGE			AS A RATIO TO INCOME OF COMMON LABORER		
	1850	1860	1870	1850	1860	1870
S. Atl.						
Del.	65	51	91	26.7	18.8	18.8
Md.	36	104	101	16.7	39.8	21.1
D.C.	—	89	94	—	28.6	—
Va.	34	46	92	16.8	18.3	29.3
W. Va.	—	—	81	—	—	20.5
N.C.	38	58	83	22.6	24.3	32.5
S.C.	40	45	109	19.5	17.6	34.7
Ga.	33	38	88	14.7	13.7	26.0
Fla.	15	43	67	4.7	11.9	18.0
E.S. Cent.						
Ky.	74	80	90	34.4	26.5	20.8
Tenn.	53	69	75	29.4	26.4	20.9
Ala.	56	87	119	25.7	29.1	31.6
Miss.	71	89	120	24.1	22.7	26.6
W.S. Cent.						
Ark.	103	94	139	44.2	29.1	32.2
La.	b	70	105	b	16.2	19.8
Okla.	—	—	—	—	—	—
Tex.	*	105	105	*	27.0	26.6
Mount.						
Mont.	—	—	742	—	—	39.8
Idaho	—	—	*	—	—	*
Wyo.	—	—	—	—	—	—
Colo.	—	—	601	—	—	77.2
N.M.	—	—	—	—	—	—
Ariz.	—	—	—	—	—	—
Utah	—	344	122	—	57.0	—
Nev.	—	—	439	—	—	47.1
Pacific						
Wash.	—	935	264	—	103.0	33.9
Ore.	—	526	306	—	—	46.4
Calif.	—	388	276	—	41.5	38.4

*Fewer than 10 persons.

aJune 1 count above yearly total.

bAggregate expenditures greater than in 1860.

Source: Appendix.

INCOME

TABLE 5
PAUPER SUPPORT: 1929-1960*

	YEARLY AVERAGE PER FAMILY				AS A RATIO TO INCOME OF COMMON LABORER			
	1929	1940	1950	1960	1929	1940	1950	1960
U.S.	$268.8	$287	$567.6	$825.6	30.6%	28.1%	28.9%	28.0%
N.E.								
Maine	554.4	298	513.6	488.4	63.5	31.7	33.6	19.6
N.H.	230.4	296	496.8	637.2	24.0	29.6	28.2	22.0
Vt.	228.0	252	412.8	476.4	27.7	28.6	25.2	18.3
Mass.	453.6	321	634.8	835.2	44.2	30.3	29.1	24.8
R.I.	376.8	343	726.0	842.4	47.2	32.4	37.1	25.7
Conn.	294.0	319	606.0	874.8	31.9	29.5	27.5	24.0
M. Atl.								
N.Y.	430.8	438	855.6	1136.4	44.9	41.3	36.8	27.3
N.J.	266.4	275	696.0	1258.8	29.3	25.0	30.3	32.8
Pa.	252.0	328	668.4	884.4	30.9	29.3	30.1	25.2
E.N. Cent.								
Ohio	274.8	203	526.8	892.8	32.5	17.5	23.2	25.0
Ind.	147.6	156	334.8	441.6	17.1	13.7	15.1	13.3
Ill.	208.8	287	602.4	1150.8	25.7	24.7	25.1	28.9
Mich.	328.8	264	588.0	1160.4	29.8	23.2	24.4	34.7
Wisc.	252.0	256	613.2	1011.6	31.2	23.7	26.7	27.7
W.N. Cent.								
Minn.	238.8	277	565.2	913.2	19.7	24.7	26.3	28.8
Iowa	193.2	195	342.0	469.2	19.2	18.1	15.7	14.1
Mo.	207.6	151	387.6	690.0	36.4	13.7	20.2	22.0
N.D.	250.8	171	465.6	646.8	19.2	—	17.9	24.9
S.D.	184.8	151	322.8	414.0	19.3	—	16.3	16.0
Neb.	262.8	140	393.6	588.0	22.3	14.0	19.7	20.5
Kan.	166.8	170	567.6	800.4	14.8	18.1	28.2	26.7
S. Atl.								
Del.	183.6	252	428.4	780.0	43.4	26.3	22.4	28.1
Md.	162.0	262	534.0	775.2	27.6	26.7	28.1	25.7
D.C.	104.0	301	541.2	883.2	72.2	—	25.3	27.0
Va.	90.0	112	289.2	502.8	17.8	15.6	20.4	24.0
W. Va.	97.2	107	267.6	375.6	10.2	9.7	14.5	14.4
N.C.	122.4	75	176.4	300.0	26.3	12.1	14.1	17.2
S.C.	74.4	107	175.2	372.0	21.4	16.7	14.8	23.8
Ga.	99.6	72	193.2	320.4	19.3	11.3	16.9	18.7
Fla.	146.4	79	181.2	393.6	30.4	12.3	13.1	17.5

TABLE 5
PAUPER SUPPORT: 1929-1960*

	YEARLY AVERAGE PER FAMILY				AS A RATIO TO INCOME OF COMMON LABORER			
	1929	*1940*	*1950*	*1960*	*1929*	*1940*	*1950*	*1960*
E.S. Cent.								
Ky.	136.8	93	279.6	398.4	25.3	10.6	17.8	17.6
Tenn.	87.6	70	152.4	206.4	18.6	10.3	11.7	10.7
Ala.	51.6	112	146.4	156.0	16.1	14.4	11.5	8.6
Miss.	69.6	70	135.6	178.8	14.1	9.7	13.0	12.3
W.S. Cent.								
Ark.	99.6	65	153.6	174.0	16.2	10.2	13.4	10.1
La.	64.8	183	388.8	609.6	10.8	25.4	27.0	28.6
Okla.	170.4	54	183.6	164.4	28.9	—	12.2	7.5
Tex.	141.6	96	231.6	315.6	21.9	12.3	15.5	14.4
Mount.								
Mont.	324.0	173	451.2	508.8	52.9	—	20.1	16.3
Idaho	193.2	177	410.4	—	29.5	—	19.1	—
Wyo.	196.8	181	542.4	792.0	32.2	—	24.2	24.7
Colo.	270.0	159	441.6	564.0	47.1	—	21.7	18.2
N.M.	148.8	90	285.6	523.2	31.3	12.5	18.3	22.3
Ariz.	265.2	170	439.2	580.8	49.6	—	24.8	21.7
Utah	151.2	256	571.2	866.4	31.9	26.1	25.8	26.5
Nev.	388.8	160	334.8	475.2	56.3	13.1	14.7	12.8
Pacific								
Wash.	231.6	170	718.8	892.8	24.1	13.5	28.9	23.5
Ore.	237.6	182	624.0	739.2	25.5	15.2	24.6	17.9
Calif.	249.6	337	544.8	708.0	25.0	28.6	23.0	18.5

Source: Appendix.

*Dollar figures for 1929, 1950, 1960 truncated; e.g. $268.8 ≈ $268.80.

APPENDIX B

(1) $$PA = f(T/W, W)$$

where PA is the average public assistance payment, T/W is the ratio of taxes to the income per constituent, and W is the constituent's income.

The equation fitted, however, is:

(2) $$T/W = b(W) \qquad 100 > T/W < O$$

Given the antiquity of tithing and charity, T/W must be greater than O. However one would expect that variations in the strength of evangelical movements, and in anticipated social disorders, would vary T/W without proportionately varying W. Equation 2 is, insofar forth, misspecified. Moreover, the equation is fitted to common labor rates, whereas W should be average earnings. Given differential changes in productivity of common labor and in the aggregate for all workers, as well as changes in the role of income from capital, it is unlikely that common labor rates will move as average earnings. Such misspecification will work to reduce the significance atributable to the coefficient of W in 2. The results for cross section fitting of data for 36 states in 1870, and 48–50 states in 1940–1960, are, therefore, all the more striking. The b coefficients (and t ratios) for the four dates were as follows:

	b	t
1870	.293	(2.76)
1940	.319	(5.10)
1950	.355	(9.10)
1960	.319	(9.50)

The great similarity between coefficients for these dates over nearly a century is striking.

An upward trend in coefficients is consistent with the textual argument in favor of earnings of constituents. Common labor rates rose by 185 percent from 1870 to 1940.

Earnings of non-farm employees rose by 155 percent, and monthly wages of farm employees, by 70 percent. Given the shift in labor force mix from 52 percent in farming to a mere 15 percent, it is clear that a combined labor force figure would show average earnings rising far more than common labor rates did. (Earnings and labor force data from the writer's *Manpower in Economic Growth*, Tables A-1, A-17, A-24, A-25.) Hence some rise in the coefficients for common labor should appear even if the ratio to constituents incomes were unchanged.

The slight upward trend and broad similarity of the coefficients is quite consistent with the text conclusion that legislators were prepared to offer 30¢ more to the poor for every additional dollar of income to common labor—and, by implication, dollar of income to their constituents. It is clear that taxes rose markedly over these decades; hence that their effective generosity would be somewhat understated. But that bias would tend to be cancelled because effective yearly unemployment probably declined.

THE MINIMUM BUDGET:
FROM "DECENCY" TO "SCIENCE"

---

*"Men cannot live decent lives nor attain
to the degree of development that befits
creatures made in the image and likeness of
God" on less than $600 a year.*
—Reverend John Ryan, 1907.[1]

"How much land does a man need?" Tolstoy asked during
his high religious phase. And he answered, in a story with
that title: "no more than enough for a grave." As the world
has industrialized, a new question was increasingly put:
"How much money does a man need?" The answer given
by American legislative practice has been noted above. But
there has been another approach. Minimum standards and
poverty lines have been set by a detailed budget of "required" items—e.g. the BLS City Workers Family Budget.
The logic behind these budgets is striking. Yet it has received little examination. How the budget relates to the
world of jobs, consumers, and legislators is a question whose
answer is fascinating, perhaps unbearably so.

I

Commentators have rarely hesitated to describe a minimum
"American" standard of living. Since Hezekiah Niles wrote
in 1817, and Matthew Carey, many such budgets have been

[1] Senator John Dryden, in almost the same year, found that "a
minimum of subsistence in conformity to the American standard of
life requires at least an annual income of $360." Cf. J. A. Ryan, "The
Standard of Living and the Problem of Dependency," *Proceedings,
National Conference Charities and Corrections* (June 1907), John
A. Dryden, *Addresses . . .* (1908), p. 125. Robert Chapin, "Influence
of Income on Standards of Life," *Publications of the American Economic Association* (1909), however, found that in the $600–700 range
33% were underfed, 51% overcrowded, and 63% underclad.

70

proposed. Personal or class bias led each writer to propose a different list of absolutely urgent items, unless it was the happenstance of the day or their knowledge.

Science, however, arrived on the scene in 1920. In that year the U.S. Bureau of Labor Statistics set forth an official budget. That budget, it declared, included those items the working man required for "health and decency."[2] There were then few items that scientists had declared requisite for health. Hence most of the budget was presumably required to achieve "decency."

So Victorian a commitment, and adjective, admitted a wide and an uncertain meaning. The BLS concluded that 23 pounds of canned peaches were required for decency but only 2 pounds of canned pineapples. Why not vice versa? That a butter knife had to be included was, perhaps, to be expected from anyone's conception of decency. So, perhaps, was the BLS assertion that a working-class family required a domestic servant one day a week.[3] But the BLS declared that a working man's family needed a lemon squeezer. Health? Or decency?

The next official effort to fix a budget, in 1947, involved a distinguished committee. That committee described its logic far more explicitly.[4] It did not even mention decency. Instead, it rested its analytic system on two pillars. One was introspective psychology; the other was brute force. It declared that its budget provided those items requisite for "the maintenance of self-respect and the respect of others."[5] Could even the most admirable national administration then (President Truman), or since (Eisenhower? Ken-

[2] Bureau of Applied Economics, *Standards of Living* (1920), p. 1.

[3] It did not deal with the fascinating question of whether domestic servants required domestic servants.

[4] BLS Bulletin 927, *Workers Budgets in the United States: City Families and Single Persons, 1964 and 1947.*

[5] "The budget therefore should represent the necessary minimum with respect to items included and their quantities as determined by prevailing standards of what is needed for health, efficiency, nurture of children, social participation, and the maintenance of self-respect and the respect of others."

nedy? Nixon? Ford?) determine which material objects Americans required to keep their "self-respect and the respect of others"? Should it? This was surely a new and instructive proposition. The second pillar on which its budget rested was far firmer. That budget, the committee wrote, "represents what men commonly expect to enjoy, feel that they have lost status . . . if they cannot enjoy, and what they insist upon having."[6] Every criterion in this eloquent sequence is dominated by the last—what men "insist upon having." Surely the great advantage of any such criterion is that no analysis is needed. Ultimately it is implemented by political pressure on the legislature—expressed in the halls of Congress and/or the streets—for which a learned committee report is all but superfluous.

Mid-Victorian "decency" had apparently failed as a standard. What men "expect to enjoy . . . and insist upon having" apparently offered no more lasting a basis. For the BLS tried again, in 1967.[7]

II

(1) In a statistical tour de force the BLS transformed a major limitation in usual budget analyses into the very rock on which it built its entire procedure. It assumed that the amount consumers spent on any "component"—e.g., clothing—was not related to what they spent on any other component, nor to their total expenditures. This novel discovery may rank in economics where Tertullian's "credo quia impossibile" does in theology. Yet half a dozen other, and no less ingenious, assumptions were also made as it developed "higher," "moderate," and "lower" budget standards. (The "lower" standard has gone forth to be used by dozens

---

[6] Lest, years later, it be concluded that reference to "men" was sexist, it should be noted that 6 of 7 persons signing the report were women.

[7] BLS Bulletin 1570-5, *Three Standards of Living . . . Spring 1967.*

of writers as a measure of the minimum needs for existence in the U.S. today.)

(2) It fixed required expenditures (by component) for the "lower"—i.e., low income—budget as whatever was spent by families in the "next lower income class" below that for the moderate standard.[8] What is the "next lower income class"? That concept has hitherto been unknown to economics. It was, in fact, defined by the person(s) who decided how many income class intervals to use in publishing the 1960–1961 expenditure data. Had Congress provided more money for that survey, there could well have been more categories published and thus a quite different "next lower group." Had the budget been smaller, fewer categories would have been published. A quite different set of minimum needs for poor people would then have been described.

Had the agency not tabulated by the intervals (in thousand dollars) $4–5, $5–6, $6–7.5, $7.5–10 but instead tabulated $4–5, $5–6, $6–7, $7–8, $8–9, $9–10 it would have arrived at a fourth and a different set of budget "requirements." Had it tabulated by $500 intervals, the elasticities would again have differed; the scientific budget requirements would have changed. For the particular dollar intervals used in publication to be wholly suitable for publishing data is one thing. That they provide an unequivocal basis for computing "points of maximum elasticity" and, thereby, budget requirements is quite another.

That problem is not discussed in any of the 5 BLS reports which describe how the budget requirements were worked out.

(3) The BLS analysis, then, fixed a standard for low income groups by reference to a "moderate" standard

---

[8] "No separate statistical analysis was made to define the consumption level appropriate for the lower and the higher living standards. Instead, budget allowances for the lower standard were most often derived at the next lower income class below the class at which the inflection point (point of maximum elasticity defined as equivalent to the moderate standard) was located." *Ibid*, p. 46.

group. How did it get the first fixed point—for the "moderate" group?

"The analysis determines the income level at which the rate of increase in quantities purchased, or expenditures begin to decline in relation to the rate of change in income, i.e. the point of maximum elasticity. The average number and kinds of items purchased at these income levels are the quantities and qualities specified for the moderate budget . . . decreasing elasticity indicates decreasing urgency. The point of maximum elasticity has been described as the point on the income scale where families stopped buying 'more and more' and started either 'better and better' or something less essential to them."[9]

What does this sequence of references to "elasticity" lead to? Expenditures for certain items were defined by the spending of one income group, while those of direct substitutes were measured by the spending of quite another income group. For example the expenditures on house furnishings were those of the $3,000–4,000 group, while house-operation expenditures were for the $5,000–6,000 group (pp. 46–47). What consumers in the $3,000–4,000 group spent on furniture and equipment apparently had nothing to do with what they spent on upkeep for such furniture and equipment. For "food eaten at home" the $2,000–3,000 group was used, but for "food eaten away from home" the $6,000–7,500 group was used (pp. 41, 47). That within any income category spending more for food away from home could affect the amount spent at home, and vice versa, is apparently ignored.

(4) The BLS procedure dealt with what it termed "components"—e.g., "clothing components"—rather than "items." It thereby apparently assumed that real families substitute one item for another within components but not across. (A mother would substitute heavy coats for light ones, but never delay replacing any worn coat in order to get the

[9] *Ibid*, p. 46.

next size shoes for the children.) If the budget principle is to determine what families "need," in some sense, then either (a) one derives a full list of items from data on spending behavior, or (b) one must resort to the ancient practice of arbitrary designation of all items. What warrant does this intermediate substitution process possess?

(5) The BLS specifically rejected family behavior in some groups but adopted it in others. Thus it stipulated that 3 families out of 4 would "at the moderate standard" own their home: the fourth would rent (p. 42). Does this mean that 3 required their own home to maintain "health and social well-being, the nurture of children and participation in community activities" (p. 1) but the ingenious fourth family, at the same expenditure level, could get away with renting?[10] Similarly, on the "lower standard" half the families in major cities are defined to require a car, while the other half do not require a car (p. 44).[11]

(6) The lower standard involved BLS intervention, on unspecified principles, in designating many of the items. The "scientific" "point of maximum elasticity" criterion was thereby ignored. For some clothing components (not specified) spending data for higher income groups were used since "there were no budget-type families having 1960–1961 after-tax incomes below $3,000" (p. 46). For personal care "allowances were obtained from two income classes below the inflection point" rather than from the canonical class (p. 47). Why? As already indicated, for "food away from home" and "alcoholic beverages" the point of maximum elasticity was apparently ignored because the income level was too high. Hence the BLS simply picked an arbitrary

[10] The absence of any logical explanation for this interesting selection scheme brought its inevitable consequence. Thus one writer concluded that the BLS low budget "assumes rental of housing because ownership is considered too costly"—a remark worth multiple rereadings. Cf. Richard Parker, *The Myth of the Middle Class* (1972), p. 100.

[11] Do those with names that begin with "a" through "l" require cars, while those with "m" through "z" don't?

interval for the moderate standard, and thereby for "next lower" class, and thereby for the "lower standard." To increase the arbitrary ingenuity, "Liquor was replaced by quantities of beer in the minimum standard" (p. 47). What price the scientific "elasticity" procedure?

(7) For some categories the BLS rejected actual spending behavior—but without considering that the balance of spending by the families would have been different if they had had to follow the BLS rules. (a) For example, the BLS excluded cigarette expenditures, and simply picked cigar and pipe tobacco spending for the $5,000–6,000 interval for its moderate standard (p. 47). (b) For food away from home and alcoholic beverages it rejected all budget data: "elasticities . . . were ever increasing, and quantities for these components at the 'moderate standard' were derived between $6,000–7,500. These moderate quantities were converted to reflect the manner of living of families at lower and higher income levels."

III

The signal advantage of an official budget is, of course, that its status enables contending parties to use it as a neutral basis for discussion. To achieve that purpose it may be desirable, or even essential, that its logic be intertwined, its procedures obscure, and its approach, oppressively "scientific." In fact the "lower" budget has been widely referred to—by leaders of large corporations, by leaders of protest movements—as a scientific minimum budget standard. Perhaps this brief foray suggests the fascinating complexities of scientific method in fixing a minimum budget. One could imagine an alternative, clearly arbitrary, list of goods that many poor families would find pleasant and that the nation could readily afford to give them. But no such arbitrary and unscientific listing could gain the eclat, or offer such serviceability, as generations of "scientific" budgets are likely to.

POVERTY AND STARVATION

> *"While it is gratifying to learn that 1.1
> million fewer people were 'officially' im-
> poverished in 1969 than in 1968, and that
> fewer people are dying of starvation, the
> point is that a wealthy society should do
> much better."*[1]

In point of fact there is no evidence that fewer people died
of starvation in 1969 than 1968.[2] Nor the reverse. For no
adequate measure of starvation in the United States exists.[3]

But it is feasible, and actually more useful, to look to
the links between poverty and malnutrition. For malnutrition is the first stage on the road to starvation. More people
will be damaged by malnutrition than are ever destroyed
by starvation. Furthermore, the malignant health consequences of malnutrition deserve action even where they
do not actually end in starvation.

I

Malnutrition has been declared endemic in American society: "when poverty was 'rediscovered' and malnutrition

[1] Frank Ackerman, et al., "Income Distribution in the United
States," *Review of Radical Economics* (1971), reprinted in Kenneth
Dolbeare and Murray Edelman, *Institutions, Policies, and Goals*
(1973), p. 233.

[2] The source given by the authors of this statement is a Census
report on income distribution. That report includes not one word
about starvation, food, or nutrition. Nor is any more relevant source
cited.

[3] The usual newspaper discussions note only a handful of cases.
Data for other nations may show a smaller percentage. In 1966 the
Government of India reported that only 7 persons died of starvation
in the state of Bihar (with its population of more than 50 million),
yet ¾ of its food crop had failed. Food failures elsewhere in India
were also substantial. Cf. Alan Berg, *The Nutrition Factor* (1972),
pp. 213, 216.

was shown to affect millions . . . they were treated as temporary paradoxes or oversights, rather than as possibly endemic features of American society."[4] Malnutrition *is* "possibly endemic" in American society—and in every other society. "Possibly endemic" is a phrase of notably high elegance, which all but defies verification. We prefer, instead, to follow Senator McGovern's precision in putting quotation marks around such words as "malnourished," "undernourished," and "hunger," thus emphasizing the lack of any scientific or general agreement on what such terms mean.[5] We shall instead use measures for specific key nutrients—calories, protein, vitamin C etc.[6]

A major 1965 U.S. Department of Agriculture survey showed that: 14 percent of American families with incomes below $3,000 failed to get enough calories. To this depressing finding, the survey added another: 10 percent of American families with incomes above $10,000 a year also failed to get enough calories.[7]

Who would doubt that the rich can afford any number of calories? Yet the difference between the two percentages lacking calories—14 percent for the very poor and 10 percent for the rich—is remarkably small. This suggests that something else is at work besides differences in income.

[4] Richard Parker, *The Myth of the Middle Class* (1972), p. xv.

[5] Cf. his introduction to *Hunger in the Classroom: Then and Now*, p. iv.

[6] One writer rejects attention to protein and caloric requirements because "the notion of 'adequate nutrition' cannot be established in any genuinely scientific fashion. . . . As one sociologist, Peter Townsend, remarked, defining what one needs for adequate nutrition is like trying to define adequate height." (Ben Seligman, *Permanent Poverty* [1968], p. 32.) We shall, respectfully, ignore the clear inference that nothing can reliably be said about the adequacy of nutrition.

[7] U.S. Department of Agriculture, Household Food Consumption Survey, 1965-1966, Report No. 6, *Dietary Levels of Households in the United States, Spring 1965*, Table 7. The official poverty line in 1964, the year to which the USDA income data relate, was $3,169 for a family of four.

Before considering other nutrient measures, we should study the immediate background of recent discussions on hunger and nutrition.

What is more basic to human existence than food? And what can generate more concern than statements about its lack? Recent warnings of widespread malnutrition in the U.S. led both to an unprecedented White House conference on nutrition and to a sequence of Congressional hearings. Some of the analyses then made were reminiscent of a report "by philanthropists and by the public press that anywhere from one hundred thousand to three hundred thousand school children (in New York City) went breakfastless to school. And, as a result of these statements, the Salvation Army undertook to give free breakfasts to school children. That program came to an abrupt halt. The reason was disclosed by a study of 4,000 New York families—which showed that only $\frac{1}{10}$ of 1 percent of the children actually went breakfastless to school"—in 1907.[8]

If even a single child had, or has to, do without breakfast, an urgent problem may exist.[9] But the appropriate public policy will differ if one child is involved or 300,000. And, similarly, a lack among adults may create a national issue and may suggest a different policy, even if there is no lack among children, or vice versa.

II

What seem to be the facts about malnutrition in the U.S. today? One result of the extended hearings held by the McGovern Select Committee on Nutrition and Human

[8] Dr. Linsly R. Williams, "Statistical Information Concerning the Physical Welfare of School Children," in *Proceedings of the National Conference of Charities and Correction . . . 1907*, pp. 160–161. The investigatory study was conducted by the New York Committee on Physical Welfare of School Children.

[9] Cf. U.S. Senate Select Committee on Nutrition and Human Needs, *Hunger in the Classroom: Then and Now* (1972), and *To Save the Children* (1974).

Needs was that the U.S. National Center for Health Statistics initiated a vast project. The Center gave health examinations to a large sample of the entire U.S. population in 1971–1972.[10] Its laboratory tests (of blood samples) reported the following:

TABLE 1

PERCENT OF AMERICANS WITH
INADEQUATE NUTRIENT LEVELS: 1971–1972

	All	In Poverty
Vitamin A (serum)	0%	0%
Protein { serum	6	5
Protein { albumin	1	0
Hemoglobin	4	6

The USDA study for 1965 reports shortages for the other nutrients, by poverty level:[11]

TABLE 2

PERCENT OF U.S. HOUSEHOLDS WITH
INADEQUATE NUTRIENTS: 1965

	All Families	Poor Families
Ascorbic acid	27%	42%
Thiamine	8	10
Riboflavin	6	10
Calcium	30	36

There are four obvious ways to bring the diets of the poor up to the level of the nation—e.g., from 14.0 percent lacking calories to 10.6 percent, from 11 percent to 10 percent lacking iron, etc.

(1) End American society, because malnutrition is a "possibly endemic factor" in it. Such a step is quite feasible.

[10] *Preliminary Findings of the First Health and Nutrition Examination Survey, U.S., 1971–72*, Tables 37, 31. The survey provides three other measures of iron in the blood, not indicating whether any one is a better measure than any other. Hematocrit percentages were 19% and 21%; serum iron, 2% and 2%; transferrin saturation, 5% and 4%.

[11] USDA Report No. 6, Tables 1, 11.

However, malnutrition may be "possibly endemic" in every other society. Since we lack these details on the nutritional status of the peoples in nearly every other society, it is difficult to predict that the change would improve health status.[12]

(2) Increase U.S. output and income. A general increase in incomes has long been urged as the prime way to accomplish that goal. But increasing incomes may not improve nutrition. Real GNP rose by $180 billion between 1955 and 1965. The proportion of families in poverty decreased. And the income of most U.S. families rose significantly. But what happened to nutrition? According to the USDA, the percent of American families with good diets actually declined between 1955 and 1965—from 60 percent to 50 percent.[13] Between 1945 and 1972 GNP rose by $437 billions—yet per capita consumption of milk products (the major source of calcium) dropped by 10 percent.[14] Higher incomes are, therefore, not necessarily the answer to malnutrition.[15]

[12] A small sample of health experts were queried on the presence of such data for "socialist" societies and "third world" societies, but were unable to suggest sources for distribution of the population by nutrient level.

[13] *Ibid.*, p. 1. The same NAS-NRC dietary standard was used for both dates.

[14] Milk equivalent (calcium content basis) declined from 249 pounds per capita to 228 pounds. Cf. USDA Agricultural Economics Report No 138, *Food, Consumption Prices, Expenditures* (1968), p. 63, and *Supplement for 1972*, p. 18.

[15] Nor do higher incomes necessarily offer a specific for particular diseases, as has been contended. Cf. "Heart disease . . . leads in the causes of death today; its causes are well known, and among them are overwork (industrial speed-up), malnutrition (unemployment), and worry over economic stability. Research is not required for the control of most heart ailments; social reconstruction, . . . which could take place only at the expense of the present 'philanthropists' is required." Ferdinand Lundberg, *America's 60 Families*, p. 340. This dazzling medical analysis seems not to have been brought to the attention of the skilled Russian researchers on heart disease.

For example, with higher incomes Americans buy more frozen peas, less garden cress. But the vitamin A units per pound come to 3,080 in frozen peas, 29,960 in garden cress. The 1965 survey demonstrates that as income goes up from the $1,000–2,000 category to the $2,000–3,000 category the amount spent for milk actually goes down.[16] Thirty percent of American families with average incomes failed to get enough calcium in 1965. Their incomes, however, were 60 percent greater than those of poor families, of whom 35 percent failed to get enough calcium. The probability of raising the incomes of the poor by 60 percent is not encouragingly high, if one may judge by the past decade. Yet even if that were done, it would apparently leave 30 percent of them still short of calcium.

(3) Expand the food-stamp program. That program quite reasonably permits people to use the money saved by stamps for other purposes. It turns out that existing recipients are less urgently concerned with being able to spend more on food than are some of those who support the program. Thus for every extra dollar given the typical recipient in food stamps he will spend only 50¢ on food, devoting 50¢ to other items.[17] The USDA can give someone food stamps; it cannot thereby make him consume the right nutrients.

(4) Direct action. Give every family the nutrients they lack. The cost would be unbelievably trivial: $50 worth of milk plus vitamin pills annually would bring every poor family up to the U.S. nutrition average. Such a diet supplement would provide for the requirements listed in Tables 1 and 2 above. It would also provide for every other "rec-

[16] USDA Report 6, Table 13.

[17] More precisely, the marginal propensity to spend on food out of income in the form of food stamps is 20 cents on the $1.00. Cf. James N. Morgan et al., *Five Thousand American Families—Patterns of Economic Progress* (1974), Vol. II, "The Allocation of Household Income to Food Consumption," by Saul Hyams and Harold Shapiro. The 50–50 split was kindly provided by Professor Shapiro, as the weighted average of data in his Table 9.7.

ommended daily allowances" of nutrients established by the National Academy of Sciences.[18]

This cost seems absolutely trivial, yet it is true that there might be even less expensive ways to achieve the same end. The government presently runs a program to keep up the price of milk—i.e., federal milk marketing orders. If that program were ended, one of the most complete foods in the American diet would be cheaper, and could be more widely consumed by the poor. However, every president, and every presidential candidate since 1948, has accepted that program. If there is a Congressman, even from an urban area, who considers that program an outrage against the poor, his vehemence has been well concealed. Hence such an alternative is unlikely to eventuate.

Given enough time, it must be admitted, dietary habits *could* change enough to achieve the same end, at lesser cost. But need we wait to save so small a sum? True, the rising popularity of soul foods could bring significant nutritional gains. Collard greens, for example, are ten times better as a source of ascorbic acid than frozen corn, and fantastically better than hearts of palm salad. An occasional choice of pork liver instead of hamburger for dinner would remedy any shortage in protein intake. Indeed, acting on the contribution to knowledge made by George Washington Carver, instead of merely listing it in history books, would do the same. For half a pound of peanuts a week per person could wipe out the protein shortage among the poor.[19] Yet this prospect is hardly likely to appear next year. It therefore does not replace the direct action alternative.

---

[18] It is these RDA's which enter into the literature on poverty, malnutrition, and hunger. There are no data on requirements for particular amino acids, trace elements, etc., much less data on whether the intake of the poor differs from the U.S. average family.

[19] As elsewhere, we refer to the excess of rates among the poor over those for all Americans. Our concern here is the impact of poverty on nutrition and not the nutritionists desire for all Americans to consume items they do not now consume.

Nations half as wealthy as the U.S. could readily afford to guarantee adequate nutrition standards to their poor if it required a mere $50 apiece in vitamin pills and milk. So could the U.S. That statement can surely be made even though the nutrition surveys exaggerate the extent to which the poor lack key nutrients. (By omitting vitamin consumption the 1971–1972 survey omitted half of all vitamin C that Americans consume. The nutrient shortage of vitamin C is therefore exaggerated. The survey ignored two thirds of vitamin A consumption in the same way.)[20]

We are left, therefore, with a set of choices for national policy. (a) We can promptly, and at moderate cost, make available nutrients to every poor family in the U.S. and bring them up to the average level for the nation. (b) Or we can continue to deplore the hunger problem. (c) Or wait for a regeneration of American society. (d) Or seek to increase our GNP by several hundred billions etc. What will the next, the inevitable, Congressional inquiry into hunger in America find the national policy choice has been?

[20] See Appendix on Data III. The 1965 and earlier surveys also excluded them.

APPENDIX

ON DATA

I

Despite the continuing importance of nutrition, and concern with the question of how many Americans lack adequate nutrition, remarkably little attention seems to have been given to the Public Health Service data that were developed as a direct result of the McGovern committee hearings on hunger.

The preliminary national findings of the First Health and Nutrition Examination survey obviously supersede the partial data from one area first reported in the Select Committee hearings.[21] The tabulations provide measures of caloric intake that are absolutely unbelievable. These are presented without comment, nor does there appear to have been any public comment on them. They indicate, for example, that 64 percent of American adults (age 18–44) who are *above* the poverty line fail to get the recommended daily allowance (RDA) of calories set by the National Academy of Sciences (*Preliminary Findings,* p. 52). The RDA used in the USDA 1965 report was 2,900 for men and 2,100 for women. The 22 intervals shown in survey data do not permit that breakdown. We use 2,749 for men and 1,999 for women—because it is the nearest figure shown by the tabulated results and because of a downward trend in RDA caloric requirements. We therefore minimize the unbelievable results of the survey, which would show even more than 64% failing to reach the 2,900 and 2,100 levels.

[21] These partial data for Texas and Louisiana show vastly greater nutritional shortage rates than does the representative U.S. sample. The estimates of Dr. Schaefer on the "alarming prevalence" rates based on the first set of examinations appear in U.S. Select Committee on Nutrition and Human Needs, *Poverty, Malnutrition and Federal Food Assistance Programs* (1969), pp. 1–4. Later data, based on a sample for the entire U.S. appear in *Preliminary Findings. . . .*

Given such findings for calories, the intake data cannot be trusted as including all the protein, ascorbic acid, etc., actually consumed by the population. The omitted calories were in food that respondents failed to remember consuming—and other nutrients must have been present in that food also. The laboratory findings are not subject to any such memory bias and are therefore the figures we use for 1971–1972. The 1965 intake data are also subject to memory bias, though they relate to seven-day intake. We show them to give some upper-bound estimate of the lack of these other nutrients.

A comparison between laboratory findings and reported intake may be made within the 1971–1972 data and against the 1965 data. It suggests that the inadequacy of the intake data to report what we are interested in arises for two reasons. First is the fact that the body accumulates needed nutrients and can provide a steady and adequate supply even where intake on a particular day may fall short. Second, apparently few but professional nutritionists seem able to remember all food intake—a hamburger eaten at a drive-in, a slice of onion on a sandwich, a piece of candy consumed at work, sauce on a piece of fish, etc. Every such omission tends to omit nutrient intake even for those improbable respondents who do remember every pat of butter and every sip of juice they consumed. And each such omission increases the estimated number of people who presumably fail to get enough nutrients.

II

The omission of vitamin usage from nutrition surveys is almost incomprehensible. People can surely report the brand of vitamin they use with at least as much accuracy as they can estimate data now promptly accepted in nutrition surveys, e.g.—how many ounces of meat (as distinct from fat and cartilage) they consume in a restaurant meal; the composition of the salad dressing they used in the plant cafeteria, etc. Given the vitamin brand, of course, quite precise information from the limited set of producers is readily available. Is it possible that nutrition surveyers really take more interest in "the farm problem" than "the hunger problem"?

III

The 1971–1972 study gives mean intake and the population count in its Table 1. The implicit aggregates are compared with unpublished consumption estimates kindly provided by Robert D. Burleson of Merck and Co. His data indicate a 1972 total of 100 trillion units of vitamin A used in food fortification and 500 trillion in pharmaceuticals. For vitamin C the figures are 3,500 metric tons. (We omit 1,000 metric tons of high-potency vitamin C production on the assumption that they were consumed by a very small part of the population. Including them would, of course, make the percentages reported above still steeper.) These data are estimated from production minus net exports and minus animal feed usage.

Some 32 percent of those examined in the 1971–1972 survey took vitamin supplements—regularly (22 percent) or irregularly (10 percent). A national survey for 1971 indicated that 53 percent of all U.S. households had 1 (or more) family members who took daily vitamin supplements—as did 43 percent of U.S. households with incomes below $5,000. Failure to allow for so widespread an intake of vitamins makes the 1971–1972 survey exaggerate nutritional deficiencies. (Data for 1971 from an Opinion Research Corporation survey for Hoffman-La Roche Inc., kindly provided by Dr. J. C. Bauernfeind and Mr. John W. Gage of that company.)

GNP AND THE GARDEN OF EDEN:
LONG-TERM TRENDS
IN U.S. REAL INCOMES

> *"I will sum up another tale . . . the death-*
> *less gods who dwell on Olympus made a*
> *golden race of mortal men. . . . And they*
> *lived like gods without sorrow of heart,*
> *remote and free from toil and grief; miser-*
> *able age rested not on them; but with legs*
> *and arms never failing they made merry*
> *with feasting beyond the reach of all evils."**

There, surely, is the ultimate legend. It appeared again, impressively, in the Bible's description of the Garden of Eden. Surely its most important secular version was Rousseau's idyll of natural man before civilization ruined his character. The legend did not lack for opposition. Perhaps the most succinct was Byron's: "The 'good old times'—all times when old are good—are gone."[2] But it was reserved for Marx to attack the legend most tellingly when he described the tremendous advance capitalism made over prior states, as humanity moved on toward socialism.

In our own day, however, a new and earnest set of romantics have appeared. Appareled in what they oddly term "Marxism," they ignore the adult Marx as they journey back to Rousseauism. And telling over each evil bead of industrialism, technology, and alienation they imply that a golden world did exist in Europe a few centuries back and on the U.S. frontier a mere century or so ago.

It is the purpose of this study to compare the physical conditions of existence in the U.S. at an earlier day with those at present. The measures used are limited. They can

---

* Hesiod, *Works and Days*, pp. 110–115.

[1] Data not otherwise footnoted are from ch. 15 in the author's *The American Economy: Income, Wealth and Want.*

[2] *The Age of Bronze.*

hardly compete with those scientific intuitions which contrast levels of happiness then and now. Our goal is a far more modest one, of trying to see for what the increased output of the U.S. economy since 1900 has been used? Where has all the GNP gone? What key items drew largely on our resources, and for which can moderately reliable statistics be computed?[3]

I

Hours of Work

> "All these writers of economics overrate the importance of work. Every man has a profound instinct that idleness is the true reward of work, even if it only comes at the end of life."
> —Yeats, *Explorations.*

The moral contribution made by work, and workmanship, has been eloquently urged by Veblen, as others in the Puritan tradition. It may be true that workers in other cultures indeed guide their lives by a virtuous instinct of workmanship. But American workers since 1900 have followed Yeats rather than Veblen: they sought a shorter work day, a shorter work week, and a shorter work year. Of course the persistent advance of productivity has enabled them both to shorten their work week and consume more. Yet if they had continued to work a 1900 work day they could have reached still higher consumption levels. It is not without symbolic importance that the greatest and most violent initial surge of U.S. worker organization occurred in 1885, under the banner of "the 8 hour day."[4] From 1900 to 1970

---

[3] GNP in investment, net exports, and government are ignored here. These may be construed as eventually permitting various types of end consumption. However, even if that were certain—and the Kuznets position on war expenditures is well known—the amount allocated to any given year would inevitably be small relative to the consumption total.

[4] The Haymarket Riot took place, of course, as a direct outcome of the Mayday demonstration for a shorter work day.

the average worker cut his work week from 66.8 to 45.0 hours, or 33 percent. It does not, of course follow that today's worker could increase his income quite that much if he were satisfied to work 48 percent more hours a week. But he could increase it very substantially.[5] That margin measures the value of increased leisure—all of it quite omitted from the GNP estimates as normally made

Weekly Hours (Scheduled)
Male Labor Force

	1900	1973	Decline 1900-1973
Total	66.8	45.0	−33%
Farm	74.0	53.9	−27
Non-farm	61.8	44.4	−28

Farmers and farm laborers—who made up 40 percent of the 1900 labor force—worked 12 hours a day for six days, and rested on the seventh with a mere 2 hours of chores. The farm work week was cut 20 hours by 1970. Farmers achieved this cut in three main ways. First, by buying tractors and gasoline instead of making hay, feeding, currying and caring for horses. Second, by buying commercial fertilizer instead of collecting and carting manure. And, third, by buying a dozen other products instead of continuing to make them in true handicraft fashion.

Urban workers cut their work week even more dramatically, as the table indicates. The overall decline for the labor force was necessarily still greater, as the center of employment moved from farm to nonfarm work. How strongly even a 10 hour work day is disliked in our own time is suggested by the glacial rate at which a 4 day, 10 hour a day, work week has been introduced. (Less than

[5] Particular emphasis on the greater efficiency of shorter hours has been given by Edward Denison. Cf. His *Accounting for United States Economic Growth, 1929-1969* (1974), Table 9-4, in which he estimates that fully half the decline in growth arising from the 1929–1948 decline in average weekly hours was compensated by greater efficiency per hour.

1% of U.S. workers are on such a work week. Nor has any national union come out favoring it.) One can surmise that the increase in wages needed to persuade workers to return to the 1900 work day would be substantial. But that great increase would mark and measure the monetary value of the hours cut since 1900, a value omitted from GNP.

Hours: Holidays, Vacations

The tedium and toil of labor can be alleviated by shortening the work day. It can also be moderated by shortening the work year. One remembers how Marx, and more recently Mandel, have attributed to capitalism the lengthening of the work year as saints days and religious holidays disappeared from the secularized calendar. How has the number of holidays taken by American workers changed? The typical 1900 worker had, at most, the 4th of July, Labor Day, and Christmas (and was probably paid for none). The typical worker in 1970 had 7 paid holidays.[6]

What of the trend in vacations? In 1900 6 percent of non-farm workers took vacations, while in 1970 some 80 percent did. The expansion took place, almost completely, after World War II.

Percent of Non-Farm Workers
Taking Vacations: 1901-1970

1901	6%
1930	1
1950	60
1960	66
1970	80

If one assumed that hardly any 1900 farm workers took vacations, the 1900–1970 rise for the entire labor force would have been from say 2 percent to 80 percent.

Surely the concentrated stretch of vacation was worth more to the typical worker than the equivalent shortening

[6] Bureau of Labor Statistics, Bulletin 1770, *Employee Compensation in the Private Nonfarm Economy, 1970,* Table A-29.

of the typical work day. So was the variety, and remission, provided by the holidays. But suppose one were to ignore that advantage, and simply compute total yearly work hours at each date. The typical American worked 3,380 hours a year in 1900—and 2,200 in 1970. The grandfather of to-day's American therefore worked 50 percent more hours each year than his grandson does. According to a usual model, these extra hours could be valued for the 1970 worker at the typical hourly wage he now receives. If so his real income is really 50 percent greater than it is reported to be.[7]

Hours of Work: Housewives

From 1900 to 1970 the work day for the typical worker fell by 50 percent, as noted above. The housewife's work day fell even more:

The Housewife's Day, 1900–1966[7a]

	1900	1966
Housework	12	5
Laundry	2	1
Cooking	6	1½
Sewing	2⎫	2½
Cleaning	2⎭	
Leisure	½ (?)	4¼
TV, radio	0	3½

"The cooking, service and 'cleaning up' of ordinary meals in a farmhouse, with the contributory processes of picking, sorting, peeling, washing, etc., and the extra time given to special baking, pickling and preserving, takes fully six hours a day." So wrote Charlotte Gilman in 1910. By 1966 cooking

---

[7] I.e., assuming his response if one were to ask him how much added income he would require to work as many hours as his grandparents did in their prime.

[7a] Sources for table appear in note 17.

time had been reduced to 1½ hours. Marketing (by urban housewives) took ⅓ of an hour. And dishwashing, all other house cleaning, sewing, and all other chores (but laundry) took 2½ hours. Time freed from all these activities went for: more child care, travel, study. And (most of all) 2 hours of conversation plus 4¼ hours a day for leisure activities such as TV. The vacuum cleaners, washing machines, and other household helps that made all this possible were not bought by her husband lengthening his work day to earn more. For his too was cut sharply. That pair of facts offers a profound comment on the U.S. economy. Whether many people would wish to return to the household work day that characterized mankind for thirty centuries is unknown. But one may surmise.

Housing: Privacy: 1

Between 1900 and today a frequent member of the American family has disappeared. In 1900 1 American urban family in every 4 sacrificed its privacy and expanded its income by taking in boarders and lodgers. By 1970 only 2 percent did so. In 1900 something like 15 percent of farm families had a resident hired hand—rarely viewed as romantically as in Frost's "The Hired Man." (Moreover, many farm families housed and fed harvest workers for short periods.)

Housewives once accepted the work of cleaning lodger's rooms, doing the extra cooking, serving, and washing. Few do so any longer. The psychological consequences of a resident outsider, and the extra work he created, apparently became too great relative to the income he provided. Two factors created this significant change. One was economic. As incomes rose, families gave up so unsatisfactory a source of income. (It is suggestive that the long-run decline reversed itself during the depression. The percent with lodgers actually rose from 11 percent to 15 percent when incomes fell between 1930 and 1934–1936.) Rates for nonwhites—with their generally lower incomes—were about double those for whites in 1930, 1960, and 1970.[8] But a second factor was at work: changing cultural patterns. Foreign-born rates were far above those for native whites and non-whites in 1910, but appear to be—there are no data for 1970, only impressions—nowhere as distinct in recent times. Thus the combination of low incomes and different cultural patterns explain 1910 rates of 11 percent for German foreign born, 18 percent for Irish, 27 percent for South Italian, and 77 percent for Lithuanians. By the third generation there exists little indication of any such differences: economic advance and the melting pot have together ended this ancient method of supplementing family income. The increased privacy families now enjoy, however, and the reduced emotional costs, fail to enter into measured GNP,[9] or into the measured increase since 1900.

Housing: Privacy, Crowding: II

The simplest indication of the increase in private space (i.e., decrease in "overcrowding") is given by the number of persons per room:

Persons per Room

Year	U.S.	White	Non-White
1910	1.13	1.11	1.30
1970	.62	.61	.77

[8] The white/non-white comparisons reported below in Part III are somewhat less reliable for other years. Thus in 1910 the nonwhite sample was very small; in 1934-1936 it was restricted to non-relief families, a quite atypical group for non-whites in those years.

[9] Because of the methods of estimate used hitherto, the value of services provided to lodgers in 1900 appears implicitly in GNP: imputed rental values for family housing were higher than they would have been if space had not been rented and then sub-let to lodgers. Presumably the family was a more efficient provider of such space and facilities than the alternatives available in the private market. It would, then, be that differential which declined over time, and the rent component of the cost of living index would have risen more in consequence of that declining differential—yielding a smaller growth in real GNP than truly occurred.

Almost 50 percent more rooms were used per person in 1970 than in 1910.[10] It is likely that the amount of cubic feet per person did not increase as much. On the other hand, the amount of privacy, and the reduction in "crowding," probably increased still more.

The level of crowding at the beginning of the century can usefully be contrasted with that in some European cities.[11] (Americans in 1910 who were foreign born tended to live primarily in cities.)

Percent of Families with
2 or More Persons Per Room

1895: Europe		1910: U.S. Foreign Born	
Paris	14%	French	6%
London	20	English	4
Berlin	28	German	9
Vienna	28	Bohemian	16
Moscow	31	Russian	43
St. Petersburg	46		

The 1910–1970 change may also be looked at by a measure of more extreme crowding. The percent of U.S. families with more than 1 person per room ran:

49% in 1910
20% in 1940
8% in 1970

Housing: Privacy: III

There was a third change in housing usage over the past three-quarters of a century. Families devoted more of their space to separate bedrooms. The 1910 Immigration Survey reported how many families customarily used every room in the dwelling unit for sleeping.

[10] The 1910 data relate to urban and rural non-farm territory. Since farms with white residents probably had somewhat more rooms per person, the extent of decline is somewhat exaggerated.

[11] Bertillon data for Europe, quoted Adna Weber, *The Growth of Cities in the Nineteenth Century* (1899), p. 416.

INCOME

Native white	1%
Negro	7
Foreign born	
English	0
Irish	0
German	1
Hebrew	5
So. Italian	7
Polish	7
Bulgarian	63

The same survey also reported what proportion of the families had 3 or more persons per sleeping room:

Native white	17
Negro	34
Foreign born	
English	13
Irish	16
German	22
Hebrew	43
So. Italian	44
Polish	50
Bulgarian	66

Both measures show highest rates for the foreign born. However rates for the three largest sources of migration—English, Irish, and German—ran close to those for native whites, and below those for Negroes. Rates for the other foreign groups ranged well upward. Their excess reflected lower incomes, larger families, and different cultural practices brought over from the old country. By 1970 the customs of sleeping in rooms other than bedrooms, and more than 3 persons sleeping in a room, disappeared: family size decreased, incomes rose, customs changed. Family budgets permitted the desire for privacy and space to dominate the "efficient" use of housing space. The spread of housing codes may also have worked to this end. The codes may have coerced the behavior of families who preferred to use space more intensively and use more of their incomes for other objects. To that extent the codes were a further force contributing to expanding privacy in the home.

It would be a fascinating inquiry to determine whether the concern about "anomie" and "isolation" increased over recent decades as the extent of privacy in the American home developed. When children ceased to be raised 3 or 4 in a room, each one instead given his own room, did publicists' concern about isolation, anomie, and rootlessness rise in proportion?

I

Housing: Facilities

It is suggestive of the extent of economic and public health advance in the past century that a key public issue in the 1970's would be the possible carcinogens in public water supply. If they were present, and if they caused a few deaths, major changes in water supply were almost certain to take place.

The problems present at the beginning of the century were staggering by any such standard of concern. As late as the 1870's "stinks arising from the Thames" would, on occasion, force members to leave the Mother of Parliaments. Deaths from water-borne disease were an inevitable part of life throughout Europe, Asia, and America. Around 1900 U.S. cities with relatively good water supplies could expect a typhoid death rate about 20 per 100,000 from causes other than polluted water. Cities that drew their raw water from polluted rivers, however, had substantially higher rates, reflecting that pollution:

Memphis	34
Washington, D.C.	48
Louisville	49
Philadelphia	51
Columbus	85
Pittsburgh	108

From 10 to 20 persons became ill from typhoid for every person who died of it. Moreover various water borne diseases significantly increased the contemporary death rate.

From 1900 to 1970 major declines in these rates took place:[12]

Deaths per 100,000

FROM

	Typhoid	Diarrheal Diseases
1900	31.3	142.7
1970	0.0	1.3

The path by which most households in the U.S. were provided with piped, clean,[13] running water can be briefly summarized:

Percent of U.S. Households
With Running Water

	U.S.	Urban	Farm	White	Non-White
1890	24%	58%	1%	(27)%	(0)%
1940	70	94	37	74	39
1970	98	100	91	98	92

More than half of the city families in 1890 had piped water. But virtually none of the farm families did—and therefore virtually no non-white family did. By 1940 most urban families had running water, while somewhat over a third of farm families did. Because of the size of the farm population, this in turn meant that 74 percent of white and only 39 percent of non-white families had such supply. The major change since 1940, therefore, has been the expansion of water supply to farm households, and the departure of many whites, and most non-whites, to urban homes that are typically provided with piped water.

[12] *Historical Statistics of the U.S.*, II, p. 26 and *1974 Statistical Abstract*, p. 62.

[13] "Clean" in terms of bacteria producing enteritis, diarrhea, typhoid, paratyphoid, etc. However, this change was achieved largely by introducing chlorine into the filtering and processing of raw water. Given that advance, the new standards of the 1970's involve concern over the impact of chlorine itself. Hence chlorine may itself be considered unclean when present in drinking water.

II

Closely related to the investment in piped water supply, and closely linked to the dramatic reduction on death rates from key contagious diseases, was the replacement of privies by flush toilets:

Percent of U.S. Households
With Flush Toilets

	U.S.	Urban	Farm	White	Non-White
1890	13%	46%	0%	14%	5%
1940	60	85	9	63	26
1970	96	99	87	97	89

I

Heating

From the most ancient times fire, and heat, were provided when lightning began forest fires. More tractable forms of heating evolved from that history. But the typical fuel used by man for many centuries, as by nature, was wood. Chopping down trees, hauling them, sawing, splitting, and seasoning, however, was a long wearying and tiresome process. As incomes rose in the U.S. less demanding fuels replaced wood:

Percent of U.S. Families
Heating by

	Wood	Coal	Oil	Gas
1880	65%	35%	0%	0%
1908	36	63	1	
1940	23	55	11	11
1970	1	3	26	56

Coal initially superseded wood because the concentration of coal deposits made the total labor and resource requirement far less. But coal itself still put heavy demands on the family: it had to be shoveled into the coal bin, into the furnace; clinkers removed at uncomfortable intervals; and ashes taken out daily. The process still demanded much labor, much discomfort for the head of the household, who typically moved coal in and ashes out. It also involved much work for the housewife, who had to clean clothing, curtains, and cellars dirtied by coal smoke. As incomes rose after the Great Depression, therefore, coal was swiftly replaced by far more convenient fuels—oil and gas. And when a combination of discoveries and federal regulation kept down the relative price of gas, that most convenient of these fuels swiftly became the primary source. By 1970 it heated about the same percentage of American homes as wood had a century earlier. But the work load within the home associated with heating had dropped markedly—and pleasantly.

II

Another change in heating mode was the extension of central heating. The traditional description of families cosily met around the winter fireside reflects the fact that the rest of the home was nearly freezing. But, however appreciated, heating in every room was not to become at all common until income levels had risen and other priorities had been met. In the United States central heating did not permit the comfortable use of every room in the dwelling until after the piping times of the honorable Woodrow Wilson and Warren Harding:

Percent of American Dwelling
Units with Central Heat

1900	0%
1910	0
1920	1
1940	42
1950	50
1960	66
1970	78

When it came, however, it came with a rush. From the early 1920's to the early 1930's the proportion went from 1 percent to near 40 percent. From 1950 to 1970 the proportion rose from half to three-fourths, with the non-white proportion rising from 40 percent to 58 percent. What the dramatic change in fuel prices in the early 1970's would do to this trend is unclear. The dollar costs of central heating were not great relative to incomes, judging by earlier standards. But the change in prices of fuel relative to other items was, of course, unprecedented. As with the change in persons per room, the extension of central heating also created more privacy, separateness, and isolation than characterized earlier, urban, days.

Consumer Durables in the Home

In considering the 1910 housewife's day, Charlotte Gilman estimated that 2 hours went for laundering, 2 hours for sweeping, cleaning, and setting "to rights."[14] Whatever the precision of her guess, it pointed to the substantial amount of time that such work required. Ever since Thomas Jefferson first began issuing U.S. patents, a thousand inventors had tried to reduce that work load, inventing sinks, washboards, washing machines, and cleaners. But housewives did not substitute machines for their own work until two things occurred. First was a rise in incomes that permitted purchases beyond the most essential. Second, of course, was the development of electricity as something beyond a laboratory curiosum. The table below suggests the rate at which the new household durables spread.

		Percent of American Families With			
	Ice	*Refrigerators* *Mechanical*	*Washing Machines*	*Vacuum Cleaners*	*Radios*
1900		0%		0%	0%
10	18%	0		0	0
20	48	1	8%	9	0
30	40	8	24	30	40
40	27	44			83
50	11	80		(54)	96
60			73	73	92
70	1	99	70	92	96

[14] Charlotte Perkins Gilman, *The Home* (1910), pp. 96–97.

After Edison, Tesla, Westinghouse, and a hundred others had done their work, the U.S. household characteristically relied on a range of electrical appliances to reduce the housewife's workload. No other nation provided its housewives with so many mechanical servants. The U.S. home used, not cold water and wash boards, but hot water in mechanical washing machines. Instead of feather dusters it had vacuum cleaners.

The widespread U.S. reliance on refrigerators—first iceboxes and then mechanical—may have saved even more work. They dramatically reduced the number of shopping trips that the housewife and/or children had to make each day, for milk, for meat, and for other items that could not keep readily without refrigeration. Work apart, the refrigerator reduced food waste, spoilage, and infection from spoiled food, just as easy-to-use washing machines led to more frequent washing and decreased disease spread by lice and thru dirty clothes.[15]

As late as 1970 the difference between the array of conveniences that assisted the American housewife and household still contrasted markedly even with Western Europe.

Percent of Households
in 1970

With:	U.S.	Western Europe
Refrigerator	99%	72
Washing machines	70	57
Dryer	45	18
Iron	100	93
Vacuum cleaner	92	61
Dishwasher	26	2
Toaster	93	21
TV	99	75
Telephone	91	33

[15] Tradition has it that the great plague of the 14th century was carried westward from bales of clothes in Genoese storehouses near the Black Sea.

III

What single item was responsible for more social change in the U.S. over the past three-quarters of a century than the automobile? Americans may have adopted it because it permitted them to carry goods at lower resource cost. But if that were its chief contribution, probably few would be in use except on farms. What did account for the rise since 1910? for the enormous rise in the single decade, 1920–1930? and for the pattern of spread shown below?

	Total	*Percent of Families with Automobiles* Urban	Farm	White	Non-White
1900	0%				
1910	1%				
1920	26	35%	29%		
1935	55	44		59%	15%
1971	80	(73)	(87)	83	53

The primary attraction of the automobile was that it expanded choice. A complicated Aladdin's lamp, it permitted families to be transported from where they were to place where they preferred to be—to stores and movies, to vacation spots, the country, the city, etc. Its ability to carry bundles of groceries, pieces of furniture, bags of cement, is purely secondary. Therefore city residents, who have more ready access to a variety of amusements and opportunities, have lower ownership rates. (That factor, together with lower incomes, accounts for some of the white-non-white differential.)

Needless to add, TV (as radio) also expands choice; the listener can visit various never-never lands, at least for the moment. The choice analogy may even maintain for electricity, which enables one to choose between a pseudo-day and a real night. And for central heating, which permits one to choose between a pseudo-summer and a real winter.

Roman emperors were careful to guarantee the steadiness of the grain supply to Rome, as well as occasional carnivals of destruction of humans and animals. Having already considered circuses (in the American form of radio and TV) we may well turn to bread, reviewing the trend in U.S. food consumption.

Food

Always the largest item in the family budget, food expenditures might be expected to change less over the course of growth than spending for many other items, such as consumer durables. Moreover, "the capacity of the human stomach is limited."[16] But the share of consumer spending for food has not declined dramatically since 1900. For housewives largely changed the way in which food was prepared.

As Table 1 indicates, families rapidly decreased their consumption of inferior foods. Salt pork, preferred in the centuries before cheap refrigeration became available, left the diet, to be replaced by fresh. Lard was replaced by butter and other fats; molasses, by refined sugar; and corn meal, by wheat bread. At the same time, families used their rising real incomes to increase their consumption of preferred foods. Ice cream and sugar consumption rose by 30 pounds 1945–1970. Beef consumption in the postwar period alone, rose by 79 percent. Poultry consumption doubled, and processed citrus intake more than doubled in that same period. One element not shown in the table is the shift to food packaged ever more conveniently—sugar no longer scooped from barrels, pickles no longer dipped from brine, etc.

But the housewife decreased her workload in the kitchen chiefly by making three major changes in her pattern of food buying. (a) In 1900 the typical housewife baked nearly half a ton (1,000 pounds) of flour each year into bread

[16] So far as food expenditures are concerned a variety of Roman emperors disproved any such statement many centuries ago.

TABLE 1

FOOD: CONSUMPTION AND PREPARATION, 1900–1970

I. PERCENT OF URBAN FAMILIES CONSUMING

	Salt Pork	Lard	Molasses	Corn Meal
1900	83%	94%	69%	—
1918	66	64	—	84
1942	9	35	7	12
1965	4	9	2	22

II. CONSUMPTION PER PERSON (LBS)

	Beef	Poultry	Ice Cream	Citrus (Processed)	Sugar
1910	56	17	2	0	77
1920	47	16	8	0	86
1940	43	18	12	4	99
1945	47	26	16	8	78
1970	84	50	26	19	108

III.

	Percent of Flour Consumed		Percent of Money Spent for Vegetables		Percent of Food Expenditure	
	at home	in baked goods	raw	prepared	at home	away from home
1900	92%	8%	96%	4%	99%	1%
1965	22	78	30	70	82	18

and other items. But by 1965, 78 in every 100 pounds of flour she bought came in the form of bread etc. already baked. (b) Over the same period the housewife increased the share of her vegetable budget from 4 percent on prepared vegetables to 30 percent. She had transferred to major corporations much of the job of shopping for her vegetables, then cleaning, coring, scraping, and cooking them. (c) And, most complete substitute of all for kitchen work. the share of family food budgets for "food away from home" rose from 1 percent to 18 percent. That increase, of course, had many components: fewer lunches were prepared at home and more eaten at work by the head of the household, and at school by the children; more meals were taken in restaurants; and more prepared food was brought home for dinner. Spending on a plethora of small appliances—toasters, timers, mixers—also reduced kitchen chores. Easier cleaning pots, and detergents instead of hard soaps, undoubtedly did so as well. But the major changes in food preparation noted above undoubtedly demanded the greatest share of increased family spending on food. They also brought the most substantial cuts in the amount of work required in the American kitchen.

One key aspect of these changes in family diet is given by two figures on time required to prepare meals in the home. An informed guess by Charlotte Gilman for 1910 contrasts with a figure from the Converse-Robinson time budget study for 1965–1966.[17] Preparing meals took 6 hours in 1910—including clean up. Cooking took 1½ hours in 1965–1966.

There are two sharply different ways to consider this (partial) record of American consumption. One is philosophical and meditative in character. It leads to the basic puzzle of what it is that societies achieve. That approach eventuates in important questions, and nearly overwhelming ones. For example, one may refer to Santayana's query: "The question was, Is material civilization worth while? Is the dull anonymous unhappiness that it steadily diffuses more tolerable than the sudden and horrible scourges that fall upon primitive peoples? Or should the question of happiness be ignored altogether. . . ."[18]

A second, albeit not alternative, approach exists. If the task of any economy is to provide the goods desired by the members of that society, then one may ask a conditional question about economic advance. Given history, as in fact it is given to this moment, how readily would the typical American give up the goods and facilities that penetrate

[17] Charlotte Perkins Gilman, *The Home* (1910), pp. 95, 133. U.S. 44 city sample for 1965 data (Converse and Robinson), reported in Alexander Szalai et al., *The Use of Time* (1972), p. 691.

[18] George Santayana, *Persons and Places* (1944), pp. 200–201.

his existence today, to return to the lower levels of 1900? Put another way, would he wish to return to the 50 percent longer work year of 1900, to do without central heating, running water, flush toilets, automobiles, TV, "a room of one's own"? And would one wish to do the work of the household in a world without mechanical refrigerators, washing machines, vacuum cleaners, sewing machines or electric light?

Both approaches raise real questions. They are probably more important than any given set of answers.

DISCRIMINATION AND POVERTY

Market discrimination actually reduces poverty—at least it does according to the kind of data widely used in discussions of U.S. discrimination. Thus 1970 Census data show:[1]

Percent of Families in Poverty in 1969

White	8.6%
Japanese	6.4

Is there any basis in theory why the very real discrimination against the Japanese should yield such results? But there the figures are. The explanation is a simple one: most models which discover that discrimination creates low family incomes are not structural ones. Moreover, few (if any) of them bother to refer to the longest malevolent U.S. experience with market discrimination—namely southern agriculture. We propose a model that goes more closely to the workings of market discrimination (in I–IV) and then review some data on farm rents (in V–VIII) which tell us a good deal about that century-long experience. Summary conclusions appear in VIII.

I

At least one member in almost every American Japanese family today was raised in a concentration camp. And most heads of these families lived in the camps during the critical years when they could have been developing labor market skills and/or being educated in schools. Moreover, that experience was the culminating point in at least half a century of life in the U.S. during which Orientals—unlike any other Americans—had been forbidden to own land, though farming constituted the largest single sector in the economy. They had, moreover, been excluded from schools, neighbor-

---

[1] U.S. Census PC2 (IG) *Japanese, Chinese and Filipinos in the United States,* Table 9. PC2 (9A) *Low-Income Population,* Table 11.

hoods, and occupations by legal as well as community pressures. That constellation of experience, for today's Japanese family heads, surely constitutes as rich a heritage on discrimination as the U.S. can offer. Yet their poverty rates fall below those for whites. Few would surmise that the explanation lies in some reverse discrimination by whites since 1945. Yet almost by an equal logic the higher poverty rate for Negro families than for whites is universally taken as cogent, and often sufficient, evidence of market discrimination, whether by employers, employees or customers.

II

The number of families in poverty is, definitionally, a function of

$$YF = f(YM_1 \ldots \ldots YM_n, YF_1 \ldots \ldots YF_n)D$$

where YF indicates the income of the family, YM_1 indicates the income of the oldest male, and YF_n indicates the income of the youngest female, with D being the impact of discrimination.

The functioning of the market at any given time does nothing to create the personnel of the family—the presence or absence of a male, a female, the numbers of each, the ages of each. The composition of the family is determined by a set of individual acts over which the management at Philco or Winnebago or Joe's Bar and Grill has remarkably little knowledge or control. Poverty in families is substantially greater where the male has disappeared. Increasing the size of the family will mean, during much of the family life cycle, more children with no corresponding increase in incomes. The combination will increase the probability of the family's being in poverty. A family, as defined by the Census and most other inquiries, is constituted by a single person. The number of additional persons added to him (or her) is of major importance in determining family income and family budget requirements. But the number of those additions is largely determined by that single person (and, subsequently, by his or her mate). It is not determined by employers, whether empathetic, discriminating, or indifferent.

For this reason, most models that seek to explain the proportion of families in poverty are unable to deal with market discrimination. By explaining "family poverty" in single equation models they confound (a) those forces which create families, and their particular age and sex composition, with (b) those forces which create the incomes of individuals of a given age and sex. Thus a model that makes family poverty a function of variables that include number of weeks worked by each family member, will obviously have its parameters affected by the age-sex composition of the family members. Three-year-olds almost never work a full year while males 40–45 almost always do. Therefore, the family with one adult male and no children will almost certainly have a higher income than one with no adult male and a 3-year-old child. A model that simply deals with the proportion of all families in poverty as a function of market variables mistakes the functional relationships at work.

Moreover, the number of family members with incomes from work is not determined by employer-worker interactions in the labor market. It is fixed primarily by family considerations. Thus, whether a mother enters the labor force is markedly affected by the age and number of children she has—all consequences of family decisions. Whether a teenager enters or an older person remains in the labor market is affected by the extent of public contributions to the family—aid to dependent children, old-age security, old-age assistance. It is further affected by the incentives to give children more schooling, which must keep them from earning income—community colleges with no admission charge, the desire of parents for their children to have more education, etc.

III

The dominant impact that private (and governmental) employers can have in creating poverty, is therefore limited to (1) the amount of employment they offer persons who enter the labor force, and (2) the rates of pay they offer those workers.

(1) The number of weeks worked per year, or hours per week, are not functions merely of employer offers, however, but are the net outcome of a schedule of such hours offered by employers and supplied by employees. For example, it is well known that many female employees seek only part-time work because of their family responsibilities. It is less well known that some employees have a greater preference for leisure than others—hence they are prepared to offer labor for fewer hours each week, fewer weeks each year. One such group includes members of college faculties, who work fewer weeks per year than the average worker. It is possible that some "low income families" include members with similar preference functions as between additional income and additional leisure.

(2) The rates of pay offered workers involve both the rate of pay for a given occupation and the opportunity to enter a given occupation. The rate of pay offered in a given occupation will vary with the employers' perception of the workers' ability and motivation—as is true in the pay of corporate officials, college faculty, football coaches, etc. It will also vary with the willingness of an employer to consider workers for employment in occupations with generally higher rates of pay—foremen as well as line assembly men, class A machinists as well as class B machinists.

Recognizing these considerations, one cannot merely accept differences in yearly earnings per worker as an indication of what the typical non-discriminating employer will offer. But it is unlikely that we shall ever be able to separate out those differences which arise from the employees' decisions, given the schedule of employer preferences plus prejudices. We shall, therefore, assume that as between white workers, Negro workers, and Japanese workers there are no group differences in ability, motivation, preference for leisure. We shall take differences in actual incomes received by those in the labor force to reflect primarily differences in employer preferences and prejudices. Thus if two groups of white and Negro workers get different average incomes, we shall assume the difference in no way reflects differences in ability, etc., but only a difference in employer prejudices.

IV

The procedure of using differences in poverty rates among ethnic groups as indicating differences in discrimination, however, leads to some extremely confusing results. For if they do, then Table 1 (A) indicates that American society apparently discriminates in favor of Japanese as against white male family heads. And Filipino and Chinese male family heads have less than half the poverty rates that Negro heads do. Such relationships are hardly consistent with our general understanding about discrimination in the U.S.

But perhaps it is wise to look at differentials within regions. After all, the official measures of the poverty line (and nearly all unofficial ones) fix a single poverty figure for the U.S. But given different wage rate levels in various U.S. regions, and given that ethnic groups are more concentrated in some regions than others, the single figure would imply differences in poverty rates—whatever the facts of discrimination. In fact, as Table 1 (B) indicates, we find that within region after region white family heads *do* have lower poverty rates than Japanese—except, oddly, in the West, where most Japanese still live.

However, turning to the detailed data by region proves to turn up a far greater puzzle. We find that the poverty rates for unrelated individuals (a) are 4 and 5 times as great as those for family heads, and (b) differ less signifi-

TABLE 1

MARKET DISCRIMINATION AND POVERTY: 1970

PERCENT IN POVERTY

A. Ethnic Group	Family Heads (Male)	
Japanese	4.3	
White	6.9	
Filipino	8.9	
Chinese	9.6	
Cuban origin	10.0	
Mexican origin	13.2	
Puerto Rican origin	16.9	
Negro	21.0	

B. Region and Ethnic Group	Family Heads	Unrelated Individuals
Northeast		
White	4.6	25.5
Negro	10.4	28.3
Japanese	4.9	27.7
North Central		
White	5.9	28.8
Negro	11.3	33.1
Japanese	7.0	36.6
South		
White	10.4	32.8
Negro	30.3	46.3
Japanese	12.2	23.5
West		
White	6.0	24.7
Negro	11.1	30.9
Japanese	3.9	26.2

Source: 1970 Population Census, PC (2)-9A, *Low Income Population* Tables 11,3.

PC (2)-1C *Persons of Spanish Origin,* Table 10.

PC (2)-IG *Japanese Chinese and Filipinos in the United States* Tables 9, 24, 39. These latter tabulations, based on the 20% sample, give data preferable to the 5% sample results in PC (2)-9A, Table 3.

cantly, and in a less systematic pattern, between the ethnic groups. If poverty rates vary among ethnic groups largely because of discrimination, why should employers discriminate far more against unrelated individuals than family heads (or, far less against family heads than unrelated individuals)? How, for example, can "discrimination" account for a poverty rate in the Northeast of 25.5 for white males (unrelated individuals) and only 10.4 for Negro males (family heads)? Why do similar contrasts appear in North Central and Western regions?

Similar questions arise if one compares poverty rates for groups that would appear similar to the untutored eye of the simple discriminator:

	Percent in Poverty, 1970[1a]
Native Negro	29.7%
Foreign stock	
Trinidad	9.9
Brit. W. Indies	10.9
Haiti	11.8
Other W. Indies	12.0
Jamaica	12.5
Domin. Republic	20.8

The answer is surely that poverty rates are affected by other forces far more powerful than ethnic differences. Hence, ethnic differences, taken broadly, may stand as proxy for other variables. The differences between family heads and unrelated individuals point to just such a set of massively important other variables. Counts of family poverty (or on total poverty—which is dominated by family poverty) will be deeply affected by personal choices made in family situations. Yet such choices tell us little about the effects of current and/or recent discrimination in the labor market in housing, or schooling. They are heavily affected by decisions of the head and his wife with respect to (a) the number of children they desire, (b) the preference for work versus leisure, (c) the number of supplementary earners in the family group, (d) incentives for work that are affected by such family composition, (e) incentives stemming from various federal programs etc.

[1a] U.S. Census, PC 2 (9A) *Low-Income Population*, Tables 3, 5.

On the other hand, when we deal with the group of unrelated individuals many of these factors do not confound our results. Yet the employer is hardly likely to manifest less prejudice with respect to the skin color or racial origin of a single man (or widowed or separated) than of a married man. For more light on the power of discrimination to create poverty, then, we may usefully study the unrelated male individual group, focussing on differences among the ethnic sub-groups within it.

The first aspect of importance revealed in Table 1 (A) is surely the vastly higher set of rates for unrelated individuals than for family heads in every ethnic group. This difference reflects differences employers perceive in the ability and motivation of such workers as compared with family heads. Because these differences appear *within* every ethnic group, they reflect factors apart from discrimination. So, one conclusion follows with respect to discrimination: differences in motivation, ability, and training between two groups can generate poverty rates 2 to 5 times greater in one group than the other. But poverty differences of this order of magnitude far exceed those between white and Japanese, or Japanese and Negro, within any region. (Or even between such groups in the U.S. as a whole.) In turn, this implies that lesser differences between poverty rates for workers in different ethnic groups may be explicable by differences in employers' perceptions of the combination of motivation, ability, and training of workers.

Suppose we take the universe of 6.4 million male unrelated individuals as a large enough category of workers within which to detect employer discrimination. Doing so, as section B of Table 1 indicates, we find that poverty rates for Japanese are higher or lower than those of whites depending on the region. (Similarly for family heads.) If we then compare Negro rates with the other two, we find such rates somewhat above the Japanese rates in three regions, and almost double those for the Japanese in the South. But if discrimination has applied as remorselessly and as vigorously against Japanese as Negroes, the Negro-Japanese poverty differentials for unrelated individuals must point to other factors—including relatively less (and lower quality) education of Negroes than Japanese, motivational differences, etc. In turn, the somewhat higher rates for Japanese than whites in the West—26.2 to 24.7—are to be compared with the reverse relationship—3.9 to 6.0—for family heads in the West. And doing so suggests that these differences reflect the combined variations in motivation, ability, and human capital which jointly account for poverty differentials far more than do ethnic differentials.

V

Studies of the empirical consequences of racial discrimination in U.S. markets have, in recent decades, focussed on nonfarm occupations and industries. These, however, are markets in which particularly complex mixtures of training, experience, and ability must be allowed for. Moreover, they are on the perimeter of discrimination: for more than three centuries most American Negroes lived and worked on Southern farms. It is worth seeing whether the extent of market discrimination in this historically important sector can be assessed. A rather simple application of rent theory does permit such measurement at two dates (1920 and 1940) after social controls in the region had generations to develop and be implemented. The results which the data suggest are not without interest.

VI

In a competitive capital market, identical rates of return will be received by investments of equivalent risk. The millions of parcels of land rented for farming, taken as a whole, would appear to constitute such a market. Stochastic elements would, of course, distort the rates paid on particular parcels, but an overwhelming tendency will develop

116

for the price to capitalize all the virtues of the land—its fertility, location, plus all other qualities apparent to buyers or sellers.

Southern land was rented under a variety of tenure arrangements. Sharecropping is perhaps most widely known, standing rent least known. But a very large block of farms were rented for cash. The cash renter assumed a greater share of risk than a sharecropper would; he was obliged to pay rent even if the crop failed. On the other hand, if a greater than expected rise in cotton prices took place, he benefitted proportionately. Moreover, he was rewarded directly and fully if he generated less than an expected level of costs. (Whereas, of course, such results under sharecropping flowed [$\frac{1}{4}$, $\frac{1}{3}$, etc.] to the owner.) One would expect the quality of cash renters to be high relative to that of sharecroppers, given their degree of confidence and given the selection by owners to reduce their own risk.

For this group of cash renters we can develop a relatively precise measure of market discrimination. Given the value of the land, if the owner charged Negroes a higher rent/value ratio than he did whites, the difference is a likely measure of discrimination.[2] If he wished to express his distaste for having any relationship with Negroes, he would charge the Negroes a higher rental rate than he would charge whites. And, given social conditions such that the tenants could move from the area only with great difficulty—because of a web of legal or social restraints—they would be forced to pay such higher rentals. The web of such restraints would be torn insofar as owners competed for the better tenants—i.e., those who would be more certain to farm well enough so that there was little risk of their defaulting on the rent. Such competition among white owners would limit the economic impact of discrimination. All might desire to discriminate. But some would, in addition, desire to rent with the least risk of default. In that

[2] The qualifications on this statement are discussed in III below.

117

competition the latter group would offer the better tenants relatively lower rents (i.e., as lower ratios to land value) and bid them on to their land, leaving other owners to take the less satisfactory tenants, either as cash tenants or as, say, sharecroppers.

It is an empirical question how far the cooperative attempt to extort higher rents from Negroes was frustrated by those owners who desired, even more urgently, to reduce the risk of default—and who cut rentals to get the best of the would-be renters. Is there any empirical material to measure the net working of such cross-purposes? Fortunately two sets of relevant data are available, one for 1920 and the other for 1940.

VII

An extensive study by the Department of Agriculture provides data on land values and cash rent charged in 1920 on 154,653 cash rented farms in 567 counties.[3] We utilize these data to compute rent/land ratios. Three exclusions from the set of counties were made to permit a clearer test of discrimination. (a) Rent-land ratios were computed only for those counties in which both white and nonwhite data were reported for at least three farms. This exclusion reduces sampling variance, without generating any obvious bias. (b) We exclude data where the tenant was kin to the land owner, as well as data for farms where kinship was not reported on. There is warrant in theory, as in the data shown in the USDA report, for believing that owners occasionally subsidized their kin by charging lower rents. Hence such data (almost wholly for whites) precludes arms length valuation. (c) Finally, we deal only with tenants who had rented their farms for more than one year. By excluding those who were renting for the first year we exclude those transactions in which both owner and tenant

[3] U.S. Department of Agriculture Bulletin 1224, Clyde Chambers, *Relation of Land Income to Land Value* (1924).

were maximally ignorant of the qualities each would bring to an owner-tenant relationship on that farm. Because ignorance in such transactions would be relatively great, one could not confidently sort out the discrimination component per se.

Having made the above exclusions, we were able to compare ratios of whites and Negroes in 126 Southern counties, and whites versus Japanese (or Chinese) in 29 Western counties. The comparison in the West is, of course, affected by the fact that Orientals were forbidden to own land in those states—giving legal support to discrimination in ways absent in the South.

Table 2 is derived from the USDA data in the following

TABLE 2

1920: RATIOS OF FARM RENT TO VALUE, BY COLOR

NON-WHITE COUNTY RATIOS

| | Number | | | |
| | Greater | Less than | Percent | Excess Rent |
		White	Greater	per Acre
South				
S. Carolina	2	—	100%	$.56*
Virginia	2	—	100	.28
Mississippi	17	1	94	3.81
Arkansas	13	2	87	2.18
Georgia	23	4	85	.62
N. Carolina	5	1	83	1.61*
Alabama	13	3	81	.99
Tennessee	4	1	80	.77*
Kentucky	3	i	75	3.71*
Texas	10	9	53	−3.13
Louisiana	4	5	44	1.33
West				
Arizona	1	—	100	7.72*
Colorado	4	—	100	3.96*
California	10	3	77	5.86
Washington	3	1	75	5.19
Oregon	1	1	50	.82*
Idaho	1	4	20	−.76

*6 or fewer counties in sample

fashion. Data for 16 counties in Alabama meet our exclusion tests above. For Baldwin county they report that the rent/value ratio for Negroes was 4.9 percent points above that for whites. There are 12 other counties in Alabama for which the sign of the excess was in the same direction, and the total of 13 is thus entered in column 1. Escambia, Fayette, and Monroe counties report white ratios above those for Negro, and therefore 3 is entered in the second column. Considering these 16 counties as a sample representative of state experience, we compute that 81 percent of Alabama counties had rent/value ratios higher for Negroes than for whites. (Ties proved absent in these data.) Similar computations refer to Negro-white differences in the South, and to Japanese or Chinese-white ratios in the West. The final column reports the excess rent, taken as the difference between the actual rent paid by Negroes (or Japanese, and that resulting from applying the white rent/value ratio to the value of land rented by Negroes (or Japanese).

The bulk of the Southern states clearly show higher rent/value ratios charged Negroes. Are these indicia of discrimination? The fact that in Louisiana and Texas the counties are about evenly split, between charging Negroes higher and lower rates, makes the question more than an a priori one. But perhaps more important is the excess rent charge per acre. If, as seems probable, Mississippi owners extorted $3.81 extra per acre from their Negro tenants, why did Georgia owners settle for a mere 62¢ and Virginia owners for 28¢? And, since we are taking these excesses as measures of the returns to owner discrimination, why did Texas owners pay Negroes $3.13 per acre (for negative discrimination—i.e. the pleasure of their company)? The presence of other factors seems indicated. But that does not preclude the presence of discrimination.

We stipulate that there should be some relationship between the amount of excess rent extorted and the amount of discrimination. If discrimination exists not merely in the mind but in the market, it should show some financial bene-

TABLE 3

DISCRIMINATION: 1920

	Excess Farm Rent per Acre in 1920	Lynchings of Negroes 1909-1918
Mississippi	$3.81	58
Kentucky	3.71	27
Arkansas	2.18	34
North Carolina	1.61	8
Louisiana	1.33	62
Alabama	.99	46
Tennessee	.77	30
Georgia	.62	122
South Carolina	.56	22
Virginia	.28	6
Texas	-3.13	74

fits to the owners of land. And the more powerfully it works the greater their financial returns should be. Since we wish to use the rent/value ratio itself as a measure of discrimination, its validity as such a measure must be tested against some other indicator.

There is an effective indicator of discrimination, of the ability of whites to discriminate in their market dealings with Negroes in the South. That indicator is the number of lynchings of Negroes. Lynchings represent an extreme indication of the ability of the white community to control and limit the actions of the Negro community. We assume that the number of Negro lynchings in a state functions as a reminder to everyone in the state that the range of acceptable behavior for Negroes is continuously monitored by members of the white community (Table 3).[4] What these data indicate is the following. Georgia, with 122

[4] Data on lynchings of Negroes are computed from the annual data by state that appear in the National Association of Colored People, *Thirty Years of Lynching in the United States, 1889-1918* (April 1919). We summarize data for 1909-1918, taking these as the years in which discrimination would be at work establishing market differentials effective at the end of that decade, in 1920.

Negro lynchings, would seem to have a higher prevailing level of discrimination and control by whites than Kentucky, with 27 lynchings. But the rent excess in Table 3 goes the other way: a $0.62 excess in Georgia and $3.71 in Kentucky. Alabama with 46 lynchings had a $0.99 excess, while Mississippi with 58 lynchings had a $3.81, and North Carolina with 8 had a $1.61 excess. Texas with 74 lynchings appears to have had a negative discrimination at work, with rent at $3.13. It hardly is likely that the harsh indications of discrimination given by the lynching data are at all consistent with the figures on excess rent per acre.[5] The issue here is not the presence of discriminatory tendencies. Those are amply demonstrated by the lynching figures, as well as other indications. The issue is whether discrimination, given competing landlords, led to discrimination in the markets where Negro tenants rented their land. The state differentials apparent in Table 3 are hardly consistent with an assumption of such market discrimination. But what other factors would account for this wide tendency of Negro renters to be charged more per dollar of land value? One factor is that suggested by Chambers: the cost of supervision.[6] Data from a contemporary USDA study of supervision costs on Southern plantations indicate it averaged $1.95 per acre.[7] According to Chambers, owner supervision costs on Southern farms was restricted to Negro tenants; white tenants typically rented from town merchants and bankers and were not supervised.[8] If the figure of $1.95

[5] The correlation between the two sets of data is trivial.

[6] *Ibid.*, pp. 56–57. Chambers uses data from the Brannen study (infra) to estimate supervision costs in 4 regional groups. We prefer the later publication, with its presumably wider sample of reports on supervision costs.

[7] C. O. Brannen, *Relation of Land Tenure to Plantation Organization*, U.S. Department of Agriculture Bulletin No. 1269, p. 77. The salary average was $1,991, with 1,021 acres supervised. The larger sample of farm managers reported a $2,100 average. The average plantation had 10 croppers of 30 improved acres apiece. *Ibid.*, p. 68.

[8] P. 57.

per acre for supervision costs be accepted, then the data for Southern states in Table 2 show Kentucky and Mississippi clearly in excess of that figure, with Arkansas just slightly above. Since Southern salaries do not appear to have differed greatly from state to state, it is not clear why the Negro "excess rent" figure in such states as Alabama, Georgia, South Carolina, Virginia, etc., fails to cover a supervision component. One conclusion would be that less supervision was given in those states than typical in plantations. The trivial excess for Virginia, and the negative figure for Texas, however, are hardly explicable even if a zero supervision cost be assumed. In any event, for the states in the South listed, the hypothesis of market discrimination in land rental to Negroes seems likely for Mississippi; possible for Kentucky despite its lack of notoriety as a scene of major discrimination; and not demonstrated by these data, given allowance for supervision costs, for other Southern states.

The data for Western states all relate to Japanese/white comparisons.[9] Chambers reports that Japanese farm tenants did not work under supervision, so that such costs need not be allowed for.[10] The excess rent figures, therefore, are suggestive of discrimination in access to land purchase and land use enforced by the legislation of the Western states.

For 1940, a similar comparison may be made. It appears in Table 4.[11] In every Southern state but North Carolina more than half the crop reporting districts showed Negro rents per $100 of value exceeded white rents.[12]

[9] The counties with Chinese farm operation reported had too few to meet our size cut-off criterion.

[10] *Ibid.*, p. 58.

[11] Data from 1940 Census of Agriculture, *Cash Rent* (1944), Table 11. Data by kinship are not available. However, computation of averages for 1920 with and without kin showed little difference; the number of kin, and average subvention, were too small to affect the averages.

[12] The crop reporting districts were groups of counties. We do not show data in Table 4 and 5 for states with less than 200 Negro

TABLE 4
1940: RENTS FOR WHITE AND NEGRO FARMERS

	RENT PER $100 FARM VALUE		Rent per Non-white Farm
	White	Negro	
Texas	$4.33	$4.31	$59.65
North Carolina	5.40	5.60	101.37
Oklahoma	5.27	5.79	72.90
Florida	6.37	7.41	55.55
Tennessee	6.04	6.60	128.83
Georgia	6.13	7.08	88.74
Louisiana	5.51	6.59	76.71
South Carolina	5.57	7.12	72.06
Virginia	4.07	5.45	70.38
Alabama	6.29	9.17	64.03
Mississippi	8.26	10.67	119.01
Arkansas	8.15	10.70	182.56

The excess rents per farm and acre are shown in Table 5. To dimension these estimates it is useful to relate them to the expected annual income of Negro tenants. There being no such data, we take instead the annual money income of farm laborers.[13] Since the average cash tenant has as an alternative such wage work, it may be assumed that the income of wage laborers offers a minimum estimate of what he would earn as a tenant. (Omitting the value of board, and being a minimum, it therefore overstates the excess rent.)

One aspect of these data stands out: the considerable variation in excess rent percentages among the states. Were excess rent solely attributable to discrimination, it would

---

farms reporting cash rent. Doing so excludes reports with excessive and unreliable variability, without changing any of the conclusions reached below. The remaining states had from 1,139 to 19,885 reporting Negro families.

[13] Data from Lebergott, *Manpower in Economic Growth*, p. 540. These are USDA monthly averages multiplied by 12. The omission of board will more than compensate for expected unemployment.

TABLE 5

EXCESS RENT: 1940

	Excess Rent per Negro Farm		Yearly Money Earnings per Farm Laborer	Excess Rent: Ratio to Yearly Earnings
	Total	Per Acre	(with Board)	
Texas	− $0.30	− $.01	$258	0%
North Carolina	3.65	.08	210	2
Oklahoma	6.56	.09	252	3
Florida	7.78	.17	192	4
Tennessee	10.95	.29	210	5
Georgia	11.89	.16	156	8
Louisiana	12.58	.39	186	7
South Carolina	15.71	.35	156	10
Virginia	17.81	.35	264	7
Alabama	20.11	.41	168	12
Mississippi	26.90	.80	174	15
Arkansas	43.45	1.32	198	22

be hard to understand why Georgia landlords, in a state with notorious chain gangs, contented themselves with an 8 percent excess, while Alabama landlords extorted a 12 percent excess. Or why Florida landlords, where peonism lasted into the 1920s, charged an extra 4 percent while Mississippi landlords took 15 percent. Or, most striking of all, why Arkansas landlords took $43, or 22 percent, while Texas landlords—by the same criterion—took 0 percent.

One element that may explain some of this variation, by accounting for a portion of the excess rent, is the provision of supervision by landlords, as well as power and fertilizer.[14] (But, of course, allowance for such factors tends to remove the very proof of discrimination—namely, excess rent.)

The possible importance of supervision in accounting for excess rent differences is suggested by the marked decline

[14] Cf. U.S. Census, *Cash Rent*, p. 3. "Particularly in the South many landlords furnish power and fertilizer to cash tenants." It may well be that power and fertilizer were furnished white and Negro tenants to an equal degree, but apparently this was less true of supervision.

in excess rent ratios from 1920 to 1940. It is possible to measure the change in excess rent from 1920 to 1940 for 47 of the 1940 crop reporting districts.[15]

In 31 districts the excess rent declines; for 16, it increases. (That difference is overwhelmingly significant at a 1 percent level.)[16] There seems to have been no corresponding decline in the desire to discriminate. Nor did the social and legal apparatus that might have assisted such discrimination obviously weaken by 1940. On the other hand, the amount of supervision could well have declined from 1920 to 1940. The reason why it may have done so is the probability that the 1940 tenant had occupied his farm a much longer time than the 1920 tenant. Negro cash tenants on plantations had been occupants an average of: 3 years, as of 1920; 9 years, as of 1936; and probably 9 years in 1940 as well.[17]

VIII

The foregoing review of differing data sets tends to emphasize the complexity of the economic and social process in

[15] We combine data for the counties reported in 1920 that were grouped into a given crop reporting district as of 1940. States typically had 9 or 10 districts. One can see that we have very comprehensive coverage for the lower South, but rather thin coverage for the border states. However, since the phenomenon of interest is discrimination, it is the totality of the 47 districts that matters, while the spread by state reduces any possible bias linked to locality. By matching districts by district, and focussing on change, we avoid problems that might arise if one simply combined state averages, independently developed for each date.

[16] Since the general trend of rates of return was down from 1920 to 1940, it is not acceptable to compare the absolute gap at the two dates—for that would unquestionably narrow. The computation is therefore based on the ratio of Negro to white ratios at each date, using data in columns 5 and 6.

[17] 1920: C. O. Brannen, *Relation of Land Tenure to Plantation Organization*, U.S. Department of Agriculture Bulletin 1269, Appendix D.

1936: Thomas J. Woofter, *Landlord and Tenant on the Cotton*

which discrimination is imbedded. That complexity makes it difficult to utilize some of the analyses typically offered for concluding much about either the dimensions of discrimination in the U.S. or changes in it over past decades. Part IV, simply noting the ethnic characteristics of families in poverty, turns up the surprising result that a smaller proportion of Japanese families than white ones were in poverty. That an entire ethnic group was put into a concentration camp for five years seems a clear and objective measure of discrimination against them. Merely raising children under conditions where they are wholly denied a cross-cultural education, has been considered by the Supreme Court to be a guaranteed method of discrimination. Many persons have inferred that higher poverty rates are an inevitable consequence. Yet the Japanese poverty rates are lower, rather than far above, the white ones. Closer inquiry suggests that the family poverty rate is a function of (a) family composition and (b) the income earned by each member of the family. Family composition can hardly be the clear or direct consequence of discrimination by employers, fellow employees, or customers. (It might be an outcome of the way the entire social process impinges on internalized values.) Furthermore, the data suggest that employers typically discern differences in the quality of workers insofar as marital status is a proxy for such quality differences. Far higher poverty rates for unrelated individuals within each ethnic and regional group appear than for family heads in the same groups. (These quality differences may reflect ability interacting with motivation with family background with education quality, etc.) Hence the wage rates offered, the occupational opportunities offered, can vary significantly merely because employers see differences in the quality of the services that workers offer the firm. The simple

---

Plantation (1936), p. 110. An increase also occurred for white tenants, but hardly as marked a one. The sample as of 1936 is considerably smaller than that for 1920, but there is no reason to believe it biassed.

differences in poverty rates for unrelated individuals and for heads of families are so great that the poverty differences between heads of families by ethnic group may in measure reflect similar quality differences—stemming from differences in quality of education received, accumulated experience, motivation, etc.

Part VII looks at data for rents paid by white and non-white farmers in 1920 and 1940. It discovers excess rents paid by non-whites at both dates. Excess rents for Japanese farmers in selected Western states in 1920 appear to reflect discrimination. Excess rents for Negro farmers at both dates may also reflect discrimination. However, the inclusion of supervision costs for the latter group makes it more difficult to take excess rent as a clear measure of discrimination. The use of this index of discrimination is additionally complicated by the extreme range between Southern states in excess rent. States with large numbers of lynchings and other evidence of extreme social discrimination are not the states with high excess rents, or vice versa. Further work may disentangle these factors.

One apparent conclusion is that state intervention in a discriminatory way can have a decisive impact on market discrimination. Thus the legal barriers to Japanese land ownership in 1920 seem associated with excess rents paid by the Japanese. At the same time the effect even of discriminatory state actions (e.g., imprisonment of Japanese-Americans, 1941–1945) may be overcompensated so far as creating family poverty is concerned—by extra endeavor and training on the part of those involved. The complex variables of training, personality, and motivation may yet be more clearly disentangled. Until then, simple discussions of the links between discrimination and poverty tell us little about either, and less about the interaction.

WHAT INCOME DISTRIBUTIONS MEAN[1]

The distribution of power, prestige, and pelf has been a topic of durable concern to most societies. In distant eras, and in simple cultures, the distribution of economic power and advantage could be fairly closely measured in simple terms—e.g., the number of the flocks in ancient Israel, or the amount of land in the Domesday Book. But recent centuries have witnessed the notable rise of urban industry. They have also seen bewildering gains in geographic and social mobility: "Men become their own fathers," making their own status. Moreover, the incentives that press the Rastignacs or Jim Bradys of the rising groups toward high consumption make their wealth only the coarsest measure of their economic advantage. Such forces have vitiated the use of data on landed wealth, or even total wealth, as a clear-cut measure of economic differences. Hence, interest in the distribution of wealth has largely given way, in our time, to interest in the distribution of income.

Uses of the Data

Income size distributions may be used as measures both of economic productivity and of welfare.

Income as a measure of productivity. For measuring productivity, the relevant income distribution is that for individuals, more particularly those engaged in production for markets. In most economies, the income received by the typical worker, peasant, or businessman reflects chiefly the quantity and quality of the goods and services which he brings to market. Such an indication of the income recipient's "productivity" measures no inherent, inalienable set of personal talents and charms. Thus, the income that a farmer receives from marketing his crops necessarily re-

[1] Adapted from the author's "Income Distribution: Size," in *International Encyclopedia of the Social Sciences* (1968).

flects, in part, the accumulated knowledge he derives from society: he can raise more rice per acre of land than his father could because better varieties of seed have been developed and because the government provides better weather information. He receives more for each bushel he raises because an improved transportation network and futures market enable him to market his crop at a time, and in a condition, that make it command a better price. Similarly, today's worker may receive a higher wage per hour for his labor than his grandfather did because of the education that his parents and society have given him and because employment agencies, unions, and newspapers help to create an efficient labor market. To the extent to which the social order and private enterprisers apply new technologies, develop cheaper materials with which the worker can labor, provide capital at lower cost—to that extent the productivity of the worker will advance, and with it the amount of product with which he is compensated.

Two obvious considerations should be noted: all is not roses and fair shares in consequence. Just as inadequacies in the social order may reduce the absolute reward of everyone in it, so government and private restrictions on entry to an industry, a region, or an occupation will tend to affect relative shares. Effective monopolies or public incentives that favor one factor of production will increase the share of those who provide that factor.

The productivity being measured pertains only to the period covered, most commonly a year. Therefore the usual income distribution will reflect differences associated with age and period in life. Thus, it is fairly typical for individuals to have relatively low-value productivity in the years just after they enter the labor force full time and just before they leave it—reflecting a combination of part-time work and low or impaired skills. Perhaps more important is the displacement of income that occurs between years, and within a lifetime, depending on the nature of the work. For example, cyclical variations in the weather and predators that affect rubber or coffee crops will swing incomes in any given year well below or above a longer-term average. If an occupation requires a lengthy training period, with both costs of training and a loss of income during that period—e.g., a machinist's apprenticeship, a physician's period in medical school—very low or zero incomes will be recorded for the individual in his younger years, with compensating higher incomes later on. The national size distribution at any time will therefore reflect the proportion of persons in these industries, occupations, and age groups.[2]

We take these as so many givens when we speak of the productivity of the individual income earner. Nevertheless, it is that productivity—however derived—which is relevant in the actual state of the labor market, both in market economies and in state-operated ones.

Income as a measure of welfare. A second common use of income data relates to the measurement of welfare. Moralists have long had difficulty equating "goods" with "the Good." And economists have become notably wary of interpersonal utility comparisons. Not only do they lack any agreed basis for translating measured income into measurable welfare, but even when a fairly extensive set of axioms is stipulated (including an assumption of equal total output), they fail to agree on whether a more equal pattern of income distribution is preferable to a less equal one.[3]

For translating income into tests of welfare we must resort to a simpler proposition: In a free consumer market,

[2] Mincer, Jacob, "Investment in Human Capital and Personal Income Distribution," *Journal of Political Economy* 66:281–302; and Dorothy S. Brady, "Individual Incomes and the Structure of Consumer Units," *American Economic Review* 48, No. 2:269–278.

[3] Strotz, Robert, Fisher, F., and Rothenberg, J., 1961, "How Income Ought To Be Distributed: Paradox Regained," *Journal of Political Economy* 69:162–180, 271–278. These conflicts are no less within other disciplines. (Cf. Roland Pennock, Ed., *Equality* [1967]). Nor have they been removed in such fine later studies as Arthur Okun's *Equality and Efficiency: The Big Tradeoff* (1975) or Robert Lampman, *Ends and Means of Reducing Income Poverty* (1971).

differentials in income will indicate differentials in the command over goods and services. (Should the state or private sellers engage in rationing—e.g., by limiting the freedom to rent or purchase housing of certain types or, in certain areas, to buy imported cars or the services of private clubs—even this premise is denied.)

As an indicator of the command over goods and services, the most informative distribution of income is that for families, not for individuals. The limitation of the latter measure is that in most societies the family acts as the primary agent for redistributing income. Children and housewives earn little or no income, but their command over goods is not equally trivial. Indeed, as the income of family heads has increased in many nations, the earnings of children have dwindled: instead of continuing to work full time in textile mills, children began to spend most of their days in school. As wives in lower income families found their husbands' incomes rising, they left full-time work to earn zero (or at most pin money) levels of income. The facility with which family members can substitute leisure for income will increase as the income of the family head, and the family, increases. Therefore the income distribution of persons tells us too little about their changing command over goods and services, including leisure as a good.

Given the primitive communism that exists within the family structure, the distribution of family income is more serviceable than that of individual income for measuring the distribution of command over goods and services. But even this distribution has important limitations.

(1) If incomes are measured before taxes, the distribution will be substantially more skewed than on an after-tax basis. The precise intent of income taxation in many nations is, of course, to contribute to such leveling. The *corvée* in 18th-century France, road labor in 19th-century Africa, conscription in 20th-century United States (given exemptions that are related to marital status and education)—each is likely to have had a differential impact by income. (Re-

cent empirical studies for several countries appear in International Association . . . 1964.)

(2) Expenditure by the state will differentially benefit families in the different income groups. Whether defense and police protection aid the well-to-do disproportionately has been argued to conflicting conclusions. There is probably more agreement that such explicit payments as family allowances, unemployment insurance, or subsidies to farmers do vary by income level.

(3) Comparisons between more and less industrialized nations (or periods in the life of a nation) are substantially affected by the amount of income received in non-monetary form. Farm and mining families have frequently received significant amounts of their real income in the form of food and shelter, making no explicit payment for them. Urban residents who receive an identical volume of such goods and services command more of the economy's real resources: the costs of transport to the city, and of the distribution of goods within it, must be covered. But whether their perceived levels of well-being are greater *pari passu* is a matter admitting of "a wide answer."

(4) The more persons who share a given family income, the less the value of goods commanded by each—even assuming economies of scale in the consumption of housing, of works of art, etc. Hence the systematic attempts since Atwater and Ammon to adjust food consumption and total budgets to an "adult male equivalent" or other standardized basis.[4] Such a scale can rest on a fairly objective basis so far as mere nutrient intake is concerned. But any allowance for food palatability or for the satisfactions from other budgeted items (clothing, amusements, etc.) tends (a) to em-

[4] Cf. J. L. Nicholson, "Variations in Working Class Family Expenditure," *Journal of the Royal Statistical Society*, Series A, Part IV, 1949. Carolyn Jackson, *Revised Equivalence Scales*, U.S. Department of Labor, BLS Bulletin No. 1570-2 (1968). J. J. Seneca and M. K. Taussig, "Family Equivalence Scales . . . ," *Review of Economics and Statistics* (August 1971).

body the investigator's personal judgments, (b) only to report (somewhat indirectly) the actual consumption levels or elasticities of a particular society at a given stage in its history, or (c) both.

Possibly more important is the implicit assumption that because welfare will be affected by the number of persons in a family, income must be measured on a per person basis. Any such assumption applies only weakly to those religious groups and entire cultures which regard fecundity per se as a goal or a moral imperative. Since such groups prefer, in principle, more children to more material goods, a per capita income measure will bluntly conflict with one of their primary values.

(5) An equal amount of income does not translate into an equal command over goods and services at all income levels. Lower income families frequently live in outlying districts, without cheap transportation. They are therefore confronted by few sellers of the goods and services they would buy. Discrimination because of caste (social, cultural, religious) may additionally restrict access to housing. Under such circumstances lower income families are confronted by higher prices for an identical budget of goods and services than are upper income families: their real incomes are therefore less than the current distribution of money incomes would indicate.

(6) Many nations seek to assure a per person minimum for particular goods and services (from zoos to well-baby clinics). These are provided without user charges, so that all persons (or all who pass a means, citizenship, and manners test) can have full access to presumably critical items. The list of such items has steadily expanded on every continent. Moreover, public social-welfare payments have increasingly replaced private charities. Many of these services are not provided by increasing money incomes—e.g., food stamps, subsidized rents (for the poor) or loans (for the middle class); access to beaches and dachas, etc. Such vexing impediments preclude the use of income distributions to

134

mark the relevant differences in command over goods and services. Given a specific, real world context, however, it may be possible to bound the impact of particular biases.

Because of the widespread receipt of assistance and income in kind—neither fully included in most income distributions—those concerned with economic welfare have found an analysis of the actual pattern of consumption a helpful supplement. Family budget surveys provide one such body of information. Data in the national accounts (on the constant dollar value of consumption) provide another such body of data. Together they remove any necessity for using the approximate statistics on income distribution to determine the extent of either grinding poverty or wealth beyond the dreams of avarice.

Changes in Income Distribution

Central to much interest in income distribution data is one question: Does the inequality in income distribution increase or decrease through time? In principle, we would answer this question by comparing the income distributions of an identical set of income receivers in different periods. Such comparisons would indicate fairly directly whether the rich were getting richer, the poor getting poorer, etc.

In fact, most analyses simply compare distributions for all income receivers at two dates, whether or not the same recipients are included at both. But between these dates, forces are working to change the underlying population. Hence the reported income distribution will change even if no one receives lower hourly wages, or higher dividends, etc. Such forces include the following:

(1) The consequences of aging and mortality. Younger persons who work part time while in school report an increase in income when they leave school and begin full-time work. Older persons retire between one period and the next, shifting down from wage to pension income levels.

(2) The demographic and social consequences of a change in aggregate economic activity. When an economy

shifts from underemployment to high employment, incomes will rise. Reported income inequality may rise in consequence. For example, the increase in U.S. incomes from the 1930s to the 1940s led elderly persons to move out of their children's homes into rooms and apartments of their own.[5] Presumably both the older persons and the families with growing children found that separate establishments provided a real advance in their welfare. Yet the usual income distribution data will report an increase in inequality: the number of "low-income families"—in the form of newly created "families" of older persons who had previously been included with their children—has increased.

Similarly, the stronger the labor market, the earlier young people find work and establish homes of their own. As a result, instead of one family being reported, with a combined income including the incomes of young persons and older persons, two families will be reported—each with a lower income.

(3) By widening the scope of income taxation, modern legislation has increased the incentives to receive income in forms other than current monetary receipts. It has thereby helped create a series of remarkable innovations whose consequences appear in the distribution of income. For upper-income groups the most significant of these innovations has probably been the conversion of ordinary income into the form of capital gains and gains from stock options. But these are typically excluded from the tabulations of income distribution. (It would indeed be difficult to decide how to include them.) Distorted results can therefore be produced by comparing income distributions between nations and between points in time when the incentives to convert income into capital gains differ (and the knowledge of techniques for doing so and the relevant legislative provi-

[5] Brady, Dorothy S., *Age and the Income Distribution*, U.S. Department of Health, Education and Welfare, Social Security Administration, Division of Research and Statistics, Research Report No. 8 (1965).

sions also differ). The distribution only of ordinary income could under such circumstances offer a singularly inadequate indication of trends in income concentration.

Other innovations that affect income distribution include the contract for deferring payment until a future date and the multiplication of nontaxable trusts. The proliferation of business expense accounts since World War II suggests that resources devoted to the feeding and amusement of entrepreneurs, and their coadjutors, have also become increasingly potent substitutes for outright income payment. An executive may find a Picasso on his office wall to be a quite tolerable substitute for the million dollars (pounds, francs, etc.) of income that he would otherwise have to earn in order to enjoy the same painting on his living room wall for a few hours in the evening. The expansion of fringe benefits to workers—in the form of contributions to pension funds, subsidized lunches, etc.—similarly distorts comparisons of reported figures on income.

(4) The expanded role of the state as a taxing agency links to its expanded role as a redistributive mechanism. Public assistance payments and Medicaid can add significantly to the resources of lower-income families, but are usually under reported in their incomes. Public guarantees of home loans and bank deposits provide middle-income families with lower interest rates, which may make the difference between owning and not owning their homes. But the saving of interest is never treated as income. The clearing of unsightly slums, the dredging of yacht harbors, and the selection of the best public school teachers for the best residential areas all benefit upper-income groups. The impact of this wandering pattern of taxation and benefit must be evaluated before simple comparisons of changes in income distributions through time can be taken to mean what they appear to mean.

(5) Finally, there are statistical problems of no mean magnitude. The amount of tax evasion is virtually unknown in most nations. Its effect in distorting reported income

distributions is even more obscure. In the single publicly available report for the United States, for 1949, something like 23 percent of taxable farm income was not reported on tax returns.[6] Of returns filed by small taxpayers (under $10,000 in adjusted gross income), one third had a change in tax liability indicated by audit. Persons owning businesses understated net profits from 7 percent (physicians) to 37 percent (hotels) to as much as 87 percent (amusement services). There is, however, no basis for assuming that tax evasion is linear with income, and hence that reported data can be so adjusted. An official report states that "under present conditions, many people in the slums, especially young black men, see illegal activity as an alternative to menial jobs paying low wages and offering no hope of advancement. A recent study of Harlem estimates that roughly 2 out of every 5 adult inhabitants had some illegal income in 1966 and that 1 out of 5 appeared to exist entirely on money derived from illegal sources."[7]

Reported income distribution figures are almost never adjusted for such evasion of taxes or understatement of income. In the very few instances in which they are adjusted (e.g., in the U.S. Department of Commerce figures), the adjustment is not differential by income level, there being no data upon which to base a reasonable differential adjustment. It is clearly captious to be concerned about the validity of data for those few nations which provide both distributions and information giving the user a fair chance to assess them. Nonetheless, intelligent use of income data must take these considerations into account.

Trends in dispersion. A long view of economic development suggests forces that would work toward and against

[6] Marius Farioletti, "Some Income Adjustment Results from the 1949 Audit Control Program," in Conference on Research in Income and Wealth, *An Appraisal of the 1950 Census Income Data* (1958), Tables 2 and 5. Subsequent IRS surveys are not publicly available.

[7] U.S. President, *Manpower Report of the President, April 1971,* pp. 2, 98. Cf. A. Dale Tussing, *Poverty in a Dual Economy,* (1975), pp. 42–45.

greater inequality of the income distribution. Some theorists have argued that as societies become more developed, the contribution of each individual becomes more specific. This enables him to receive greater rent on his ability, thereby increasing inequality.[8] History does indeed suggest a trend toward concentration, to be surmised from periodic confiscations—the redistribution of the land under Solon, of monastic wealth under Henry VIII and the sans-culottes, and of property in land and slaves under Tsar Nicholas and President Lincoln. But no less significant has been the long rise in prices generated by the discovery of silver in the Old World and of gold in the New World. This trend has, in Sir Josiah Stamp's phrase, brought the unseen robbery of generations. By eroding existing accumulations of wealth, it has offered later generations the fair prospect of more equal chances to earn and to accumulate income.

Kuznets' review of a mass of 19th- and 20th-century data on income distribution in many nations concludes that there has been some long-run tendency toward leveling.[9] The expansion of public education, the opening of occupations to children of lower class origin, the widening of credit facilities, the cheapening of transport (destroying local monopolies)—all these raised the income levels of the lower income groups and thereby made for greater equality in the income distribution.

The Formation of Income Distributions

The mechanism that creates the distribution of income has been explained in ways that range from historical-sociological theories of great generality to hypotheses of sharply de-

---

[8] Lachmann, L. J., "The Science of Human Action," *Economica* New Series 18:412–427.

[9] Kuznets, Simon, "Economic Growth and Income Inequality," *American Economic Review* (1955), 45:1–28. Cf. also his "Income-Related Differences in Natural Increase," in P. A. David and M. W. Reder, eds., *Nations and Households in Economic Growth: Essays in Honor of Moses Abramowitz* (1974).

fined stochastic process.[10] One hypothesis, first suggested many decades ago, was that the Gaussian normal distributions (which fit many human characteristics, such as height, weight, IQ) might apply to income as well. But records for many societies, despite their unreliability, agree in suggesting that this is not so. Broadly speaking, two types of explanation developed subsequently. One premises the normal distribution as a starting point, then seeks to explain how that distribution was truncated or otherwise forced so that the usual skewness of income distributions developed. The second category of explanations premises that the underlying distribution is lognormal, or Poisson. Some specialists have sought primarily to find a single function that could describe many existing distributions. Others have been more concerned with understanding what economic processes could reasonably produce the distributions and then have more or less systematically proceeded to fit various functions to data.

Among the analyses concerned with explaining how income distributions arise from the incentives and institutions of typical economies, many have emphasized the arithmetic normal distribution as the starting point. A substantial bias in that distribution may be assumed to result from the impact of property inheritance, from differentials in parental interest and ability to invest in training for their children, and from the consequences of inherited social position. High incomes are then explicable by the greater potential some persons have for earning income (given their advanced training and status) or for acquiring it (i.e., returns from inherited property). The impact of inheritance has been emphasized by Pigou and Dalton. Marxist critics have focused also on status and sociological differentiations.

While inheritance of property was vital in Britain, income from such inheritance in most Western nations is not such

[10] Recent skilled reviews include: *Review of Income & Wealth* (Sept. 1970), A. S. Blinder, *Toward an Economic Theory of Income Distribution* (1974).

as to make it likely to be a significant factor per se in explaining the skewness of income distributions. On the other hand, the inequality of training and contacts among young persons beginning their work career is surely relevant, particularly given the recent literature that emphasizes private monetary returns to investment in education. To the extent that all this is simply an application of the Biblical stipulation "to him who hath shall be given," one would expect to see mounting inequality over time. Such a trend is not apparent, either in the West or in underdeveloped nations. (However, such a tendency could be masked by the consequences of concurrent attempts to redistribute income and to widen access to education, which often first take place in a nation during the very periods for which the first data become available, permitting comparison of its income distributions through time.)

It has recently been contended that abilities to earn income in fact form a truncated arithmetic normal distribution—whose apparent skewness in some societies reflects the fact that credit-granting agencies provide capital to persons with high money-making abilities (thus enabling them to compound these to attain very high incomes), whereas these agencies truncate the other end of the income distribution by denying credit to most large-scale speculators, whose skills would otherwise enable them to develop large risky enterprises that would lose large sums of money and generate large negative incomes.[11]

An important group of analysts stipulate that there are really two underlying distributions. Thus Tinbergen (1956) has suggested that persons who possess great ability for certain jobs (e.g., artists, craftsmen) will have a particularly strong desire to engage in them and will therefore lower their wage demands in order to enter them, whereas workers with lesser abilities will choose more widely, taking those jobs which command higher monetary returns. Fried-

[11] Lebergott, Stanley, "The Shape of the Income Distribution," *American Economic Review* 49:328-347.

man (1953) has emphasized not two classes of individuals but two classes of actions—more and less venturesome—in which individuals engage. Greater possibilities of very high incomes inhere in the more venturesome (job choices, investment choices, gambles). If a mechanism exists for redistributing the proceeds of quasi lotteries, one can generate some extremely high incomes without generating negative ones—since entry to the lottery requires only a small admission fee. The model is thus consistent with the usual skewed distributions. It will be noted that both models require some rather strong corollary assumptions for them to apply to recent periods or to modern nations—e.g., that highly skilled people are willing to take unusually low wages, that some widespread redistributive mechanism exists to take from the poor(er) to give to the rich(er). Neither assumption is descriptive of behavior in many labor markets or of the impact of the usual governmental taxing and redistributive mechanisms.

Another group of analysts has emphasized the contribution made to the shape of the over-all income distribution by its component distributions. Since Mill and Cairnes pointed to the presence of "non-competing groups," it has been clear that the distribution of incomes for a peasant group, for a wage-earning group, and for the sons of the rich will each have a characteristic shape. If, then, all persons in a given country are taken together, the over-all distribution will reflect the symmetry or, more generally, the actual shape of the underlying distributions.[12] Such considerations are, of course, consistent with an over-all distribution ranging from the near-symmetrical to the wildly skewed.

Probably the most widely attempted explanations in recent years involve those which specify the income distribution as lognormal, with the logarithms of income normally

[12] Hayakawa, Miyoji, "The Application of Pareto's Law of Income to Japanese Data," *Econometrica* 19:174–183; and Miller, Herman P., 1964, *Rich Man, Poor Man,* New York: Crowell.

distributed even though income itself is not. Originally sparked by Gibrat's pioneering study (1931), this distribution has received repeated attention in recent decades.[13] These writers assume that a Markov process is at work in which the incomes received, e.g., in a given year, will change by some percentage from that year to the subsequent year, the size of that percentage being independent of the income in the initial year. Given that the probabilities of such changes are independent, application of the central limit theorem enables us to conclude that as sufficient time passes the original shape of the distribution will no longer be significant. What we will then come to observe is the skewed lognormal distribution. The simpler models of this sort imply vast increases in income inequality, for each of the assumed random changes will add to the variance of the distribution.[14] Such increasing inequality, however, does not appear in most sets of empirical data of reasonable validity. Various additional side conditions have been specified to prevent the model from leading to such a conclusion.[15] One substantial difficulty with these amended models is that they fail to fit recent reliable income distributions. It is also to be noted that by premising random percentage increments, they stipulate a pattern of random reward in the income acquisition process that seems uncharacteristic

[13] Gibrat, Robert, *Les inegalites Economiques,* 1931. Kalecki, Michael, "On the Gibrat Distribution," *Econometrica* 13:161–170; Champernowne, David G., "The Graduation of Income Distributions," *Econometrica* 20:591–615; Aitchison, John and Brown, J. A. C., *The Log-Normal Distribution: With Special Reference to Its Uses in Economics,* Cambridge University Press, 1957; Bjerke, Kjeld, "Some Income and Wage Distribution Theories: Summary and Comments," *Weltwirtschaftliches Archiv* 86:46–66; Mincer, Jacob, "Investment in Human Capital and Personal Income Distribution," *Journal of Political Economy* 66:281–302.

[14] Kalecki, Michael, "On the Gibrat Distribution," *Econometrica* 13:161–170.

[15] Champernowne, David G., "The Graduation of Income Distributions," *Econometrica* 20:591–615.

of many societies. Most economies structure income receipt with respect to economic contribution (e.g., such as marginal productivity of labor), or social status, or some combination of known economic incentives and social restraints.

Measurement

Modern analysis of income distribution begins with Vilfredo Pareto. Somewhat earlier Quetelet, Leroy Beaulieu, and others had given brief consideration to data then flowing from various taxing systems. But it was Pareto, one of the group of economists engaged in transforming a branch of natural philosophy into a rigorous system of analysis, who first observed how similar many income distributions were when evaluated in terms of what is still called the Pareto coefficient.[16]

The Pareto coefficient. The Pareto coefficient is a in the equation $\log N = \log A - a \log x$, where N is the number of persons with incomes at least as large as x. Pareto's review of data for various countries suggested to him that the coefficient was approximately 1.5 in every instance, although in fact he reports data ranging from 1.24 to 1.79. This putative fact led to the inference that a natural constant had been discovered: "A decrease in the inequality of incomes cannot come about . . . except when total income increases more rapidly than the population."[17] Following Pareto, even very modern writers, noting that the parameter ranges from 1.6 to 2.4, infer that such a narrow range, although referring to widely separated countries and occasions, would seem to indicate a common underlying mechanism. Massive differences between economies, centuries, and continents are submerged by this measure into

[16] Pareto, Vilfredo, *Cours D'economie politique Professe a l'Universite de Lausanne*, 2nd edition, Paris: Giard & Briere, 1927, Vol. 2, p. 305. A comprehensive and lucid review of these measures appears in James Morgan, "The Anatomy of Income Distribution," *Review of Economic Statistics* (August 1962).

[17] Pareto, *op. cit.*, pp. 312, 320.

a simple single coefficient, originally offered (and frequently taken) as a kind of ultimate social law.

The theoretical limitations of this measure were canvassed by Macaulay and Mitchell, and others.[18] One difficulty is that the formula will estimate an infinite number of recipients for incomes greater than a near-zero amount: it must therefore be used only to estimate the number above some level arbitrarily chosen to give sensible results. It is, at the very least, a signal difficulty that one function should hold above some income level picked by the analyst on an *ad hoc* basis, while another presumably explains the distribution below that arbitrary level. Another difficulty is that differences in the coefficient which appear small on casual inspection, and therefore lead to the assumption of its constancy, may not be small so far as any serious economic or political issue is concerned. (Thus the ratio of wives to husbands is fairly close to 1.0 in most Western nations. Yet one can be certain that any community in which the ratio was 1.01 would have an interesting basis for tea-time discussion and police action.) In this respect the position of Harold Davis, while extreme, was more reasonable when he declared that small variations in the coefficient made the difference between revolution and peace in many a historic situation.[19]

In fact, Pareto's equation does not fit distributions recorded in recent years at all well, and even his original fit was to a mixture in which data for both individuals and corporate bodies were included. It may be a more reasonable inference that the coefficient is simply insensitive to major differences in concentration if our criterion of

[18] Macaulay, F., and Mitchell, W., eds., "The Personal Distribution of Income in the United States," Volume 2 in National Bureau of Economic Research, *Income in the United States: Its Amount and Distribution, 1909–1919* New York: Harcourt, 1922.

[19] Davis, Harold T., *The Analysis of Economic Time Series*. Cowles Commission for Research in Economics, Monograph No. 6. Bloomington, Ind.: Principia Press, 1941.

stability in the coefficient is casual inspection. However, the coefficient is a convenient smoothing device and in recent years has frequently been used for computing income aggregates from distributions.

Pareto's premise, and that of some later writers, that the constancy of his *a* demonstrated that redistribution was impossible and that incomes could be improved only by an increase in total product, is an interesting example of a theorist drawing policy conclusions from an empirical observation—with no theory behind his speculation. It was pardonable that half a century of subsequent redistribution through progressive tax systems had not been revealed to him as demonstrating the contrary, but the lack of an analytic model stipulating why no shift was possible was less warranted.

Lorenz curve. Another measure widely used—in part because it is associated with a simple graphic presentation—is the Lorenz curve.[20] Total income is measured on one axis and total population on the other. For each percentile point the cumulated income and cumulated population are recorded. If all members of the distribution were to receive the same income, a simple diagonal would appear on the graph, running from the origin (southwest) to northeast. As it is, the Lorenz curve always reports that income is not distributed equally. This discovery is hardly one of unusual moment (1) because ocular standards rather than formal tests of significance are involved and (2) because the standard of perfect equality is used, rather than some actual reality, such as, say, the average distribution for several high employment years or that for a nation with an active policy of redistribution, etc. But the curves are most commonly used to demonstrate the degree to which the distribution has shifted toward or away from equality from one period to the next, or differs from equality from one nation to the next. Since the extent of movement may be

[20] Lorenz, Max O., "Methods of Measuring the Concentration of Wealth," *Journal of the American Statistical Association* 9:209–219.

considered trivial to one temperament and significant to another, the significance of a difference between two curves is best assessed by comparison with the difference between two other curves—e.g., is the change from period 1 to 2 greater than that from 2 to 3? In comparisons between nations it is, of course, essential that comparable populations be contrasted. A contrast between a distribution of income taxpayers in one nation and the total population in another, or between two tax-paying populations with different levels of exemption, may produce fierce findings of difference in the measures despite a total lack of difference in the actual distributions.

The Gini index. For the study of capital formation, class warfare, and related purposes, the index of concentration developed by Corrado Gini has been widely used.[21] It is a straightforward measure based on the area of the triangle under the line of perfect equality: the area between the Lorenz curve and the diagonal of perfect equality is taken as a percentage of the total area in the triangle. It is computed from the equation $\log N = \delta \log Y - \log c$, where N measures the number of individuals with incomes above a given amount "z" and Y measures the aggregate of incomes above z (δ is commonly termed the Gini coefficient). Gini's N is a function of S, the total of incomes above z, whereas Pareto's N is a function of z itself.

In Conclusion

Income size distributions are almost inevitably measured in money. A money income measure is, of course, both succinct and precise—e.g., $20 thousand, $10 million, etc. That very precision, however, fluently transmits clear messages to the tax gatherer, to rivals, to the covetous. All of which in no way denies that money is a useful contrivance in producing wealth. But it does imply that measure-

[21] Cf. Joseph L. Gastwirth, "The Estimation of the Lorenz Curve and the Gini Index" *Review of Economics and Statistics* (August 1972).

ment in money will create distributional consequences. As these accumulate, they eventually destroy the precision with which money can measure income. An increasingly greater premium comes to be put upon receiving real income in forms less susceptible to simple measurement than money income so obviously is.

In capitalist societies when tax rates increase special occupations develop to facilitate the consumption of goods without their purchase, as well as to transform income (which is taxable) into capital (which is usually not taxable). But new social orders also arise. These provide more persuasive long-run solutions. In most societies, of course, leaders will enjoy power and prestige and bodily comforts. But in command societies a step forward occurs. Their leaders need not acquire high money incomes, as under capitalism, in order to enjoy a corresponding flow of admiration, comfort, and sense of power. They can directly secure special housing, personal servants, access to imported motor cars, foods, etc. One essential condition for such receipt is, in fact, that they do not receive high money incomes.

If numerical measures were ever developed that could summarize the total flow of power, prestige, and real services as cogently as money can summarize the flow of real incomes, then these persistent personal purposes would be sought through other social modes. Meanwhile, money income continues to provide a basis for measurement in most societies. And its apparent comprehensive exactness continues to support contention over the equity and equality of any income size distribution.

THE CONCENTRATION OF
WEALTH: SOME ECONOMIC
ASPECTS OF ETHICS

Once upon a time, according to Irish legend, there was "a rich man of great age who had bribed the people on the other side of death to leave him here."[1] Now perhaps riches cannot bring off any such Faustian bargain. But the belief that they can do so reflects a nearly universal fascination with the powers of wealth. The ethical aspects of those powers are twofold: (1) ones that concern equity between rich and poor in a given generation, and (2) ones that concern equity between current and future generations.[2]

That a morally unacceptable wealth distribution exists in the United States, if not in any other country, seems widely believed. But that belief springs from a more fundamental belief—namely, that there exists a morally unacceptable saving function. Neither theologians nor ethicists appear to have studied such a saving function. We consider it below.

Before doing so, however, we must distinguish the ethics of wealth concentration from those of income concentration. We will here take the concentration of income, after tax, as given. For our inquiry asks: what ethical issues arise when the concentration of income changes the concentration of wealth? Part I deals with the intra-generation issues. Part II treats of transfers between the generations.

Given any income distribution, how is it possible for the wealth distribution to become *more* or *less* socially acceptable? Chiefly by differential savings rates. To the extent that men differ in their propensity to save, and in the

[1] Maurice Collis, *Somerville and Ross* (1968), p. 150.
[2] Focussed on the economic consequences of concentration, the analysis is neutral as between those who prefer "equity" as the suitable noun and those who prefer "envy."

length of their lives, wealth distributions will come to differ from income distributions. If all men had the same savings function,[3] then changes in the distribution of wealth would reflect the flow of income distribution. No additional problems in equity would arise. The belief that the distribution of wealth is even less acceptable than the distribution of income presumes that savings functions cannot be ethically neutral and that morally unacceptable ones exist.

I

What economic consequences, then, are created by the fact that the rich not only "are different" but save differently? To answer that question we first determine how these savings rates differ (in A) and then look to the consequences (in B).

A

Nineteenth-century attacks on the rich focussed on savings functions. The rich escaped their fair share of taxes, it was argued, because the existing tax system rested primarily on tariffs. As one knowledgeable critic wrote: "The middle class find it difficult to save more than 10 per cent. But the savings of the rich proceed upon a rapidly increasing ratio . . . there are well known instances of persons whose income exceeds $1,000,000 whose expenditures do not equal 2 per cent of their income. Such persons are practically exempt from all taxation by the Federal Government."[4]

Shearman surmised that those with incomes above $1 million saved 84 percent of those incomes. For the top 1 percent of all income recipients his data indicate a saving rate of 41 percent.[5] When arguing for passage of the income tax, Senator Borah declared that a rich man "did not pay as

[3] Including the rate of return on their savings.
[4] Thomas G. Shearman, *Natural Taxation* (1895), p. 34.
[5] *Ibid.*, p. 35. We interpolate his Class VI data linearly.

much to support the National Government as one of his employees." Implicitly he argued this occurred because the rich consumed less.[6] More recent attacks have likewise emphasized high savings rates by the rich.[7]

We have only one fairly solid estimate of the saving rate by the rich. But it does suggest their rate is far above average. (Lampman uses Kuznets' studies to infer that the top 1 percent of income recipients saved 43 percent of their incomes since the 1920's.[8] Ratios somewhat below 43 percent appear to have prevailed in more recent years.[9]

B

Two important economic consequences flow from higher savings rates by the rich.

(1) The more they save, the less they consume. They thereby leave more of the current flow of goods and services to be consumed by those with lower incomes. Moreover, by not bidding for as many goods as their incomes would

[6] *Congressional Record* (August 27, 1913), p. 3807. "A short time ago there was an estate probated in this country for $87,000,000. The man who possessed that estate, in my judgment, did not pay as much tax to support the National Government as one of his employees who took care of his building. The employee undoubtedly paid all the way from 5 to 10 or 15 percent of his annual income into the Treasury of the United States while the man with the $87,000,000 estate at that time did not pay nearly so much in proportion to his income." Borah argued that because the primary federal revenue source was the tariff, and the tariff taxed consumption, the rich man did not contribute appropriately: his saving function was too different.

[7] Cf. *inter alia* Gabriel Kolko, *Wealth and Power in America* (1962).

[8] Robert Lampman, *The Share of Top Wealth-Holders in National Wealth, 1922-56* (1962), p. 236.

[9] Dorothy Projector, *Survey of Changes in Family Finances*, FRB Technical Papers (1968), pp. 7, 9. It should be added that there exists only one actual survey in which savings for the rich were reported —the 1963 FRB survey. That survey reported negative saving for those with incomes of $100,000 and above in 1963. Cf. Table S8, p. 214, in *ibid.*

permit they, insofar forth, keep down the prices of the goods bought by those with lower incomes. Their saving, for their selfish purposes, results in more goods and lower prices for persons with lower incomes than if they had invaded the market with their full incomes.

Consider the behavior of Andrew Carnegie and his partners after they had sold out to U.S. Steel. His partners had low savings rates. Their careers of riot are detailed and reprimanded in Gustavus Myers' sermon on *The History of the Great American Fortunes*, and Matthew Josephson on *The Robber Barons*. They indulged in gala suppers of champagne and pigs knuckles. They bought bracelets and creations by Monsieur Worth for ladies as charming as Lillian Russell. They lit cigars with $100 bills. (A writer once described the free spending rich as "devoted 'to pleasure regardless of expense.' He was gently corrected by the late Colonel Waring. 'What these people do is to devote themselves to expense regardless of pleasure.' ")[10] The unbelievable excesses to which the high consumption rich went in Carnegie's time were catalogued by contemporary writers.[11] Every cigar they bought decreased the concentra-

[10] Ralph D. Paine, "Are Riches Demoralizing American Life?" *World's Work* (1903), Vol. 6, p. 3913. A more apt description of a low propensity to save would be hard to achieve.

[11] "Indeed, there is something abnormal about the lives of the owners of privilege at every turn, to wit: One multi-millionaire has a telephone at his bedside, and before rising every morning he receives from his office all important telegrams . . . and gives preliminary orders and directions" (p. 68). "In the fall of 1904 the first big (automobile) race was held . . . for a silver cup offered by W. K. Vanderbilt . . . one participant was killed outright. . . . Many other fatalities have since attended high speeding. Would this imply that our Princes of Privilege have brutal tastes? What I assert is that, lifted above interest in normal things, our princes as a class crave unusual stimulants. So far has this appetite advanced that women of the privileged order are now seen at prize fights" (p. 75).

"And what are the offsets to this seeking for excitement . . . one lady . . . has the teeth of her pedigreed pet gold-filled . . . then

tion of wealth. Every cigar that Carnegie failed to buy increased it. His greater abstemiousness increased savings, and thereby the concentration of wealth. (In due time, of course, Carnegie gave his fortune away—to firemen who saved little children, to public libraries, to the Carnegie Foundation. But meanwhile his crabbed restraint tended to increase the concentration of wealth while their free-handed expenditure decreased it.)

The differences between high-spending partners and more abstemious millionaires were specified several centuries ago by Abraham Cowley. There are, he declared, two kinds of avarice. One seeks gain "not for its own sake but for the pleasure of refunding it immediately through all the channels of pride and luxury. The other is the true kind . . . an unsatiable desire of riches not for any farther end or use but only to hoard, and . . . perpetually increase them . . . he can give no reason or colour, not to the devil himself, for what he does; he is a slave to Mammon, without wages."[12]

Society may prefer (a) a Rockefeller, with dour Baptist principles, who ate dry biscuits, cleaved to a single wife, and thereby increased the concentration of wealth.[13] Or (b), it may prefer Henry Hyde, who feted many ladies, consuming resources from the common stock in lordly fashion, but thereby decreasing wealth concentration. The

---

there are those who choose snakes, lions, pigs and bears for pets. At other times there is the very madness of inanity: valentine dinners, golden-dish dinners, bull and bear dinners . . . and Egyptian desert dinners . . . where each guest dug up jewels with tiny pick and shovel" (p. 79). Henry George, Jr. *The Menace of Privilege* (1905). The entire chapter on "Amusements, Dissipations and Marital Relations" of the rich is studded with examples of high consumption.

[12] Abraham Cowley, "Avarice" J. R. Lumby, ed., *Prose Works* (1909), p. 142.

[13] "Artemidorus, reckoning his fortune at many times ten thousand, and spending nothing, leads the life of mules, who often, carrying on their backs a heavy . . . load of gold, only eat hay," *The Greek Anthology* (Loeb Ed.), iv, 261.

choice surely turns on which savings function society considers to be most moral—an issue on which economics has little to say. (It may, indeed, mutter a bit about savings as a source for investment and growth.)

(2) But if high savers are indeed "slaves to Mammon without wages," they must face the question of what to do with their acquisitions. The times are long past when the rich kept their savings in strong boxes, French peasants or eccentric millionaires notwithstanding. America's rich drive for a return upon their savings. And they do so no less sedulously than they originally fought for higher incomes.

But to achieve a return they must put their funds into capital markets. A Bradley Martin could waste his (father-in-law's) substance on such massive consumption items as a ball on horseback at the Waldorf. But William Astor, Payne Whitney, and a thousand others saved a substantial share of their income, then invested that share for further returns. By so doing the rich expanded the supply of loanable funds. Such expansion must tend to drive down interest rates.

Who benefits from the resultant decline in interest rates? One likely candidate is suggested by the century-long cry of American populists for cheap money, for bimetallism, and for any other means of lower interest rates. Which suggests that when the rich avariciously invest, rather than consume, they end up benefiting the populists—presumably to the confusion of each. The most recent comprehensive study of the debt status of American families reported: [14]

Average Family Debt (Dec. 1962)

Head self-employed	$8,214
Head employed by others	$4,286

Active entrepreneurs, farmers and small businessmen, therefore benefit more from an increase in loanable funds than

[14] Federal Reserve Board, *Survey of Financial Characteristics of Consumers* (1966), p. 132.

do the poor, or the middle classes.[15] Lavish saving by the rich has helped keep down interest rates for small businessmen. It may, indeed, have given them more help than the better publicized endeavors of such populists as Mary Lease, Sockless Jerry Simpson, or even Wright Patman.

II

A

The second issue of moral urgency concerns the transfer of wealth from one generation to the next. If all millionaires consumed their wealth, or left it to charity, no issue would arise. But the rich do propagate. And, as their inferior brethren, they then strive to bestow asset claims on their children. Those transfers could be prevented. Andrew Carnegie (when he was childless) proposed that the state wipe out every great estate when its creator died. Later thinkers, agreeing that "the advantage owned by the children of the rich is almost insurmountable," have been willing to settle for "a 90 percent inheritance, gift, and estate tax" instead of a 100 percent tax.[16]

The limitations of classical economic theory, with its individual utility maximizing process, have been widely noted. But is there any clearer disproof than the fact that today's youth are most outspokenly prepared to end, or hobble, inheritance—i.e., precisely whose who, by definition, will inherit this generation's wealth?

Could one imagine a more humane, and a more useful, policy in today's world than "a 90 percent inheritance, gift

[15] Data from the same source (pp. 110, 130) indicate that the ratio of debt to income was about 2% for the lowest and highest income groups. It was the $5,000 to $50,000 groups that sought, and could get, high debt-income ratios.

[16] Jack Newfield and Jeff Greenfield, *A Populist Manifesto* (1972), p. 106. This study has been described, by a well-known millionaire, as "a program for the millions of ordinary men and women who believe that government ought to serve the people, not just the special interests." *Ibid.*, p. 1.

and estate tax" in the U.S.—with, say, the proceeds given to the United Nations Development Fund in aid of developing nations? Such a gift by the U.S. young would break the inheritance chain. Moreover, by helping nations in acute need, it would advance the cause of peace as well. To be effective, as Newfield and Greenfield note, an equal tax must apply to gifts. (Otherwise parents could still transfer capital in the form of heavy expenditures on education, automobiles, stereo sets, airplane tickets, etc.)[17]

B

But perhaps few American youth are willing to deed their inheritance to foreigners. The apparent objections of the young to inheritance (and some of their middle-aged spokesmen) may not be as strong as their rhetoric. The rhetoric may conceal a division of class interest between (a) those who only expect to inherit less than an average amount from the older generation and (b) those who hope to inherit an above average amount. It is, of course, a perfectly rational policy, and wealth maximizing, for those who would gain by redistribution to urge redistribution.

But let us assume that American youth really is ready to give their inheritance over to needy foreigners. Let us, further, assume universal agreement that everyone in the younger generation should have "an equal start" in life. How would one go about creating "an equal start in life" for everyone in the young generation?

A more unlikely method than U.S. inheritance legislation since 1826 (when Louisiana began taxing inheritances) could hardly be figured out.

For if our goal is "an equal start" for those beginning the race, why tax those in the previous race? Why not tax those who now receive inheritances—to equalize *their*

---

[17] Since we are dealing merely with the ethical aspects, any administrative problems of taxation are ignored here—as in other hortatory literature, populist and reactionary.

potential? Our present legislation declares it beneath the notice of the state when someone acquires $1,000,000 by inheriting from several sources. But it taxes severely the same acquisition if it comes as an inheritance from a single affluent source. This is all unhappily reminiscent of medieval judicial ruling—in which an officer of the court was ordered to whip an offending river, or tree, or animal. U.S. inheritance laws efficiently lash out at the bloated, but already dead, rich. But if our goal were to insure an equal start for all members of the next generation, the tax should not be oriented to the wealth of those who have passed on.[18] Should it not, instead, be dimensioned to aggregate wealth claims received by a given heir, from whatever combination of rich and poor relatives?

C

Our present progressive inheritance taxation has another fascinating oddity, and a more important one: its attitude toward what constitutes "an equal start." For it implies that all men have an equal start except when their money inheritances differ. It unerringly taxes a dead rich man who left his son $80,000. But it looks the other way when a live rich man gives his son $80,000 worth of education (nursery school through professional school). Yet such a sequence of education creates a far greater income potential then does $80,000 inherited by a 35- or 45-year-old.

Does our society really seek an equal start? We have a simple test—namely, the way it treats two groups. The first are blind children. That the blind are massively handicapped, there can be little question. What child with no prospects of any money inheritance would change places with a blind child? What Appalachian boy or black girl would do so? Yet our public programs provide each blind

---

[18] For practical administrative purposes the Treasury would, of course, utilize probate reports, and the estate transfer process, to guarantee collection. But the shape and size of the tax to be levied is the issue under discussion here.

person $1,248 a year.[19] This is not a starting level for a
new program. Aid to the blind has been a national program
for a third of a century. And in that period hundreds of
humane souls have—rather noisily and publicly—discovered
Sensitivity Analysis, Human Rights, and the Disadvantaged.
Yet aid to the blind remains at so modest a level. That
figure tells us more cogently than newspaper stories do what
national values on an equal start actually look like.

There exist a second set of children whose life chances
are far below average: the mentally retarded. Only one
of every five such children is enrolled in a special school
program.[20] (And that such minimal programs create equal
life chances even for the 1 in 5 seems most unlikely.)

Programs for the blind and the mentally handicapped
seem to have been created by a minimalist philosophy. The
majority has surely not done so because of the usual political
dilemma when efficiency wars with equity. For no moral
hazard arises. Neither blindness nor mental handicap are
within control of the individual. In contrast to welfare or
aid to dependent children or unemployment insurance, there
is little likelihood of anyone choosing either status in order
to get free assistance. All of which we take to indicate
that society has not decided to give the young an equal
start in life. Indeed it has recently done the contrary. Prospects for the young were most sharply changed in recent
years by one program expansion—namely free college education. Which youngsters benefited by that expansion?
Those who already were guaranteed better than average

---

[19] More accurately the blind who qualify. *U.S. Statistical Abstract,
1971*, p. 294.

[20] Approximately ½ million children were enrolled in programs
for the mentally retarded in 1966. (*U.S. Statistical Abstract, 1971*,
p. 108.) The total number of children aged 5–17 was about 50 million.
(*Ibid.*, p. 105.) Given the usual shape of the IQ distribution, we
may assume that the bottom 5% of that distribution were severely
handicapped by IQ and by the interaction with IQ of education
designed for average children.

life chances—by above-average intelligence, application, motivation.[21]

We conclude that attacks on the concentration of wealth because it creates unequal life chances for the young are wide of the mark. True, some people do favor equalization. And still others are busy trying to improve the chances for particular pressure groups. But the major social programs developed over decades in a democracy do pretty well reflect its dominant values. And the programs developed over the past half century offer (1) trivial assistance to those youngsters with the objectively worst life chances, (2) substantial assistance to those already ahead in the race.

Pleas for higher inheritance taxation are typically no less diversionary. Such taxation now tries to equalize the past generation beyond what death has already accomplished. And its focus is restricted to redistributing less than 1 percent of society's capital stock—mostly to Defense.[22] A program to give "an equal start" to severely disadvantaged youth would draw upon all the resources of an affluent society and would reallocate to such youth, not to the Defense Department.

Adequate explanation of these diversionary discussions and of the choice of social policies lies outside economics. For it is only the theologian who can explicate the concept

[21] The point was clearly made by J. E. Meade, *Efficiency, Equality and Ownership of Property* (1964), p. 62. Education expenditures might be so allocated as "to equalize the future earning power of different students. . . . Taken to its logical extreme . . . (this) principle would mean concentrating educational effort . . . on the dullards to the neglect of the bright students until the educational advantages of the former just made up for the greater inborn abilities of the latter in the future competition for jobs." Meade drops the entire topic with these few lines, though he brilliantly and empathetically pursues many other moral aspects of social policy, including eugenics. The point is vigorously pursued by Edward Denison, "An Aspect of Inequality of Opportunity," *Journal of Political Economy* (Sept.-Oct., 1970).

[22] Inheritance taxes go into the general revenues of the Treasury, from which the largest single claimant is the Defense Department.

of an immoral saving function. And it is probably only the psychoanalyst who can explain our inheritance customs. It may not be irrelevant to mention an ultimate inheritance tax. One anthropologist, noting a "widespread belief in both aboriginal America and pre-Christian Europe" in the "dangerous character of all inherited rights," describes how these societies coped with their fears: They simply destroyed the property that the dead left behind them.[23]

[23] Jack Goody, *Death, Property and the Ancestors* (1962), p. 306. Goody describes this custom, present in Africa as well, as "a social projection of guilt feelings generated within the holder-heir situation" (p. 307).

THE NOUVEAU RICHE AND
UPWARD MOBILITY

How long has upward mobility been commended as the sovereign medicine for democratic societies? And for how long have the carriers of such mobility, the nouveau riche, been denigrated? Certainly since Balzac and Marx they have been regularly described as vulgar, pushing, greedy, and coarsely aspirant. Such adjectives by now make up a ritual cadence—testimony, of course, to the impressive battery of inventions by those master dramatists. But the resultant formula for aversion has shifted attention almost wholly to the two establishments: the historic rich and the permanent poor. That fixed focus has prevented adequate analysis of the actual circulation of elites in U.S. society.

To what extent have the top wealth groups in the U.S. actually been recruited from lower wealth classes? A review of new data on this question turns out to yield conclusions for widely different temperaments. Reactionaries will presumably accept the finding that between one and two thirds of the top U.S. wealth group in any generation is recruited from lower wealth groups. Radicals will presumably accept the estimated probability that any given person will so rise, from lower wealth to the top 1 percent, is less than .00002.[1] The basis for these conclusions rests on a review, in Part C below, of over a century of American experience.

I

We begin with four conclusions on changes in U.S. wealth distributions. Two are tested empirically below (in Part C), while the others are from Chapter 13.

(1) Of the families who make up the top 1 percent of the wealth distribution in one U.S. generation, about 40

[1] So, presumably, will mathematicians.

percent fail to have heirs who appear in the next generation's top group.

(2) The share of U.S. personal wealth owned by the top 1 percent of the U.S. wealth distribution has neither clearly increased, nor decreased, over the past century.

(3) It follows from the two preceding statements that the top 1 percent of wealth holders in recent generations has been heavily recruited from lower wealth classes. Given a minimum 40 percent attrition rate among established wealth holders, the nouveau riche will constitute over one-third of the top group, and may make up as much as two-thirds of the top group.

(4) The probability that anyone will rise from the lower 99 percent to the top 1 percent of the wealth distribution is less than 0.0002—or about as great as the chance of winning a top prize in the typical state lottery.

II

Various authorities have discovered the U.S. distribution of income to be "radically unequal," or "outlandishly skewed," or having an "enormous concentration," and that "material inequality has remained great."[2] These strenuous adjectives and adverbs lead directly to Robert Heilbroner's question: "Why social peace persists in the face of an outlandishly skewed distribution of income is a perennial puzzle, especially in a democratic society. Why do so many acquiesce in an income distribution that accords so much to so few?" That question applies no less forcibly to the distribution of wealth, which is even more unequal. Three possible explanations may exist, not mutually exclusive.

[2] "A radically unequal distribution of income has been characteristic of the American social structure since at least 1910." (Gabriel Kolko, *Wealth and Power in America* [1962], p. 49.) "Outlandishly skewed." (Robert Heilbroner, "The Clouded Crystal Ball," *American Economic Review, Papers and Proceedings* (May 1974, p. 123.) "Remained great." (Tom Christoffel et al., *Up Against the American Myth* (1970), p. 9.)

(1) Americans may not define "radically" or "outlandishly" or "greatly" by any *a priori* standard. They may measure those adverbs and adjectives against the real worlds of other times and other nations. Thomas Weisskopf has found that "capitalism has historically always been characterized by great inequalities in the distribution of income and wealth."[3] While Tom Christoffel has declared that "the income structure in America has remained virtually static since 1910," Gabriel Kolko observed that it has been "radically unequal . . . since at least 1910."[4] All of which implies that Americans have been accustomed to the present "radically unequal" distribution for more than half a century. And, moreover, that capitalist societies all over the world, and back to the 17th century, have also manifested "great inequalities in the distribution of income and wealth." But surely any such phenomenon that has characterized every one of the many capitalist nations, and has done so for several centuries, tends to be taken for granted after a while. It may be as abhorrent in its inequality as death in its equality, but it is hardly outlandish or unusual.

(2) However, Americans may match U.S. wealth inequality against "material inequality . . . and the power to decide" in noncapitalist societies.[5] The "power to decide" is obviously important: from Savonarola to Stalin, from Torquemada to the Generals that rule in Latin America, Greece, Africa, or Asia, men have traded some wealth for some "power to decide." Where differences in wealth in-

[3] Thomas Weisskopf, "Capitalism and Inequality" in Richard C. Edwards et al., *The Capitalist System: A Radical Analysis of American Society* (1972), p. 126.

[4] Christoffel et al., *op.cit.*, p. 9. Kolko. *loc.cit.* Christoffel's source is Kolko. Kolko's source is an NICB report from the late 1930's. The NICB's source, as its procedures, are unknown to living man. We surmise they were based on guesses of W. I. King—from data for Wisconsin at one point versus data for the U.S. at another.

[5] "Material inequality has remained great and the power to decide has grown more unequally distributed than ever before." Christoffel, *op.cit.*, p. 9.

equality are offset by differences in "the power to decide" Americans may not seek that alternative.

Yet concentration of wealth exists in socialist nations as well. For example, the largest item of personal wealth in socialist nations is the automobile. And data on its owner-ship[6] show the following:

TABLE 1

AUTOMOBILES: 1971

	Total in Nation %	Percent Owned by the Top 1% of Population %
U.S.S.R.	100	60
Poland	100	59
East Germany	100	13
U.S.A.	100	3

Because far more consumer durables are owned in the U.S. than in these other nations (e.g. washing machines, refrigerators, vacuum cleaners, minor appliances), the ownership concentration of all durables would be still greater in the socialist countries noted above. And allowance for the imputed value of homes and dachas provided elite groups, such as party officials and artists, would make total private wealth still more concentrated in those nations than in the U.S. The top 1 percent of U.S. families owned 20 percent of U.S. private wealth in 1971. There is, therefore, a fair possibility that private wealth is more concentrated in the

[6] Data from the United Nations, *Statistical Yearbook*, 1972, Tables 19, 135, and 150. For the U.S.S.R. no ownership data are available. The production of passenger automobiles over the past 14 years was therefore used, assuming no net loss from depreciation. The procedure would appear to understate the true extent of concentration. The procedure for Poland, for example, compared the number of passenger cars (556,000) with the number equal to one percent of the population (330,000). The use of passenger cars as taxis is a further reason why these estimates understate wealth concentration in socialist nations.

U.S.S.R. and Poland than in the U.S., and in East Germany as well.

(3) But the third factor explaining why "social peace persists in the face of an outlandishly skewed distribution of income" may be more important. And that is simply the attraction of that faint, but distinct, prospect of becoming one of the nouveau riche. The attraction of a lottery is not the mathematical expectation of winning—but the chance of the glittering prizes. The recent florescence of bingo games under clerical auspices, and of lotteries under state auspices, reminds us of what illegal lotteries have demonstrated for years—that millions of people are prepared to hazard on such terms. (That the new state lotteries offer an even lower prize return per dollar wagered than do the illegal lotteries merely accentuates this point.) The wagering of a few dollars does not dimension the willingness of men to accept an economic system. The fact merely focusses attention on men's willingness to engage in "money making" activities even where the mathematically expected value of the returns is below that of costs to the typical participant. However, the opportunity to join the nouveau riche constitutes a more striking, multifaceted prize. It may be one reason why some of the many participants in our market economy acquiesce in the current distribution of wealth.[7]

III

There exist various lists of the very rich at different points in American history. They share a common characteristic: a substantial portion of the names on any list would not have been on a similar list a generation before, and often a mere decade before. The actual percentage will vary from time to time, as will the precision with which it can be estimated. We therefore proceed from the more recent data,

[7] This, of course, is quite different from their very fair odds of achieving higher real incomes, and higher wealth, than did their parents.

for which the most precise estimates can be made, back to earlier periods.

Distributions of top wealth holders by age are available for 1922, 1953, and 1969 from recent studies by Robert Lampman and the Internal Revenue Service.[8] By applying appropriate mortality rates to the distribution in 1922, we can estimate the number of survivors to 1953, roughly a generation later. And similarly we can estimate survivors to 1969 from the 1953 group. Given such estimates we are then able to compute the percentage of newcomers to each group. We concentrate on the older age groups— which hold the lion's share of U.S. wealth. Those aged 71 and over owned nearly $300 billion dollars of wealth in 1969. Those aged 55+ owned $847 billion dollars.

We make the computation initially for those persons aged 40 and older.[9] Age 40 is selected on the assumption that the transfer of inheritances to the younger generation would have been essentially completed by the time that generation had reached aged 40.[10] Therefore, those aged 71 and over in 1953 would consist only of survivors of the rich in 1922 plus recruits from those in lower wealth classes in 1922.

Of those aged 71 and older in 1953 (age 40+ in 1922) some 76 percent were additions to the top group since 1922 (Table 2). And in 1969 some 85 percent of those 55 and

[8] The 1922 and 1953 distributions by age from Robert Lampman *The Share of Top Wealth-holders in National Wealth, 1922–56* (1962), pp. 250, 110. The 1969 distribution is from Internal Revenue Service, *Statistics of Income, 1969, Personal Wealth*, Tables 24 and 25. The mortality rates used are from Lampman, pp. 248 and 48.

[9] Cf. Appendix.

[10] For his pioneering study, *Income and Welfare in the United States* (1963), James Morgan and associates secured data on amounts inherited by age of the heads of a national sample of spending units surveyed in 1960. Through the kindness of Professor Morgan I have been given access to tabulations from that study, which indicate that of all those who reported receiving an inheritance 14% were under 34. The median was 54 years. Our use of age 40 as the cutoff below which little inheritance had taken place seems, therefore, not unreasonable.

TABLE 2
RECRUITMENT OF THE RICH

Age 70 and older
1953 top wealth holders
Number aged 70 and older

Total	255,000
Survivors from 1922	
top wealth holders	62,000
Nouveau riche	193,000
Percent nouveau riche	76%

1969 top wealth holders
Number aged 70 and older

Total	1,392,000
Survivors from 1953	
top wealth holders	259,000
Nouveau riche	1,133,000
Percent nouveau riche	81%

Age 55 and older
1969 top wealth holders
Number aged 55 and older

Total	4,238,000
Survivors from 1953	
top wealth holders	624,000
Nouveau riche	3,614,000
Percent nouveau riche	85%

older (40+ in 1953) were additions since 1953. If we were to assume that inheritances had been largely passed on at a lower age, say age 30, then we would arrive at slightly larger percentages of new recruits in the top wealth groups.

These data are more representative, but less graphic, than individual lists of the rich. However, reference, say, to *Fortune's* list of "the Richest of the Rich," in 1968, reveals the same phenomenon. Hughes, Hunt, Land, Ludwig, Ahmanson, Fairchild, Hess, Hewlett, Packard, Kennedy, Mars, Newhouse, Abercrombie, Benton, Carlson—name after name proves to have gained wealth within the present generation.[11]

[11] Arthur M. Louis, "America's Centimillionaires" *Fortune* (May 1968). Louis notes that "perhaps a third were men of modest means

Were the top wealth groups recruited from below less frequently prior to this 1922–1969 experience? Data that reach back a century earlier are less comprehensive. Yet they do not change the judgment that at least half our wealthy families at any time were not represented in the top wealth group a generation earlier.

We consider below data for earlier periods.[12]

1916–1922. The U.S. Bureau of Internal Revenue has published data on the origins of top incomes in 1922 (Table 3).[13] The 537 persons who reported top incomes (i.e., over $300,000) in 1922 are classified in Table 3 by their prior year incomes, reaching back to 1916. Over half had been

TABLE 3

Top Income Recipients in 1922, by Their Incomes 1916–1921

Income Class in Given Year	1922	1921	1920	1919	1918	1917	1916
$300,000 & over	537	172	174	215	219	242	246
200,000 to 300,000		77	77	72	63	63	59
100,000 to 200,000		112	97	115	89	78	78
50,000 to 100,000		78	64	63	61	50	48
10,000 to 50,000		56	56	38	68	57	47
5,000 to 10,000		8	7	11	4	7	4
Under $5,000		34	62	23	33	40	55
Percent of 1922 top group with lower incomes in given year		32%	32%	40%	41%	45%	46%

and obscure reputation a decade ago" (p. 52). Half of these 66 individuals with $150 million or more did not appear on a 1957 *Fortune* list of the richest at that time (p. 62).

[12] An informative cohort study of thirds of the income distribution in 1961 by Katona, Lininger, Morgan and Mueller shows (*1961 Survey of Consumer Finances*, p. 76) that of the top third (by income) of spending unit heads aged 55–64 in early 1961, half had been in the bottom two thirds of the 1929 (and the 1940) distribution for this group. Data are also presented for younger groups, other earlier dates, show similarly marked recruitment.

[13] U.S. Bureau of Internal Revenue, *Statistics of Income*, 1922, p. 14.

recruited from lower income intervals in the 1916–1922 period; 68 percent had lower incomes in 1921, and 54 percent had lower incomes in 1916. (Changes in income, of course, are not very close proxies for changes in wealth. But the availability of this matching for high income recipients in 1922 is not to be ignored; and it proves to be consistent with findings on wealth change in later and earlier periods.)

1913–1924. A list of top taxpayers in 1924 can be compared with a list of top wealth holders in 1913 (Tables 4, 5).[14] Such familiar names as Astor and Rockefeller appear. But the very rich in 1913 failed to include Fords, Bakers, Dodge, or Curtis. Nor did they include such vanished luminaries as Cutten, James, Foster, or Hancock. Some 60 percent of this top taxpayer group in 1924 had no representatives on the 1913 list. If one reaches back to an 1892 list of mere millionaires (infra) the figure is over 60 percent.

1892. A list of 4,047 millionaires as of 1892 was published by the *New York Tribune*, with considerable detail on the source of wealth, including whether inherited or not.[15] On the basis of that list, Table 6 was prepared, giving for specified cities and states, the proportion of millionaires having inherited their wealth.[16] Table 6 indicates that 84 percent of the 4,047 millionaires in 1892 were nouveau riche, having reached the top without benefit of "inherited

[14] The 1924 list was published in various newspapers. This particular list is from Albert A. Atwood, *The Mind of the Millionaire* (1926), p. 255. The 1913 list, developed by the *New York World*, was published in the Appendix to *Congressional Record* for August 1913 as part of the discussions on the passage of the first income tax.

[15] W. Sidney Ratner, *New Light on the History of the Great American Fortunes* (1953). Ratner also publishes a 1902 list from the *New York World*. Since the latter does not give detail on whether or not inheritance was involved, it is not serviceable for present purposes.

[16] Every name listed as "partly" inheriting was also included. Since it is likely, for example, that such men as Oakes and Oliver Ames became millionaires with little reference to whatever they may have inherited, this procedure provided an upper-bound estimate of the inheritance count—hence goes against the present hypothesis. Simi-

TABLE 4

Top Income Tax Payers:
Taxes Paid in 1924

	($000)
John D. Rockefeller, Jr.	$6,278
Henry Ford	2,609
Edsel Ford	2,158
Andrew W. Mellon	1,883
Payne Whitney	1,677
Edward S. Harkness	1,532
R. B. Mellon	1,181
Anna R. Harkness	1,062
Mrs. H. E. Dodge	993
Wm. Wrigley, Jr.	837
Frederick W. Vanderbilt	793
George F. Baker	792
Thomas F. Ryan	792
George F. Baker, Jr.	783
Edward J. Berwind	722
Vincent Astor	643
James B. Duke	641
Doris Duke	252
Cyrus H. K. Curtis	584
J. P. Morgan	574
Claude H. Foster	570
Eldridge R. Johnson	543
George Allan Hancock	544
H. H. Timken	540
Arthur W. Cutten	540
Arthur C. James	521

wealth." (The percent who were self-made millionaires was clearly much the same.)

One additional aspect of Table 6 is worth noting. And that is the special role of New York, Boston, and Philadelphia. These were enclaves where 59 percent of all U.S. heirs to wealth clustered. The rates of heirs to millionaires

---

larly we include as inheritors (a) all millionaires rated as having gotten money from their wives (assuming that such money derived from their father-in-laws); as well, of course, as (b) women described as related to wealthy men of a prior generation.

TABLE 5
Top Wealth Holders: 1913

Above $35 Million	($ Millions)
John D. Rockefeller	$500
Andrew Carnegie	300
William Rockefeller	200
Estate of Marshall Field	120
George F. Baker	100
Henry Phipps	100
Henry C. Frick	100
William A. Clark	80
Estate of J. P. Morgan	75
Estate of E. H. Harriman	68
Estate of Russell Sage	64
W. K. Vanderbilt	50
Estate of John S. Kennedy	65
Estate of John J. Astor	70
W. W. Astor	70
J. J. Hill	70
Isaac Stephenson	74
Jay Gould Estate	70
Mrs. Hetty Green	60
Estate of Cornelius Vanderbilt	50
Estate of William Weightman	50
Estate of Ogden Goelet	60
W. H. Moore	50
Arthur C. James	50
Estate of Robert Goelet	60
Guggenheim estate	50
Thomas F. Ryan	50
Edward Morris	45
J. O. Armour	45

$25 to 35 Million

James Stillman	Nathaniel Thayer
J. H. Schiff	Estate of H. H. Rogers
Charles M. Pratt	Estate of Robert Winsor
J. H. Flagler	Estate of George Smith
Quincy A. Shaw	Estate of W. B. Leeds
E. T. Bedford	Estate of W. Scully
E. T. Stotesbury	Estate of John Arbuckle
John Claflin	Estate of J. Crosby Brown
Henry Walters	Estate of John F. Dryden
E. C. Converse	Estate of W. L. Elkins
Clarence H. Mackay	Estate of O. H. Payne

TABLE 6
The Nouveau Riche in 1892

	Total Number	Nouveau Riche	Inheritors	Percent Nouveau Riche
Number of Millionaires				%
U.S.	4,047	3,321	726	82
New York				
New York City	1,103	763	340	69
Rest of State	405	324	81	80
New Jersey	124	81	43	65
Boston	217	172	45	79
Philadelphia	209	175	34	84
Chicago	316	309	7	98
Rest of U.S.	1,673	1,497	176	89

in those cities were 31 percent, 21 percent, and 16 percent. Prior to World War I these cities were resorts of fashion, amusement, and security for the rich. They drew heirs to wealth. But the men who were still making their fortune, or had just made it, were more apt to live in less elegant, less couth, locations. The rate for that brawling mid-continent city celebrated by Sandburg was only 2 percent. And the rate for all the rest of the U.S. was 6 percent. Hence the many studies that focus on wealth distributions in New York City, Boston, and Philadelphia will yield exaggeratedly high estimates of the importance of inheritance, and inherited wealth, in the U.S.

Finally we may refer to Edward Pessen's studies of "the rich" in Boston and New York in 1828–1848.[17] Pessen defines the 1848 rich in Boston as those with estates of $50,000 and over.[18] Of this group about 60 percent were new ar-

[17] Edward Pessen, "Did Fortunes Rise and Fall Mercurially in Antebellum America?" *Journal of Social History* (Summer 1971), Tables 1, 4.

[18] "By 1848 . . . the minimum value of estates required for qualifying as 'rich' had gone up to $50,000, and 477 individuals possessed estates of at least this value." (*Ibid.*, p. 343.) It is to be noted that the phrase— "required for qualifying"—refers not to the original Boston lists but to Pessen's own standard for what was "rich."

rivals since 1833, according to his data.[19] (Reference to a basic published source for 1848 permits us to estimate that about 75 percent of those with estates of $100,000 and over did not inherit their wealth.)[20] His figures for New York City relate to 1828 and 1845. Defining the rich in 1845 as "those having $45,000 and over," he finds that 235 of the 1,000 in that group had either been among the rich in 1828 or had been "members of well known wealthy families," even though themselves impecunious.[21] Some 75+ percent of the 1845 rich in New York City were thus new entrants since 1828.[22]

IV

We summarize the above review in Table 7. Its percentages differ. But they all range upwards of 60 percent, for varying periods in American history, and by different criteria of "the rich." For the broadest estimates of wealth

[19] Since Pessen does not provide comparable income intervals, it is necessary to say "about." He reports 477 persons who had $50,000 or more in 1848, of whom 174 had $40,000 or more in 1833.

[20] The listing is that of 'Our First Men' A Calendar of Wealth, Fashion and Gentility . . . (Boston, 1846). This list, covering 398 persons, is called "largely accurate" by Pessen on the basis of his comparisons with tax data. ("Did Fortunes. . . ," p. 343.) We take any reference by the generally loquacious compiler to "inherited," or to established status and wealth in a prior generation of the family, as indicative of inheritance.

[21] He defines the rich in 1828 as those with $50,000 and over. (Ibid., p. 350.) Pessen provides a list entitled "New York City's 'Wealthiest One Thousand' in 1845" (in his "The Wealthiest New Yorkers of the Jacksonian Era: A New List," New York Historical Society Quarterly [1970] Vol. 54, pp. 161–72), including those with $45,000 or more in that year. He defines "the rich of 1845" as those with $45,000 and over on p. 351 of his later article.

[22] Had he used the same dollar criterion for "the rich" at each data, rather than $45,000 for the earlier date and $50,000 for the later, the percentage would presumably be slightly higher. I am indebted to Professor Pessen for a letter explaining that he "treated property-owning relatives of 1828 wealthholders as distinctive wealthholders in their own right," designating them by asterisks in his Table 4.

WEALTH

TABLE 7
PERCENT NOUVEAU RICHE AMONG THE RICH

			Arrived Since
1969:	top wealth holders (estates of $60,000 & over) age 55+	85%	since 1953
1953:	top wealth holders (estates of $60,000 & over) age 70+	76%	since 1922
1924:	top income recipients (income tax of $500,000+)	60%	since 1913
1913:	top wealth holders (wealth $25 million and over)		since 1892
1892:	top wealth holders (wealth $1 million and over)	84%	did not inherit wealth
1848:	Boston rich (Estates of $50,000+)	60%	since 1833
1846:	Boston rich (Estates of $100,000+)	75%	did not inherit wealth
1845:	New York City rich (Estates of $45,000+)	75%	since 1828

holding—the U.S. in 1969, 1953 and 1892—they range from 75 percent to 85 percent.[23] These findings consistently indicate that newcomers in U.S. history steadily elbowed their way into the charmed circle of wealth. That the proportions are so great is consistent with our earlier observations that (1) attrition among the existing wealthy classes was persistent, and (2) that the percentage of total wealth concentrated in the top group has not obviously risen or fallen over the past century.

[23] Although the data relate to a biased sample, of World War II air cadet volunteers, it is of interest that 51% of those in the upper earnings decile in 1969 were recruits from those in lower deciles in 1955. Cf. Paul Taubman, "Schooling, Ability and Nonpecuniary Rewards. . . ," Conference on Research in Income and Wealth (May 1974). Ratio computed from data in his Table 9.

If the top wealth group is defined as including only say 1 percent of the population, simple arithmetic forces an inference from the above observations. The chance that anyone will rise from the bottom 99 percent into the top 1 percent of the wealth-holding group is minute. Even were the top 1 percent to disappear completely every generation, the probability that anyone from the remaining 99 percent would move into the new top 1 percent would be a trivial .01.

That the prospect of joining the top 1 percent has a probability under .00002 will persuade many that "the system" has naught to attract them. That perhaps 40 percent to 60 percent of the top wealth group has been recruited from below in recent generations is a potent attraction to others. Which is right? Or may not each be right—for themselves? On these questions economists have strong feelings, but economics offers little wisdom. The questions must, therefore, be left either to those more "In Tune with the Infinite" or to the judgment of the many participants.

APPENDIX

To estimate the recruitment rates to the upper wealth groups it is first necessary to establish some basic demographic characteristics of these groups. On the basis of various 1970 Census and IRS data we stipulate the following for the top wealth groups: [24]

(1) The typical rich man marries at age 25.

(2) He dies at age 69.

(3) His first child is born when he is 26, the last when he is 37, and his median child at 31.

(4) Therefore the typical top estate is inherited when the primary heir is 38 years old (69–31).

The 38-year figure is consistent with survey findings by James Morgan. (cf. n. 10 *supra*.)

---

[24] (1) 1970 Census, *Age at First Marriage*, of white males 45–54 with incomes of $25,000 or more was 24.8. Given the steady rise in age with income, a 25-year figure for the top wealth holders would be a minimum.

(2) IRS, *Statistics of Income, 1969, Personal Wealth*, Table 24, gives data indicating the median year of death for married top wealth holders is 69.3.

(3) 1970 Census, *Women by Number of Children Ever Born*, Table 53, shows that white wives aged 45–49 with incomes of $25,000 and over had 3,093 children born per 1,000 mothers. But while this figure reliably reflects completed fertility, it also reflects differential mortality. Taking the averages for younger ages we find a peak of 3,210 for age 35–39, not significantly increased thereafter. We therefore take the mid point, 37.5, as the age at which the last child was born to the median top wealth holder. And 1 year after marriage at age 23.8 (1 year less than the husband's age), or 25, is age of first child. The median child was born between age 26 and 37 for the mother. Taking that 11-year difference as 100%, we assume it was born at the 40% point, at the mother's age 30.4 (and father's age 31.4). The 40% ratio is based on the sequence of averages in number of children born per 1,000 white women in urbanized areas aged 44. (Data for ages, 43, 42, 41, 40 given similar results, *Women by Number of Children Ever Born*, Table 29.) These data show the peak number of children ever born 29 years after marriage; the median number, 11.5 years after marriage, 11.5/29.0 being 40%.

TABLE 1
Top Wealth Holders*: 1922–1969
(000)

A. 1922 and 1953

Age	Number in 1922	Survivors to 1953	Number in 1953	Survivors from 1922
40–50	109	44	383	
50–60	124	18	425	
60–70	96		340	
70–80	54		188	44
80+	16		67	18
Memorandum:				
Age 70+			255	62

B. 1953 and 1969

	1953		1969	
Age	Number in 1953	Survivors to 1969	Number in 1969	Survivors from 1953
40–50	383	306		
50–55	220	59		
55–60	206	118	1,052	⎱306
60–65	188	84	981	⎰
65–70	152	47	819	59
70–75	113	10	634	118
75–80	75		392	84
80–85	41		220	47
85+	27		147	10
Memorandum:				
Age 55+			4,245	624
Age 70+			1,393	259

*Possessing gross estates of $50,000+ in 1922, $60,000+ in 1953 and 1959.

We apply appropriate mortality rates to the distribution of top wealth holders by age in 1922 to infer the number of remaining wealth holders still alive in 1953. Now the wealth holders aged 40–50 in 1922 who were still alive in 1953 were then aged 71–81. If one deducts the survivors of the 40–50 year group in 1922 from the reported number aged 71–81 in 1953, one arrives at the number of nouveau

177

riche who make up the 71–81 age category in that year. We make similar computations for each age group 40+ in the population. (Because we conclude—on the basis of 1–4 above—that the typical heir received his wealth by age 40, the ratio we thus compute for those aged 71 and older in 1953 will not be biassed by inheritances received in the interval.)

ARE THE RICH GETTING RICHER? TRENDS IN U.S. WEALTH CONCENTRATION

> *"I wonder is he still a millionaire . . . I know*
> *they're getting a bit scarce. There's such a*
> *lot of people down on them.*
> *'Scarce as polecats,' I said. 'I've heard they're*
> *going to be stopped,' said Walter. 'It's quite*
> *likely they'll stop themselves,' I said."*
> —Cary, *The Horses Mouth*

> *"One thing's sure and nothing's surer*
> *The rich get richer and the poor get children. . . ."*
> —Fitzgerald, *The Great Gatsby*

Literature shades into litany in discussion of many an emotionally charged subject, not least the distribution of wealth. Such shading has one great advantage: it often puts prevailing beliefs into superbly succinct form. Thus, the compact statement that "the rich are growing richer and the poor poorer."[1] We propose to assemble some new evidence on trends in U.S. wealth concentration. When tested by a simple model of wealth accumulation (Part I) this evidence sharply contradicts the conclusion that "the rich get richer." The reasons for the contradiction inhere in the wider structure of U.S. society (Part II). The continuing process of wealth exchange since the early 19th century offers further empirical confirmation, and is reviewed in Part III.

[1] "The forces of capitalist society, if left unchecked, tend to make the rich richer and the poor poorer." Nehru, "Credo," *New York Times* (September 7, 1958).

The "epigrammatic assertion that the rich are growing richer and the poor poorer . . . is a wandering phrase, without paternity or date. De Laveleye, the Belgian economist, attributes it to Gladstone; others credit it to Lasalle." C. D. Wright, "Are the Rich Growing Richer and the Poor Poorer?" *Atlantic Monthly* (September 1897), p. 301.

179

It may be universally true that a man who gets "to the top of the greasy pole" desires to establish his estate as a permanency. But it is far from universally true that everyone else in the world bows or bends to that desire. Yet unless widow, sons, daughters, and other would-be wealthy men all collaborate to his material purpose, his riches may not be perpetuated. Widows must not dissipate fortunes in mere consumption, nor in unwise second marriages. Sons must consume with some prudence, must see that the estate is successfully invested, and not give themselves wholly over to leisure, to joy, and/or to social welfare. For the very very rich, such requirements may be easily met. For those with fewer millions, the chapter of accidents becomes more important. We describe below the actual record for the "top wealth holders" over the generation from 1892 to 1922, that from 1922 to 1953, and from 1953 to 1969. That record demonstrates that these other variables in the equation for perpetuity failed to work out. The top wealth holders over these periods failed to hand along their wealth in ways that gave their descendants an increasing share of the nation's wealth.

I

The plausible reasons why wealth must increasingly concentrate range from the very nature of capitalist society to meritocratic bias and coercive conspiracy. The Rockefellers and DuPonts surely do possess quite unbelievable amounts of wealth. And the world has surely never before seen a fortune like J. Paul Getty's. But examples prove little. After all, where are the heirs of Stephen Girard and Captain Billy Gray, the wealthiest Americans in the early 19th century? Or Morgan Reno, worth over $200,000 in 1860?[2] Or the millionaire, J. C. Tullis, manufacturer of "the rebounding ball"?[3]

[2] Robert P. Swierenga, *Pioneers and Profits* (1968), p. 103.
[3] W. Sidney Ratner, *New Light on the History of Great American Fortunes* (1953), p. 42.

ARE THE RICH GETTING RICHER?

There are two non-anecdotal modes of demonstrating that wealth concentrates increasingly. One is to state that, given private property, a basic process tends to concentrate wealth under capitalism.[4] Sherman states that "some one-fourth of all American privately owned wealth (in 1956) was owned by only ½ of 1 percent of all Americans . . . just 1.6 percent of the people held 32 percent of the wealth, including 82 percent of all stock.

"Notice the cumulative and self-reinforcing nature of the concentration of wealth and income. The high concentration of stock ownership leads to a high concentration of income from profits. This income is so concentrated that its recipients are in the highest income brackets. But it is only these higher income brackets that are able to save significant amounts. Therefore, they are the ones who make large investments, thus increasing their stock ownership. In other words, large ownership of stock leads to high income in the form of profits; but high income leads to more stock ownership."[5]

What is the proof of "the cumulative and self-reinforcing nature of the concentration of wealth and income"? Appar-

[4] "Ordinary economic forces tend toward a progressive concentration" (in the ownership of productive capacity). "Wealth does breed; 'To him who hath shall be given, and from him that hath not shall be taken away.' If such a trend is not empirically prominent, it is because of various sorts of social interference, equally numerous 'accidents' and perhaps factors analogous to those which make any mass unstable." Knight adds, in another paper: "all productive capacity—whether owned 'property' or personal qualities—is essentially 'capital.' . . . And those who already have more capacity are always in a better position to acquire still more, with the same effort and sacrifice. . . . The tendency goes beyond the individual life, from generation to generation, through the family and transmission of advantages. It is modified but hardly mitigated, and certainly not simplified, by the large element of 'luck' in human affairs." (Frank Knight, "Statics and Dynamics" in *On the History and Method of Economics* [1956], pp. 200–271.)

[5] Howard Sherman, *Radical Political Economy, Capitalism and Socialism from a Marxist-Humanist Perspective* (1972), pp. 51–52.

ently, that the concentration in stock ownership leads to disproportionate profits; that profits in turn are "saved in significant amounts"; that when reinvested in stock they produce still more excessive profits. Thus the grand round continues. (Sherman's description thus proves to be more explicit, if not more pungent, than Marx's "Accumulate, Accumulate, that is Moses and the Prophets.")[6] But this theoretical model is, however, still subject to verification. We may still ask: given the wealth possessed by a given group of wealthy Americans at a point in time, how has their share of "privately owned wealth" actually changed?

The second mode of demonstrating increased concentration is to look to some variety of empirical materials. The method of approach, however, is not obvious. To demonstrate that the concentration of wealth in the U.S. increased "with each passing season," and rose "after a generation or two," we must have some agreed upon definition and criterion.[7]

We begin from a simple model of wealth accumulation—(1) and (2) below—and use exactly the same data on which Kolko, Sherman, and others rely. Doing so, we immediately arrive at a paradox: wealth concentration does not increase over the past third of a century. It decreases. And a similar test for the previous generation of 32 years also shows a decrease.

If concentration is to take place, the share of U.S. personal sector wealth owned by "the rich" must increase. The inequality in (1) would then maintain:

$$(1) \qquad \left[\frac{W_1}{W_{us_1}} - \frac{W_0}{W_{us_0}} > 0 \right]$$

[6] To the connoisseur of ethnic attitudes "it is no accident" (in the Marxist phrase) that Marx misquoted the original phrase—which was, of course, "The Law and the Prophets."

[7] The phrases are from Edward Pessen, "The Equalitarian Myth and American Social Reality: Wealth, Mobility and Equality in the Era of the Common Man," *The American Historical Review* (October 1971), p. 1027.

(W represents the aggregate holdings of the rich at time 0 and time 1 respectively. W_{us} represents the nation's total personal sector wealth.)

In (2) a straightforward model of wealth accumulation stipulates that W_1 (the wealth of the rich at time 1) is a function of W_0, initial period wealth; r, the rate of return; R, the proportion retained and not consumed; E, earnings during the period; and S, the proportion of earnings saved:

$$(2) \qquad W_1 = W_0 + \Sigma_{t_0}^{t_1} [(W_0 R)^r + (ES)^r].$$

For an initial empirical estimate we follow populist and radical literature by assuming that the rich, like the lilies of the field, toil not. Therefore $(ES)^r$ is taken as zero. (Nearly everyone with an income over \$1 million does, in fact, work. But since less than 5 percent of the adjusted gross income of millionaires comes from salaries, the approximation is adequate for present purposes.) [8]

Whether the rich become richer then turns on R and r in (2). Following C. Wright Mills "coma" theory, in which the tightfisted rich automatically hold on to their wealth, we take R as equal to 1. [9] And for r, the rate of return, we assume that the rich earned 8 percent a year. [10]

[8] IRS, *Statistics of Income, Individuals, 1970*, p. 14. Some 77% of the group have wages or salaries. And 38% have net profits from business (sole proprietorship, partnership, or farm). No recent data are available on the extent of overlapping sources. Were we to allow for $(ES)^r$ our conclusion would, of course, be even stronger.

[9] "If you bought only \$9,900 worth of General Motors stock in 1913 and . . . had gone into a coma . . then, in 1953, you would have had about \$7 million. And if you had . . . merely put \$10,000 into each of the total of 480 stocks listed in 1913 . . and then gone into a coma until 1953, you would have come out worth \$10 million. . . . Once you have a million, advantages would accumulate—even for a man in a coma." (*The Power Elite* [1956], p. 111.) Mills did not apply his theory to the men who bought stock in Reo or Packard rather than General Motors.

[10] Something like 10% would appear to be warranted for 1919, 1929, and 1939 total capital stock. (Cf. Simon Kuznets, *Capital in the Amer-*

(That modest rate is actually below the 9.2 percent real rate of return that Brittain estimated for a representative stock portfolio, 1919–1965.[11] Hence, its use will make more likely the conclusion that indeed "the rich are becoming richer.") For W_1 and W_0 (in billions) we then use the same data source (Lampman) as used by the commentators quoted above.[12]

The result is to give:

$$W_{1953} = 101 + \Sigma_{t_{1922}}^{t_{1953}} [(101)(1)^{.08}]$$
$$= \$1,086.$$

Thus, if the 1922 rich earned 8 percent on their holdings, they would have accumulated $1,086 billions by 1953.[13] However, total U.S. personal wealth was then only $1,105 billions. And the top 1 percent then owned only 27 percent

---

ican Economy [1961], Table 3, and his National Income and Its Composition [1941], Vol. 1, Table 22.) Eight % is approximately the rate Becker estimated for return on business capital, 1948–1954, and that Denison estimates for all private domestic assets in 1957. (Cf. Edward Denison, The Sources of Economic Growth in the United States and the Alternatives Before Us [1962], p. 34.)

[11] John Brittain, "The real rate of interest on lifetime contributions . . . ," in 90th Congress 1st Session. (Joint Economic Committee, Old Age Income Assurances, Part III [1967], p. 120.) Brittain used the Moody and Cowles components as his portfolio.

[12] Robert Lampman, The Share of Top Wealth-Holders in National Wealth, 1922–56 (1962), Table 106.

[13] As Representative Dan V. Stephens (Nebraska) remarked in 1913, "The Nation must protect itself from the menace of abnormal fortunes that corrupt the morals of the people and that will ultimately absorb all the wealth of the Nation. . . . Capital at 6 percent will increase three hundred and forty and one-half times in 100 years . . . the great fortunes, if unchecked, will have abserbed all the property in the world in another century at their usual rate of earnings . . . a rate as high as even 6 percent means bankruptcy to the people, and no one will dispute that these great fortunes have increased at a greater rate than 6 percent annually." Comments on the income tax bill, in Congressional Record, Appendix, 63rd Congress 1st Session, pp. 78–79.

of U.S. personal wealth[14]—far below the 98 percent which projection by (2) indicates.

What accounts for this startling failure of the top wealth holders to grow richer? Allowing for their earnings would only have projected a still larger share than 98 percent. That, therefore, offers no help. Allowing them a more realistic rate of return than 8 percent also offers no help, for a higher rate would yield a still greater 1953 share. (Nor is there any problem of incomparability. Both 1922 and 1953 shares comes from the Lampman estimates.)

One may make a similar calculation for 1953–1969, using the recent estimates by James Smith for the top 1 percent of the wealth distribution.[15] Similarly, these data show that if the assets of the top 1 percent in 1953 earned 8 percent they would generate a 1969 total for the top 1 percent far in excess of their actual 1969 total.[16] And this during one of the longest stretches of prosperity in U.S. history, with inflation steadily pushing up the asset values of the rich.

And it is possible to make a similar, but cruder, estimate for the thirty years preceding 1922. In 1892 there were approximately 4,000 millionaires, according to a widely used list.[17] Probate data indicate that these averaged $3 million each, giving a total of $12 billions for the group.[18] For

[14] Lampman, loc.cit., p. 227.

[15] James D. Smith and Stephen D. Franklin, The Concentration of Personal Wealth, 1922–1969 (American Economic Review, May 1974), Table 1 data. We use net worth data, as being most precise for this purpose; assets data would also reveal a discrepancy. Smith's 1953 total differs from Lampman's, but is consistent with his 1969 figure.

[16] Smith's data permit us to estimate 1953–1969 changes in net worth. Assuming an 8% rate of return on his 1953 net worth total for the top 1% leads to a 1969 net worth total 27% greater than the one he estimates.

[17] The New York Tribune listing, discussed below.

[18] This average is based on data for estates probated 1912–1923 in selected counties. (Cf. Federal Trade Commission, National Wealth and Income [1926], p. 58.) The Commission provides data for estates probated 1918–1923, when the prosperity of World War I would

the balance of the top one percent, an additional $6 billion must be added.[19]

If the top one percent in 1892 earned 8 percent on the $18 billion they owned, they would have ended up in 1922 with assets that vastly exceeded the Lampman total for the top one percent in that year.

Hence, over three lengthy periods the richest 1 percent of the population accumulated far less than equation (2) indicates they should have. Why the rich failed to increase their share in wealth over two thirds of a century (1892–1969) is to be explained by R in (2).

II

A

To understand the determinants of R, the retention rate, we must go beyond the rather mechanical economic explanation offered by neo-Marxists. Millionaire fortunes do not simply multiply themselves from one generation to the next by any inevitable "coma" process. No man may choose in the untrammeled air how he will dispose of his estate. He must allow for the interests of wife, sons, daughters. Nor can the rich man readily ignore cogent claims by the state for taxes, and by benevolent spokesmen for charitable purposes. Wealth is transmitted by a human being in a social order whose laws and mores shape his purpose and actions. Most of the rich exist, as well, in a family. (Over 95 percent of American millionaires have been married.)[20] The family

have created a proportionately greater number of small estates, which would dominate the average for millionaires as a group. G. K. Holmes, "The Concentration of Wealth," *Political Science Quarterly* (December 1893), p. 593, also assumes $3 million for this group of millionaires.

[19] G. K. Holmes, *loc.cit.* estimates $25,000 per family for the top 1,000,000 families, exclusive of millionaires. For the top 122,000 families—i.e., the top one % minus millionaires—a considerably higher average should be assumed. We adopt $50,000.

[20] P. A. Sorokin, "American Millionaires and Multimillionaires," *The Journal of Social Forces* (May 1925), p. 629, reports 97%.

constitutes a powerful constraint on his choices. In the most capitalistic of societies, during the most Byzantine stages of its decadence, the family still constitutes an island of primitive communism. The U.S. offers no exception.

The contribution of these constraints is distinguished in (3), where the avenues of effect are indicated:

$$(3) \quad R = [RMF + RS_1 + RS_2 \ldots RS_n + RD_1 + \\ RD_2 \ldots RD_n + RO] + C - E$$

The retention rate (R) for the wealth of any top wealth holder is a function of the retention rates of: the widow times her percentage of the estate (RMF); the eldest son times his share (RS_1); the remaining sons and daughters times their shares $(RS_2 \ldots RD_n)$; other relatives times their share (RO); and C, the percentage share given to charity.

B

(1) The retention rate R is negatively related to the number of terms within the brackets: as the estate gets divided up among more and more persons, the probability diminishes that any of them will thereby become rich. Only if much of the estate is left in entail—(E)—can there be any strong guarantee of financial immortality. There is really only one name in American history that stands for wealth enduring since the early 19th century: Astor. And the Astors appear to be one of the very few wealthy families whose founder tied up his estate in entail, and his son followed suit.[21]

Models that simply assume zero for all terms but RS_1 and RD_1 will, of course, be more likely to predict the in-

[21] A 1964 study of those with incomes $10,000+ reported that only about 6% of those who had received an inheritance are restricted in its use by the terms of the inheritance. Cf. R. Barlow, H. E. Brazer, and J. N. Morgan, *Economic Behavior of the Affluent* (1966), p. 231.

creasing concentration of wealth.[22] Hence the absence of such a trend in the U.S. will derive from the work of those factors which these additional terms represent—as well as the ability of people to make (or lose) money within their own lifetimes.

If all terms are zero except one, so that a single person inherits the entire estate, then that estate may well expand. But how often does that occur? Less than 5 percent of all million-dollar estates go to one heir,[23] for the typical millionaire has a wife and four children.[24]

(3) The grand aggregate of inheritances passed along to widow, sons, and daughters will also help decide whether the estate will expand. Obviously, estates of the kind left by Payne Whitney, or John D. Rockefeller, will almost surely remain above the million-dollar level. But trends in wealth concentration for one or a dozen families have only limited interest. What about the 120,652 millionaires, to use the 1969 figure?[25] If millionaires typically left estates greater than $5,000,000, then even an equal estate division among wife and four children would make them all millionaires. But the average millionaire leaves an estate well below $5,000,000 (Table 1).

[22] Cf. Alan Blinder, "A Model of Inherited Wealth," *Quarterly Journal of Economics* (November 1973). Blinder assumes no inheritances go to wives or collateral relatives, no gifts to charity, and the estate divided between one son and one daughter (*ibid.*, pp. 610, 614). Moreover, his model implicitly permits a maximum of about 30% "equalization" in one generation no matter how estates are fissioned between the heirs, and no matter how many millionaire heirs marry paupers. (Cf. his equation (10) and Table i.)

[23] *Statistics of Income for 1946, Part I*, p. 376, and *1947*, p. 396.

[24] Sorokin, *op.cit.*, p. 631, reports 3.84 children (18 and older) per deceased millionaire, for a sample of 222. His figure for living millionaires is 2.56—but here the fact that the data do not relate to completed fertility probably more than offsets any trend toward lower birth rates. Our sample of NYC millionaires, from Weeks, averages 3.0.

[25] Internal Revenue Service, *Statistics of Income, 1969, Personal Wealth*, p. 19.

TABLE 1
Estates of Millionaires

Year	Average size (000)	Proportion under $2 million
1912–1923	$3,565	n.a.
1946	$2,250	68%
1947	$2,476	65%
1953	$2,364	67%
1965	$2,113	65%

Source: For 1912–1913, W. I. King collected data on 43,512 estates in 13 states that had been probated in 1912–1923 and 540 New York City, Philadelphia, and Chicago estates probated in 1918–1923. (Federal Trade Commission, *National Wealth and Income* (1926), pp. 58, 67.) The respective averages are $2,975 for the wider and earlier sample, $3,860 for the latter. We combine using a weight of 33 percent for the latter—based on the proportions in the 1892 millionaire list, and 1962 data from the Internal Revenue Service *Personal Wealth, 1962*, p. 55. Data for other years come from the *Statistics of Income, Individuals, Part 1, 1946*, p. 362; *1947*, p. 382; *1953*, p. 74; and *Fiduciary, Gift and Estate Tax Returns, 1965*, p. 70.

(4) The same impact on concentration will arise because some wealthy men never marry. In 1969 the proportion of male top wealth holders (estates over $100,000) who never married was 8 percent, while the proportion for females was 10 percent.[26] The percentage of unmarried millionaires appears, if anything, to be somewhat greater.[27] One of our two billionaires, Howard Hughes, is divorced and never had any children. George Eastman, never married, left nearly $75 million, his estate, to educational institutions. Stephen Girard, perhaps the richest man in the U.S.

[26] Statistics of Income 1969, *Personal Health*, Tables 27, 28. For 1962 the similar IRS report indicates 8% for men and 18% for women.

[27] Comparable data for the living estate tax population are not available. However, *Statistics of Income for 1953*, Part II, pp. 76–78, gives data by marital status and estate size for decedents. These data indicate a greater proportion for millionaires than for all estates.

just after the Napoleonic wars, left $3 million to educate poor Philadelphia boys—with the remainder of his estate ($140,000) going to other charities and to some relatives. Matthew Vassar, also unmarried, left most of his fortune to Vassar College. Johns Hopkins left $7 of his $8 million fortune to Johns Hopkins University and Hospital. John G. Johnson put most of his $3 million accumulation into works of art, left them to the city of Philadelphia.[28]

C

Let us now consider the individual terms in (3). Doing so will help explain how it was that the accumulated wealth of the top 1 percent in 1953 failed, and by so wide a margin, merely to equal the 1922 wealth of the top 1 percent plus a modest rate of return during the interim. Of these elements the first is RM.

Widow (RM). Many societies have attempted to prevent what one might term the Margaret Dumont phenomenon, in which a wealthy widow dissipates her husband's fortune among various feckless fortune hunters.[29] Thus Roman legislation as far back as B.C. 169 forbid women to inherit the estate of any man in the wealthiest assessment category.[30] But no such laws have been at work in the United States. Millionaires have left large portions of their estates to their wives with no legal hindrance nor social impediment.[31] In so doing, some millionaires have guaranteed the prompt dissipation of the great fortunes they had accumulated. Margaret Sage, for example, inherited the vast

[28] Data from appropriate sections of *Dictionary of American Biography*, *The National Cyclopedia of Biography*.

[29] We allude, of course, to the great lady who simpered her way through various Marx brothers films, her dignity far surpassing her acuity.

[30] The Lex Voconia is briefly described in *The Institutes of Gaius*, Ed., Francis de Zulueta (1946), Part I, pp. 145–147.

[31] Before 1789 common law appears to have limited wives and widows in their financial dispositions more severely than later statute law or practice. Cf. R. B. Morris, *Studies in the History of American Law* (1959), pp. 135ff.

estate put together by her husband. Apart from a tiny fraction for her living expenses, she converted the entire estate to one or another charitable enterprise. And when George Lorillard's widow (tobacco) married Count Di Agreda, or Mrs. Hamersley (real estate) became the Duchess of Marlborough, or Mrs. Isaac Singer became the Duchess de Camposelice, decumulation surely succeeded upon accumulation.

But there is a more powerful reason why widows tend to dissipate their husband's accumulations: they live on after their husbands die. Wives of the rich typically die almost 12 years (11.7) after their husbands.[32] (Does achieving wealth shorten the life of rich males relative to their wives?) During this decade one would expect wealthy widows to consume the inheritances rather than add to them. Married men with taxable estates left 60 percent of their estate to their wives; married millionaires left 30 percent (Table 2).[33] A substantial share of the estates that millionaires fiercely accumulate is destined to be slowly consumed away during

[32] *The U.S. Statistical Abstract for 1971*, p. 53, indicates that the expectation of life at age 60—close to the median age of top wealth holders—was about four years more for white females than for males in 1959-1961.

IRS, *Statistics of Income for 1947, Part I*, Table 9, and *Statistics of Income, 1953, Part I*, Table 5, and IRS, *Statistics of Income, 1969, Personal Wealth*, Tables 24, 25, provide data by marital status of decedents for whom estate tax returns were filed. We take the median age of death for married decedents to be that for husbands, and the median age of widow decedents as that at which their wives eventually died. For 1969 we use data for married males and for widows. For 1947 these ages were 66.6 and 78.8; for 1953, they were 68.8 and 79.9; for 1969, they were 69.3 and 81.0.

[33] *Statistics of Income, 1965, Fiduciary, Gift and Estate Tax Returns*, Table 9, reports the number of returns with distributable estate given to wives. Assuming that within each of the 22 estate-size categories the average size of distributable estate was the same for men with wives as all persons filing, we use the percentage distribution for the numbers of returns with (monetary) "distributions to wives" to compute aggregates for estates of married men. These are then related to the SoI total for "distribution to wives" to give the data shown in Table 2, panel B.

TABLE 2

INHERITANCES IN 1966

A ALL DECEDENTS	All Wealthy Decedents		All Millionaires	
	($000,000)			
Total Estate	$21,575		$5,773	
Debts		1,151		261
Economic Estate	20,606		5,512	
Legal & Funeral exp.		945		214
Taxes		2,694		1,399
Charity		1,309		824
Left to persons	15,658		3,075	
Wife		5,062		840
Others		10,593		2,235

B MARRIED MEN	All Wealthy Decedents		Married Men Millionaires	
	($000,000)			
Economic Estate	$8,507		$2,094	
Left to Wife	5,062		840	
Percent to wife		59.5%		40.1%

Source: *A* Statistics of Income, 1965, *Fiduciary, Gift and Estate Tax Returns,* Table 9. These data relate to 97,339 returns filed for gross estates of $60,000 and more.

B Derived from *ibid.* See text.

twelve years of widowhood. Should the widow marry a fortune hunter, the estate can be consumed more gaily and faster.

D

$RS \ldots RD_n$. If the rich man's estate is to be reliably transmitted, and to grow in size, he must have children. True, collateral relatives prove willing to shoulder the burden of inheriting great wealth, as *Middlemarch, Cousin Bette, Bleak House,* and a hundred other 19th-century novels describe in lamentable detail. However, rich men appear substantially more willing to give to charity if it is at the expense of collateral relatives than if they have children of their own. We do not follow the practice of upper-class representatives in ancient Rome, or modern Japan, of adopting some likely young man to carry on the family name and fortune. When, therefore, data (for the 13,000 top estates in 1947) indicate that nearly one fourth of the rich and 27 percent of the millionaires had no children of their own, we can see why a very significant share of top wealth holdings may well go to charity—to dissipation or to destinations other than the perpetuation of family wealth.[34]

But even families with children divert funds—to taxes, charities, and wife. As a result, only 20 percent of the entire value of the estates of married men goes to children, plus other relatives.[35]

Of the $22 billion accumulated by those rich decedents, married plus unmarried, who died in 1966, less than 10 percent ($1.7 billion—Table 2) went to children who might carry on the family fortune. Some of the men—perhaps 10 percent—never married. Of those who married, perhaps 25 percent never had children and of those who had children, prior claimants for their estate existed: the tax gatherer, their wives, and charity.

Daughters (RD)   In the summary view of Ogden Nash:

"There are several things standing in the way of
    a natural distribution of wealth, but if you want to
    know which is the chief thing, well, I will tell you which:
The rich marry only the rich.

[34] IRS, *Statistics of Income for 1947*, Part I, Table 10. We summarize data for married, widowed or divorced or separated decedents. Data for estates of widows give much the same ratio, but are not relevant since they relate to estates which, in most instances, have already been reduced in size by being shared out among children. Unfortunately, data for any year later than 1948 are not available. Given that most top wealth holders were well beyond draft age, however, the happenstance of a postwar year should not affect the data on that account.

[35] Table 2 indicates that about 20% of the economic estate of all wealthy decedents went for legal and funeral expenses, taxes, and charity. Applying the same ratio to the $8.5 billion economic estate of married wealthy decedents (using data in the same table) indicates that not over $1.7 billion went to children and other relatives.

It is one of our national disasters
That, broadly speaking, Astors and Vanderbilts and
   Rockefellers and Morgans never marry anybody but
   Morgans and Rockefellers and
   Vanderbilts and Astors
Whereas if they only bestowed their affections on
   somebody in a lower crust
Why money would be distributed over this broad land
   of ours like dust."[36]

Nicholas Georgescu-Rogen makes the same point, somewhat differently: "the gene of low fertility tends to spread among the rich. . . . On the whole, the family with very few children climbs up the social ladder, that with more than the average number of offspring descends it. Besides, since the rich usually marry the rich, the poor cannot but marry the poor. The rich thus become richer, and the poor poorer because of a little suspected interplay of economic and biological factors."[37]

There is much to be said in favor of the position expounded by Nash and Georgescu-Rogen. Certainly, many cultures continue the concentration of family wealth, and tradition, by marrying daughters into families of "appropriate" social status. That tradition is ancient, ubiquitous—but it is un-American.

Like marries like in most cultures. Daughters of wealthy American families, however, have chosen their husbands with considerable freedom. And their choices have not always fastened upon men of an equivalent social stratum. As a result, noteworthy accumulations of wealth have been decimated.[38]

Daughters of pecunious American magnates married impecunious European noblemen at the end of the 19th century. In so doing, their memory was immortalized by Henry James—but not their fortunes. Miss Huntington (railroads

<hr>

[36] His "The Song of Songs."

[37] His *Analytical Economics* (1966), p. 102.

[38] The impulse to exogamy is, of course, hardly restricted to the U.S. For example, an able study has shown a long-term rise in the

became Princess Hatzfeld; Isabella Andrews (tanning) became Countess Von Linden; Miss Winnaretta Singer (sewing machines) became Princess Scey-Montbeliard; Miss Anna Gould became the Countess de Castellane.[39] But when all this happened, the noble gentlemen thus enriched demonstrated greater skill in conspicuous consumption than ardent accumulation. The wealth piled up by one generation ran swiftly down by the end of the next generation.

Sons (RS_1). The practice of transmitting virtually the entire inheritance to the eldest son has dominated much of the history of the wealthiest classes in England, France, and other nations. But entail has not been customary in the U.S., nor primogeniture the rule. Estates of millionaires appear to have been divided so that the eldest son has typically gotten an equal or somewhat larger share than the other children, rather than the entire bulk. (The entail arranged over generations of the Astor family stands out by virtue of its rarity among American millionaire families.)

Whatever the shares given sons, their retention ratio will limit how much lasts in perpetuity. Unfortunately for individual character, but fortunately for the goal of equalizing the wealth, the inheritance of great wealth affects individual character. As Frank Knight has somewhat cryptically written: "the possessor of a vast fortune, especially if it has been inherited, can hardly have the same motives and interests as one just achieving business success."[40] Or in Robert LaFollette's words: "When a fortune has passed from the dead to his successor . . . (the latter) would require years of training and experience to make it as great a menace as it was in the hands of the man who accumulated it."[41]

---

proportion of the Swedish nobility marrying commoners—from 2% in 1690-1699, 44% by 1860-1869. Cf. Sten Carlsson, "The Dissolution of the Swedish Estates, 1700-1865," *Journal of European Economic History* (winter 1972) 1:600.

[39] Marital details from *New York Tribune*, in Ratner, *loc.cit.*

[40] *On the History and Method of Economics* (1956), p. 200.

[41] Robert LaFollette, in *Congressional Record* (August 27, 1913), p. 3821. Senator Williams, at the same time, expressed his "fear a sort of habit . . . has grown up among a few of the great rich fami-

Many sons of hard-driving businessmen decided that there were more important things in their lives than devoting energy to equal hard work, and to further accumulation.

Thus the Manvilles accumulated a fortune, passed on to a son. But T. Franklyn Manville joyously dispersed that fortune—among 11 wives and other acquaintances.[42] Frederic Mott accumulated many millions in General Motors. His son dispensed millions for interesting charitable activities even before he reached middle age. Henry Hyde made millions in Equitable Life. But his son, after the insurance investigations of 1905, sold the company for 2½ millions and fled to France,[43] and there for the next quarter century he consumed the bulk of that fortune. Leonard Case, Senior, left millions to Junior. But the latter, who never married, "gave the bulk of his estate to the Case Library and the Case School of Applied Science."[44] Frances Lowell put together a great fortune from mercantile and manufacturing enterprise. But James Russell Lowell diverted himself with poetry and editorship. And later Lowell's descendents, unto the third generation, committed themselves to literary and other salutary enterprises.

RO. Beyond the inheritance treatment of the immediate family is that of other relatives. The Romans sought to guarantee the concentration of wealth, and thereby class stability, by forbidding legacies to other persons that would aggregate to more than that left the heir.[45] And when such legislation proved difficult to enforce they stipulated (to the same end) that the sum of all legacies could not exceed

---

lies of America of not permitting their fortunes to be divided equally between their children, but leaving them to the best moneygrabber in the family."

[42] *New York Times* (October 9, 1967). Manville left no children.

[43] Mark Sullivan, *Our Times* (1930), III, pp. 44–45.

[44] *National Cyclopedia of Biography, Dictionary of American Biography*.

[45] Cicero, *The Speeches, Pro Balbo*, VIII:20 (Loeb ed., p. 648). Cf. also H. H. Scullard, *A History of the Roman World from 753 to 146, B.C.* (1951), pp. 358, 183.

three-fourths of the net estate.[46] No such legislation has functioned in the United States. The result must have been a greater division, and therefore dissipation, of concentrated wealth than in societies that seek such an end via effective mores or legislation.[47]

Charity (C). The origins of the charitable impulse are difficult to define. Charity has been described as a public good. It may be a means of perpetuating one's name. It may pursue one's purposes after death.[48] What we know for certain is that upbringing and experience lead the rich to give to charity. They thereby hack away at the corpus of their estate, reduce the likelihood that their children will perpetuate the family fortune, or expand it. In 1965, wealthy decedents left 7.7 percent of their distributable estate to charity. Millionaires left 25 percent, or 5 times the 4.7 percent share left by those 1916 millionaires exposed to the icy blast of the first estate-tax law.[49] Whether that increase marks a substitution of charity for the tax collector and/or other changes in attitudes of the very rich is, of course, unclear. But it has helped stay the further accumulation of wealth from estates of the rich.

[46] W. W. Buckland, *A Textbook of Roman Law from Augustus to Justinian* (1950), p. 342.

[47] In a study of Wisconsin inheritance tax, Wallace Edwards found "that estates valued at $100,000 and over had an average of more than nine beneficiaries per estate. He also found that the movement of property is 'what might be described as downward by somewhat less than one generation,'" in part because of such fission. R. J. Lampman, *The Share of Top Wealth-Holders in National Wealth, 1922–56* (1962), p. 238 n.

[48] It is an interesting speculation, for example, what proportion of Ford Foundation expenditures would have been acceptable to Henry Ford. The effective charitable choice, however, was a contribution to a charity *or* to the Treasury of the United States.

[49] U.S. Statistics of Income, 1965, *Fiduciary, Gift and Estate Tax Returns*, p. 81. (There had, of course, been earlier, transient, laws taxing legacies.) U.S. *Statistics of Income . . . for 1920* (1922), p. 41. The first IRS tabulation included all returns filed for 1916 through 1922.

III

We turn now from top wealth holders as a group to a look at particular cohorts of the rich. Doing so enables us to review information for other periods in American history, and to look more closely at the micro-foundations of these changes.[49a]

A. 1892 to 1924

A fairly comprehensive long view of trends in concentration can be developed on the basis of lists of the rich—one for 1892, the other for 1924. The first lists 4,047 millionaires in the United States in 1892.[50] Prepared by 1,500 local correspondents of the *New York Tribune* over a year and a half, it was revised on the basis of corrections from readers and persons on the list.[51] The adequacy of this list is suggested by its widespread use by G. P. Watkins, Spahr, and other contemporary economists, as well as its inclusion of every name subsequently designated by writers on the great fortunes. (Being a millionaire in the 1890's does not appear to have carried quite the social stigma among learned and activist circles that it does today.[52] Hence the listing need not have had the downward bias perhaps inevitable in a list prepared in later years.)

In 1925 Congress stated that totals for taxes on high income individuals should be made publicly available. The newspapers of the time promptly listed top tax payers throughout the country.[53] The first step in the 1892–1924

[49a] Significant historical studies not cited below include: Soltow in J. D. Smith, Ed., *The Personal Distribution of Income & Wealth* (1975), and Gallman in L. Soltow, Ed. *Six Papers on the Size Distribution of Wealth and Income* (1969).

[50] Sidney Ratner, *New Light on the History of the Great American Fortunes* (1953).

[51] *Ibid.*, pp. xviii-xix, 3–4.

[52] The Manhattan telephone book for 1900 listed Russell Sage as a "capitalist." Would any large investor volunteer such a description for an equivalent public listing today?

[53] *New York Times*, issues of September 5-15, 1925.

TABLE 3
MILLIONAIRES IN 1892 AND 1924

	Number	Percent
Total in 1892	4,047	100
Surviving names in 1924	610	
Sons	600	15
Adjustment for married daughters	150	4
Millionaire heirs in 1924	750	19

comparison was to match the list of names in 1892 against the list of those who paid $500 and over in taxes on 1924 incomes.[54] The results for San Francisco, for example, indicate that of the 192 names on the earlier list only 7 still appeared in 1924: Crocker, Hearst, Phelan, Spreckles, Talbot, Williams, Wilson.[55] (It follows, of course, that most of the San Francisco high tax payers in 1924 were new names—from Alexander, Anderson, and Bentley thru to Wallace, Wachter, and Zellerbach.) Of the 13 Columbus, Ohio, millionaires in 1892 not one remained to the 1924 list—Moneypenny, Mithoff, Hoster, M'Une, and the others having all disappeared from the upper ranks. The lowest attrition rates proved to be those for New York City, Boston, Philadelphia, as was perhaps to be expected.

Table 3 indicates that 610 of the names on the 1892 list reappear in 1924, as having paid· an income tax of $10,000 or more, and hence likely to have been millionaires.[56] That

[54] This comparison was made for each 1892 city listing and the relevant 1924 IRS district. For example, the 192 San Francisco names on the earlier list were matched against the San Francisco listing for 1924. They were also checked against the New York and Florida lists at the later date, to locate persons who might have migrated to the centers where the wealthy moved.

[55] Ratner, op.cit., pp. 6–8, New York Times, September 5, 1925, p. 10.

[56] A tax of $10,000+ implied an income of $50,000+ in 1924. At a 5% rate of return, a $1-million estate would yield such a sum. We therefore derive an upper-bound estimate for the number of heirs, since allowance for earned income, at a higher rate of return, would reduce the count of heirs.

count, however, fails to include some daughters of million-aires—namely those who had received a very substantial inheritance, had married, and had survived to 1924. We estimate their numbers as follows:

(1) Given the concentration of 1892 millionaires and their widows in the upper age groups almost none would have been likely to survive to 1924. We assume no more than 10 were included in the 610 count.[57]

(2) The 600 matching names (610 − 10) would include sons and unmarried daughters that had inherited substantial sums. We estimate an upper-bound value for married daughters in 1924 on the basis of data on estate ownership in 1922.[58] These indicate that 24 percent of top wealth holders aged 40 and under were female.[59] Top wealth at such early ages almost always comes from inheritance. Hence the ratio should offer a reliable measure of the ratio of female to total children who inherit substantial sums. Some of these women would be unmarried, and hence previously included in the 600 count. Parents would have been somewhat more likely to give such inheritances to unmarried than married daughters. It would seem a minimum estimate that 20 percent (of the 24 percent) of millionaires' children were married daughters who should be added to the 600 as heirs.[60] The adjusted total number of heirs is then (600 ÷ .80) or 750.

The generation from 1892 to 1924 lived through a high

[57] For 1922, the earliest year for which there are adequate distributions of the rich by age, mortality rates would have been less than the 1892–1922 average, given the downward trend in mortality rates. Yet the 1922 rate of 3.1% would imply that 99% of the 1892 rich had died by 1922. The 1922 data are from Robert Lampman, *The Share of Top Wealth-Holders in National Wealth, 1922–56* (1962), p. 54, and Mendershausen in Raymond Goldsmith, *A Study of Saving in the United States* (1956) III:320, 338.

[58] Lampman, *op cit.*, p. 250.

heirs. The 600 total includes some cousins and collateral heirs, so

[59] The 1950 percent is virtually identical, at 24.7%. *Ibid.*, p. 251.

[60] Here, too, we seek an upper-bound estimate for the number of that 150 would be somewhat too great an estimate for qualifying daughters.

tide of prosperity plus a wartime boom. Nonetheless, the various forces dividing up millionaire estates noted above were at work in the form of various familial and charitable claimants for shares of those estates. So too was the unwillingness (and inability) of heirs to work as effectively and aggressively as had their parents for more and more wealth. The combined forces dropped 4 out of every 5 millionaire heirs from the millionaire class. Only about 20 percent of the original set of millionaires had descendants who were themselves millionaires. Regression to the mean was forcefully at work.

B. 1863 to 1892

For the period from the Civil War to the turn of the 20th century, retention rates can be developed for the two cities where about a third of American millionaires lived in 1892—New York and Philadelphia. We compare lists of high income residents in both cities based on the Civil War income tax returns with a list of millionaires in 1892 (Tables 4, 5).[61] Simon Arnold was the sole Philadelphian with an 1864 income above $500,000 ($617,817), but no Arnold appears on the 1892 list. Two of the four persons in the next size group do appear, and 42 percent in the next lowest category. (The percentage for the entire $100,000 and over group is also 42 percent.) When we go beyond the 36 persons with these very high incomes, the rates fall rapidly, to 19 percent, and then to 10 percent.

Within a single generation, the erosion from the wealthiest 1 percent or 5 percent of Philadelphians in 1864 was substantial. Capitalizing 1864 incomes at a moderate 5 percent would suggest that at least three-fourths of the Civil War millionaires had ceased to be millionaires by 1892.

[61] *Income Tax of the Residents of Philadelphia and Bucks County for the Year Ending April 30, 1865* (Philadelphia 1865). For 1892 the *New York Tribune* list of millionaires is reprinted in Sidney Ratner, *New Light on the History of Great American Fortunes* (1953). The income totals correlate sufficiently well with wealth totals in recent years for high income groups to suggest these data reasonably reflect retention rates.

TABLE 4
WEALTHY PHILADELPHIANS: 1864 AND 1892

1864 INCOME

	All $50,000 and over	Over $500,000	$250,000 to 499,999	$100,000 to 249,999	$75,000 to 99,999	$50,000 to 74,999
Total in 1864	138	1	4	31	32	70
Millionaires in 1892	28	0	2	13	6	7
Not on 1892 list	110	1	2	18	26	63
Percent on 1892 list	20%	0	50%	42%	19%	10%

The erosion of the New York City wealthy group from 1863 to 1892 was equally marked (Table 5). A. T. Stewart, probably the American with the highest income in 1863, left no children. Two in the top wealth group—LeGrand Lockwood and Moses Taylor—disappeared in the mists of time. Two others—William Astor and Cornelius Vanderbilt —remain enshrined in every classic list of millionaires. In sum, of the 5 families in the $500,000+ income group in NYC in 1863, the names of only 2 reappear in the 1892 list. The retention rates for the other top intervals are not strikingly dissimilar to those for Philadelphia. The proportion of the entire $50,000+ income group reappearing on the 1892 list was 25 percent.

For both Philaldelphia and New York the 20–25 percent retention rates include only sons, unmarried daughters (plus, of course, surviving widows and millionaires). An allowance must be added for married daughters and collateral relatives who received large inheritances. Details provided by the 1892 listing indicate that such allowance would increase the 20–25 percent figures to 25–31 percent.[62]

C. 1828 to 1848

What can be said of retention rates at other points in American history? For the Jacksonian era it is possible to discern

---

[62] The listing locates, for example, the married daughters of Moses Taylor who were millionaires, nieces such as Hetty Green, etc., since it reports sources of inherited wealth.

TABLE 5

WEALTHY NEW YORKERS: 1863 AND 1892

1863 INCOME

	All $50,000 and over	Over $500,000	$250,000 to 499,000	$100,000 to 249,999	$75,000 to 99,999	$50,000 to 74,999
Total in 1863	225	5	7	51	58	104
Millionaires in 1892	57	3	3	15	12	24
Not on 1892 list	168	2	4	36	46	80
Percent on 1892 list	25%	60%	42%	28%	20%	26%

something useful from lists of the wealthiest New Yorkers and Bostonians. These lists were developed with great skill and pertinacity by Edward Pessen "to test empirically . . . de Tocqueville's statement that 'most of the rich men were formerly poor.' "[63] Utilizing his data for two of the three cities which were homes for most millionaires gives the data in Tables 4 and 5.

For every group a regression to the mean occurs: families fall from the top wealth groups while lesser wealth categories provide recruits to the upper intervals.[64] Every top NYC wealth category in 1828 includes people whose fortunes waste away by 1845. (Moreover, because Pessen's

[63] Edward Pessen, "The Wealthiest New Yorkers of the Jacksonian Era: A New List," *New York Historical Society Quarterly* (1970) 54; 145–172 and his "Did Fortunes Rise and Fall Mercurially in Antebellum America?" *Journal of Social History* (summer 1971), Table 4.

[64] Because Pessen does not provide comparable income intervals for both dates, for either city, we have had to make some combinations to provide a basis for judging mobility. And because his 1845 transcriptions for NYC did not include those worth less than $25,000, further combination was required. Pessen provides data for one additional NYC group—those with $7 to $25,000 in 1828. But since the lowest wealth category he provides for 1845 is "Not in 1845 tax list or worth less than $25,000," no measure of downward mobility can be inferred. Similarly, for Boston he shows a $6,000–$20,000 group in 1828, but only three categories for 1848—over $50,000; "in 1848 tax list, but not among the rich" and "not in the 1848 tax list." No definition is given for the scope of these two latter categories.

TABLE 6

THE WEALTHIEST NEW YORKERS IN 1828, CLASSIFIED BY 1845 WEALTH

WEALTH IN 1828

Wealth in 1845	$250,000 & over	$100,000 to 250,000	$70,000 to 100,000	$50,000 to 70,000	All $50,000+
Total	10	49	152	309	520
$100,000+	9	27	61	68	165
$45–100,000	1	8	35	92	136
Under $45,000	0	14	56	149	219
Retention Rate	<90%	<66%	<63%	<50%	<54%

TABLE 7

THE WEALTHIEST BOSTONIANS IN 1833, CLASSIFIED BY 1848 WEALTH

WEALTH IN 1833

Wealth in 1848	$100,000+	$70–100,000	$40–70,000	All $40,000+
Total	83	54	166	303
$50,000+	62	31	81	174
Under $50,000	21	23	85	129
Retention Rate	<75%	<57%	<49%	<57%

Source: Computed from Pessen, *J. Social History* and *N. Y. Historical Quarterly*.

intervals are not precisely comparable the percentage declines are understated for the top three groups.)[65] Every Boston wealth category also includes substantial proportions of people in 1833 who drop to lower wealth levels by 1848. We are able to distinguish the top ten NYC wealth owners in 1828 by tabulating Pessen's original data, and the decline for that group—while apparent—is relatively small.[66] (While not relevant to our present concern, it may be noted

[65] They may also be understated for the fourth, but that is less obvious.

[66] His lists appear in the *NY Historical Society Quarterly, loc.cit.*

that upward mobility from the lower wealth groups likewise appears, as one would expect in this general regression to the mean.)

In both New York and Boston over 40 percent of the upper wealth groups lost their financial footing, falling to lower wealth categories in the 15–17-year span covered. Such rates, of course, cannot readily be compared with the 75 percent decline from 1892 to 1924.[67] Yet they suggest that a larger percentage of the wealthiest American families suffered wealth declines in the first third of the 20th century than in the first third of the 19th century.

D

Tables 8 and 9 note the erosion from the millionaire income group over the brief interval of World War I.[68] Table 8 follows the fortunes of the 57 persons who reported $1 million dollar incomes in 1914. After five years, only 60 percent remained in the upper income interval.[69] The most striking aspect of this table is its indication of how incomes of the "old" millionaires (i.e., 1914) declined during the peak prosperity years, 1916–1920. Even as purchases by the Allied purchasing missions reached all-time highs, and as American war production peaked, the incomes of these groups of millionaires were decreasing. Surely, none of them entered the poorhouse. But even in these piping times of

[67] NYC and Boston are hardly the nation; rates of monetary supply and price expansion differed; one period is 15-17 years and the other 30 years; etc.

[68] The aggregate number of millionaire incomes in each year is given by Edward White. (cf. Table A.) The history of the 1914 group appears in his Table F.

[69] The true retention rate may have been still smaller. For there were in all 60 millionaire incomes reported in 1914. These data pertain to the 57 persons of the 60 who had incomes above $300,000 in every year 1914–1919. Given the general downward income trend, it is likely that the 60 in 1914 had dwindled to fewer than 23—hence, less than 40% by 1919.

TABLE 8

1914 MILLIONAIRES, BY NET INCOME IN EACH YEAR, 1914–1919

Income class	1914	1915	1916	1917	1918	1919
$1,000,000 and over	57	53	51	44	32	23
$300,000–$1,000,000	...	4	3	10	13	20
$100,000–$300,000	...	...	2	1	5	6
Under $100,000	...	...	1	2	7	8
Total in group	57	57	57	57	57	57
Retention rate		93%	89%	77%	56%	40%

Source: Edward White, "Income Fluctuations of a Selected Group of Personal Returns," *Journal of the American Statistical Association* (March 1922), p. 78.

TABLE 9

1916 MILLIONAIRES, BY NET INCOME IN EACH YEAR, 1916–1919

	1916	1917	1918	1919
$1,000,000 and over	151	≤95	≤35	≤42
Below $1 million	0	≥111	≥171	≥164
Total in group	151	151	151	151
Retention rate		≤63%	≤23%	<28%

Source: Text, p. 37, n. 70.

war, the long-run tendency for high incomes to regress to the mean persisted. And declines for the top income cohort were substantial, steady, and without significant reversal over the period. Table 9 describes the experience of those who became millionaires in 1916 ("new millionaires") along the crest of wartime prosperity.[70] Their number was actually reduced by at least two thirds—from 151 to less than 42—and in a mere three years.

[70] We estimate this table as follows, using White's Tables A and F. Deducting 44 (the number of persons in the 1914 group who were still millionaires in 1917) from 141 (the total count for that year) gives 95. Since some of these 95 could have become millionaires for the first time in 1917, it is clear that 95 is an upper-bound estimate for the number of the 1916 millionaires who remained millionaires in 1917. Similarly, the 67 total count of millionaires in 1918 minus the 32 survivors from 1914 gives a maximum of 35 persons who first became millionaires in 1916 and were millionaires in 1918, etc.

In Table 10 the incomes of these millionaires are summed. The sharp income declines for 1914 millionaires after 1916 were similar to those which afflicted the newer 1916 millionaires. But the table also points to a decline in income even in the peak prosperity year of 1920. Nor did any net recovery (from the 1919 level) appear by 1920–1924, when the available data end. Such attrition of the upper income group is particularly striking, for it took place during the unbuttoned prosperity of World War I and the inflationary aftermath. That fact points to the fundamental forces that erode any given high income group, and do so even as other persons are seizing opportunities and climbing into that group. These forces of incompetence, of diminishing returns, and of inattention evidence themselves for these millionaire groups by income declines. Every income source but two reflects mild declines. And business profits, 1916–1917, and dividends, 1917–1918,[71] reflect massive declines.

TABLE 10
INCOME TREND FOR MILLIONAIRES

	Number				Net Income (1916 = 100.0)					
Millionaires		1916	1917	1918	1919	1920	1921	1922	1923	1924
as of 1914	57	100	91	59	60	n.a.	n.a.	n.a.	n.a.	n.a.
as of 1916	121	100	76	57	57	47	40	45	47	51

Source:

1914: Edward White, "Income Fluctuations of a Selected Group of Personal Returns," *Journal of the American Statistical Association* (March 1922), p. 71.

1916: 69th Congress 1st Session Senate Report 27, Part 2 *Investigation of the Bureau of Internal Revenue*, pp. 3, 11. Data relate to the 121 out of 206 millionaires in 1916 whose returns were available through 1924.

A special study by the Joint Committee on Internal Revenue Taxation measured the attrition among those who were millionaires in 1924—in the midst of the boom of the 1920's.[72] It indicated the count of 1924 millionaires to

[71] Senate Committee Report, p. 11, and White, *ibid.*, p. 72.

[72] U.S. Joint Committee on Internal Revenue Taxation, *Million-Dollar Incomes* (1938), pp. 8–9.

have been as follows: TABLE 11

Number of millionaires

in 1924	75
in 1924 and 1925	60
in 1924 and 1936	2

About 20 percent of the 75 had fallen to lower income levels within a single year despite the fact that the economy was moving up to the boom level of 1925. (Virtually all 75 had, of course, left the group by the depression year, 1936.)

F

Given the striking regression to the mean shown by millionaire incomes during the prosperity of a World War, the still more rapid decline in millionaire incomes during the Great Depression was only to be expected. But the 1929–1933 decline for the entire upper income group was also comprehensive. Table 12 summarizes Mendershausen's findings.[73] In the median city surveyed, some 72 percent of the upper income group ($7,500+) in 1929 declined to a lower income interval by 1933. But, since the $7,500 and over interval is an open-end category, only income declines great enough to drop families completely out of this group will appear. Another study suggests even greater declines 1929–1932.[74]

G

In sum, the above sets of data indicate the continuing tendency for the value of estates held by top American wealth holders, and even millionaires, to decline. Some of those

[73] Data computed from Horst Mendershausen, *Changes in Income Distribution during the Great Depression* (1946), Appendix B.

[74] G. Perrott and S. Collins, "Relation of Sickness to Income and Income Change in 10 Surveyed communities," *Public Health Reports,* Vol. 50, No. 18, p. 603. The PHS survey, together with the Department of Commerce surveys used by Mendershausen, represent the basic material on income change during the depression.

TABLE 12

RETENTION RATES FOR THE UPPER INCOME GROUP
1929–1933

City	*Survey Families with Income of $7500+* in 1929	*1933 and 1929*	*Percent Remaining by 1933*
Atlanta	241	88	36%
Birmingham	202	19	9%
Boise	16	3	19%
Butte	85	24	28%
Cleveland	1,167	343	29%
Dallas	125	39	31%
Des Moines	82	36	44%
Erie	74	21	28%
Indianapolis	211	64	30%
Lansing	31	6	19%
Lincoln	60	16	27%
Little Rock	89	26	29%
Minneapolis	255	80	31%
Oklahoma City	151	33	22%
Peoria	98	31	32%
Portland, Me.	87	35	40%
Portland, Ore.	103	27	26%
Providence	157	56	36%
Racine	47	6	13%
Richmond	141	55	39%
Sacramento	89	25	28%
St. Joseph	55	22	40%
St. Paul	30	14	47%
Salt Lake City	116	34	29%
San Diego	138	29	21%
Seattle	197	44	22%
Springfield	25	4	16%
Syracuse	40	16	40%
Topeka	49	17	35%
Trenton	29	5	17%
Wheeling	31	6	19%
Wichita	74	13	18%
Worchester	93	44	47%
Median city			28%

Source: Computed from Horst Mendershausen, *Changes in Income Distribution during the Great Depression* (1946).

declines occurred within their own lifetimes; others occurred during the next generation. The historic data report such attrition in all periods surveyed—from 1828 to 1845 for the rich in Boston and New York; from 1863–1865 to 1892 for the rich in Philadelphia and New York; from 1892 to 1924 for the 4,047 millionaires of 1892; and for millionaires at various points in the period since 1914, even including the boom years of the 1920's. That such regression to the mean should occur[75] is perhaps not remarkable except to those who focus their attention on the financial fate of the top .0001 percent, who largely do retain their position. But so far as concerns the top 1 percent (or 2 percent-5 percent-6 percent), or the set of millionaires, the historic evidence points to one clear conclusion: time and circumstance broke up the estates of many of them in the course of a single generation, and still more within the next generation.

IV

The rate of return that very rich achieve, r, is hardly as high as might be assumed, nor is it as uniform. No doubt there exist those completely prudent millionaires who entrench themselves behind the remorseless arithmetic of compound interest, and then watch their money accumulate. But it is surely an empirical question how many millionaires in a given society are dominated by just the neat combination of rationalism and obessionalism needed to achieve such a result. Schumpeter's description of the classic entrepreneur, and Marx's, emphasize his ceaseless vigor, his drive for more and more. Such materialism makes it probable that he is involved in far risker enterprises than those dear to the pure rentier. Table 13, for example, indicates for the U.S. in 1970 the massive contribution made by inherently irregular, and relatively risky, sources of income to the total received by millionaires.

[75] The subject is discussed at length in Simon Kuznets, *Shares of Upper Income Groups in Income and Savings* (1953), pp. 131ff.

TABLE 13
INCOME SOURCES OF MILLIONAIRES: 1970
($000,000)

Total adjusted gross income	$1,419
Business profit	17
Business loss	− 14
Partnership profit	100
Partnership loss	− 32
Sale of capital assets	648
Dividends	523

Source: IRS, *Statistics of Income, Individuals, 1970,* Table 4

And, as noted above with respect to the fortunes of World War I millionaires, the commitment to such venturesome sources as business enterprise both leads to high incomes—and, for a subset, to subsequent sharp declines in income as profits fall and dividends are cut.

The children of the rich in America tend to regress toward mean incomes—and thereby prevent the increasing concentration of wealth. That history was anticipated with painful accuracy by George Mason of Virginia. Addressing the Federal Convention in 1787,[76] he spoke in favor of democratic elections for the larger branch of Congress because: "We ought to attend to the rights of every class of people. [I have] often wondered at the indifference of the superior classes of society to this dictate of humanity and policy; considering that, however affluent their circumstances, or elevated their situations . . . the course of a few years . . . certainly would distribute their posterity throughout the lowest classes of society . . . therefore every family attachment ought to [lead them to] . . . provide no less carefully for the rights and happiness of the lowest, than of the highest order of citizens."

[76] Jonathan Elliott, *Debates on the Adoption of the Federal Convention* (1845), v:136.

THE AMERICAN ECONOMY

INCOME, WEALTH,
AND WANT

THE DISTRIBUTION OF WEALTH
IN 1970

It has not been established as a natural law that discussion of the increased concentration of wealth, or the impact of inflation, varies inversely with the amount of reliable data on the subject. Yet where are the facts to warrant multiplied assurances that the concentration of wealth in the U.S. is increasing? Or has moderated? Or that inflation hits the middle class more than the rich? Or less? In point of fact, we barely have comprehensive data on the distribution of wealth for a single year, much less a set for testing changes over time. Moreover, available data either relate to a tiny fraction of the distribution or prove to have serious flaws.

The present study provides estimates of the distribution of U.S. wealth, by family income, for 1970. The procedures developed are novel in several respects. They permit regular and current estimation, in future years, of wealth data directly comparable with the IRS income data on which the national income accounts largely rest, and many tax analyses. Such estimates can be made at low cost, rather than the $½ million plus cost of comprehensive field surveys of wealth. (They provide less data, but more reliable data, than most field surveys.) Finally, they permit linkage to the widely used annual Census surveys of income distribution. Part I contrasts the basic approach with that used in key estimates currently available. Part II outlines present procedures, while Part III reports the estimates themselves.

I

A

Discussions of U.S. wealth distribution that go beyond urgent and anecdotal evidence of rich men and poor families rely on three types of estimates.

(1) A major survey for 1962 by the Federal Reserve Board, with field work by the Bureau of the Census.[1] The comprehensive skill and assiduity manifest in that survey probably achieved as much as any field survey in eliciting surmises on the quantum of wealth that respondents owned. Nonetheless, the intelligent expenditure of thousands of dollars, plus a good many years of skilled work, yielded results that fail to match control figures for aggregate wealth—and do so with such variation by wealth type as to cast serious doubt on the reliability of the underlying distributions. These problems are discussed below in B.

(2) Data for the shares of wealth held by the top 1 and top 5 percent of the wealth distribution have been developed by Kuznets and Lampman.[2] Their results provide much information of interest. Yet they do not purport to afford us detail for the remaining 95 percent of the income distribution. To say anything useful about the effects of price inflation on different classes of wealth holders, therefore, or to comment on anything more than the mere tip of the iceberg, we must add to the results of their admirable endeavors.

(3) Approximate indications of distribution have been drawn from estate tax reports beginning with the work by Spahr, King, Mendershausen, and others.[3] The most recent reliable studies of that type are by James Smith and the Internal Revenue Service.[4] Their data apply to dece-

[1] Dorothy Projector, Gertrude Weiss and Ervid Thorkelson, *Report on the Survey of Financial Characteristics of Consumers* (1966).

[2] Simon Kuznets, *Shares of Upper Income Groups in Income and Savings* (1953); Robert Lampman, *The Share of Top Wealth-Holders in National Wealth, 1922–56* (1962).

[3] The early work is reviewed by C. L. Merwin, Jr. in *Studies in Income and Wealth*, Vol. 3 (1939). Charles Stewart reviews and applies the income capitalization method, used here, in the same volume of *Studies*. The later leading study by T. R. Atkinson on Wisconsin incomes is well known. Mendershausen's impressive attempt appears in Raymond Goldsmith, *A Study of Saving*, Vol. III.

[4] U.S. Internal Revenue Service, *Statistics of Income, 1969, Personal*

dents leaving estates of $60,000 and over. How large a share of the population are they thereby discussing? According to Lampman's estimates, this group constituted less than 1 percent of the adult population prior to 1946, and less than 2 percent later.[5]

In sum, the estate tax and upper income family data, constituting two of the three basic sources often used, relate to the wealth of 5 percent or fewer American families. Even if they offered precise reports, even if they permitted ready and accurate extrapolation in estimating the holdings of the living from those of the dead, these data still describe only a tiny proportion of the wealth distribution. Yet the lower and middle classes do exist. Detail for them is not unimportant. We therefore turn to the question of the adequacy of the one source that does encompass the entire distribution—the FRB survey—before outlining an alternative approach.

B

The FRB survey was planned and executed with care, intelligence, and zeal of a kind probably never exceeded in any household survey. Its techniques built upon those carefully worked out over many income surveys by the Bureau of the Census and many surveys of consumer finances (under FRB auspices) by the University of Michigan Survey Research Center. The interviews and repeated follow ups for non-respondents were standard. Whatever could be elicited in a field survey by ingenious, astute, and hard work was surely elicited by this survey. Hence the biasses apparent in its final results suggest the inherent limits of field surveys of consumers in this area. Short of providing interviewers with sodium pentothal ampoules for respondents, it is hard

---

Wealth, and James Smith and Stephen Franklin, "The Concentration of Personal Wealth, 1922–1969," *American Economic Review* (May 1974).

[5] Lampman, *op.cit.*, p. 201. Smith (*loc.cit.*) provides data for the top 1% (and ½ of 1%) of persons, utilizing estate tax data.

NEW DATA

TABLE 1

U.S. WEALTH IN 1962:
EXTENT OF COVERAGE BY FRB SURVEY AND BY ESTATE TAX RETURNS

		SURVEY AS PERCENT OF	
	Flow of Funds Total ($ billions)	*Flow of Funds*	*Estate Tax Returns (Survey Data for those with Assets of $60,000+)*
Bank accounts and currency	$272	57%	50%
Bonds	83	63	60
Stocks	373	101	94
Mortgages and notes	32	139	88
Insurance equity	92	84	74
Interest in personal trust	85	64	—
Real estate	—	—	59
Equity in non corp. bus.	291	59	—
other assets	—	—	187*
Automobiles	90	64	—

*The total for "other assets," including non-corporate equity, is $324 billion.

to see how household interviews could have gotten better wealth data from respondents.

What were the results? Most disturbing were the contrasts carefully and professionally reported in the survey publication itself, comparing the implicit survey aggregates with control totals from the FRB flow-of-funds accounts.[6] Column 2 in Table 1 is based on these data. Column 3 compares estate tax results and survey results for units with assets of $60,000 and over.[7]

[6] *Institutional Investor Study, Report of the Securities and Exchange Commission, Supplementary Volume 1* (1971), p. 379, provides dollar data from these sources as compiled in a study by John Bossons. We use these as being somewhat more comprehensive and detailed than the original FRB publication. There is no need to assume that the flow-of-funds data are without fault to believe that they offer a reasonable check on the validity of the implicit survey totals.

[7] *Ibid.*, p. 385.

218

Since portfolio composition is not random by income level, a mere proportionate adjustment for under-reporting by wealth type could well misrepresent the shape of the wealth distribution. However, whether errors for one asset type are concentrated in certain income levels, and those for another class of assets at different income levels, is beyond the knowledge the survey provides. (Indeed, had the survey provided any basis for reasonable adjustment, we may assume that the FRB survey report would have made such adjustments—or at least indicated their direction.)[8]

C

Some evidence of location and nature of bias can, nonetheless, be derived. One way is to compare survey data with Internal Revenue Service reports on the income flows associated with wealth holdings. A second is to refer to internal evidence from the survey. We look first at data on ownership of different types of assets. (Tables 2–ff.)

Stock Ownership (Table 2)

The FRB proportion owning publicly traded stock is contrasted in Table 2 with the IRS proportion reporting dividends.[9] The broad conformity, by income level, between the FRB and IRS summary columns is surely striking. What of the exceptions? A breakdown of the FRB data by age of family head tells us something about the way in which the total rates develop. For the $5,000–7,500 interval, the FRB figures are all above IRS—and may well be preferable.

[8] The survey report (p. 61) states: "SFC data do not yield a good estimate of market value for closely held corporate businesses" and therefore used a book value figure for company stock totals—giving $306 compared to $384 billions for FOF stock. Bossons doubles such book values to infer market ones, giving the 101% in this table.

[9] Federal Reserve Board, *Survey of Financial Characteristics of Consumers* (1966), pp. 114–116. U.S. Internal Revenue Service, *Statistics of Income, 1962, Individual Income Tax Returns*, p. 5 reports returns with dividends received, while p. 36 reports total returns.

TABLE 2
PERCENT OF FAMILIES OWNING CORPORATE STOCK: 1962

		FRB SURVEY[11]			
Income Level	IRS Returns[10]	All Ages	35–54	55–64	65+
Total	12%	16%	17%	20%	16%
$0–2,999	6	7	2	15	8
3,000–4,999	7	8	5	9	17
5,000–7,499	9	15	13	19	28
7,500–9,999	15	19	17	22	37
10,000–14,999	30	32	34	22†	66
15,000–24,999	58	52	53	56	43Δ
25,000–49,999	77	83	77	94*	81
50,000–99,999	89	88	80	97	85
100,000 +	95	97	92	96	99

Source: IRS 1962, Table C, p. 5, and Table 3, p. 36. FRB, pp. 114–116.

What of the other intervals? For the $25,000–50,000 income interval how likely is it that the survey 94 percent* does exceed the rates for either the younger or older age groups by so much? Or, that the rate for the oldest age group in the $15,000–25,000 interval (43Δ) should dip so much below that for the younger age intervals? Or, for the $10,000–15,000 interval, that the 22 percent rate for the central age group should be a third below that for the younger age group, two thirds below the older group? Is the sequence reported for the $0–3,999 interval—2 percent, 15 percent, 8 percent—really credible?

Such irregularities may merely testify to the force of factors other than current-year income. On the other hand, the irregularity may suggest, e.g., that reports from the 196 persons in the FRB $25,000–50,000 interval provided less valid data than did the far greater number reported to IRS.[12] (Thus, if the survey count of persons aged 55–64 in this income group had been 60, instead of 50, the FRB and IRS proportions owning corporate stock could readily

[10] Data refer to receipt of dividends.
[11] Data refer to ownership of publicly held stock.
[12] IRS count from *op.cit.*, p. 33; FRB, *op.cit.*, p. 150.

TABLE 3

FRB SURVEY:

RATIO OF CORPORATE STOCKS TO TOTAL ASSETS

		AGE OF OWNER			
Total Income	Under 25	25–34	35–44	45–54	55–64
Below $3,000	7%	2%	—%	2%	10%
3,000–4,999	13	1	3	5	12
5,000–7,499	5	11	6	5	13
7,500–9,999	0	3	9	6	18
10,000–14,999	0	27	6	18	12Δ
15,000–24,999	19	19	24	24	31
25,000–49,999	66	9*	46	56	52
50,000–99,999	0	72	74	66	51
100,000 +	0	0	83	72	78

Source: Unpublished tabulations of FRB results made by John Bossons.

have been the same. Since FRB sampled 1 in 4,000 for this cell, such a possibility seems not totally unreal.)

(In a model methodological analysis by Robert Ferber of stock ownership, the dimensions of erroneous stock reporting proved substantial. That study, sponsored by the FRB as a follow-up of the above survey, indicated that when a sample of families, all of whom actually did own stock, were questioned, some 31 percent failed to report ownership.)[13]

Another view of the variability in the FRB survey results appears in Table 3.[14] Survey proportions for the upper income holders, who account for the bulk of total stockholdings, swoop and drop without plausibility. How probable

[13] Robert Ferber et al., "Validation of Consumer Financial Characteristics: Common Stock," *Journal of American Statistical Association* (June 1969), p. 429. Cf. also p. 431, which notes the extent to which the implicit aggregates in two FRB surveys fell below the flow of funds totals.

[14] SEC *Study*, p. 394. These data include both publicly held and privately controlled companies.

is it that the ratio of stocks to total assets rises steadily with income for the 55–64 age group, but falls to 12 percent △ in the $10,000–15,000 income interval? Or that for the 25–34 group the irregular upward trend should show a decline to 9 percent* as income rises to $25,000–50,000—or that the highest income group in this age interval should own no stock at all? We take it for granted that the irregularity for the youngest age group has no particular meaning, with gifts and inheritances producing an odd pattern. But before accepting any such explanation for the older age groups, we would have to dispose of the more probable contribution of sampling variability. Since these groups own the bulk of wealth in the U.S. it is possible that variations in the grand totals, where they differ from the IRS results, are variations in survey results rather than in reality.

The corresponding table for ownership of business (farm or equity in profession) is Table 4.[15] Here the overall percentages are identical—17 percent and 17 percent. But in each of the lower income intervals the IRS turns up more reports indicating ownership—perhaps of part-time businesses that were not really considered "business" in the FRB survey responses. More striking, however, is the IRS 69 percent for the top income group—almost double the FRB rate, but almost identical with IRS (and FRB) for the $50,000–100,000 interval. The FRB proportions for age group 35–54 change little over the five lowest intervals— then almost triple to the 71–77 percent range for the remaining three intervals. For the 55–64 group, an abrupt difference separates the six lowest income intervals from the top three. And while one might expect still lower rates for the age 65 and older group, it is hard to understand why only 11 percent in the top income group had business equities when 61 percent and 51 percent of those in the next

[15] For IRS we use the proportion of returns that reported incomes or loss from sole proprietorships and from partnerships, both farm and non-farm (S of I, 1962, pp. 36–37). We assume that income from each legal form was exclusive.

TABLE 4

PERCENT WITH EQUITY IN BUSINESS: 1962

		FRB (FAMILIES)				
	IRS			AGE OF OWNER		
Income	(Filers)	Total	Under 35	35–54	55–64	65+
Total	17%	17%	10%	19%	22%	13%
$0–2,999	17	12	8	18	20	8
3,000–4,999	16	12	6	13	18	15
5,000–7,499	14	17	9	17	22	41
7,500–9,999	15	18	13	18	21	23
10,000–14,999	19	22	25	20	28	12
15,000–24,999	42	26	29	26	27	23
25,000–49,999	64	64	57	71	54	61
50,000–99,999	69	70	95	72	81	51
100,000 +	69	35	—	77	73	11

Source: FRB Study, pp. 110–111; IRS 1962, pp. 36–37.

highest groups did so.[16] Finally, we may note that the FRB percentages presumably include those who held stock in closely held corporations as well as the proprietorship group covered by the IRS—hence FRB rates at every income level should be above those for IRS, particularly so at upper income levels where such corporations are more common.[17]

II

The present wealth distribution estimates are derived in Sections A–C below. Section A gives the sources used for control totals of U.S. aggregate personal sector wealth, by type. Section B proffers some general comments on the use of IRS data to provide data for allocating these control totals by income level. Section C then outlines how each wealth component was allocated.

[16] The 35% rate shown by the FRB for all ages replaces the 27% rate it had before adjustment for non response. Cf. *ibid.*, pp. 60, 110.

[17] Cf. Survey, pp. 45, 61. Professor Bossons estimates that the value of closely held stock exceeds that of publicly held stock for those in the $25,000–49,000 and $50,000–100,000 income intervals.

A

Most components for aggregate household wealth in 1970 were taken from the Flow of Funds accounts.[18] Unpublished estimates for the value of consumer holdings of automobiles and of other durables were kindly provided by Stephen Taylor of the FRB.[19]

Estimates for three other wealth aggregates were derived by extrapolating to 1970 the 1968 aggregate estimates made by Raymond Goldsmith and Helen Tice:[20]

(1) For equity in unincorporated business the FoF data on gross investment in 1969 and 1970 were added to the Goldsmith-Tice figure for December 31, 1968.[21]

(2) A preliminary estimate of the value of structures owned by individuals was estimated by depreciating the December 1968 estimate of Goldsmith and Tice[22] for two additional years at a rate of 2.3 percent per year.[23] The purchases of new residential structures in 1969 and 1970 (as estimated in the national income accounts)[24] were then added, giving a total of $616 billions for December 1970.

(3) The value of land in 1970—$271.4 billions—was estimated by extrapolating the 1968 Goldsmith-Tice figure by

[18] Federal Reserve Board, *Flow of Funds Accounts: Financial Assets and Liabilities Outstanding, 1945–1971* (June 1972), p. 8. Data are as of December 31.

[19] These were estimated as of April 1973.

[20] *Institutional Investor Study, Report of the Securities and Exchange Commission, Supplementary Volume I* (1971), p. 310.

[21] *Flow of Funds Accounts: Annual Flows, 1946–1971* (August 1972) p. 15, farm (line 3) plus non-farm (line 4). A simple summation of the flow of funds figures for 1961–1968 almost exactly reproduces the Goldsmith-Tice change for 1960–1968, and hence comparability is indicated.

[22] SEC study, *op.cit.*, p. 310.

[23] *Ibid.*, p. 254, assumes a 2.2% rate for 1–4 family non-farm housing; 2.7% for multi-family and 1% for farm.

[24] *Survey of Current Business* (July 1972), p. 37, Table 5.2. The $616.2 total was rounded to 616 to adjust for residential property bought by non-individuals.

the USDA index for the value per acre of farm land and buildings.[25]

B

Personal income tax returns constitute the primary source for data on the bulk of the wealth distributed by income size below. Two aspects of these returns are to be noted.

(1) The coverage of the individual income tax with respect to income is now quite comprehensive. In the past few decades, as inflation has taken its toll, and as productivity advances have moved so large a proportion of Americans up beyond the filing minimum, the coverage of IRS returns has become almost universal. Thus in 1970 the IRS personal income tax returns provided data for approximately 195 million persons—as compared with the estimated 192 million persons in the Census income survey.[26] The IRS returns reported $632 billion in adjusted gross income, as compared with the $644 billion estimated by the Census income survey for its money income concept.[27]

(2) Were the IRS distributions used as is to infer wealth distributions, they would slightly understate the wealth of the lowest income groups, who are exempt from filing.[28] The family wealth distributions we have developed therefore translate IRS distributions into ones adjusted to the actual Census distributions of family units by income size,

The direction of bias in field surveys of wealth ownership, it is to be noted, is just the opposite—but more substantial. Field surveys notoriously have difficulty in locating, and in getting cooperation from, high income respondents—

[25] *1972 Statistical Abstract*, p. 595.

[26] *Individuals 1970*, p. 91, deducting the age 65 and over exemptions. Census, *Household Income in 1970* . . . , P-60, No. 79, Table 1, multiplying the household count by the size intervals indicated.

[27] IRS, *ibid.*, Census, *idem.*, multiplying the Census mean income by the number of households.

[28] Since our estimates suggest that those with incomes under $3,000 had 7% of aggregate wealth, the impact of such understatement would nonetheless be small.

who, however, own most of the wealth. Estate tax returns reflect a somewhat different bias, but one also positively correlated with income and wealth: transfers are made in anticipation of death, while changes in portfolio composition are made for the same cause.

C

Corporate Stock

The control total for personal wealth held in corporate stock is allocated by the distribution of dividends and other distributions reported on 1970 individual income tax returns.[29] If upper income groups achieve a higher proportion of their return in capital gains than lower income recipients, the results would be biassed. However, as noted in D below, no such bias obtrudes when one applies this procedure to their holdings for 1962, then compares that distribution with the distribution of FRB stock ownership. That comparison indicates the dividend and stock ownership distributions to have been much the same—or at least, that no particular income-linked bias appears. It is, of course, more than likely that upper income recipients prefer, ex ante, to take a relatively large share of their proceeds in capital gains. But it may be no less true that lower income people succeed in investing in dubious stocks—penny ante, fly-by-night, uranium-gold combinations—so that their dividend share proves to be "relatively" low. Whatever the reasons, however, the FRB-IRS comparison suggests that no clear bias by income level in fact arises from using 1970 dividends to allocate 1970 stock ownership.[30]

This capitalization procedure for dividends would have been considerably less satisfactory some years back, when the reporting of dividends on personal income tax forms was less comprehensive. However, the introduction of

[29] U.S. Internal Revenue Service, *Statistics of Income, Individuals, 1970* (referred to henceforth as *IRS 1970*), p. 54, col 2.

[30] *Per contra* the FRB survey reports variability by income level that is itself suspect. Cf. Table 2 above.

source documents on dividend receipt has gradually increased reporting coverage on the personal tax forms.

The distribution of dividends in 1962 broadly paralleled the FRB's value of publicly traded stock:[31]

TABLE 5

INDICIA FOR DISTRIBUTION OF U.S. STOCK OWNERSHIP: 1962

	Aggregate Dividends (IRS)	Market Value of Publicly Traded Stock (FRB Survey)
Total	100%	100%
Under $3,000	4	6
3,000–4,999	8	4
5,000–7,499	7	8
7,500–9,999	7	11
10,000–14,999	11	13
15,000–24,999	14	10
25,000–49,999	18	18
50,000–99,999	14	12
100,000+	17	19
Memorandum:		
$15,000 and over	63	59

The similarity is considerable, and tends to support the empirical acceptability of assuming the same capitalization ratio at each income level.[32] (The fact that the survey "data do not yield a good estimate of market value for closely held corporate businesses" led the FRB to include such businesses at book value.[33] Since distributions by such corporations would, however, be included in the IRS total, the higher proportion of IRS dividends going to the incomes over $15,000 may therefore be consistent with the true distribution of total stock holdings.[34])

[31] IRS data from *Statistics of Income, Individuals, 1962*, p. 5 FRB data from *Survey*, p. 136.

[32] Apparently, the survey also used a constant capitalization ratio (across income levels) to fill in data for a limited number of respondents on the asset value of their publicly traded stock. Cf. *Survey*, pp. 54–56.

[33] *Ibid.*, pp. 45, 61.

[34] Professor Bossons also rejected the original FRB survey reports:

Bank Deposits, Bonds, Mortgages, Notes, Currency

These credit market instruments yield a fixed interest sum as their primary return.[35] The IRS tax returns report interest as an income source.[36] Its distribution by AGI level is used to allocate the total for household investment in these securities. We thereby assume that the net value of capital gains on such instruments, by income level, correlates closely with the receipt of interest. No other source appears to provide data on currency held by income level, nor even a reliable aggregate for holdings by persons. (The flow-of-funds accounts combine banks deposits and currency in a single total.) We therefore accept the flow-of-funds total for these items, inclusive of currency, on the surmise that cash tends to be held because it offers liquidity, and is held differentially by income level as other fixed value securities are.[37]

Real Estate

For real estate we rely on the fact that real property in the U.S. is universally taxed by the municipalities and counties within which it is located. Real estate tax data provide the basis from which one can estimate the value of such real estate. Some 82 percent of all persons with incomes of $10,000 and over who filed federal income tax returns for 1970 itemized their deductions. (Some 91 per-

---

to approximate market value he doubled all the book values for equity in closely held corporations (SEC *Report*, p. 380). His results, however, imply ratios of (a) closely held, to (b) publicly traded holdings of: 86%, 120%, 222%, and 42%, as one goes up the income scale from $15,000–25,000 to $100,000. Although we do not know the payout ratio for these corporations, it seems doubtful that the IRS figures are in fact consistent with such a sequence of ratios.

[35] For currency this obviously is not true. We assume, however, that the holdings of cash by income level parallel those of deposits—each being in portfolios primarily to provide liquidity and security.

[36] *1970 IRS*, p. 15, col. 35.

[37] Fixed, of course, apart from the impact of general price trends.

TABLE 6
REAL ESTATE TAXES PER $1,000 AGI[38]

Income (000)	Average Tax	Returns Filed
$6 to 7	$27	1,248,095
7 to 8	26	1,512,490
8 to 9	27	1,764,724
9 to 10	27	1,924,834
10 to 11	28	1,943,331
11 to 12	28	1,724,688
12 to 13	27	1,324,888
13 to 14	26	1,582,714
14 to 15	26	1,421,300
15 to 20	26	4,192,670
20 to 25	27	1,564,855
25 to 30	27	646,790
30 to 50	24	788,265
50 to 100	20	311,147
100 to 200	17	58,058
200 to 500	14	11,553
500 to 1,000	14	1,608
1,000 and over	7	600

cent of the $15,000 and over group did so. And, 74 percent of all filers in the income interval $10,000–15,000.) Their itemization included detail on real estate taxes paid.

For each of 24 AGI income intervals we take those who itemize deductions to be a representative sample of those at that income level, then use their reports to estimate ratios of real estate taxes paid per dollar of adjusted gross income.

To rely on the ratios derived from these samples we must make one further assumption—namely, that the geographic mix, and the assessment-value mix, does not change the tax-value ratio as one moves from income level to income level. If, say, all persons with $50,000–100,000 incomes lived in counties with high assessment-value ratios, while those

[38] *Statistics of Income, 1970, Individuals,* Tables 35, 38, 68. Weights for those aged under and over 65 are from Tables 4 and 67 and are used here to weight to a U.S. average.

with $100,000–200,000 incomes lived in counties with low assessment-value ratios, this inference would be unacceptable. But given what the IRS data show about the state and metropolitan area distribution of filers by income level, as well as Census geographic data, such a result does not appear. On the contrary, the geographic mix at each income level is extremely wide, and—what is important here—does not seem to shift from income level to income level in ways that would bias the tax-value ratio (cf. step 6 below).

The ratios by income level are given in Table 6, using the actual data reported by those itemizing deductions:

The extraordinary stability in the rate through the 12 lowest intervals is clear.[39]

The estimating procedure adopted had 6 steps.

(1) The ratios of real estate taxes paid to income received were computed, by AGI level, for persons itemizing deductions.

(2) These ratios were then applied to total AGI income reported at each level (by those itemizing and those not itemizing). The resultant distribution enables us to allocate the value of real estate ownership by income level.[40]

(3) Different proportions of older filers itemized their deductions at lower income levels than did younger filers because of the old-age exemption. Therefore, taxes per dollar of AGI were separately computed for persons under and over 65, then weighted by universe counts of filers under and over 65.[41] As could be expected, perhaps, the adjustment makes no change at upper income levels; the tax/AGI ratios for each age group differed hardly at all

[39] Can Engels laws maintain in an FHA-HUD world?

[40] Internal Revenue Service, *Statistics of Income, Individual, 1970*, pp. 113, 123.

[41] *Ibid.*, pp. 210–211, provides data for those over 65. Combining these with the data noted above permits us to estimate tax/AGI ratios for those under and over 65. These were weighted at each AGI level by the number of filers under and over 65, using data from the same source, pp. 14, 203.

for the upper income levels. The adjustment creates its impact at lower levels where the tax advantage to older persons stems not merely from extra exemptions but from medical deductions.

(4) For income intervals below $10,000 a special check estimate was made. In these intervals the proportion of U.S. families filing returns obviously dwindles. The representativeness of the average tax per return on which deductions are itemized may therefore be inadequate. Moreover, the proportion of owners in the population may not as surely be assumed the same as that in the filing population (even though the latter includes both those who itemize as well as those who do not).

The check estimate was made from the 1970 Census of Housing.[42] As indicated in Table 7 below, the proportion of Census families who own homes and the proportion of IRS itemizers with real estate taxes prove to be much the same. The differences do not indicate that the data for the IRS under $10,000 group are biassed for our purposes.[43] They are explicable by factors that, taken together, are *not closely correlated with income: one ratio relates only* to owned home, the other includes real estate as well; one relates to stock as of April 1970, the other relates to assets at any time during 1970; one relates to the tax return unit, the other to the family as defined by Census, etc. We conclude that the proportion of real estate owners reported for each IRS income interval (for returns with itemized deductions) does offer an unbiassed measure of the proportion in the universe, and that the variation in average tax per filer from level to level is no less adequately indicated.

[42] 1970 Census of Housing, *Metropolitan Housing Characteristics,* HC (2)-1. The data used relate to all housing, not merely metropolitan housing.

[43] The higher IRS proportions presumably reflect ownership of land and structures by renters.

TABLE 7
REAL ESTATE: 1970

Income (000)	IRS Real Estate Tax per return*	Census Families: Percent Owning Homes	IRS Returns: Percent with Real Estate Tax*
$0–1	$438⎫	49.2%	50.8%
1–2	356⎭		
2–3	360	50.9	56.4
3–4	330	50.2	54.7
4–5	337	50.3	51.4
5–6	318	51.0	55.2
6–7	320	53.1	56.9
7–8	306⎫		
8–9	332⎬	61.3	70.0
9–10	345⎭		
10–11	368⎫		
11–12	387⎪		
12–13	412⎬	72.6	81.6
13–14	432⎪		
14–15	451⎭		
15–20	526⎫		
20–25	673⎬	80.5	85.9
25–30	824⎭		
30–50	1,032⎫		
50–100	1,498⎪		
100–200	2,436⎪		
200–500	4,377⎬	84.5	89.1
500–1000	7,913⎪		
1000+	15,887⎭		

*For returns itemizing deductions.

Sources: Columns 1 and 3: IRS, *Statistics of Income, Individuals, 1970*, Tables 35 and 38. Column 2: 1970 Census of Housing, *Metropolitan Housing Characteristics*, HC (2)-1, p. 1–8.

(5) The distribution of real estate taxes, thus estimated for the entire U.S. filing population, was used to allocate aggregate real estate wealth to the separate income levels.

(6) Are real estate parcels held by the rich assessed at the same rate as those held by the poor—as this procedure

implies? It has been contended that the rich escape equitable assessment. Moreover one might hypothesize that the rich tend to be established, geographically stable for longer periods. If so, since older houses tend to be reassessed less promptly in line with current market values, that relationship alone could produce a bias.

These tendencies could well be at work. However, in an efficient market over time such predictable biasses on the part of the tax authorities would be recognized, by both buyers and sellers. If so, the biasses would be capitalized into the value of the real estate properties involved, and we could safely use taxes for projecting market values.[44] (Had a massive housing boom or collapse taken place during 1965–1968, say, the transients in this relationship could produce some bias. It did not.)

As one approximate test of whether the market does efficiently adjust for this potential bias, we rely on data from the 1967 Census of Governments.[45] That Census provides data on the median assessment ratio for non-farm single homes sold during a six months' period in 1966. We assume that within a state those local areas with relatively high assessed values are those with higher average incomes. For example, Westchester, N.Y. (with a $12,319 average assessed value for non-farm single-family homes) is a higher income community than Syracuse (with an average of $5,347); and Glendale, California (with $6,268) higher income than Long Beach (with its $4,348 average). As a test of the efficiency with which real estate markets revalue assets to reflect any income-linked bias displayed by tax assessment authorities, we correlate the median assessment ratio (for measurable sales of single family homes) with the assessed value of homes. The units of observation are individual communities in each of three states—New

---

[44] A succinct discussion of the factors shaping assessment error appears in J. T. Romans, "On the Measurement of Assessment Error," National Tax Journal (March 1970).

[45] 1967 Census of Governments, Taxable Property Values, Table 19.

York, California, and Illinois.[46] The results were as follows:

			$\bar{R}^2$
Illinois	AR = 43.02	+.000725 AV	.029
		(.00547)	
New York	= 20.22	+.002652 AV	.165
		(.000909)	
California	= 18.46	+.000424 AV	.005
		(.000376)	

"t" ratios for the AV coefficients were 1.325 for Illinois, 2.915 for New York, and 1.126 for California. The lack of significance for Illinois and California and the significance for New York (at .05) suggest some possibility for market imperfections. However, this very simple model takes area differences in market value to mark area differences in income, while it is the latter variable in which we are actually interested. A close analysis by David Black of assessment results within the city of Boston reports that the assessment ratio was not significantly related to median family income within tracts when other factors were included in the equation. (But it did prove to be positively related to mean property value.)[47] Utilizing the data for the Survey of Consumer Finances for 1948 and 1953, Maynes and Morgan concluded that "no systematic relationship was found" between median effective rate of real estate taxation and money income of home owners.[48]

We take these various indications as a basis for concluding that, over the entire nation, assessment ratios for real estate holdings do not vary by income class. In part, this conclusion rests on the assumption that the Astor phenomenon

[46] Data from 1967 Census of Governments, *loc.cit.* We utilize data for all areas for which the Census reports data—39 in N.Y., 46 in California, and 26 in Illinois.

[47] David Black, "The Nature and Extent of Effective Property Tax Rate Variations Within the City of Boston," *National Tax Journal* (June 1972), p. 207.

[48] E. Scott Maynes and J. N. Morgan, "The Effective Rate of Real Estate Taxation: An Empirical Investigation," *Review of Economics and Statistics* (February 1957), p. 18.

is at work: some rich persons hold parcels of very small unit value. Moreover, other rich persons hold parcels in assessment districts scattered throughout their state and nation. In part, the conclusion rests on the consistency of the Maynes-Morgan and Black results and the Census data with the theory of an effectively functioning capital market, in which systematic biasses of income tax authorities are capitalised in the market value of the properties involved.

Business Equity

The aggregate estimated above was allocated, by income level, using IRS data for net profit (minus net loss) of business or profession, farms, plus partnerships.[49]

Consumer Durables—Automobiles

The total[50] was allocated to the separate income intervals as follows: The Census Survey of Consumer Buying Expectations provides a distribution, by household income level, of the cars owned by model year.[51] In turn, these ownership data were allocated by original purchase price as reported in the Survey of Consumer Finances.[52]

[49] IRS, *Statistics of Income, 1970, Individuals*, p. 14.

[50] Based on unpublished estimates as of March 1973 kindly provided by Stephen Taylor. For a similar estimate, different approach, see Wolfhard Ramm, "Measuring the Services of Household Durables: The Case of Automobiles," American Statistical Association, Business and Economic Statistics Section, *Proceedings*, 1970, p. 155.

[51] Unpublished data in somewhat greater detail than published were kindly provided by Jack McNeil of the Census Bureau. Published information appears, for example, in Census Current Population Report, P 65, no. 28, *Special Report on Household Ownership and Purchases of Cars . . . 1968* (1969), p. 7.

[52] George Katona, et al., *1969 Survey of Consumer Finances* (1970), p. 54. Earlier SRC surveys in this series—especially 1965, p. 71—were used to amplify the detail so that estimates could be made for each purchase year 1959–1969. No detail was available for 1970 purchases, the annual survey having been discontinued. Data from a more recent but much more limited study did not provide any real increase in information over the prior distributions. For the 1970 segment, we

The SCF distribution of purchases by amount paid per new car was used to compute averages paid for each cumulated group in the purchase population. For example, in 1969 53 percent of the cars were purchased by persons who paid $3,500 or more per car (at an average of $4,455) and 23 percent by those paying $3,000 to $3,500 (at an average of $3,250). Therefore, the most expensive 76 percent of the cars were bought by those paying an average of $4,090. These averages were graphed and interpolated to give an average for each cumulated percentage point in the distribution of car purchases. The Census data on actual purchases by income level were then similarly cumulated from the top down and matched against the SRC-derived data to estimate amounts paid by income level. In effect, this assumes that on average, for the nation as a whole, the highest income persons bought the most expensive cars, and so on down the income scale. Because we are estimating total expenditures for cars, the fact that some of the very rich may have bought relatively modest "estate wagons" presents no problem because they bought, on average, more cars than did lower income families. The average purchase price figures for each year were then depreciated using the 25 percent annual rate implicit in the Flow of Funds computations for our control total for 1970 stock value, and cumulated.[53] Although the estimates were made for each year back to 1959, it is clear that the bulk of the current stock value derives from only the most recent years. The distribution by income level of these stock values was

---

therefore extrapolated the 1965–1969 trend in the distribution of purchases by prices paid—the actual number of cars bought, of course, coming from the Census survey.

[53] While it was desirable to use the same depreciation rate as that used in deriving the FRB control total, it may be noted that Cagan's rates based on price ratios in the mid 1950's run to 25% for low-price Fords and Chevrolets, 21% for medium eights. Cf. Phillip Cagan, "Quality Changes and the Purchasing Power of Money," in Zvi Griliches, ed., *Price Indexes and Quality Change* (1971), p. 227.

then adjusted to the FRB 1970 total to give the final distribution of depreciated auto stock by income level actually used.

The procedures used for estimating auto equity by income level, when applied to 1962, yield different results from those of the FRB survey for that year. Thus they report a steady rise in equity from income level to income level because of the underlying Census data on ownership, and the assumption as to purchase price leads to that consequence. The FRB survey, on the other hand, reports auto equity, e.g., declining from $2,835 to $2,292 as one goes up from the $50,000–100,000 income interval to the $100,000+ interval.[54]

Consumer Durables—Other than Automobiles

The Flow of Funds total for this item was distributed by income level using a procedure similar to that adopted for automobiles.[55] While the results are cruder than those for automobiles, they do reflect with sufficient accuracy a pattern of family asset ownership that is different from that for other assets. Hence including them in the total distribution is preferable to working with a total which, by ignoring them, tacitly presumes them to have the same distribution as the total for other assets.

Other Assets

The present estimates omit certain wealth items (as do those of the FRB, Lampman, Smith, et al.). The most important are pension and life insurance reserves. Unlike other wealth items, these can be monetized only by growing old,

[54] Survey, *ibid.*, p. 110. The same decline appears for families with heads aged 35–54 and those with heads under 35.

[55] The Census data, on purchases of specified major appliances, were combined with the SCF data on the average expenditure for TV's and the average expenditure for kitchen appliances, each of the latter sets of averages then being weighted by the SCF number of purchases.

or dead. If they were to be included in a wealth distribution, the result would be to make that distribution less unequal than the one we show.

D

The data in Tables 9–12 relate to the universe of IRS returns. That is a less familiar universe than that of families and individuals. Estimates were, therefore, also developed (in Tables 14–16) for consumer units as defined in the Census income reports.[56] For this purpose we need only a single set of ratios from the data developed for Tables 9–12— namely, wealth per dollar of income, by income level (in Table 13). By applying these ratios to Census data we assume, e.g., that the 1970 IRS sample of 41,000 returns with incomes of $15,000–20,000 represents an adequate sample for estimating wealth per dollar of income for families and unrelated individuals reporting such incomes in the 1970 Census survey.[57]

We make one change in the Census income distribution, however, for Tables 14–16; that is to reject the Census estimate of $35,680 for the mean income of families in the open-end income interval of $25,000 and over. For the Census did not derive the average for this vital high income group from any enumerative process; it relied, instead, on fitting a Pareto curve.[58] We prefer, instead, to use the IRS average of $48,123 for that interval. Since IRS filers split family incomes, $48,123 is, if anything, too low. We conclude, therefore, that the Pareto curve produces a conspicuously low figure, and for this purpose there appears to be no reason to cling to a function in preference to actual

[56] Cf. *Money Income in 1971 of Families and Persons in the United States*, Series P-60, No. 85, p. 9.

[57] The IRS sample for this interval included 25,122 non-business returns plus about 16,000 business returns. Cf. IRS, *op.cit.*, p. 296, and Table 15. The entire Census reporting income sample was not much greater. Cf. P-60, No. 85, p. 20.

[58] Census, P-60, No. 66, p. 9.

IRS data. When the wealth-income ratios are weighted by the Census distribution of families (rather than by the distribution of tax returns, from which they were derived), the wealth aggregate, somewhat surprisingly, proves to be within 1 percent of that in Table 9. We adjust the wealth-income ratios by this trivial proportion to make the consumers' unit data in Tables 14–15 directly usable with the widely used Census income distribution.[59]

It is to be emphasized that the wealth/income ratios are merely used to convert 1970 data from IRS income level classification for returns to a Census income level classification for consumer units. The wealth-income ratios show virtual stability in the entire range of $6,000–20,000 incomes. Their increase in the still lower income categories presumably reports the relatively great impact of transients in those groups: entrepreneurs with temporarily low incomes, and older persons with newly lowered incomes, who retain wealth "appropriate to" higher permanent levels of income. The ratios of wealth per dollar of income estimated for 1970 exceed those for the FRB for 1963, as one would expect given 7 years of rising asset prices. It may be worth contrasting the present ratios with those of the FRB for

[59] The Census consumer unit distribution used was that from P-60, No. 80, p. 1. To split the p. 1 figure for $25+ between the $25,000–50,000 and the $50,000 plus interval, the family data from p. 57 were utilized. The difference may arise because of limitations in the Census distribution. Thus in 1971 the Census income data aggregate to only 88% of control totals. Cf. P-60, No. 85, p. 21. Their limitations have been scrupulously and helpfully discussed by various census experts. In particular, Herman Miller, *Income Distribution in the United States* (1966), and Mitsu Ono, "Current Developments . . . ," in the 1971 *Proceedings of the ASA Social Statistice Section*, may be noted. Comparison between Tables 10 and 15 shows that the Census data indicate a smaller percentages of wealth held by the top 1%. They do so because the Census counts fewer units with $50,000 + income than does the IRS. Yet the latter count is affected by income splitting. We believe, therefore, that the percentage based on IRS data for the top 1% of returns (19.86) is more precise than the Census (17.01).

1963 and of a special Survey Research Center study for 1959 of upper income groups: [60]

TABLE 8

WEALTH PER DOLLAR OF INCOME

Income Interval (000)	1970 Present Estimates	1963 FRB Survey	1959 SRC Survey
$25–50	7.7	8.4	
50–100	10.9	10.7	
100+	15.7	10.7	
20–29	5.5		8.0
30–49	8.6	(8.4)	6.7
50+	12.8	10.7	12.5

We conclude that the present procedure appears to yield higher wealth estimates in proportion to income than does the comprehensive 1963 FRB survey, and higher figures than the net worth data from the earlier SRC surveys would suggest.[61]

[60] FRB, *Survey* . . . , pp. 149, 110. SRC: George Katona and John Lansing, "The Wealth of the Wealthy," *Review of Economics and Statistics* (February 1964), p. 3. The SRC data are ratios of mean net worth to income, and therefore likely to be somewhat lower than the other figures. However, the FRB data on debt by income level suggest that the difference for these income groups would produce little incomparability.

[61] Katona and Lansing, p. 4, indicate how much lower these ratios were in the 1953 Survey of Consumer Finances, and imply considerable understatements of net worth in the earlier SRC surveys.

TABLE 9

WEALTH IN 1970,
(PERSONAL SECTOR)
BY AGI INCOME LEVEL

Adjusted Gross Income	Total Wealth	Cor- porate Stock	Short- Term Claims, etc.*	Real Estate	Business Equity	Consumer Durables	
						Auto	Other
			($billions)				
Total	$3,145.80	$763.06	$785.03	$887.40	$432.60	$106.30	$171.40
None	}41.61	6.10	7.22	—	−23.75	}1.15	}2.79
$1–999		2.37	6.75	39.20	−0.22		
1,000–1,999	82.01	7.10	21.27	45.10	2.60	1.41	4.53
2,000–2,999	116.38	16.41	40.27	46.90	5.45	1.78	5 57
3,000–3,999	114.51	17.09	40.74	37.40	8.83	2.59	7.86
4,000–4,999	124.51	17.32	47.42	35.90	11.59	3.26	9.02
5,000–5,999	122 24	20.76	38.31	36.20	11.77	4.50	10.70
6,000–6,999	116.88	16.33	32.74	37.60	13.63	5.23	11.35
7,000–7,999	128.31	18.31	37.29	39.80	15.23	6.04	11.64
8,000–8,999	127.32	17.40	31.48	45.20	15.44	6.68	11.12
9,000–9,999	132.06	17.63	31 72	49.30	14.02	7.53	11.86
10,000–10,999	130.01	17.17	31.09	49.80	14.45	7.60	9.90
11,000–11,999	124.83	15.57	30.15	48.30	14.45	7.19	9.17
12,000–12,999	114.53	16.25	26.14	43.30	13.89	6.58	8.37
13,000–13,999	105.49	15.80	25.51	38.20	12.55	5.94	7.49
14,000–14,999	93 79	13.96	20.41	34.80	12.63	5.34	6.65
15,000–19,999	353.87	68.22	86.20	113.20	49.71	15.51	21.03
20,000–24,999	213.47	54.33	51.89	52.50	39.71	6.50	8.54
25,000–29,999	133.22	37.77	31.95	25.90	30.71	3.04	3.85
30,000–49,999	292.16	99.81	63.74	37.70	80.97	4.50	5.44
50,000–99,999	252.20	109.72	47.02	21.30	68.47	2.64	3.05
100,000–199,999	114.19	69.67	19.78	6.40	16.66	0.79	0.89
200,000–499,999	63.67	48.00	9.81	2.30	2.90	0 31	0.35
500,000–999,999	21.92	17.47	3.30	0.60	0.35	0.09	0.11
1 million +	26.62	22.51	2.83	0.50	0.56	0.10	0.12
Memorandum·							
$25,000+	903.98	404.95	178.43	94.70	200.62	11.47	13.81
50,000+	478.60	267.37	82.74	31.10	88.94	3.93	4.52
100,000+	226 40	157.65	35.72	9.80	20 47	1.29	1.47
Top 1%	624.70	322.00	113.00	47.00	130.00	5.90	6.80

*Includes cash, deposits, bonds, mortgages.

NEW DATA

TABLE 10
WEALTH IN 1970,
(PERSONAL SECTOR)
PERCENT DISTRIBUTION BY AGI

Adjusted Gross Income	Total Wealth	Cor-porate Stock	Short-Term Claims, etc *	Real Estate	Busi-ness Equity	Consumer Durables Auto	Consumer Durables Other	PERSONAL TAX RETURNS
Total	100.00%	100.00%	100.00%	100.00%	100 00%	100.00%	100 00%	100 00%
None	}1.32	0.80	0.92	—	−5.49	}1.08	}1.63	}8.31
$1–999		0 31	0.86	4.42	−0.05			
1,000–1,999	2 61	0.93	2.71	5.08	0.60	1 33	2 64	8.46
2,000–2,999	3.70	2 15	5.13	5 29	1.26	1.67	3.25	7.54
3,000–3,999	3.64	2 24	5.19	4.21	2.04	2.44	4.59	6.92
4,000–4,999	3.96	2.27	6 04	4.05	2.68	3 07	5.26	6.84
5,000–5,999	3.89	2.72	4.88	4.08	2.72	4.23	6.24	6.41
6,000–6,999	3 72	2.14	4.17	4.24	3.15	4.92	6 62	6.27
7,000–7,999	4.08	2 40	4 75	4.49	3.52	5 68	6.79	5.96
8,000–8,999	4.05	2.28	4.01	5 09	3.57	6.28	6.49	5.77
9,000–9,999	4.20	2.31	4.04	5.56	3 24	7.09	6.92	5 62
10,000–10,999	4 13	2.25	3.96	5 61	3.34	7 16	5.78	4.96
11,000–11,999	3.97	2.04	3.84	5.44	3 34	6.76	5.35	4 39
12,000–12,999	3.64	2.13	3.33	4.88	3.21	6 19	4.88	3.76
13,000–13,999	3.35	2.07	3 25	4.30	2.90	5.59	4.37	3.19
14,000–14,999	2.98	1.83	2.60	3.92	2.92	5.02	3.88	2.70
15,000–19,999	11.24	8.94	10 98	12.74	11.49	14 61	12.28	7.46
20,000–24,999	6.78	7.12	6.61	5.92	9.18	6 11	4.98	2.57
25,000–29,999	4 23	4.95	4.07	2 92	7.10	2.86	2.25	1.03
30,000–49,999	9.29	13 08	8.12	4.25	18.72	4.23	3.17	1.24
50,000–99,999	8.02	14.38	5.99	2.40	15 83	2.48	1.78	0 47
100,000–199,999	3 63	9 13	2 52	0.72	3.85	0.74	0.52	0.084
200,000–499,999	2.02	6 29	1.25	0 26	0.67	0.29	0 20	0.017
500,000–999,999	0 70	2.29	0.42	0.07	0.08	0.08	0.06	0.0024
1 million +	0.85	2.95	0 36	0.06	0.13	0.09	0 07	0 0009
Memorandum.								
$25,000 +	28.74	53.07	22 73	10.68	46 38	10.77	8 05	2.84
50,000 +	15 22	35 04	10.54	3.51	20.56	3 68	2.63	0.57
100,000 +	7 20	20 66	4 55	1.11	4.73	1 20	0.85	0.10
Top 1%	19 86	42.20	14 39	5.30	30 03	5.55	3.97	1 00

*Includes cash, deposits, bonds, mortgages

TABLE 11
AVERAGE WEALTH IN 1970—PER IRS RETURN,
BY AGI INCOME LEVEL

Adjusted Gross Income	Total Wealth	Corporate Stock	Short-Term Claims, etc.*	Real Estate	Business Equity	Consumer Durables	
						Auto	Other
Total	$42,351	$10,273	$10,569	$11,947	$5,824	$1,431	$2,307
None	} 6,736	14,615	17,298	—	−56,902	}186	}452
$1–999		411	1,172	6,805	−38		
1,000–1,999	13,042	1,129	3,383	7,172	413	224	720
2,000–2,999	20,750	2,926	7,180	8,362	972	317	993
3,000–3,999	22,247	3,320	7,915	7,266	1,716	503	1,527
4,000–4,999	24,479	3,405	9,323	7,058	2,279	641	1,773
5,000–5,999	25,675	4,360	8,046	7,603	2,472	945	2,247
6,000–6,999	25,106	3,508	7,033	8,077	2,928	1,123	2,438
7,000–7,999	28,969	4,134	8,419	8,986	3,438	1,364	2,628
8,000–8,999	29,722	4,062	7,349	10,552	3,604	1,559	2,596
9,000–9,999	31,642	4,224	7,600	11,813	3,359	1,804	2,842
10,000–10,999	35,321	4,665	8,446	13,529	3,926	2,065	2,690
11,000–11,999	38,277	4,774	9,245	14,810	4,431	2,205	2,812
12,000–12,999	41,047	5,824	9,369	15,519	4,978	2,358	3,000
13,000–13,999	44,545	6,672	10,772	16,131	5,299	2,508	3,163
14,000–14,999	46,764	6,960	10,176	17,351	6,297	2,663	3,316
15,000–19,999	63,893	12,318	15,564	20,439	8,975	2,800	3,797
20,000–24,999	111,813	28,457	27,179	27,499	20,800	3,405	4,473
25,000–29,999	173,410	49,165	41,589	33,714	39,975	3,957	5,011
30,000–49,999	318,192	108,703	69,419	41,059	88,185	4,901	5,925
50,000–99,999	718,564	312,612	133,969	60,688	195,083	7,522	8,690
100,000–199,999	1,828,005	1,115,309	316,647	102,454	266,701	12,647	14,248
200,000–499,999	4,962,588	3,741,231	764,614	179,267	226,033	24,162	27,280
500,000–999,999	12,518,561	9,977,156	1,884,637	342,661	199,886	51,399	62,821
1 million +	41,464,174	35,062,305	4,408,100	778,816	872,274	155,763	186,916
Memorandum:							
$25,000 +	427,395	191,457	84,360	44,773	94,852	5,423	6,529
50,000 +	1,116,482	623,723	193,017	72,550	207,480	9,168	10,544
100,000 +	2,914,146	2,029,219	459,776	126,142	263,483	16,604	18,921
Top 1%	841,009	433,496	152,127	63,274	175,014	7,943	9,155

*Includes cash, deposits, bonds, mortgages.

NEW DATA

TABLE 12

PORTFOLIO COMPOSITION, 1970
PERCENT DISTRIBUTION OF WEALTH BY AGI INCOME LEVEL

Adjusted Gross Income	Total Wealth	Corporate Stock	Short-Term Claims, etc *	Real Estate	Business Equity	Consumer Durables Auto	Consumer Durables Other
All incomes	100.0%	24.3%	25.0%	28.2%	13.8%	3.4%	5.5%
$<999	100.0	20.4	33.6	94.2	−57.5	2.8	6.7
1,000–1,999	100.0	8.7	25.9	55.0	3.2	1.7	5.5
2,000–2,999	100.0	14.1	34.6	40.3	4.7	1.5	4.8
3,000–3,999	100.0	14.9	35.6	32.7	7.7	2.3	6.9
4,000–4,999	100.0	13.9	38.1	28.8	9.3	2.6	7.2
5,000–5,999	100.0	17.0	31.3	29.6	9.6	3.7	8.8
6,000–6,999	100.0	14.0	28.0	32.2	11.7	4.5	9.7
7,000–7,999	100.0	14.3	29.1	31.0	11.9	4.7	9.1
8,000–8,999	100 0	13.7	24.7	35.5	12.1	5.3	8.7
9,000–9,999	100.0	13.4	24.0	37.3	10.6	5.7	9.0
10,000–10,999	100.0	13.2	23 9	38.4	11.1	5.9	7.6
11,000–11,999	100 0	12.5	24.2	38.7	11.6	5.8	7.3
12,000–12,999	100.0	14.2	22 8	37.8	12.1	5.7	7.3
13,000–13,999	100 0	15 0	24 2	36.2	11.9	5.6	7.1
14,000–14,999	100.0	14.9	21.8	37.1	13.5	5.7	7.1
15,000–19,999	100.0	19.3	24.4	32 0	14.1	4.4	5.9
20,000–24,999	100.0	25.5	24.3	24 6	18.6	3.0	4.0
25,000–29,999	100.0	28.4	24.0	19.4	23.1	2.3	2.9
30,000–49,999	100.0	34.2	21.8	12.9	27.7	1.5	1 9
50,000–99,999	100.0	43.5	18.6	8.5	27.2	1.1	1.2
100,000–199,999	100.0	61.0	17.3	5.6	14.6	0.7	0.8
200,000–499,999	100.0	75.4	15.4	3.6	4.6	0.5	0 5
500,000–999,999	100 0	79.7	15.1	2.7	1.6	0.4	0.5
1 million +	100.0	84.6	10 6	1.9	2.1	0 4	0.5
Memorandum:							
$25,000 +	100.0	44.8	19.7	10.5	22.2	1.3	1.5
50,000 +	100.0	55.9	17.3	6.5	18.6	0.8	0.9
100,000 +	100.0	69 6	15.8	4.3	9.0	0.6	0.7
Top 1%	100.0	51.5	18.1	7.5	20.8	0.9	1.1

*Includes cash, deposits, bonds, mortgages.

TABLE 13

WEALTH AND INCOME PER IRS RETURN: 1970

Income Level	Wealth	Income	Wealth per $ of Income
	PER RETURN		
No AGI ⎱ $1–999 ⎰	$ 6,736	$ 108	62.37
1,000–1,999	13,042	1,498	8.71
2,000–2,999	20,750	2,488	8.34
3,000–3,999	22,247	3,507	6.34
4,000–4,999	24,479	4,506	5.43
5,000–5,999	25,675	5,496	4.67
6,000–6,999	25,106	6,493	3.87
7,000–7,999	28,969	7,496	3.86
8,000–8,999	29,722	8,490	3.50
9,000–9,999	31,642	9,497	3.33
10,000–10,999	35,321	10,487	3.37
11,000–11,999	38,277	11,487	3.33
12,000–12,999	41,047	12,488	3.29
13,000–13,999	44,545	13,487	3.30
14,000–14,999	46,764	14,486	3.23
15,000–19,999	63,893	17,064	3.74
20,000–24,999	111,813	22,109	5.06
25,000–29,999	173,410	27,151	6.39
30,000–49,999	318,192	37,163	8.56
50,000–99,999	718,564	65,836	10.92
100,000–199,999	1,828,005	130,543	14.00
200,000–499,999	4,962,588	282,431	17.57
500,000–999,999	12,518,561	670,596	18.67
1 million +	41,464,174	2,210,912	18.75
Memorandum:			
25,000 and over	427,410	43,715	9.78
50,000 and over	1,116,482	87,431	12.77
100,000 and over	2,914,146	184,989	15.75

NEW DATA

TABLE 14

AGGREGATE WEALTH OF CONSUMER UNITS IN 1970—BY INCOME LEVEL
($ BILLIONS)

Income Level	Total Wealth	Corporate Stock	Short-Term Claims etc	Real Estate	Business Equity	Consumer Durables Auto	Consumer Durables Other	Number of Consumer Units (000)
Total	$3,145.80	$763 06	$785.03	$887.40	$432.60	$106.30	$171.40	67,305
Under $1,000	18.91	3.71	6.02	16.94	−9.43	.47	1.20	2,652
1,000–1,999	65.30	5.75	16.95	36.03	1.89	1.08	3.60	4,990
2,000–2,999	91 78	13.17	31 80	37.14	3.93	1.35	4.39	4,412
3,000–3,999	92.22	14.05	32.96	30 34	6.52	2.01	6.34	4,148
4,000–4,999	95.54	13.60	36.62	27.80	8.17	2.41	6.94	3,913
5,000–5,999	102.69	17.84	32.40	30.70	9.08	3.65	9.02	4,011
6,000–6,999	100.14	14 35	28.31	32 60	10.76	4.33	9.79	4,010
7,000–7,999	118.28	17.32	34 70	37.14	12.93	5 39	10 80	4,106
8,000–9,999	248.21	34.39	61.05	91 53	25.96	13.15	22 13	8,137
10,000–14,999	596.88	84.85	141.30	227.85	65.75	33.19	43.94	14,894
15,000–24,999	722.15	160.36	177.76	213.88	105.05	27 15	37.95	9,550
25,000–49,999	537 63	180.01	123.15	82.08	131.17	9.30	11.92	2,162
50,000+	356 07	203 67	62.01	23 37	60.82	2.82	3.38	320

TABLE 15

WEALTH OF CONSUMER UNITS IN 1970—
PERCENT DISTRIBUTION BY INCOME LEVEL

Money Income Level	Total Wealth	Corporate Stock	Short-Term Claims etc	Real Estate	Business Equity	Consumer Durables Auto	Consumer Durables Other
Total $ billions	$3,145.80	$763 06	$785.03	$887.40	$432.60	$106.30	$171.40
Total percent	100.00%	100.00%	100.00%	100.00%	100.00%	100.00%	100.00%
Under $1,000	0.60	0.49	0.77	1.91	−2.18	0.44	.70
1,000–1,999	2 08	0.75	2.16	4.06	0.44	1.02	2.10
2,000–2,999	2.92	1.73	4.05	4.19	0.91	1.27	2.56
3,000–3,999	2.93	1.84	4.20	3.42	1.51	1.89	3.70
4,000–4,999	3.04	1.78	4 66	3.13	1.89	2.27	4 05
5,000–5,999	3.26	2.34	4.13	3.46	2.10	3.43	5.26
6,000–6,999	3.18	1.88	3.61	3.67	2.49	4 07	5.71
7,000–7,999	3.76	2.27	4.42	4.19	2.99	5.07	6.30
8,000–9,999	7.89	4.51	7.78	10.31	6.00	12.37	12.91
10,000–14,999	18.97	11 12	18.00	25.68	15.20	31.23	25.65
15,000–24,999	22.96	21.02	22.63	24.10	24.28	25 54	22.14
25,000–49,999	17 09	23.59	15.69	9.25	30.31	8.75	6.95
50,000+	11.32	26 68	7.90	2.63	14.06	2.65	1.97
Top 1%	17.01	35 79	12 71	4.85	24.77	5 24	3.68

TABLE 16

AVERAGE WEALTH PER CONSUMER UNIT:
FRB FOR 1962 AND PRESENT ESTIMATES FOR 1970
($000)

	STOCK		REAL ESTATE		BUSINESS EQUITY		LIQUID ASSETS	
	Traded	*All*						
Income Level	*1962*	*1970*	*1962*	*1970*	*1962*	*1970*	*1962*[a]	*1970*
$0–2,999	*	2	4	7	1	−1	2	4
3,000–4,999	*	3	4	7	1	2	2	9
5,000–9,999	2	4	7	9	2	3	3	8
10,000–14,999	5	6	11	15	4	5	5	10
15,000–24,999	10	16	21	22	10	12	15	19
25,000–49,999	71	82	63	38	62	66	81	57
50,000–99,999	162	313	58	61	277	195	131	134
100,000+	956	2,029	139	126	288	263	272	460
Memorandum: Aggregate for U.S. Households[b] (billions)	$377	$763	$594	$887	$172	$433	$181	$785

*Under $1,000.

[a]Includes closely held corporations.

[b]1962 survey totals from Bossons in SEC, p. 379.

1970 estimates from Table 1, *supra.*

Sources: Table 14, *supra,* and FRB, pp. 110, 118.

LONG-TERM TRENDS IN THE U.S.
STANDARD OF LIVING

*"So it is with human felicity, which is
made up of many ingredients, each of which
may be shown to be very insignificant"*
—Boswell, *Life of Johnson*

I

How has the U.S. standard of living changed since 1900?
And for what has the increase in personal consumption
expenditure gone? To answer these questions we develop
data on various aspects of the change in personal consumption. But the economic elements in the standard of living
include more than personal consumption expenditure, or
services from assets. A very substantial increase in personal
consumption from 1900 to 1970 was foregone, to permit,
instead, a substantial cut in the work day and work year.
We therefore take note of the declining work day for members of the labor force, and the declining work load—and,
possibly, work day—for housewives (whose labor is not
included in the labor force count).

Hours of Work

If one wishes to mark the major switch between work
and leisure, it is probably most meaningful to compare the
regular work week for the typical worker. For this purpose
we estimated regular hours in 1900 and 1973. Since there
were relatively few females in the labor force in 1900, and
since women at both dates tended to work short work
weeks, the comparison is made for males only.

(Hours actually worked by any individual worker will
vary from those scheduled regularly on his job. They will
be less insofar as he takes time off because of illness, for
vacations, for other reasons. They will also be lower insofar

248

as the production is interrupted—whether because of failure of supplies to be delivered, or brief cycle impacts that cut demand and bring temporary cuts in the work week. But a worker's hours will be higher than scheduled insofar as he takes a second job to add to his income, or insofar as pressure of demand makes his employer offer overtime work. To make meaningful long-run comparisons of average hours actually worked, therefore, would involve allowing for these multiple factors, if, in fact, it could be done.)

1900. For employees in manufacturing the estimates by Albert Rees are used; for construction, BLS; for transportation, Wolman's.[1] For trade we use the work of Harold Barger.[2] His estimate for trade is likewise used for service industries, for they operate in a similar manner, and for non-farm self-employed as a group.

For the non-white average we weight the industry averages cited above by the 1900 Census counts of non-white gainfully employed by occupation.[3] The average for whites is then computed as a residual.

1973. Hours of work for non-farm employees on full-time schedules are reported from the Current Population Survey for 1973.[4] The same source reports 53.9 hours for all farm workers with no distinction by sex or color on full-time status. However over 80 percent of the farm worker group were male wage and salary or self-employed

---

[1] Albert Rees, *Real Wages in Manufacturing, 1890–1914* (1961), p. 33. Paul Douglas, *Real Wages in the United States, 1890–1926* (1930), p. 163 for mining, p. 196 for government. For construction: G. W. Hanger, in Bull. 54 of the U.S. Department of Labor, (1904) pp. 1120ff., averaging data for key occupations. Leo Wolman quoted in John Kendrick, *Productivity Trends in the United States* (1961), p. 512, estimates 60 hours for steam railroads. We use this figure, for the major component of transportation, for all transport.

[2] Harold Barger, *Distribution's Place in the American Economy Since 1869* (1955), p. 11.

[3] 1900 Census, *Occupations*, Table 2.

[4] U.S. Bureau of Labor Statistics, *Employment and Unemployment in 1973*, Special Labor Force Report No. 163, Table A-26.

workers aged 16 and over.[5] It seems reasonably safe, therefore, to use this average as applying to adult males on full-
time schedules. We assume, further, that the same average
applies to white and non-white workers. Using counts of
workers by farm/non-farm status, crossed by sex by industry, from the 1970 Census, we can weight these hours figures to yield those shown in Table 1.[6]

TABLE 1

WEEKLY HOURS (FULL-TIME SCHEDULES)
MALE LABOR FORCE

	1900	1973
Total	66.8	45.0
Farm	74.0	53.9
Non-farm	61.8	44.4
White	66.7	45.1
Non-white	67.6	41.9

Holidays

Little information seems available on the number of paid
holidays in 1900. It seems a reasonable assumption that
Christmas Day, Thanksgiving Day, and the Fourth of July
were widely given as holidays. Moreover, by 1905 some
36 states celebrated Labor Day. It seems unlikely that more
than 2 of these were typically paid holidays, although evidence is lacking.

In 1970 the typical worker had 7 paid holidays, and may
well have celebrated Patriots Day, Forefathers Day or
Shakespeare's Birthday on his own.[7]

Vacations

It is likely that few farmers or farm workers took
vacations prior to recent years, if then. There are, however,

[5] *Ibid.*, Table A-21.
[6] 1970 Census, *Industrial Characteristics*, Tables 37, 38.
[7] Bureau of Labor Statistics, Bulletin 1770, *Employee Compensation
in the Private Nonfarm Economy, 1970*, Table A-29.

data of some reliability for non-farm workers. They lead to the figures shown in Table 2.

TABLE 2

U.S. Non-Farm Workers: Percent Taking Vacations¨ 1901–1970

Year	
1901	6%
1930	1
1950	60
1960	66
1970	80

Sources: *Eighteenth Annual Report of the Commissioner of Labor, 1903* (1904), p. 291. *Abstract of the Fifteenth Census of the United States* (1933), p. 461. Census, Current Population Reports, *Annual Report of the Labor Force, 1950,* Tables 9, 12. BLS, Special Labor Force Report 14, *Labor Force and Employment in 1960* (April 1961), pp. A-29, A-36; #129, *Employment and Unemployment in 1970,* pp. A-21, A-22.

The estimates for 1950–1970 were derived as follows. CPS data on the average number of workers with a job but not at work because of vacation are given for every month in these years. Taking the ratio to the civilian labor force, one can then compute what percent of workers were on vacation. But that percentage will vary because the duration of their vacation will determine the probability that they are reported on vacation status during the Census survey week. To adjust for this, one must determine the duration of vacations. For this purpose we compute the median duration of paid vacations from data in a comprehensive BLS survey.[8]

II

Housing

Privacy: The Lodger

Since 1900 one major trend in family expenditure has been to provide more privacy. Whatever the psychological

[8] Bulletin 1770, *ibid.,* Table A-30.

NEW DATA

stimuli, or sociological results, the persistent trend shown
in Table 3 is unmistakable. In 1900 1 in every 4 urban

TABLE 3

URBAN HOUSEHOLDS WITH BOARDERS OR LODGERS: 1900-1970

Year	All	Total	Native	Foreign	Non-White
		WHITE			
1900	23%	23%	22%	26%	—
1910	17	17	12	33	20
1930*	11	10	10	10	23
1934–1946 (non-relief)	15	15	—	—	11
1941	14	—	—	—	—
1960*	4	3	—	—	9
1970*	2	2	—	—	4

Sources: 1900: U.S. Commissioner of Labor, Eighteenth Annual Report,
1903, *Cost of Living and Retail Prices of Food* (1904), p. 261.

1910: U.S. Immigration Commission, *Immigrants in Cities* (1911)
Vol. 1, p. 139. *Immigrants in Industries,* Part 23, Vol. 2, pp.
414, 424. We average ratios from the two portions of this
study, then weight them by urban population data from 1910
Census, *Population,* Vol. 1, p. 189.

1930: U.S. Census of Population, *Families,* VI: 24.

1934–1936: BLS Bulletin 638, *Money Disbursements of Wage Earners and
Clerical Workers, 1934–36* (1940), pp. 18–20, 95.

1941: BLS Bulletin 822, *Family Spending and Saving in Wartime*
(1945), pp. 91, 94.

1960: U.S. Census of Population, *Families,* pp. 196–197.

1970: U.S. Census of Population, *Family Composition,* pp. 246–247.

*Lodgers only.

families had boarders and/or lodgers as a means of supplementing their incomes. Given that most wives were at home
anyway taking care of children, and given that meals had
to be prepared anyway, the incremental financial cost of
caring for a lodger's room and feeding him was small—indeed very small compared to what he paid for such facilities. The sacrifice made by the family as a whole was in
the lack of privacy, and the penumbra of psychological
consequences associated with a resident "outsider." While
there were undoubtedly some benefits from such a presence,

there was surely, on balance, a net cost to the family. The cost, in terms of added work as well as psychological results, was undoubtedly greatest on the wife.

TABLE 4

URBAN HOUSEHOLDS IN 1900 AND 1910: PRIVACY

| | 1900: PERCENT SHARING HOUSEHOLD WITH | 1910: PERCENT SHARING HOUSEHOLD WITH | |
| | | *Boarders or* | |
	Boarders or Lodgers	*Lodgers*	*Another Family*
Native White	22%	14%	3%
Negro	—	32	4
Foreign Born	26	33	—
Bohemian	—	15	2
Canadian	27	—	—
English	26	—	—
German	24	11	3
Hebrew (Russian)	—	43	2
Irish	31	18	3
Italian (South)	20	27	9
Lithuanian	—	77	—
Polish	—	38	1

Sources: 61st Cong., 2nd Sess. S.D. 338, Report of the Immigration Commission, *Immigrants in Cities* (1911) Vol. 1, p. 139; Vol. 2, p. 384. Commissioner of Labor, *Eighteenth Annual Report, 1903* (1904), p. 261. The 1900 data relate to samples of Irish and German foreign born that are more than 4 times as great as the 1910 samples.

Table 4 suggests that the financial stimuli led about 22 percent of native white families to share their household with a boarder and/or lodger, and somewhat more Negro families. The ratios rose among various foreign-born groups, with 31 percent for the Irish, somewhere around 40 percent for Russian Jews and for Poles, rising to 77 percent for Lithuanians. (Since income averages for Lithuanians do not run below those for Poles and Bohemians, a further element in terms of differing desires for privacy relative to income is obviously at work.) While the proportion for South Italians appears to be somewhat lower, the difference from, e.g., Russian Jews and Poles is explicable by another cultural aspect: the willingness to accommodate another family, as distinct from the usual unmarried male lodger.[9]

But Table 3 indicates what happened with rising real incomes. Urban families sloughed off boarders and lodgers. The decline from 1900 to 1970 is obvious, considerable, and all but complete. Indeed, the temporary halt in that decline during the depression (perhaps an actual increase) helps to emphasize that the trend was created by families using rising real incomes to get rid of the lodger rather than to keep him and have still higher incomes.[10] The 70-year impact of this trend, then, was to reduce the work load of the wife in many urban families and to increase the privacy and comfort for all family members within their household.

For farm households the declining proportion with lodgers may be roughly estimated as follows:

1900	17%
1970	1

The 1970 estimate is precise, and based on the Census of Population.[11] For 1900 we use the ratio of farms with gross farm incomes of $1,000 or more.[12] Farms below $500 in gross income were excluded because they averaged $18 (or less) in the entire Census year for hired labor, inclusive of wages and value of board provided to hired labor.[13] In

[9] Because a substantial number of South Italian immigrants during 1900–1910 were married men who had migrated ahead of their family, working until they had made enough to buy tickets for their family, some of these lodgers might well have provided more stability than the usual unmarried male.

[10] The 1934–1936 data relate only to non-relief families. Because the ratio among the large relief group would be higher, a U.S. average for 1934–1936 would be at least back to 1910 levels.

[11] 1970 Census of Population, *Family Composition*, PC (2)-4A, Table 23. We compute the proportion of all households whose head was a farmer or farm manager that had 1 or more lodgers.

[12] Specifically, those with $1,000 or more in value of products not fed to livestock. 1900 Census, *Agriculture*, Part 1, Table 17.

[13] *Ibid.*, p. 231, and the schedule on p. 750.

1899 the average daily farm wage, without board, averaged $0.99.[14] We assume that 18 dollars of paid labor—18 days at $1 a day—characterized farms that hired only for a brief period at harvest time. Farms with gross incomes of $500 to $999 averaged $52 in labor costs. At $19.97 per month (for farm labor without board) they could, therefore, have hired 1 farm laborer for the equivalent of slightly less than 3 months. But since they, too, would have hired day labor for the harvest they could not have hired weekly or monthly farm labor for more than say 1 or 2 months. We, therefore, assume that only farms with $158 or more in annual hired labor costs (i.e., those with $1,000 or more in gross incomes) frequently had resident farm laborers. That group constituted 17 percent of all farms in 1900.[15]

Congestion

The combination of low incomes and national mores is evident in Table 5.[16] One method of providing more sleeping space was to have beds, sofas, or blankets in every room—and from 2 percent to 41 percent of various nativity groups chose that approach. Another method was to have more and more people sleep in each "bedroom"—and the ratios here ranged from 19 percent for Irish families to 57 percent among Slovenian.

Space

The first comprehensive and reliable estimates of housing space become available with surveys for 1901 and 1910.

1901, 1910. For these years we utilize two major surveys. The 1901 data appear in the *Eighteenth Annual Re-*

[14] U.S. Department of Agriculture, BAE, *Farm Wage Rates, Farm Employment and Related Data* (January 1943), p. 35.

[15] In sum, we use the top 2 of the 8 income intervals for which the Census reports data, one actually being $0.

[16] To some extent, as well, the size of family is a factor—presumably smaller urban Negro families at this date were responsible for the low Negro percentage.

NEW DATA

TABLE 5
HOUSEHOLDS IN 1910: CONGESTION

	Percent with 3+ Persons per Sleeping Room	*Percent with Persons Sleeping in Every Room*
Native white	17%	0.5%
Negro	34	6.8
Foreign Born	39	5.1
English	13	0
Irish	16	0.1
Bohemian	39	1.4
German	22	1.1
Hebrew	43	4.7
Italian (South)	44	6.9
Polish	50	7.4
Slovak	55	5.7
Bulgarian	66	63.3
Roumanian	81	9.1

Source: 61st Cong., 2nd Sess. S.D. 338, Report of the Immigration Commission, *Immigrants in Industries* (1911) Part 23, Vol. I, pp. 160, 162.

port of the Commissioner of Labor, 1903 (1904), p. 371. Those for 1910 appear in 61st Congress, 2nd Session, Senate Document 633, Reports of the Immigration Commission, *Immigrants in Industries*, Part 23, Vol. 1, p. 155, and Part 23, Vol. 2, pp. 551–560.

The 1901 survey provides data for about 12,000 native families, the 1910 survey for about 16,000 foreign-born families. Although both surveys in fact provide data for both nationality groups, their samples in some categories are not equally adequate. The survey results were therefore combined as follows. The 1901 survey includes a fairly substantial number of the major foreign-born nativity groups—Irish and Germans. Weighting its results together for these two groups gives an average of 1.03 persons per room, or virtually the same figure as the 1.02 per room reported for those nationalities by the 1910 survey. From this fact we infer that there was no significant change in persons per room between the two dates.

For native born, therefore, we utilize the 1901 average of .926 for native born, based as it is on a much larger sample for that group than the 1910 survey. (The reported 1910 average for those with both parents native born is .87.)

For foreign born we do not use the reported average given by the immigration survey because the industrial composition of their sample does not necessarily reflect that of the nation, and nativity differences—which are industrially linked—are marked. We therefore reweighted as follows. (a) Consistent estimates of wage earner employment by major industry group were taken from Solomon Fabricant, *Employment in Manufacturing, 1899–1939* (1947), Table B-1. (b) The proportion of foreign born to total employment in each manufacturing industry was computed from the 1910 Census of Population, *Occupations*, Vol. IV, pp. 336ff. (c) The number of foreign born was computed by multiplying the ratios from step b by the counts from step a. (d) The numbers from step c were then used as weights to combine the persons-per-room figures for the foreign born employed in individual manufacturing industries as shown in the Immigration Commission *Reports*, Part 23, Vol. 1, p. 259, giving an average of 1.37. (e) The .926 native average and the 1.37 foreign-born average computed above were then weighted together by 1910 Census data to give a U.S. white average of 1.11. The non-white figure of 1.30 is taken from *Reports*, Part 23, Vol. 1, p. 157, weighted with the white average to give a U.S. average. (Population weights are from the 13th Census, *Population*, Vol. IV, p. 64, using data for population 10 and older. Other data for 1910 are derived from *Reports*, Part 23, Vol. I, pp. 153, 157, 160.)

1940–1960. 1960 Census of Housing, Vol. 1, Part 1, pp. 1–10, 1–43, 1–213, 1950 Census of Housing, Vol. 1, Part 1, pp. xxx, 1–21; and 1960 Census, *Families*, p. 190.

1970. 1970 Census of Housing, HC(7)-3. *Space Utilization of the Housing Inventory*, Tables A-1, A-4, A-11.

These sources and estimates lead to the figures in Table 6 below.

TABLE 6

AMERICAN HOUSING: 1910–1970

AVERAGE NUMBER OF PERSONS PER ROOM

	1910	1940	1950	1960	1970
U.S. total	1.13	.74	.68	.60	.62
White	1.11			.56	.61
Native	.93				
Foreign Born	1.37				
Non-white	1.30			1.12	.77

PERCENT OF FAMILIES WITH 1+ PERSONS PER ROOM

1.0+	48.8%	20.3%	15.8%	11.5%	8.0%
1.5+		9.0	6.2	3.6	2.0
2.0+	8.9				

Home Ownership

The physical amenities available from housing can be provided by rental housing as well as ownership. But the desire for possession has always been a factor in the scarcely veiled warfare between landlords and tenants. Supporters of capitalism inevitably accept, or applaud, ownership. Detractors of capitalism on occasion demonstrate its failures by the "inadequate" ownership rate among certain groups. What seems assured is that home ownership in the U.S.—tax benefits aside—is a relatively low return form of investment. Moreover, it seems to induce much ancillary expenditure—on rugs, painting, lawn rakes, garden books, barbecue pits, and porch furniture. It therefore marks a capital intensive method of consuming housing services. As such the trend shown in Table 7 is suggestive of an important trend in resource use. The perceptible break in trend after 1940 presumably stemmed from the G.I. bill loans for soldiers of World War II, and other public efforts to subsidize home ownership. The trend for whites may be presumed to have been much the same as that for the nation. For non-whites,

TABLE 7

HOME OWNERSHIP, 1890–1970:
PERCENT OF U.S. FAMILIES OWNING THEIR HOME

Year	All	Urban	White	Negro
1890	48%	37%	51.5%	18.8%
1900	47	37		
1910	46	38		
1920	46	41		
1930	48	46		
1940	44	41		
1950	55	53		
1960	62	58		
1970	63	58	65.2	41.5

Sources: 1890 Census, *Report on Farms and Homes* (1896), pp. 19, 558. 1960 Census of Housing, Vol. 1, Part 1, *U.S. Summary*, Table 9. 1970 Census of Housing, *General Housing Characteristics*, HC(1)-A1, Tables 3, 10, 13.

however, it is not unlikely that the major rise from 18.8 percent occurred well after World War II, with the gain to 41.5 percent taking place in the late 1950's and the 1960's.

Facilities

The additional facilities present in today's dwelling unit, and not present in that of 1900, account for about 25 percent of the cost of the structure, apart from land.[17] In part the new items were put in at the expense of both the size and the quality of the core house. The number of rooms in the typical non-farm dwelling unit decreased from 4.76 to 4.26 between 1919 and the "1945 or later category."[18]

Fairly detailed expenditure analyses[19] indicate the ratio

[17] Leo Grebler, et al., *Capital Formation in Residential Real Estate, Trends and Prospects* (1956), p. 118.

[18] *Ibid.*, p. 120.

[19] *1913, 1919:* United States Department of Labor, *Report of the United States Housing Corporation* (1920) Vol. 1, p. 219. Estimates relate to a "modern six-room frame house," using unit price for Boston at both dates.

of such specified costs to total labor and materials costs.
See Table 8.

TABLE 8

SINGLE FAMILY HOUSING: SHARE OF COSTS

	1913	1919	1931–1932	1968
Plumbing	11%	10%	10%	10%
Heating	6	5	7	5
Electrical	2	2	5	5
Total Labor and Materials	100	100	100	100

The typical American in 1900 lived in a house or apartment that had no running water, bathtub, or flush toilet;
no central heating; and no electricity. These cost break-
downs then permit one approximate estimate. And that is
that approximately 20 percent of the rental value of American housing in 1970 went for facilities lacking in the typical
1900 dwelling unit. Given that $90.9 billion went for rent
in 1970 (actual or imputed), we may estimate that $18
billion was spent by Americans for basic housing facilities
that were lacking in 1900—a sum roughly equal to what
they spent for physicians and dentists and almost equalling
what they spent for gasoline and oil.[20]

Facilities and Durables

As a rough basis for dimensioning the changes noted below
in facilities and durables as the nation grew, it may help

1931–1932: National Resources Committee, Housing Monograph
series no. 3. *Land, Materials and Labor Costs* (1939), p. 57. These
estimates rest on BLS data for 15 cities. Somewhat similar figures,
based on estimates by type of house, appear in President's Conference on Home Building and Home Ownership, *House Design, Construction and Equipment* (1931), pp. 34–35.

1968: FHA data in *Report of the President's Committee on Urban
Housing, Technical Studies* (1968) Vol. II, p. 183. Almost identical
figures are given in the same source based on replied by builders.

[20] Consumption expenditure data from *Survey of Current Business*
(July 1974), p. 24.

to contrast the U.S. and Western European percentages today.[21] See Table 9.

TABLE 9
Percent of Households with Specified Item in 1970

	U.S.	Western Europe
Refrigerator	99%	72%
Washing machine	70	57
Dryer	45	18
Iron	100	93
Vacuum cleaner	92	61
Dishwasher	26	2
Toaster	93	21
Automobile	80	47
TV	99	75
Running cold water	93	91
Running hot water	87	61
Central heating	66	26
Telephone	91	33

Running Water

The importance of clean water supply in keeping down the deaths from typhoid is perhaps hard to recognize in an era when few Americans die of typhoid. But it was not easy to recognize through most of the 19th century. When members could not sit comfortably in Parliament as late as the 1860's because of the "stink rising from the Thames," the importance of clean water supply and its twin—adequate sewage treatment—had hardly become generally accepted. Boston, Philadelphia, and some New England cities had established public water supply relatively

[21] U.S. percentages derived below except telephone. Bell telephones per 1,000 population rose 17% from 1960 to 1965, while the proportion of households with phones rose 8%. The ratio of one percentage to the other was applied to the 22% rise, 1965–1970, in Bell phones per 1,000 population. Data from *1971 Statistical Abstract*, pp. 482–483. The heating and water percentages are as of 1960. The European data are from The Readers Digest, *A Survey of Europe Today, The Peoples and Markets of Sixteen European Countries* (1970).

early. In most instances that supply was also a clean supply; Philadelphia was a notable exception.

A

As of 1900, approximately $800 million had been invested in water works, about a third private and two-thirds public.[22] That sum protected most of the urban residents of the nation from water-borne typhoid and related diseases. As can be seen from Table 10 most of these plants had been built since the Civil War. Since Boston and New York had built some plants earlier, the proportion of total urban population protected was somewhat greater, somewhat earlier, than these data indicate. The investment of $1 billion in water supply systems reflects in no small measure the desire not to die of typhoid. Typhoid death rates of 20 per 100,000 could be expected from causes other than water—since cities with good water supplies had rates about that level (Boston, 21; Chicago, 16; Detroit, 21; New York, 16). Cities with raw water taken directly from polluted rivers and streams had rates such as the following:

Washington, D.C.	48
Louisville	49
Memphis	34
Philadelphia	51
Columbus	85
Pittsburgh	108
Allegheny	127

The difference measured the absence of a clean water supply.[23] However, additional costs existed—in the form of other deaths due to polluted water supply, and from 10

[22] U.S. Commissioner of Labor, Fourteenth Annual Report, 1899, *Water, Gas and Electric-Light Plants Under Private and Municipal Ownership* (1900), p. 12.

[23] Data used above from R. B. Dole, "Effects of the Purity of Industrial Water Supplies on Their Use," in *Report of the Inland Waterways Commission* (1908), pp. 444-446.

TABLE 10

WATER WORKS IN THE U.S. 1899, BY DATE OF CONSTRUCTION

1795–1799	2
1800–1804	5
1805–1809	0
1810–1814	0
1815–1819	4
1820–1824	4
1825–1829	3
1830–1834	6
1835–1839	3
1840–1844	9
1845–1849	7
1850–1854	23
1855–1859	30
1860–1864	26
1865–1869	81
1870–1874	179
1875–1879	176
1880–1884	415
1885–1889	865
1890–1894	1318

Source: *1795-1849:* Tabulated from U.S. Commissioner of Labor, Fourteenth Annual Report, 1899, *Water, Gas, and Electric-Light Plants Under Private and Municipal Ownership* (1900), pp. 44–132.

1850-1894: F. Turneaure, *Public Water Supplies* (1911), p. 12. Turneaure's estimates begin in 1850. The Commissioner's figures are below Turneaure, particularly after the Civil War. However, they are probably correct indications of the very low counts before 1850.

to 20 persons sick from typhoid for every one who actually died from it.[24] (Not to mention turbidity, odor, and color from polluted water supply.)

B

Judging from Tables 10 and 11 it seems likely that less than 5 percent of American homes had running water at

[24] *Idem.*

the end of the Civil War. The advance of scientific knowledge about the role of infection in creating typhoid, and other diseases, which had taken place during the period 1820–1850 particularly, led to action in the 1860's, both in Europe and the U.S. That the implementation of such knowledge demanded huge construction projects was a perception not wasted on a variety of public entrepreneurs, such as one-eyed Connolly and his colleague Boss Tweed. The surge of construction from 1865–1889 (which helped moderate the depression of 1873–1879) had brought running water to 58 percent of the urban population (Table 11).

TABLE 11

PERCENT OF U.S. HOMES WITH RUNNING WATER: 1890–1970

	TOTAL			URBAN			RURAL		
	All	*White*	*Negro*	*All*	*White*	*Negro*	*All*	*White*	*Negro*
1890	24%			58%			1%		
1920							10		
1930							16	18%	1%
1940	70	74%	39%	94	96%	68%	37	41	6
1950	83	84	57	96	97	81	58	61	12
1960	93	94	80	99	99	95	79	83	28
1970	98	98	92	100	100	99	91	93	55

By the 1930's virtually the entire urban population had running water, while most of the rural population did not. Since that time, most rural homes have been equipped with running water. The combination of movement off Southern farms, plus improved urban housing, doubled the proportion of Negro homes with running water between 1940 and 1960.[25]

The data in Table 11 were derived as follows.

1890. We estimate the proportion of homes with running water on the basis of an extensive Census report.[26]

[25] The improved urban housing was a combination of some new construction, some installation in existing homes, but also some shift of older housing previously occupied by white families.

[26] *Report on the Social Statistics of Cities in the United States at the Eleventh Census: 1890* (1895), p. 32.

Although these data report information for 97 cities, it was necessary to adjust for the bias in sample used.[27] The resultant 58 percent urban rate was then combined with an arbitrary 1 percent rate for farms with running water—a not unreasonable figure given the farm ratio of 16 percent in 1930, 10 percent in 1920.[28]

1940–1970. The data are computed from various reports of the U.S. Census of Housing.[29]

1934–1936. Data are available for an extensive BLS expenditure survey of cities of 50,000 population and over.[30]

The results for these cities are above the 1940 Census average for cities of 50,000 population and over, as well as above those for the urban U.S.[31] We conclude that they represent a biassed sample, in part because of the BLS exclusion of relief families. A less biassed sample, because it was of housing per se is provided by the Real Property Inventories conducted in the early 1930's.[32] Even when reweighted for the correct regional distribution of housing, these results likewise gave somewhat higher figures than does the 1940 Census.[33] Since between the early 1930's and

[27] Since a detailed adjustment was made in the estimate for flush toilets, as discussed below, we used the reported Census 97 city average of 1.251 water taps per house connection to adjust the estimate of 46% of urban families having flush toilets to 58% with running water.

[28] The 1920–1930 data are from the 1930 Census, *Agriculture, IV,* p. 540.

[29] U.S. Census of Housing, 1940, Vol. II, p. 16; U.S. Census of Housing, 1950, Vol. I, Part 1, pp. 1–6; U.S. Census of Housing, 1960, Vol. I, Part 1, pp. xxxvi, xxxviii, xliii, 1–225; U.S. Census of Housing, 1970. HC (1) A-1, *U.S. Summary,* pp. 1–16, 1–41.

[30] U.S. Department of Labor, BLS Bulletin 638, *Money Disbursements of Wage Earners and Clerical Workers, 1934–36* (1941), pp. 242–245.

[31] The BLS Survey reports rates of 98% for urban families, 100% for urban whites, and 75% for urban Negroes—as compared with 1940 Census rates of 94%, 96%, and 68% respectively.

[32] Summarized in Peyton Stapp, *Urban Housing* (1938).

[33] The survey sample overweighted New York City, etc.

1940 the housing stock should have lost relatively more older houses, which typically had less in the way of plumbing facilities, the 1930–1934 figures should have reported a lower proportion of houses with running water, and not higher.

Households with Water Closets

1860. The order of magnitude of a rate for 1860 is unquestionable even though the estimate is per se more difficult and dubious than the comprehensive benchmark estimate for 1880. That conclusion is reached because the true proportion is clearly somewhere between zero and 2 percent. That conclusion is reached on the basis of the following bits of evidence.

The bulk of the population was resident in rural areas, where flush toilets were nonexistent as late as 1890. What were the ratios for those urban centers where running water was introduced early and other sanitary improvements nearly as early? Data collected by Martin[34] permit us to estimate the following rough figures for key cities:

PERCENT OF FAMILIES WITH
WATER CLOSETS IN 1860

New York City	10%
Albany	1½
Boston	30
Charleston	1¼
Baltimore	2

Discounting the representativeness of Boston (it introduced public water supply as early as 1652), given the 2 percent level in one of the largest cities in the South, Baltimore, and 0 percent for rural areas, a weighted average of 1 percent for all U.S. households is probably somewhat high.

[34] Edgar W. Martin, *The Standard of Living in 1860* (1942), pp. 111–112, 127. We estimate in general 6 persons per family, reduce the NYC population to allow for persons in group quarters. Martin's data are for 1860 except for NYC, which is 1856.

(That figure includes very few flush toilets, including mostly water closets with pans.)

1880. The 1880 Census provided an extensive review of various aspects of history and conditions in various cities. It incidentally provided information on the proportion of families that relied on various types of privies, indoor water closets, the extent of sewer availability and connections etc.[35] Estimates were derived for each state by making estimates for every major city in the state (e.g., Portsmouth, Boston, Providence, etc.) and for each city size class—using from 2 to 5 size classes. For each size class the average of reported proportions for cities in that size class was used.[36] Because of the weighting given to the largest cities detailed estimates were made for each.[37] In a few instances sources other than this Census were used, in particular regressions of plumbers per city versus water closets per city provided some rough control on the estimates.[38]

---

[35] 1880 Census, *Social Statistics of Cities, passim.*

[36] In some instances the Census merely used words, such as "largely," "some," "majority." These were ignored in favor of the averaging procedure noted except where supporting data helped bound the estimate. For example, Biddeford is labeled as "some" while Lewiston had 1/3. Since Biddeford reported no house sewer connections in 1890, a nominal 5% was used for 1880.

[37] For Boston the Census (p. 133) reports a rate based on a sample of 9 blocks in different parts of the city in 1878; for Worcester a description of "most" was translated to 60% on the basis of a 66% rate shown for 1890; for New York the 66% rate for Brooklyn was increased to 85% on the basis of the respective ratios of water taps per dwelling unit in each city in 1890; for Pittsburgh the 1890 home connection rate was used, being virtually identical with the Philadelphia 1880 rates. For Memphis a new sewer system was begun in January 1880, while New Orleans had no sewers in 1890; both were taken at 0 for 1880.

[38] For Chicago the Census' "nearly half" was translated to 45%, the Chicago Department of Health having estimated that one-third of the city population in 1886 relied on privy vaults. (Cf. Bessie Louise Pierce, *A History of Chicago* (1957) Vol. 3, p. 53.) For Cleveland the same rate was used, the two cities having about the same ratio of plumbers to population. For farms a rate of zero was used, the rate being only 9% some sixty years later.

1890. In this year an extensive survey by John Shaw Billings for the Census Bureau provides data on the number of house connections (to sewers) in each of 97 cities.[39] For the cities in size groups 10–15 thousand, 15–25 and 25–50 thousand, the ratios of house connections to population were taken from the Census.

For about half the cities with over 50,000 population, the Census provides individual city data, which were used, For each of the remaining cities in this category estimates were made by regressing (a) the number of house connections to sewers against (b) the number of water taps, using all the data for cities in this size group.[40] The regression relationship was sufficiently close to provide an adequate basis of estimate. Comparison of the regression estimates against 1890 rates, and against the ratios of plumbers to population, did not lead to altering any of the regression estimates.

The ratios of house connections to population were then adjusted to ratios of water closets per family on the basis of 1890 Census data on population per dwelling unit.[41] The rural population was assumed to have no indoor water closets, given that their rate was only 9 percent as late as 1939.

A non-white estimate for 1890 was derived on the basis of the distribution of the non-white population by size of city and as between farm and non-farm.[42] The rates for each of these size groups were those for the total population used above in deriving a U.S. average. The resultant figure of 6.8 percent is presumably somewhat of an overestimate since non-whites within a given city size group probably had lower incomes and fewer facilities. However, since sew-

[39] Census Office, *Report on the Social Statistics of Cities, 1890* (1895), pp. 32–33.

[40] Data from *ibid.*, p. 33.

[41] 1900 Census, *Population*, Part 2, p. clvii; 1890 Census, *Social Statistics of Cities*, p. 7.

[42] Population distribution as of 1890 from 1900 Census, *Supplementary Analysis*, pp. 601–604.

age facilities were typically lacking for all residents in the Southern cities and farm districts where non-whites were concentrated, such potential bias is small. We round down to 5 percent to acknowledge its presence. The white estimate was then calculated on the basis of the U.S. average.[43]

1900. For 1900 we extrapolate the 1880–1890 rate of change by its ratio to the rate of change of the number of plumbers.[44]

1920. A 1930 count of dwelling units with flush toilets is reported below. That figure was reduced to a 1920 level by deducting the 1920–1929 manufacturer's shipments of lavoratories.[45] The 11.6 million pieces shipped are reduced 10 percent to allow for exports, for some replacement in buildings subject to fire and tornado, and for some construction of units with more than 1 bathroom.

1925–1926. An estimate of 82 percent for urban areas is indicated in a survey by the General Federation of Women's Clubs.[46] The sample is not described but it seems likely to have been biassed toward upper income homes.

1930. Data for farms, but not urban areas, are available from the 1930 U.S. Census.[47] For the urban areas we rely on the Works Progress Administration Real Property Inventory for 203 cities.[48] For non-whites we rely on the 1930

[43] Population weights were from the 1900 Census, *Supplementary Analysis, loc.cit.*

[44] The increase in the number of plumbers between 1880 and 1890 was 54% of that between 1880 and 1900. Applying that 54% ratio to the 1880–1890 increase in households with water closets gives a 2.36 million figure for 1900—equal to 15% of all households.

[45] Shipments figures are reported in David Wickens, *Residential Real Estate* (1941), p. 49.

[46] Quoted by Leo Wolman, *Recent Economic Changes in the United States* (1929), Vol. 1, p. 66.

[47] 1930 Census, *Agriculture*, Vol. IV, p. 533.

[48] These are weighted and summarized by Peyton Stapp, *Urban Housing, A Summary of Real Property Inventories Conducted as Work Projects, 1934–1936* (1938), p. 19. The 15% of the urban population classed as sharing *or* having no toilet facilities is here assumed as having none. (It may be noted that the National Resources Com-

Census data for operators; on studies by the Bureau of Home Economics for Negro families in small cities and villages in the Southeast in 1935–1936; and on the Bureau of Labor Statistics data for Negro families in large cities in 1935–1936.[49] The rate for whites is that implicit in the 51 percent for the U.S. and 23 percent for non-whites.[50]

1940–1960. These data are taken from the Censuses of Housing for the respective years.[51]

1970. The 1970 data can be derived, with minor adjustment, from the 1970 Census of Housing.[52]

---

mittee, *Urban Planning and Land Policies* [1939] Vol. 2 of the *Supplementary Report of the Urbanism Committee*, p. 183, reports an 82.9% rate of dwelling having indoor water closets, using data from 64 cities in the 1934 Real Property Inventory.)

[49] Fifteenth Census, *Agriculture*, Vol. iv, p. 533. We use the Census report for dwellings with water piped into bathrooms as a measure of those with flush toilets. U.S. Department of Agriculture, Miscellaneous Publication No. 399, *Consumer Purchase Study, Family Housing and Facilities, Five Regions*, by Hazel Kyrk, et al. (1940), *p.* 79. And BLS Bulletin 638, *Money Disbursements of Wage Earners and Clerical Workers, 1934–36*, by Faith Williams and Alice Hanson (1941), p. 244. These BLS data refer to cities of 50,000 and over (*idem.*, p. 15). The small city data refer to those to 2,500 to 25,000, while villages had below 2,500: National Resources Committee, *Consumer Incomes in the United States* (1938), p. 43. The number of non-whites in each of these city size categories, and on farms, was derived from the U.S. Census, *Negroes in the United States, 1920–32*, p. 49. We assume that the rural farm operator rate of 0.5% applied to the entire rural population. The Southeast sharecroppers shown by BHNHE had 0%, and Southeast villages reported in the same source, 3.2%.

[50] The white count for 1930 includes that for white and Mexicans, *Abstract of the Fifteenth Census, 1930* (1933), p. 84.

[51] 1940 Census of Housing, Vol. 2, p. 16; 1960 Census of Housing, Vol. 1, pp. xxxviii and xliii.

[52] 1970 Census of Housing, HC (1)-A1. *U.S. Summary*, pp. 1–53, 1–56, and HC (1)-B1, *U.S. Summary*, pp. 1–280. For whites the Census provides no precisely comparable data: we therefore deduct from the U.S. all-year-round housing units those occupied housing units with Negro heads.

The vast differences between city and farm dwellers, white and non-white, North and South, that prevailed as late as the mid 1930's are documented in Table 12. From

TABLE 12

PERCENTAGE OF UNITS WITH INSIDE FLUSH TOILETS

		Total	White	Non-White	White minus Non-White
I.	1935–1936				
	All urban	85.7%	92.2%	56.4%	35.8%
	100,000+ population	91.6	94.3	66.3	28.0
	North and West		95.5	79.5	16.0
	South		92.7	48.7	44.0
	25,000–100,000 population	77.2			
	North and West	82.1			
	South	70.4	76.3	21.9	54.4
II.	1935–1936: South				
	Small cities—NC & SC		91.2	15.2	76.0
	Villages—NC & SC		80.8	3.2	77.6
	Farm operators				
	NC & SC		2.3	0.0	2.3
	Ga. & Miss.		0.4	0.0	0.4
	Share croppers				
	NC & SC		0	0	0
	Ga. & Miss.		0	0	0
III.	1936: South (Plantations)				
	North Carolina		4.2	0.1	4.1
	South Carolina		3.5	*	3.5
	Mississippi		3.3	0.1	3.2
	Louisiana		3.0	0.1	2.9
	Georgia		2.3	0.1	2.2
	Arkansas		1.8	0.1	1.7
	Alabama		1.2	*	1.2

a high of 95.5 percent for whites in large cities of the North to 1.2 percent on Alabama farms, and from 79.5 percent to 0 percent for non-whites, the major role that urbanization played, together with higher incomes in the North, is apparent. Non-white rates were lower in every city size or rural location for which data are available, while the U.S. difference would be far greater given the concentration of the non-white population on Southern farms and small towns. These differences had been largely removed by 1970.

The data in panel I are derived from an extensive survey by the U.S. Public Health Service—being weighted together to give urban totals by the survey sample counts reported in that study.[53] The data in panel II come from studies by the U.S. Bureau of Labor Statistics and the U.S. Department of Agriculture.[54] The results are not wholly consistent with the Public Health Service study but do provide additional contrasts for the south. Panel III reports data from a study of a sample of plantations by the Works Progress Administration.[55]

TABLE 13

PERCENT OF U.S. HOUSEHOLDS WITH INSIDE FLUSH TOILETS: 1800–1970

Year	Total	Urban	Farm	White	Non-White
1800	0%				
1860	1				
1880	7	34%	0%		
1890	13	46	0	14%	5%
1900	15				
1920	20				
1925–1926		82			
1930	51	85	8	54	23
1940	60	85	9	63	26
1950	71	87	28		
1960	87	94	62	88	69
1970	96	99	87	97	89

[53] U.S. Public Health Service, Bulletin 261, *Analysis of Sanitary Conditions* (October 1942), pp. 1608–1609.

[54] U.S. BLS Bulletin 638, *Money Disbursements of Wage Earners and Clerical Workers, 1934–36, Summary Volume*, pp. 103, 245, 370, and USDA Consumer Purchases Study, Misc. Pub., 339, *Farm Housing and Facilities* (1942), pp. 69, 75, 79.

[55] WPA Research Monograph V, Thomas J. Woofter, *Landlord and Tenant on the Cotton Plantation* (1936), p. 228.

FUEL

A

1880. The proportion of American families that relied on wood for heating their dwellings in 1880 ran to 65 percent, according to data in a Census report.[56] If we assume that 95 percent of rural families still relied on wood—the use of coal being restricted to urban areas by reason of its price—the implicit percentage for urban families would have been 16 percent.[57]

1890. Some 33 percent of a large sample of families of cotton and wool factory workers used wood for fuel.[58] This high rate presumably reflects both their low income and the concentration of these mills in rural territory.

1908. An extensive Forest Service survey for 1908 indicated that 70 million cords of firewood were consumed on U.S. farms.[59] Given 5.6 million farm families relying

[56] C. S. Sargent, *The Forests of North America*, in 1880 Census, Report Vol. 8, p. 489. His count of "number of persons using wood for domestic fuel"—based on letters to every town in the U.S.—equals 64.5% of the total population.

[57] The ratio of farm families to total in 1880 we take as 74%, the ratio of residents in country districts to total as given in 1900 Census, *Supplementary Analysis*, p. 50. The ratio of farmers plus male farm laborers aged 16 and over to all families in 1880 was about 2/3 (1880 Census, *Population*, pp. 669, 724, 730). We reduce the 74% rate to 70%, to allow for farm families who relied on coal because they lived near mines in Pennsylvania, Missouri, Alabama, Ohio, etc. A 100% rate of wood use for 70% of the population and a 64.5% rate for the entire nation implies a 15.5% rate for the urban population.

[58] U.S. Commissioner of Labor, *Seventh Annual Report*, Vol. II, Part III (1890), Table VII. It was necessary to exclude from the tabulation those families who were residents of foreign countries. We estimate the ratio of wood users to total for specified fuel users for American families—assuming that the "not specified" fuel group was best omitted from the calculation. The report also includes data for iron manufacturing employees—with an obvious bias because of their residence near coal mines.

[59] Forest Service Circular 181 (September 1910), Albert Pierson, *Consumption of Firewood in the United States*. The circular was

on wood that year, an average of 12.44 cords consumed per farm family is implicit.[60] The survey also estimated that 14.2 million cords of wood were consumed in towns and cities.[61] Industrial wood consumption would have been relatively unusual by 1908 except in smaller towns. We therefore assume an arbitrary 12 million cords for household consumption. Given the higher cost of wood in cities, we assume 10 cords per urban household using wood for fuel, which implies 12 million non-farm households using wood. These figures imply 35.7 percent of all U.S. households, and 9 percent of urban households using coal.

Coal: 1880, 1908

If all "coal destined for sale to ultimate consumers" had been consumed by households, the 1908 household average would have been about 7½ tons.[62] That average therefore represents a maximum estimate of average coal consumption by households relying on coal. The coal tonnage thereby computed per household is consistent with a report by a visiting group from the British Board of Trade: the "general testimony of (Chicago) workpeople is that they burn 1 ton (2,000 pounds) per month and 6–7 tons in the cold season."[63]

We can arrive at an 1880 figure by taking the above estimate of 35 percent of U.S. households that used coal for heating in 1880, dividing the 3.5 million user total into

---

based on inquiries "sent to more than 48,000 county and crop correspondents of the Bureau of Statistics" USDA, together with supplementary investigation by agents of the Census (cf. pp. 1-2). The number of replies is, understandably, not mentioned.

[60] We estimate that 30.69% of U.S. households in that year were farm households, that being the ratio in 1910. (Household data from *Historical Statistics*, II, p. 15.) We allow 5% of the 5.920 million farm families as coal consumers because of their proximity to coal mines, leaving 5.625 million farm households relying on wood.

[61] *Ibid.*, p. 3.

[62] William H. Shaw, *Value of Product Since 1869* (1947), p. 262.

[63] Great Britain: Cost of Living in American Towns, *Report of an Enquiry by the Board of Trade into Working Class Rents . . .* (1911), p. 149, Command. 5609.

Shaw's 1879 figure—to yield an average of 8½ tons.[64] Since these averages relate to different periods, they imply a fair consistency between the two quite different methods of estimating the underlying figures for proportion of households consuming coal versus wood. We conclude that consumption by households using only coal probably averaged 7 tons a year.

1914. By 1914 improved distribution and concentrated markets had made coal a widespread substitute for wood in cities, and to a considerable extent on farms as well. Department of Agriculture surveys indicate that farm families who bought no coal consumed approximately 15 cords of wood a year.[65]

The 1918 BLS survey enables us to contrast this farm average of 15 cords with one of 8 for urban families who also depended solely on wood for heating.[66]

The difference between 15 cords for rural and 8 for urban families presumably reflects lesser urban usage because of (a) distribution costs added in getting fuel to cities, (b)

[64] Household data from *Historical Statistics*, II, p. 15 and coal production data from Shaw, *idem*.

[65] U.S. Department of Agriculture, Farmers Bulletin 635, *What the Farm Contributes Directly to the Farmer's Living* (1914), pp. 14–15, and Department Bulletin No. 1338, *The Family Living from the Farm* (1925), pp. 8–9. Data for 1914 average 14.0 cords, 17.8, and 14.3 for farms in North Carolina, Vermont, and Georgia respectively, and 13.7 for New York farms not using coal. Data for 1918 indicate 12 for one county in New Hampshire, and one in Ohio; while 16 for white farmers in Georgia and 13 for non-whites are reported. For other states where significant amounts of coal were purchased, lower averages appear. Most data for 1919ff. in Bulletin 1338 are not reported together with total fuel expenditures, so there is no way of knowing the relative importance of wood to other fuel sources.

[66] This latter estimate is based on reports for families in Portland and Astoria, Oregon and Green Bay, Wisconsin who did not buy coal or other fuel. In these cities close to major timber sources, we would expect to find timber relatively cheap and used in greater volume than the rest of the U.S. The combined price and income effects of changes from 1914 to 1918 would perhaps cancel so that 8 applied equally well to 1914. BLS Bulletin 357, pp. 334, 357, 376.

smaller homes and better insulated ones in cities than on farms.

B

1918. Expenditure data for these years are derived from the BLS expenditure survey in this year.[67]

TABLE 14

HEATING FUELS IN AMERICAN HOMES: 1880–1970

		U.S. TOTAL				URBAN		FARM	
		Wood	*Coal*	*Oil*	*Gas*	*Wood*	*Other*	*Wood*	*Other*
A.	Percent of families using specified heat source								
	1880	65%	35%	0%	0%	16%	84%	98%	2%
	1908	36	63	1		9	91	95	5
	1940	23	55	11	11	6	93	67	33
	1950	10	35	26	29	5	95	40	60
	1960	4	12	32	48	1	99	13	87
B.	Average family expenditure for each fuel								
	1918					$4	$33	$36[a]	$15
	1935–1936					2	38	30[a]	17
	1941					2	42	3[b]	20

[a] Includes imputed value of farm supplied wood.
[b] Does not include imputed value of farm supplied wood.

1935–1936. Data are from the large scale BLS urban survey in this period.[68]

1941. Expenditures data are provided by the BHNHE and BLS surveys for this year.[69]

[67] BLS Bulletin 357, *Cost of Living in the United States* (1924), p. 391.
[68] U.S. BLS Bulletin 638, *Money Disbursements of Wage Earners and Clerical Workers, 1934–36*, p. 252.
[69] U.S. Bureau of Human Nutrition and Home Economics, *Rural Family Spending and Saving in Wartime*, USDA Misc. Publication 520, p. 48, which shows $17 for coal and fuel oil, and coke; $3 for purchased wood; and $30 for value of home produced fuel and ice. BLS Bulletin 822, *Family Spending and Saving in Wartime* (1945), p. 79, reports the urban and U.S. data.

1940, 1950, and 1960. These data are from the Census of Housing.[70]

Central Heating

The expensive and pleasant development of central heating began to spread during the 1920's. In 1920 the proportion of U.S. homes with central heating was about 1 percent. By 1960 it had risen to 66 percent.

1920. For this year we rely on an estimate to be derived from the 1918 BLS Cost of Living Survey.[71] For 92 individual cities in the United States that survey reported the average rooms per family and the average rooms equipped for central heating, separately for families in houses and those in flats, by income level. For the upper income interval "$2,500 and over" with houses there were 27 cities in which the sample consisted of 1 report. Nine of these had central heating—or one-third. For the same income interval there were 7 cities with 1 observation for flats, of which 2 had central heating. For the next lower income interval ($2,100 to $2,500) the proportions were 21–2 and 11–2. These cities were scattered throughout the nation, and included large and small towns. We infer that one-third of all dwellings occupied by persons with $2,500 income and over had central heating; 10 percent of the houses and 20 percent of the flats for those with incomes of $2,100–2,500 did; that 10 percent of those with the $1,800–2,100 income interval and living in flats did as well.

Applying these percentages to the BLS distribution of all U.S. urban families by income interval and tenure gives a rate of 2 percent having central heating. Assuming a rate of close to zero for rural families—the rate was only 9 percent in 1940—gives an overall U.S. average of slightly over 1 percent.

[70] Sixteenth Census, *Housing*, II, p. 42. 1950 Census of Housing, Vol. I, Part 1, 1–9. 1960 Census of Housing, Vol. I, Part 1, 1–44.

[71] BLS, *Cost of Living in the United States*, Bulletin 357, Table D.

1940, 1950, 1960. Data are derived from the Censuses of Housing.[72]

1945. Data are from a special Census survey.[73]

1970. Data computed from 1970 Census of Housing, HC(7)-4, *Structural Characteristics of the Housing Inventory*, Tables A-8, A-24. No separate data for farm and urban are reported. For farm we therefore use the data for units with employed heads who were farm workers. (The 1.8 million count for this group compares with 1.6 million persons in the experienced civilian labor force who were family heads and either farmers or farm laborers or foremen. 1970 Census, *Occupational Characteristics*, Table 33.) Deducting this group from the total for all dwelling units gave a sub total then used for urban.

TABLE 15

AMERICAN FAMILIES
PERCENT WITH CENTRAL HEATING; 1900–1970

	Total	Urban	Farm	White	Non-White
1900	0%	0%	0%		
1910	0	0	0		
1920	1	2	0		
1940	42	58	10		
1945	36	41	15		
1950	50	63	18		
1960	66	76	36	69%	40%
1970	78	79	56	80	58

Lighting

The primary lighting source of U.S. homes 1900–1970 is indicated in Table 16. The 1900 data are derived in the last chapter, Service Expenditures in the United States Since

[72] Sixteenth Census, *Housing*, II, pp. 99, 100. Census of Housing: 1950, Vol. I, Part 1, 1–9. 1960 Census of Housing, Vol. I, Part 1, 1–42, 1–227.

[73] Quoted in U.S. Department of Agriculture, Misc. Publication 653, *How Families Use Their Incomes*, p. 37. They are weighted together by population data from Census, Current Population Reports, Series P. 20, No. 11.

1900.[74] Estimates for 1910–1950 are derived below in the section in Electric Lighting. For 1960 and 1970 they rest on industry sources.[75]

TABLE 16
AMERICAN HOMES BY LIGHTING SOURCE: 1900–1970

	1900	1910	1920	1930	1940	1950	1960
All families	100%	100%	100%	100%	100%	100%	100%
Primary lighting source:							
Kerosene and coal oil	88						
Gas	9	85	65	32	21	6	1
Electricity	3	15	35	68	79	94	99

Electric Lighting

1900. For 1900 we estimate that 3.1 percent of dwelling units had electricity. The first official Census figures are for 1907, but because of the speed at which electricity was adopted, that ratio will obviously be too high. The 1900 rate was estimated on the basis of the 1902–1907–1912 trend in the number of meters.[76] (The 1902 Census of Electrical Industries indicates that "a rough assumption . . . might be made that each meter represented a customer."[77] How-

[74] The number of families using each source is estimated there. The percentages are related to 16.0 million households, using the count from *Historical Statistics*, II, p. 15.

[75] The 1957 proportion of dwelling units with electric service to all dwelling units was 98.8% (*Historical Statistics*, II, p. 510). It was assumed that 99% was reached by 1960, and that 1% of homes are still lighted by sources other than electricity.

[76] In 1907 and 1912 the ratio of (a) dwelling units with residential service to (b) the number of customer's meters came to about 90%. Cf. U.S. Census, *Central Electric Light and Power Stations and Street and Electrical Railways . . . 1912* (1915), p. 57, for an estimate of meters. The estimate of families derives from the U.S. Census, *Historical Statistics*, II, pp. 510, 15. The number thus estimated for families in 1900 with residential service (500,000) proves to be 3.1% of all families—or closely in line with what a simple extrapolation of rates of change would have indicated.

[77] U.S. Census, *Central Electric Light and Power Stations, 1902* (1905), p. 74. The report stipulates "Leaving arc lighting patrons

ever, because of the transition away from a period in which numbers of customers paid a flat rate, rather than being metered, we did not use the number of meters as a direct estimate for the number of consumers.) Since only 2 percent of farms had electricity as late as 1920, we assume a zero rate for rural dwellings in 1900. The implicit urban rate is 7.85 percent.[78]

1910. The 1912 Census of Electrical Industries reports rates of 8.0 percent for 1907 and 15.9 percent for 1912.[79] We estimate a 1910 rate of 15 percent based on a curve freely fitted to 1900, 1907, and 1912 rates. Using population distributions, and a zero rate for farms, yields 33 percent for urban dwellings.

1920, 1930. Data derived from the Censuses are used here.[80]

1940, 1950. Rates are taken from the Census volumes.[81]

1970. No inquiry on electricity was made in the 1970 Census of Housing. We estimate 99 percent on the basis of data from industry sources.

TABLE 17

PERCENT OF FAMILIES WITH ELECTRIC LIGHTING 1900–1970

	U.S.	Urban	Farm
1900	3%	8%	0%
1910	15	33	0
1920	35	47	2
1930	68	85	10
1940	79	96	31
1950	94	99	78
1970	99		

out of consideration." Since the latter were municipalities (street lighting), commercial, and industrial establishments, that exclusion is desirable for our purposes.

[78] We weight by rural-urban population figures.

[79] *Historical Statistics*, ɪɪ, p. 510.

[80] As presented in *Historical Statistics*, ɪɪ, p. 510.

[81] Sixteenth Census, 1940, *Housing*, Vol. ɪɪ, p. 23. Census of Housing: 1950, Vol. 1, Part 1, *U.S. Summary*, pp. 1–9.

Washing Machines

1920. The cost of living survey for 1918 reported 3 percent of all surveyed families buying washing machines.[82] If that rate applied to the entire set of U.S. families, then about 750,000 would have bought washing machines. However, the survey applied only to urban families, and the distribution among urban families was, in addition, biassed toward upper income levels. An uncertain proportion of this group would have been purchasing for replacement, so that users as of 1920 cannot be inferred from this estimate alone.

The number of users of washing machines in 1924 came to 3.5 million; in 1928, 5.7 million; and in 1930, 7.2 million, according to industry sources.[83] Given this trend, and the 1918 sales figures, we infer that 2 million families had washing machines in 1920—or 8 percent of U.S. families.

1930. We use an industry estimate of 7.2 million—or 24 percent of U.S. families.[84]

TABLE 18

PERCENT OF U.S. FAMILIES WITH WASHING MACHINES: 1900–1960

1900		0%
1920		8
1930		24
1941		
Farms	35	
Rural non-farm	44	
1960		73
1970		
All families		70
Home owners	86	
Renters	42	

[82] U.S. Bureau of Labor Statistics, *Cost of Living in the United States* (1924), p. 401.

[83] Quoted in Harry Jerome, *Mechanization in Industry* (1934), p. 432.

[84] *Electrical Merchandising*, quoted in Jerome, *ibid.*

1941. These data are based on an extensive survey by the Department of Agriculture.[85]

1960, 1970. These data are derived from reports by the Census Bureau.[86]

Refrigerators

Since we live in an era when 99 percent of American families rely on mechanical refrigerators, it is difficult to think back to a period when none existed. Although we need go no farther back than Woodrow Wilson or Warren Harding, it is still more difficult to recognize that in the prior decades of our national existence any refrigeration whatever was a rarity. A 1915 study of the standard of living in New York City, summarizing various detailed budgets, actual and recommended, did not include any expenditures whatever for ice.[87] Nor does the well-known Heller model budget for wage earners include such an expenditure as late as 1927.[88] The Bureau of Labor Statistics budget providing "health and decency" for a 1920 worker's family in Washington, D.C., however, projects an ideal goal for many items, and includes twenty five pounds of ice daily for four months.[89]

What was the actual extent of refrigeration in earlier decades? Estimates are made below for percentages of families with refrigeration—defined as either mechanical or ice. The estimates for ice effectively measure those who used ice refrigeration during the summer months. For by the time that incomes and habits reached a point where any

[85] U.S. Department of Agriculture, *Rural Family Spending and Saving in Wartime*, Misc. Publication 520, p. 70.

[86] 1960 Census of Housing, Vol. 1, Part 1, p. xxxix; Census, *Special Report on Household Ownership of Cars, Homes, and Selected Household Durables*, Series P-65, No. 33 (1970), p. 8.

[87] New York City Bureau of Standards, *Report on the Cost of Living for Unskilled Laborer's Families in New York City* (1915), pp. 14, 16, 24, 39–42 and *passim*.

[88] Bureau of Applied Economics, *Standards of Living, A Compilation of Budgetary Studies*, Vol. II (1932), pp. 43–46.

[89] Bureau of Applied Economics, *Standards of Living* (1920), p. 5.

large proportion of ice users were able to consider year round consumption—the mid-1920's—the mechanical refrigerator had begun its swift supersession of ice boxes.

1910. For 1910, we estimate the number of households with ice refrigeration on the basis of the Census count of ice dealers times a ratio of 500 households per dealer.[90] That ratio was derived on the basis of data for 1930 and 1940. The 1930 implicit ratio is 611.[91] That for 1940 is 520.[92] We reduce the 1930 ratio (611) down to 500 for 1910, since the 1910 ratio should reflect a substantially greater volume of ice deliveries to breweries and saloons. The resultant figure implies that 18 percent of U.S. families in 1910 had ice deliveries. Given that these were virtually all non-farm families, the proportion implies that 38 percent of non-farm families had ice delivered.

1920. The proportion of households with mechanical refrigerators was estimated at under 1 percent. Early sales data indicate that the first Kelvinators were sold in 1918; the aggregate of all makes sold in 1923 ran to only 18,000, while only 30,000 were sold in 1924.[93]

The number of ice boxes sold from 1923 to 1929 averaged close to one million a year.[94] We assume one million for 1920 as well. Given a twelve year life for ice boxes implies some 12 million owners in 1920, or 48 percent of the number of households in that year.[95]

[90] The number of dealers is reported in the 1910 Census, *Occupations*, p. 422. The number of households is from Census, *Historical Statistics*, II, p. 15.

[91] 1930 Census, *Occupations*, p. 570, reports the number of dealers. Households with ice are estimated below. (See 1930).

[92] 1940 Census of Housing, II, p. 36, reports the number of households with ice refrigeration. Alba Edwards, *Comparative Occupation Statistics* . . . (1943), p. 51, indicates a 10% declines from 1930 to 1940 for the combined fuel and ice dealer groups, and we apply the same percentage decline to the 1930 Census count of ice dealers.

[93] American Society of Refrigerating Engineers, *The Refrigerating Data Book* (1936), pp. 484–485.

[94] *Idem.*

[95] A 12-year life for appliances is taken from Raymond Goldsmith,

Some rough validation of the sales figure for 1920 is given by the BLS consumer expenditure survey of that year. The survey indicated the average family spent $16 at retail for an ice box.[96] A distributive spread of about 46 percent for furniture and appliances in 1919 is indicated by Barger's estimates.[97] Hence, a manufacturer's price of about $8 an ice box is indicated. The manufacturer's shipments total for 1919 was $10.8 million.[98] Hence, these data suggest something like 1.35 million ice boxes sold to consumers and added to distributor's inventories.

Because 1919 was a year of considerable prosperity, we believe that the actual sales must have included first purchases as well as replacements. Therefore, the one million estimate is not likely to be an underestimate of replacement sales.

The 48 percent figure thus derived for 1920 is consistent with a study by the USDA Bureau of Home Economics in 1927–1928, which reported that 57 percent of homemakers in their study had ice-cooled refrigerators and 7 percent had mechanical refrigerators.[99] Given the probable upward income bias in their reporting sample, we cannot infer that the proportion with ice in the mid-1920's was actually well above that for 1920. But it may have been.

1930. Annual sales of ice boxes in the late 1920s ran about one million units.[100] Assuming a 12-year life for ice

---

A Study of Saving (1955), Vol. I, p. 689. The household count is from *Historical Statistics*, II, p 15.

[96] U.S. Bureau of Labor Statistics, *Cost of Living in the United States* (1924), p. 397.

[97] Harold Barger, *Distribution's Place in the American Economy Since 1869* (1955), p. 92.

[98] Simon Kuznets, *Commodity Flow and Capital Formation* (1938), p. 86.

[99] Unpublished data cited in President's Conference on Home Building and Home Ownership, Vol. V, *House Design Construction and Equipment* (1931), p. 279.

[100] American Society of Refrigerating Engineers, *The Refrigerating Data Book* (1936), p. 485, estimated about 7 million homes having

boxes (*supra*), there would have been 12 million ice box owners. To that figure we must add an allowance for the total number of domestic mechanical refrigerators sold from 1921 through mid-1930, or 2.448 million.[101] Given 30 million households in 1930, these figures lead to an estimate of 40 percent with ice boxes and 8 percent with mechanical refrigerators.

1940, 1950. Data are reported by the Censuses of Housing for these years.[102]

1960. A Census survey as of January 1960 indicates that 98.1 percent of home owners owned refrigerators, while 66.4 percent of renters did so.[103] However, additional renters were provided refrigerators with their apartment or house.

We therefore turn to the industry estimates of wired homes with refrigerators. Adapting these data we estimate 90 percent for 1960.[104]

1970. For 1970 census data indicate a rate of 99 percent.[105]

---

mechanical refrigeration, indicating the figure was probably on the high side. It is obviously an undepreciated total of yearly sales itemized from 1923 through 1934. We deduct sales back to the spring of 1930, adjust for improper inclusions of refrigerators that lacked either high or low side, to infer under 2 million—or 6% of the 30 million families at the Census date.

[101] *Idem.*

[102] 1940 Census, *Housing,* Vol. 2, p. 36. Census of Housing: 1950, Vol. 1, Part 1, U.S. *Summary,* pp. 1-9.

[103] U.S. Census Bureau, Current Population Reports, Series P-65, No. 33, *Special Repot on . . . Ownership . . . ,* Table 6.

[104] *The U.S. Statistical Abstract for 1971,* p. 67, indicates 49.6 million homes with refrigerators and 42.0 with washing machines in 1960. We apply the ratio of one to the other to the Census of Housing total for occupied homes with clothes washing machines (1960 Census of Housing, Vol. 1, Part 1, pp. 1-28). We then take the resultant figures as a percent of Census occupied units.

[105] U.S. Census Bureau, Current Population Reports Series, P-65, No. 40, *Household Ownership . . . 1971,* p. 3, reports a "saturation level" of 99.1% for July 1971.

TABLE 19

PERCENT OF U.S. FAMILIES WITH REFRIGERATION: 1910–1970

	Total	Ice	WITH Mechanical Refrigeration
1910	18%	18%	0%
1920	48	48	*
1930	48	40	8
1940	72**	27	44
1950	91	11	80
1960	90		
1970	99	*	99

*Under 1%.

**Includes 1% with refrigeration other than ice or mechanical.

Vacuum Cleaners

Industry studies report 5.0, 7.7, and 9.1 million users of vacuum cleaners in 1924, 1928, and 1930 respectively.[106] About 1 million vacuum cleaners were produced in 1919, 1923, 1925, and in 1927.[107] Given that fairly steady rate we assume that the 1920–1924 change equalled that from 1924 to 1928, yielding a 1920 figure of 2.3 million homes, or 9.4 percent, with vacuum cleaners. Numbers of households are estimated by the Census Bureau.[108] The proportion of farm homes with vacuum cleaners in 1920 was approximately twice as great as the U.S. average. However 9.0 percent had electric vacuum cleaners, while another 8.4 percent had "hand-power vacuum outfits."[109]

The 1953–1970 data are based on industry sources.[110]

[106] *Electrical Merchandising*, quoted in Harry Jerome, *Mechanization in Industry* (1934), p. 432.

[107] Quoted by Leo Wolman, "Consumption and the Standard of Living" in President's Conference on Unemployment, *Recent Economic Changes* (1929), Vol. I, p. 57.

[108] *Historical Statistics*, II, p. 15.

[109] A survey of 10,000 families by the USDA, quoted by E. L. Kirkpatrick, *The Farmer's Standard of Living* (1929), pp. 137–38.

[110] 1971 *Statistical Abstract*, p. 677, reports the percentage of wired homes with vacuum cleaners. For 1953 the ratio was adjusted in

PERCENT OF HOMES WITH VACUUM CLEANERS: 1900-1970

	U.S.	Farm
1900	0%	0%
1910	0	0
1920	9	9
1930	30	
1953	54	
1960	73	
1970	92	

Radios

The percent of families with radios in recent decades is reported by the Census and industry sources for 1930ff, while a General Federation of Women's Clubs' survey give a 1925 ratio.[111]

PERCENT OF HOMES WITH RADIOS: 1900-1970

1900	0%
1920	0
1925	24
1930	40
1940	83
1950	96
1960	92
1970	96

Electrical Appliances

The advent of electricity reduced the labors of the housewife and otherwise changed life in the family—but not at once. By 1912, 16 percent of all homes had electric lighting. But virtually the only electrical appliances in those homes were toasters. Two decades later on, in 1932, the typical American home had at most only two electrical

accord with the percent of homes that were wired. For the later dates percentage wired were so close to 100% that the ratios were used without change.

[111] 1925: Quoted in Paul Nystrom, *Economic Principles of Consumption* (1929), p. 481. 1930–1960: Census of Housing, Vol. 1, *States and Small Areas* Part 1, p. xl. 1970: Industry sources indicate a rise of 3.7% points from 1960 to 1970 in the percent of wired homes having radios. (1971) *Statistical Abstract*, p. 677. We add that point change to the Census 1960 figure to give a 1970 estimate.

appliances, the toaster and the iron. (About a third had washing machines, vacuum cleaners, and toasters.) But after another two decades, of which only one was prosperous, the proportions for many major appliances ran to well over 50 percent. By 1917, of course, ownership ratios upwards of 90 percent characterized nearly all the appliances shown.

With major appliances. Estimates from industry sources on the proportion of wired homes with specified appliances are available.[112] These were adapted to apply to all homes by the ratio of wired to occupied units.[113]

TABLE 20

HOMES WITH ELECTRICAL APPLIANCES: 1932–1971

	1912	*1932*	*1953*	*1971*
All homes	100%	100%	100%	100%
With major appliances				
Vacuum cleaners	0	30	54	92
Washing machines	0	27	70	92
Refrigerators	0	12	82	100
Ranges	0	4	22	56
Dishwashers	0	1	3	26
With minor appliances				
Irons	0	65	82	100
Toasters	0	27	65	93
Coffeemakers	0	19	47	89
Radio	0	61	94	100
TV	0	0	43	99

[112] Data for 1932 are from *Electrical Merchandising*, reprinted in National Resources Committee, Urbanism Committee, *Urban Planning and Land Policies* (1932), Vol. II, p. 192. For 1953 and 1971: *Statistical Abstract, 1971*, p. 277. The 1930 Census counts of radios and occupied units were adjusted to 1932 levels by adding the 1930–1932 change in non-farm households as estimated by Census, and of radios and families with radio sets as estimated by industry sources. 1960 Census of Housing, Vol. I, Part 1, p. xl, *Historical Statistics II*, pp. 15, 491.

[113] The 1932 data in the source cited apply to "all houses." The 1953 and 1971 counts of wired homes and households are from *Historical Statistics*, II, p. 15, and *1971 Statistical Abstract*, pp. 673, 677, 36. It was assumed that the industry ratios for "all houses" in 1932 and "wired homes" in 1971 represented universe estimates.

Automobiles

1910. The ratio of passenger registrations to families in 1910 is just over 2 percent. Allowing for business use we estimate 1 percent for families.

1920. The number of farms with passenger cars was reported in the 1920 Census.[114] On the assumption that no laborers resident on farms had cars in that year we can compute a 29 percent ratio for farm families. If we apply to 1920 the 1930 ratio of family to total passenger car registrations we arrive at a U.S. ownership rate of 26 percent. The U.S. rate is thus slightly below the farm rate in 1920—as it was in both 1960 and 1970. (For 1942 we would expect the U.S. rate to fall well below the farm rate: the impact of the depression should have cut auto use by urban workers heavily. Most of them did not require their cars for production, as farmers did.) The implicit ratio for urban families in 1920 is 35 percent.

1930. The number of automobiles belonging to private households is estimated as 78 percent of passenger car registrations in 1930.[115] That percentage is the ratio to be derived for 1941 by comparison between (a) the number of cars reported by families and (b) the total registration of passenger cars for that year.[116] Ratios of about 80 percent were utilized by William Lough, who worked from R. L. Polk figures of 6 to 8 percent for passenger registrations in business names.[117] Our ratio is, however, somewhat higher than the 70 percent ratio derived from various Public Roads Ad-

---

[114] *Statistical Abstract of the United States,* 1923, p. 148 reports motor cars, and 1930 Census, *Population,* vi, p. 12 reports farm families.

[115] Registration data from *Historical Statistics,* ii, p. 462.

[116] The number of cars is computed from data on the percentage of families reporting ownership and the number of families and single consumers. BLS Bulletin 822, pp. 68, 86. Registration totals (from *Historical Statistics,* ii, p. 462) are adjusted downward by the ratio of 1941 population to 1941 full spending units, to allow for the transfer of titles among family units, and for deaths.

[117] William Lough, *High-Level Consumption* (1935), pp. 251, 271.

ministration studies by the Bureau of Foreign and Domestic Commerce, and used by both Kuznets and OBE for all years.[118]

TABLE 21

PERCENT OF FAMILIES WITH AUTOMOBILES: 1900–1971

Year	Total	Urban	Farm	White	Non-White
1900	0%	0%	0%	0%	0%
1910	1	—	—	—	—
1920	26	35	29	—	—
1930	60	—	—	—	—
1935–1936	55	44	—	59	15
1942	58	55	69	—	—
1960	75	69	77	—	—
1970	79	73	87	—	—
1971	80	—	—	83	53

1935–1936. The BLS study of money disbursements of wage earners reports a 44 percent ownership rate for automobiles in urban areas, which compares reasonably well with a 55 percent rate for the U.S.[119] (The latter was calculated as the rate for 1930 was.) The BLS rate for non-whites in urban areas is 15 percent—implicitly leaving a white rate of 59 percent.[120]

1942. Data are from the extensive BLS and BHNHE surveys for this year.[121]

1960, 1970, 1971. Data are taken from Census surveys for these years.[122]

Food

Since food is the largest item in the consumer's budget, changes in resource use for food are likely to be both obvi-

[118] Simon Kuznets, *National Product since 1869* (1946), p. 25.

[119] BLS Bulletin 638, p. 313.

[120] Nonwhite rate from *ibid.*, p. 314. Non-whites were 10% of the U.S. population (*Historical Statistics*, II, p. 8).

[121] U.S. BLS Bulletin 822, *Family Spending and Saving in Wartime*, p. 86.

[122] U.S. Census Bureau, Current Population Reports, Series P-65, No. 33, *Special Report on Household Ownership of Cars . . . 1970, 1969 and 1960*, p. 5 and Series P-65, No. 40, p. 8.

ous and important. Two primary trends do appear since 1900:

(1) Americans have decreased the pounds of food they consumed, decade after decade. "The capacity of the human stomach is limited," a point repeatedly made in support of projections of decreased demand resulting from the consequences of cybernation, automation and so on.

(2) Americans have largely increased the amount of food they consumed—both in terms of quality and in the real resources of labor, capital, and land required to produce it.

Table 22 and 23 indicate the sharp declines in inferior foods and rises for preferred foods over time. For inferior foods, consumption has gone down as incomes have gone up.[123] Thus in 1900 some 94 percent of urban families consumed lard. Probably 99 percent of all U.S. families did so, reckoning in farm families as well. But by 1965 only 9 percent of all U.S. families still consumed lard. The proportion who consumed corn meal in 1900 must have been at least 90–95 percent, for it was still 84 percent in 1918. But by 1970 less than 10 percent of families consumed corn meal. For salt pork and molasses milder, but equally clear and impressive declines appear.[124] The per capita consumption figures for these goods confirm the downward slide. GNP in later decades rose because consumers insistently preferred other sources of fats to lard—butter, margarine, mayonnaise, or cooking oils—and because they preferred fresh pork to salt pork, and sugar to molasses.

Special note must be taken of the decline in flour and meal consumption. For consumption of flour and meal was nearly cut in half—but the amount bought for home use

[123] The fact that their prices have not risen relative to their substitutes is, of course, requisite for a demonstration that they are inferior goods.

[124] For 1900 an average of 3.6 gallons per family of 5.31 persons is reported in the Commissioner of Labor, op.cit., pp. 647–648. At 13 pounds per gallon, a per capita poundage of 8.8 is indicated.

fell over 85 percent.[125] The housewife has pretty well ceased making the family's bread. It was and is romantic, natural, and ecological. But it also required hours of work each week by the housewife—who now prefers to get her bread by a few added minutes each week in the grocery.

Bread in 1900 cost 5¢ for a one pound loaf.[126] By 1970 the price of the average 1 pound loaf had reached 24.3¢[127]

The USDA per capita flour and cereal product average of 300 pounds per capita in 1909 was extrapolated to a 1900 level of 240 pounds by the Census data for grain production and population.[128]

The 1903 survey was reweighted to indicate that 156 pounds of flour and meal plus 46.4 loaves of bread per capita were consumed in survey families.[129] On the basis of the above price data, we assume these to average 1 pound loaves. Since bread weighs approximately 50 percent more than its flour content, given the addition of water, etc., the flour content of the bread is taken as 23 pounds—making total per capita consumption of 179 pounds of flour and meal. Hence survey families made about 87 percent of their flour and meal into bread at home, only 13 percent being consumed indirectly in "store bought" bread. Farm families

[125] Total consumption from USDA *Agricultural Economic Report 138*, p. 83.

[126] Cost of Living *Report*, p. 656, gives the figure of .0492¢ for the price of a loaf as reported in family budgets and .0545 for the retail price average, while pp. 690–691 indicate that the retail prices were for loaves with a medium (and modal) size of 1 pound.

[127] USDA *Food Consumption, Prices, Expenditure, Supplement to Agriculture Economics Report No. 138 for 1970*, p. 69.

[128] 1900 Census, x, *Manufactures*, p. 365, and 1920 Census, x, *Manufactures*, p. 110. Population data from *Historical Statistics*, ii, p. 9. The 1899–1909 decline is consistent with William Shaw, *Value of Product since 1869* (1947), p. 174. The 1899 average of 234 was raised to 240 for 1900.

[129] Commissioner of Labor, *op.cit.*, p. 648. These regional averages were reweighted by population data from the 1900 Census, *Supplementary Analysis*, p. 17. They were then divided by the U.S. population per household, from U.S. Census, *Historical Statistics*, ii, p. 16

in 1913 consumed about 220 pounds of flour per capita and purchased about $1 worth of bread and pastries.[130] At 5¢ a pound loaf of bread it is clear that in 1913 not over 5 percent of farm family flour was consumed indirectly. For 1900 it seems a safe assumption to set the rate at zero. Weighting the averages derived from these two studies by the U.S. rural/non-rural population proportions gives the data shown in Table 22 for per capita consumption in 1900.[131]

The major shifts in the American diet since 1900 reflect also, in part, income gains. (a) The shift to preferred foods is well marked (Table 23) by declines in three proportions, as salt pork, salt beef and lard were replaced by more expensive and preferred foods.[132] (b) A similar quality advance is evidenced by the decline in potatoes and the substitution of other vegetables. The salted meat and potato diet was well suited to the centuries before refrigeration was available, and before incomes had risen, but no longer. The expansion of consumption horizons is equally apparent in the declining share of coffee and tea in non-alcoholic beverages, as the market for colas and ades of every description expanded.

Three ratios in Table 23 mark the decline in work by the housewife, as food preparation shifted outside the home. Of total flour and meal consumption at the beginning of

---

[130] USDA Farmers Bulletin 635, *What the Farm Contributes to the Farmer's Living*, p. 11. Because of the variability of the data we take the median value for the 10 states reported.

[131] Population data from *Historical Statistics*, II, p. 14.

[132] *Eighteenth Annual Report of the Commissioner of Labor, 1903* (1904), p. 648. Data for meals away from home, and the ratio of oleo to butter, are weighted averages computed from Great Britain, Board of Trade, *Cost of Living in American Towns, Report of an Enquiry . . . into working class rents, housing and retail prices* (1911) Cd. 5609, pp. 404ff. U.S. Department of Agriculture, Household Food Consumption Survey 1965-66, Report No. 12, *Food Consumption . . . 1965-66*, Tables 1-19. The 1910 meals-away proportion is assumed to apply equally in 1900.

NEW DATA

TABLE 22

U. S. Consumption Trends, Inferior Foods: 1900–1970

| | PERCENT OF URBAN FAMILIES CONSUMING | | | | CONSUMPTION PER CAPITA (LBS.)[b] | | | | Flour and Meal | |
| | Salt | | Molas- | Corn | | Molas- | Corn | Pota- | | in Purchased |
Year	Pork	Lard	ses	Meal	Lard	ses	Meal	toes	Direct	Baked Goods
1900	83%	94%	69%	—	15.9	8.8	95	—	195	18
1910	—	—	—	—	12.5	1.3	53	184		
1918	66	64	—	84%	11.8	1.9	50	162		260
1942	9	35	7	12	12.8	1.1	20	118		201
1965	4	9	2	22	6.4	0.3	7	84	27[c]	94[c]
1970	—	—	—	—	4.7	0.2	7	74		119

Sources: a· 1900:   U.S. Commissioner of Labor, *Cost of Living and Retail Prices of Food* (1904), pp. 494–495.

1918:   Bureau of Labor Statistics Bulletin 357, *Cost of Living in the United States* (1924), pp. 118–119.

1942:   U.S. Department of Agriculture Miscellaneous Publication 550, *Family Food Consumption in the United States, Spring 1942* (1944), Tables 26–28.

1965·   U.S Department of Agriculture, *Food Consumption of Households in the United States, Seasons and Year, 1965–66,* Report 12, (1972), pp. 72, 65, 76, 68

b: 1900:   U.S. Commissioner of Labor, *Cost of Living and Retail Prices of Food* (1904), pp. 642–648. For flour and meal see text.

1910ff.   U.S. Department of Agriculture, *Food Consumption, Prices, Expenditures;* Agricultural Economic Report 138 (1968), pp. 82, 83, 84, 64 and *Supplement for 1971,* pp. 18, 29.

c: Unpublished estimates of the U.S. Department of Agriculture based on 1965 *Household Food Consumption Survey* (a letter of June 26, 1972 from Helen Eklund, U.S Department of Agriculture, reports 27 pounds for direct. We deduct 27 from the published USDA total of 121 for flour and meal to give 94 for consumption in purchased baked goods.)

the century, over half was eaten in the form of home baked bread; by 1965, spending for flour had dropped to 19 percent of the combined total. Spending for prepared vegetables—selected, cleaned, cored, scraped, and often pretty well cooked—rose from less than 5 percent of the vegetable bill to nearly 70 percent over the period. Correspondingly, of course, came a decline in the share of the household's

TABLE 23

PREFERRED FOODS: U.S. CONSUMPTION TRENDS, 1910–1970
(POUNDS PER CAPITA)

Year	Beef	Poultry	Ice Cream	Citrus (processed)	Sugar
1910	56	17	2	0	77
1920	47	16	8	0	86
1930	39	18	10	1	116
1940	43	18	12	4	96
1945	47	26	19	8	78
1950	50	25	19	11	101
1960	64	34	23	15	98
1970	84	50	26	19	107

Source: See Note b, Table 22 (ice cream includes ice milk).

vegetables that the housewife still had to prepare. Finally, the total task of food preparation moved increasingly out of the home, including dish and pot washing and cleanup. For the proportion of food spending that went for meals away from home rose from less than 1 percent to 18 percent, or to the equivalent of one meal out of every five.

For four key items of nutrient intake it is possible to note the trend over the past half century. Table 24 reports farm and non-farm averages, and computes them as a ratio to the 1964 NAS-NRC recommended daily allowance.[133]

Higher meat and milk consumption moved the urban averages up. The chief change in farm diets has been to reduce caloric intake as the consumption of potatoes, breads

[133] Nutrient intake data for a sample of 11,900 urban workingmen's families in 1918 and 1,331 farm families in Kansas, Kentucky, Missouri, and Ohio in 1922–1924 were computed by the U.S. Department of Agriculture from field survey diet reports. The results appear in Ellis L. Kirkpatrick, *The Farmer's Standard of Living* (1929), pp. 91, 86–89. Data for urban and rural farm nutrient intake in 1965 are from U.S. Department of Agriculture, Agricultural Research Service, *Dietary Levels of Households in the United States, Spring 1965* (Household food consumption survey, 1965–1966, Report No. 6, Table 3). The NAS-NRC standards are implicit in a comparison of the heading in Tables 7, 8, and 11 of that report.

TABLE 24
Changes in Diet: 1900–1965

	PORK	BEEF	LARD
			Percent of Lard
	Percent Salted	*Percent Salted*	*+ butter + oleo*
1900	50%	10%	25%
1965	3	0	9

		POTATOES	COFFEE & TEA
			Percent of beverages
		Percent of Vegetables	*(non-alcoholic)*
1900		41%	95%
1965		23	51

	FLOUR & MEAL	PREPARED VEGETABLES	MEALS AWAY FROM HOME
	Percent of bread	*Percent of*	
	+ flour + meal	*all vegetables*	*All food*
1900	57%	4%	*%
1965	19	70	18%

*under 1%.

and fats declined.[134] At the later date more detailed information is available, that indicates the following proportions of the households in the U.S. below recommended daily allowance levels: about 5 percent for energy, 50 percent for protein, 10 percent for iron, and about 30 percent for calcium. One factor in these shortages is economic; a more important one is general reluctance to drink as much milk as dieticians and parents recommend.

III

The data reviewed above tell us something about the elements in the growth of GNP over the past half century

[134] The decline in caloric intake was implicitly proposed by well known budget studies: one for 1920 set 786 pounds of potatoes as scientifically required per person, while one for 1947 set only 391 pounds as required. Cf. 1920 Bureau of Applied Economics, *Standards of Living*, Bulletin No. 7 (rev. December 1920), pp. 4, 24. This standard is referred to in Bureau of Labor Statistics, *How American Buying Habits Change*, p. 238 (1947). BLS Bulletin 927, *Workers' Budgets in the United States . . . 1946 and 1947*, p. 31.

TABLE 25

TRENDS IN NUTRITIVE VALUE OF U.S. DIETS: 1920–1965

	URBAN		FARM	
Nutritive Value	*1920*	*1965*	*1920*	*1965*
I. Typical diet				
Energy (calories)	2,741	3,131	4,370	3,620
Protein (grams)	82	106	121	111
Calcium (mg.)	650	1,090	1,220	1,210
Iron (mg.)	14	19	21	21
II. Typical diet—as percent of NRC standard allowance				
Energy	95%	108%	151%	125%
Protein	117	151	173	159
Calcium	81	137	153	151
Iron	140	190	210	210

or century. They reflect changes that made heavy drafts on human energy, that accounted for a very large portion of the increase in real consumer expenditures.

They indicate a major reduction in weekly hours worked. (Had those hours not been reduced so sharply, GNP would have risen vastly more than it actually did.) That reduction for members of the labor force was probably not matched by anything like an equivalent reduction in hours worked by housewives.

However, a major share of the increase in real GNP went for more durables and better housing facilities that did reduce housewives' labor. The introduction of coal, then of central heating, ended the typical task of the housewife in the mid-19th century—preparing kindling, sometimes chopping firewood, and bringing in tons of firewood during the year. The mechanically powered washing machine has markedly reduced the effort, as well as time, once devoted to hand rubbing, washing, rinsing, the family wash. The introduction of piped cold water, and then of hot water, has removed the housewife's former task of pumping water from a well outside the house, carrying bucket after bucket indoors, and then heating them on a stove for washing. The expanded use of ice, and then the nearly universal adoption of mechanical refrigeration, has reduced waste of food and improved its quality. But, particularly for urban housewives, it has reduced the frequent trips to the grocery store required when the preservation of food in urban dwellings for more than a day was difficult, where it was not impossible.

Changes to provide amenities desired by the family demanded massive increases in resources for housing. The growth of central heating, the replacement of privies by flush toilets, the introduction of running water, bath tubs, fixed sinks, represent such changes. These expenditures helped cut death rates from typhoid and cholera—diseases once a part of daily life, but now almost unheard of in the U.S.

The automobile, and the universal presence of radio and TV, have so sharply changed life for all Americans that even their major share of GNP hardly indicates their impact on society or the options they opened to virtually all Americans. Finally, the great decline in consumption of potatoes, flour, lard, molasses, and their replacement by many other more preferred items in the diet, is well known.

It is unnecessary here to applaud these as advances in the wellbeing of Americans, or to regret the passing of the natural, unalienated, way of life in which housewives pumped gallons of water, chopped the kindling, baked several hundred pounds of bread a year, canned vegetables, and so on. What the above review indicates, instead, are directions of change created decade after decade by American families as they spent their incomes. That these choices reduced the work load of the housewife, reduced deaths from unsanitary conditions, brought a more varied diet, made available more "bread and circuses," and created more privacy, all give us some insight into American values in these decades.

WHITE AND NON-WHITE INCOME
DISTRIBUTIONS: 1900–1970

Despite the considerable interest in contrasting white and non-white income distributions, data for this comparison do not exist for the years prior to 1947. As a result, it is difficult to understand changes in one distribution relative to the other since 1947. For example, are the changes since 1962 similar to those which occurred in prior peacetime periods? Or are they significantly greater? Do they report a rate of change that merely continues longer trends? Or do they indicate a sharp reversal resulting from newer social forces?

To assist in the study of such problems, we have developed white and non-white family income distributions for 1900 and for 1935–1936. The choice of these dates derives largely from the fact that extensive field surveys were conducted at both dates. It is therefore possible to prepare income distributions for them on the basis of fairly comprehensive and representative statistical materials. We describe below the methods used in deriving the 1900 and the 1935–1936 distributions, together with the sources for the 1947ff. data shown in Tables 1 and 2.

1900

Separate distributions for white and non-white farm operators' families were based on the reported Census of Agriculture distributions of the value of farm products (produced and not fed to livestock).[1] From these distributions the proportion non-white was computed for all farm operators cumulated from the lowest income level—e.g., 22.73 percent of those with $0 value produced were non-white; 32.8 percent of those with value of $1–50 were non-white; and

[1] 1900 Census, *Agriculture*, Part I, p. 30.

299

TABLE 1
INCOME OF U.S. FAMILIES: 1900 TO 1970 BY COLOR

	1900			1935–1936			1944			1954			1971		
	All	White	Non-White	All	White	Non-White	All	White	Non-White	All	White	Non-White	All	White	Non-White
Total Number (000)	15,964	14,064	1,900	30,430	27,632	2,798	33,314	30,328	2,986	41,934	38,170	3,764	53,296	47,641	5,655
Percentage Distribution															
All	100.0%	100.0%	100.0%	100.0%	100.0%	100.0%	100.0%	100.0%	100.0%	100.0%	100.0%	100.0%	100.0%	100.0%	100.0%
$0–999	80.8	78.6	97.3	38.3	33.4	85.6	13.5	11.5	33.5	8.8	7.6	21.6	1.5	1.3	2.9
1000–1999	19.2	21.4	2.7	35.8	38.2	12.1	20.5	19.5	29.7	11.0	10.0	21.5	2.6	2.1	6.6
2000–2999				15.1	16.4	1.9	25.4	26.2	17.8	11.9	11.3	17.1	4.2	3.5	9.9
3000–3999				5.2	5.8	.3	17.3	18.1	9.1	15.4	15.2	17.9	4.8	4.3	8.7
4000–4999				2.0	2.2	.1	9.7	10.2	4.5	15.6	16.1	9.8	5.4	5.0	8.9
5000–5999				1.0	1.1		6.1	6.6	1.6	11.9	12.6	4.7	5.7	5.4	8.1
6000–6999				.6	.7		2.6	2.6	1.6	8.5	9.0	3.4	5.5	5.4	7.1
7000 +				2.0	2.2		4.9	5.3	2.2	16.9	18.2	4.0	70.2	73.0	47.9

TABLE 2
MEDIAN U.S. FAMILY INCOME

Year	Total	White	Non-White	Non-White + White
1900	$705	$745	$390	52%
1935–1936	1,240	1,296	690	53
1947	3,031	3,157	1,614	51
1948	3,187	3,310	1,768	53
1949	3,107	3,232	1,650	51
1950	3,319	3,445	1,869	54
1951	3,709	3,859	2,032	53
1952	3,890	4,114	2,338	57
1953	4,233	4,392	2,461	56
1954	4,173	4,339	2,410	56
1955	4,421	4,605	2,549	55
1956	4,783	4,993	2,628	53
1957	4,971	5,166	2,764	54
1958	5,087	5,300	2,711	51
1959	5,417	5,643	2,917	52
1960	5,620	5,835	3,233	55
1961	5,737	5,981	3,191	53
1962	5,956	6,237	3,330	53
1963	6,249	6,548	3,465	53
1964	6,569	6,858	3,839	56
1965	6,957	7,251	3,994	55
1966	7,500	7,792	4,674	60
1967	7,974	8,274	5,141	62
1968	8,632	8,937	5,590	63
1969	9,433	9,794	6,191	63
1970	9,867	10,236	6,516	64
1971	10,285	10,672	6,714	63

so on. These successive proportions were then graphed against the cumulated proportion of all U.S. farms by size of value produced. A curve fitted to these points was then used to interpolate the proportion non-white at the appropriate operator's income intervals.[2]

[2] Thus, 9.8% of all farm operators produced $0–200; 24.0% produced $0–$300 and so on. From the fitted curve, the proportion non-white—27.2%—(at the point which included the bottom 9.8% of

For farm laborers the ratio of non-white to total married male agricultural laborers was computed for each state, using Population Census data.[3] These ratios were then applied to the number of farm laborers in the appropriate states, as allocated to 1900 family income level in connection with the 1900 family income distribution.[4] Implicitly, this procedure assumes that the average for white and non-white farm laborers for each state was the same. This assumption is acceptable because—but only because—virtually all the male married non-white farm laborers worked in a few Southern states, and earnings averages for farm laborers in those states would reasonably reflect those for non-whites.

For non-farm family heads the proportion non-white at each income level was estimated as follows. The numbers of non-white married widowed and divorced males, in major non-farm occupations, was used as a set of weights to combine the separate BLS earnings distributions for men in those occupations.[5] The occupations selected included the bulk of male non-white non-farm employment—e.g. laborers, servants, draymen, porters, sawmill employees.[6] (Conversely non-whites accounted for from one third or more of total employment in the most important of these occupations.)

The resultant distribution of earnings by male heads has two biasses as used for family incomes, biasses which were assumed to be roughly cancelling. (a) On the one hand, the use of male earnings tends to understate Negro family income, by excluding significant contributions in earnings

---

farms) was then taken to be the proportion for all operators in the $0–200 farm operators' income group.

[3] 1900 Census, *Occupations*, Table 41.

[4] See p. 310 ff.

[5] The occupation data are from the 1900 Census, *Occupations*, p. 60. The occupation earnings distributions are from the LS Report, pp. 264–280.

[6] The 5 occupations specified received 80% of total weight. The balance of the weights were for carpenters, masons, painters, miners, merchants.

of the wife, children, and payments by boarders and lodgers. Thus in 1900 over 40 percent of non-white females worked, as compared to 15%–20% for foreign-born whites and somewhat less for native whites.[7] The 1910 Immigration Survey reports data consistent with these figures, indicating even higher rates for urban negro families.[8] Negro females (18 and over) earned $207 in 1910 as compared with $465 earned by negro male heads of family.[9] Hence the exclusion of wives' incomes from the negro family income distribution is likely to understate the income figures. (b) On the other hand, incomes of non-whites within the occupations selected would have been toward the lower end of the distribution, rather than proportionately distributed. This point is not to be exaggerated for the particular occupations selected, since foreign-born whites constituted very large proportions of the totals for such occupations.[10] And 1910 data suggest that the foreign-born in urban occupations earned about the same average incomes as Negroes.[11]

Therefore, a tendency toward compensating biasses is apparent, plus some likelihood that omitting income from family members other than the head probably does more to understate Negro family incomes than the upward bias in the husband's earnings figures overstates them. Differences between the broad income intervals shown—i.e., percent $0–499; percent $500–999—however, probably have little bias.

[7] 1900 Census, *Supplementary Analysis*, p. 446.

[8] Reports of the Immigration Commission, *Immigrants in Cities*, Vol. 1 (1911), *ibid.*, p. 139.

[9] *Ibid.*, pp. 138, 140.

[10] 1900 Census, *Occupations*, p. 11.

[11] Immigration Commission, *ibid.*, p. 140, shows average family head earnings of $465 for urban negro, and $452 for foreign-born family heads. Because the sample of negro heads was small, one can make no more of this than the lack of any obvious difference in earnings rates for family heads in the two groups. Foreign-born heads engaged in mining probably earned more than these urban averages, while the large group of track workers probably earned less.

1935–1936

Data for all families, non-relief and relief, are given in various publications of the National Resources Committee.[12] Distributions for Negroes and for other non-whites were derived as described below, then deducted from the above total distribution to give that for whites.

Negro. (1) Non-relief families were allocated by weighting 5 city-size-region distributions for the South, and 2 for the North Central, by the NRC weights.[13] The resultant weighted distribution accounts for some 93 percent of the final Negro non-relief distribution.

(2) For the small Negro group in New England and the Mountain and Pacific states in 1935–1936 we estimate a 24,000-family total, to which the metropolitan North Central distribution used above was applied. The population count is derived by estimating the Northeast, Mountain, Pacific ratio of non-relief to total Negro population. That ratio ranges from 91 percent in Southern farm areas and 75 percent in Southern urban, to 37 percent in the North Central states.[14] We adopt a 37 percent rate for Negroes in the 3 regions noted, and apply to the population count of 67,000 to give 24,000.[15]

(3) For non-relief Negroes in North Central cities (below 100,000 in size) we estimate 84,000 families, and use a weighted average of the distributions available for North Central metropolises and large cities.[16]

[12] *Family Expenditures in the United States*, pp. 1, 108; *Consumer Incomes in the United States*, p. 97, Table 8B.

[13] *Consumer Incomes*, p. 100, gives distributions for Negroes in large, middle-sized, small cities, all farm families, and rural non-farm families in the South; for metropolises and large cities in the North Central region. Corresponding population weights appear on page 102.

[14] *Consumer Incomes*, pp. 76, 102.

[15] Count from *ibid.*, p. 76.

[16] *Family Expenditures*, p. 18, gives a total of 154-thousand Negro families (relief plus non-relief) in North Central communities under

(4) For Negro relief families a count of 574,000 is more
or less implicit in the NRC data.[17] The count was distributed according to the income distribution of those relief
families with incomes under $1,000.[18] Apparently only a
single volume of the many in the Consumer Purchases Study
actually shows the distribution of Negro relief families—
namely that for Chicago.[19] That distribution indicates that
92 percent of Chicago Negroes on relief had incomes of
under $1,000. It is a likely inference that in other cities,
where prevailing income medians and levels of relief tended
to be lower, the proportion of relief Negroes with incomes
above $1,000 could not be significant.

However, we have a further guide. The National Health
Survey, which provided the underlying basis for the National Resources Committee estimates of proportions on relief, gives data for a host of individual cities.[20] A review
of those for which separate data for Negroes is reported
indicates that in the Southern and North Central cities
(where Negroes on relief were concentrated) the propor-

100,000. We estimate the proportion on relief at 45%, using as a
guide the 48% ratio for communities over 100,000 in the region
(*Family Expenditures*, p. 18, and *Consumer Incomes*, p. 102) and
the small differential in relief rates by size of north central city as
shown in U.S. Public Health Service, *The National Health Survey:
1935–1936*, Preliminary Reports, Bulletin No. C, (1938), p. x. Two
thirds of the resultant 84,000 total was used as an added weight for
the NC metropolitan distribution, one third for the large cities
distribution.

[17] *Consumer Incomes*, p. 76, gives 2,664,000 total families. Deducting
from that total the sum of non-relief families as shown for the South
noted above, as well as the 108,000 estimated above for regions not
specified, gives a total of 2,090,000, leaving 574,000 as the estimate
of Negro relief families.

[18] The distribution for all relief families appears in *Consumer Incomes*, p. 98, Table 13B.

[19] Bureau of Labor Statistics, Bulletin No. 642, Vol. 1, *Family Income In Chicago, 1935–1936*, p. 110. Professor Duane Evans of Cornell
University, who worked on the study, confirmed this gap.

[20] U.S. Public Health Service, *The National Health Survey
1935–1936*, Bulletin No. A.

tions with incomes under $1,000 for families *not* on relief ranged from 30 to 60 percent. (In the South .3 of 2.1 million families were on relief; in the North Central region, .23 of .48 million.) It is not unreasonable to assume, given the relief gap, that 100 percent of Negro families on relief were in the under $1,000 interval.

Other non-whites. This group of 248,000 (compared to the 2,665,000 total Negro families) was distributed by the Negro income distribution derived above.[21] Of the "other non-white" group, 37 percent were Indian, 18 percent Filipino, 21 percent Chinese, and 22 percent Japanese. Examination of the 1930 occupational distributions indicates an overwhelming concentration of Chinese, Japanese, and Filipinos in farm labor and service work. Given such a distribution, and given later Indian Service studies on Indian incomes, we allocate the entire "other non-white" group to income levels by the Negro income distribution. (It is to be remembered that we are adding only 9 percent to a group of 2.7 million families.)[22]

1944–1971

These data are all from the annual money income surveys of the Bureau of the Census.[23] By these years the proportion

[21] The total number of families in the NRC study classed as "other color groups" ran to 372,000 (*Family Expenditures*, p. 18). That category, however, included Mexican-Americans, a group classified as white in all Censuses but that of 1930, but classified as non-white in that Census and therefore in the BLS Study of Consumer Purchases. From the 1930 Census, *Occupations*, p. 74, we take the details of the number of gainfully occupied males who were Mexican, Indian, Chinese, Japanese, Filipino, etc., and compute the proportion of this subgroup that were Mexican. Applying that proportion to the NRC 372,000 gives us 248,000, the figure used as the size in 1935–1936 of the non-white group other than Negro.

[22] The occupational distribution suggests that the higher incomes characteristic of Chinese and Japanese families since 1946 did not characterize them in 1935–1936.

[23] Current Population Reports, Series P-60, No. 2, Table 1; No. 20, Table 2; No. 85, Table 27.

WHITE AND NON-WHITE INCOME

TABLE 3
U.S. FAMILIES, BY INCOME AND COLOR: 1900

	Total	White	Non-White
Number (000)	15,964	14,064	1,900
Percentage Distribution			
Total	100.0	100.0	100.0
$0–199	7.9	5.4	26.8
$200–299	6.3	5.4	13.1
$300–399	5.5	4.8	10.8
$400–499	7.0	6.2	13.2
$500–599	10.4	9.9	14.0
$600–699	12.2	12.4	10.6
$700–799	12.9	13.8	5.2
$800–899	12.3	13.7	2.3
$900–999	6.3	7.0	1.3
$1,000–1,099	5.9	6.6	1.0
$1,100–1,199	4.2	4.7	0.5
$1,200–1,299	1.5	1.6	0.4
$1,300 and over	7.6	8.5	0.8

TABLE 4
NON-FARM FAMILIES BY MONEY INCOME AND COLOR: 1900

	Total	White	Non-White
Number (000)	9,403	8,571	832
Percentage Distribution			
Total	100.0%	100.0%	100.0%
$0–299	1.9	0.5	16.1
300–399	2.5	1.5	12.5
400–499	6.0	4.6	20.1
500–599	12.9	11.9	23.2
600–699	16.0	15.8	17.3
700–799	18.0	19.2	6.7
800–899	17.8	19.2	2.9
900–999	7.6	8.3	0.6
1,000–1,099	7.4	8.1	0.2
1,100–1,199	4.5	4.9	0.1
1,200–1,299	1.4	1.6	0.1
1,300 and over	4.0	4.4	0.2

NEW DATA

TABLE 5
Farm Families by Income: 1900

	Total	White	Non-White
Number (000)	6,561	5,493	1,068
Percentage Distribution			
Total	100.0	100.0	100.0
$0–199	18.4	13.6	43.0
$200–299	13.6	13.3	15.3
$300–399	9.8	9.9	9.6
$400–499	8.5	8.6	7.9
$500–599	6.8	6.8	6.9
$600–699	6.8	7.1	5.4
$700–799	5.3	5.5	3.9
$800–899	4.5	5.0	1.9
$900–999	4.5	5.1	1.8
$1,000–1,099	3.8	4.2	1.6
$1,100–1,199	3.8	4.4	0.8
$1,200–1,299	1.5	1.7	0.6
$1,300 and over	12.7	14.8	1.3

TABLE 6
Farm Operators by Family Income: 1900

	Total	White	Non-White
Number (000)	5,690	4,906	784
Percentage Distribution			
Total	100.0	100.0	100.0
$0–199	14.9	12.6	28.8
$200–299	9.6	8.6	15.4
$300–399	9.1	8.6	12.8
$400–499	9.1	9.0	9.9
$500–599	7.8	7.6	9.4
$600–699	7.8	7.9	7.4
$700–799	6.1	6.2	5.4
$800–899	5.2	5.6	2.6
$900–999	5.2	5.7	2.4
$1,000–1,099	4.4	4.7	2.2
$1,100–1,199	4.4	4.9	1.1
$1,200–1,299	1.7	1.9	0.8
$1,300 and over	14.7	16.7	1.8

of families in agriculture had dropped to so small a percentage of the total that the Census exclusion of imputed farm incomes does not overstate the proportion of low income families very markedly. Moreover, since our focus is on contrasts between white and non-white distributions, that distortion is reduced to a relatively small level.

THE INCOME DISTRIBUTION

IN 1900

A more detailed family income distribution, and probably a more reliable one, can be developed for 1900 than for any year prior to 1936.[1] The existence of two extensive studies account for this somewhat surprising potential. One is the 1900 Census, which provided more detail on gross farm income and expenses than is available for any year prior to 1940.[2] (Farming then occupied a third of our labor force.) The other is the survey by the U.S. Commissioner of Labor, which reports 1900–1902 income data for a larger sample of urban families than has been surveyed in any year before 1936, or since.[3] These data provide an unusually solid base for developing estimates of the distribution of family incomes.

I. FARM

A

For farmer's incomes in 1900 we utilize the 1900 Census distribution of 5.7 million farms by value of product to allocate 4.9 million farm operators by net income. A variety of adjustments were then needed to convert value-of-product estimates into estimates of net income of farm operators. (These adjustments changed the shape of the distribution hardly at all.)

(1) The Census provides totals for expenditures on labor, and on fertilizer by value-of-product level. Both of these

[1] The 1929 distribution by Leven, though utilized in the original Brookings report and later in publications by others, is no obvious exception to this assertion.

[2] Twelfth Census of the United States, Volume v, *Agriculture*, Part 1.

[3] Eighteenth Annual Report of the Commissioner of Labor, 1903, *Cost of Living and Retail Prices of Food* (1904).

were then deducted from the value of product (not fed to livestock) at each value-of-product level.

(2) National aggregates for repairs, for net change in livestock inventories, and for gross rental value of farm dwellings are given by Towne and Rasmussen.[4] These aggregates were distributed to the 1900 value-of-product intervals on the basis of relevant Census data.[5]

(3) Taxes and interest were derived from various USDA totals, then allocated by Census data.[6]

(4) Ginning costs as estimated by Towne and Rasmussen, were distributed by Census data for Southern farms.[7] The impact of these adjustments may be seen by comparing columns 2 and 3 in Table 2—the one reporting the Census average value of farm products (not fed to livestock) while the other measures net income to farm operators from farming.

B

To the above figures it is necessary to add the imputed income that farm operators derived from home-grown food,

[4] Marvin Towne and Wayne Rasmussen, "Farm Gross Product. . . ," in Conference on Research in Income and Wealth, *Trends in the American Economy in the Nineteenth Century* (1960), pp. 266, 272.

[5] Repairs were distributed in proportion to the value of implements and machinery in each product value interval, net rental by the value of buildings, and change in livestock inventories by value of livestock.

[6] USDA totals for farm taxes are reported in the U.S. Census, *Historical Statistics of the U.S.*, II, p. 283. USDA figures for interest in 1910 are reported in the same source, as is the value of land and buildings in both 1900 and 1910 (*ibid.*, pp. 278, 286). The 1900–1910 trend in value was used to extrapolate the 1910 total for interest paid. Interest and taxes were then allocated to the 1900 product intervals, using the 1900 Census distribution of value of land and improvements.

[7] Towne and Rasmussen, *op.cit.*, p. 272. These were allocated to value-of-product intervals, using the distribution of value of product on farms in the South Central division. Cotton farms constituted a larger proportion of all farms in that division than any other. (Furthermore, the South Central division raised the bulk of U.S. cotton.)

rental of farm house, and fuel from the farm woodlot. Median incomes of farm operators and farm laborers differ—but not so largely as one might first think, for capital gains from land investment were a critical element in the total return to farms.[8] Median *imputed* incomes of farmers and of farm laborers would have differed even less: farm laborers typically lived in the same farmhouse and ate at the same table as members of the farmer's family.

We therefore take the difference between earnings of farm laborers with board and those without board as a reasonable market reflection of the value of board and lodging. Such valuation would be at cost to the farmer. As such it would be directly additive to the (market valuations of) the value of products sold off the farm.

Is there any way of testing the adequacy of imputed income of farm operators as inferred by the difference between average wages to farm laborers with and without board? Fortunately, two independent checks exist. The more substantial is provided by the large-scale survey of the farmers standard of living in 1922–1924.[9] This survey, of 2,886 farm families, secured data for farm operators (owners and tenants) and farm laborers.[10] The average value of home consumption was $684.[11] The 1922–1924 USDA data for the wage differential (monthly, with and without board) multiplied by the number of persons per farm family shown by the USDA survey provides a home

[8] W. I. King has asserted that "usually the farmer is not only a producer but also a land speculator. Indeed, it is rather upon the increase in the value of his land than upon the sale of his produce that the farmer rests whatever hope he cherishes of growing rich." W. I. King, in Wesley Mitchell, ed., *Income in the United States, Its Amount and Distribution, 1909–1919* (1922) Vol. 2, p. 298.

[9] U.S. Department of Agriculture, Department Bulletin 1466, E. L. Kirkpatrick, *The Farmer's Standard of Living* (1926, 1930), p. 29.

[10] Of the 2,886 white families surveyed 1,950 were owners; 867 were cash and share tenants, including croppers; 69 were hired men or managers. *Ibid.*, p. 7.

[11] *Ibid.*, p. 29. The figure constitutes 43% of the value of all goods consumed.

consumption figure of $630 per farm family.[12] The survey estimates are therefore within 10 percent of the imputed income derived by our use of the wage differential.

Another check, based on a small sample but on a more nearly contemporary (pre-World War I) one, yields a figure of $421—to be compared with one of $380 from the 1914 farm labor wage differential.[13]

Since the wage rate differentials for 1899 and 1909 are virtually identical—$5.93 per month and $6.11 per month— we can utilize for 1900 the 1909 figure that Goldenweiser derives (and King accepts) from the USDA source noted above.[14] The USDA report reckons on the probability that the Census enumerators had included in the value of product totals a proportion of meat and vegetables consumed on the family farm, hence reduces the required addition to $260 per family.[15]

This average value of imputed income for all farm operators has to be varied by net product level.[16] Imputed income

[12] USDA, Bureau of Agricultural Economics, *Farm Wage Rates, Farm Employment and Related Data* (January 1943). We average 1922, 1923, 1924 differentials. Size of family from Kirkpatrick, *op.cit.*, p. 21. The monthly differences were, of course, multiplied by 12 to give a yearly total.

[13] Estimates from the USDA Farmers Bulletin of December 1914, based on "the monetary affairs of 483 farmers in 10 well scattered localities" quoted by W. I. King, *op.cit.*, p. 301.

[14] King, *op.cit.*, pp. 300-302. A. Goldenweiser, "The Farmer's Income" *American Economic Review* (March 1916), p. 43. We substitute for the average imputed value of owned home, however, a figure equal to 10% of the value of farm buildings. This procedure is the same as the USDA uses for 1910ff.—and therefore provides comparability with that source. (Cf. USDA, *Agricultural Statistics, 1942*, p. 660.)

[15] Reference to the 1900 Census of Agriculture, Vol. v, Part 1, p. 762, shows that the Census questions explicitly asked for the value of animals slaughtered on the farm for home use, and for the value of milk, etc., consumed on the farm. Presumably, the value of farm product was arrived at by summing the individual product items, although—since it came first on the schedule—this is no certainty.

[16] One alternative would be to use the 1922-1924 study, varying

was varied in proportion to the average value of land and building per farm in each interval.[17] The first reason for doing so is that a large proportion of the imputed income not already included in gross product was in the form of imputed rent. Secondly, imputed returns would have tended to vary with the asset status of the family, best indicated by the asset value of land and buildings, rather than by any current income flow. These figures, when added to net income from farm operations, gave net income of farm operators. (The amount of off-farm income to farm operators' families in 1900 was assumed to have been so small that it could be ignored, the income from assisting in family farm, of course, having already been included.)

C

Farm laborers. The 1900 Census reported 5.7 million farm families—a figure virtually identical with the 5.7 million farms.[18] The Census therefore excluded families of farm laborers from its total for farm families.[19] We estimate their number in 1900 by computing the ratio of (a) married, widowed, and divorced males who were gainfully employed as farm laborers to (b) the number of farmers who were married, widowed, or divorced males, applying that ratio to the number of "farm families" (i.e., farm operators' families.)[20]

The income distribution for farm laborers is unusually easy—in that data for this group in any year, including

the ratio of imputed to cash income by total income level in accord with those data. However, the pattern of variation in ratios differs from that in subsequent expenditure surveys; moreover, it yields an improbably low income figure in the lower intervals.

[17] Data from the extensive 1922–1924 survey indicate that the proportion of total consumption furnished by the farm was virtually identical in all size groups. (Kirkpatrick, *op.cit.*, p. 54.) The proportion ranged from 38% to 43%, with 42.9% for farms with less than 25 acres and 37.9% for farms of 525 and more acres.

[18] 1900 Census, Agriculture, p. lxviii, discusses the minor differences.

[19] This is confirmed in a letter from the Census Population Division in January 1971.

[20] Data from 1900 Census, *Occupations*, pp. 52, 58, 62.

1970, are not of any high reliability. Hence the 1900 data for this sector may be as good as those for 1970.

The 1901 BLS survey recorded incomes for families of 100 farm laborers—presumably those living in small towns. The median earnings figure for that group was $240.[21] Average monthly earnings in 1899 for U.S. farm laborers who did not receive board averaged $19.97—or $239.63 on an annual basis.[22] It is difficult to understand why these two wholly independent sources should agree so closely. But there is no point in looking a gift statistic in the mouth. We take $240 to represent the average yearly earnings (including the value of imputed rent and food) for farm laborers in 1900, arbitrarily rounding up to $250 to include the contribution of other family members. (Since a great many farm laborers were unmarried—and we are developing a distribution for all farm laborers' families, whether single persons or married—the average contribution of other family members would be small.) All farm laborers in each state (other than family members) were then assumed to earn 12 times the average state monthly wage (without board) in 1899, the state figures then being combined to give a U.S. distribution of laborers.[23] The resultant distribution obviously lacks the variance of one not based on state means. However, its pattern is sufficiently similar to that for the farm laborers enumerated in the BLS expenditure survey, and its weight in the total is small enough, to warrant its use.

II. Non-farm

A

The report by the Commissioner of Labor (henceforth referred to as the LS report) provides income averages and

[21] LS, p. 264.

[22] Data from BAE, *Farm Wage Rates, Employment* . . . , (1943, mimeo.), p. 23.

[23] The number of laborers is from 1900 Census, *Occupations*, Table 32, while the average wage by state is from the BAE, *Farm Wage Rates*. . . .

distributions. We begin from distributions, by state, of the incomes of 11,156 families.[24]

One advantage of using these state distributions is that they may be tested against other data to learn something about their biasses. For this purpose we compared the average state income shown by the LS data both with the average income by state as estimated by Richard Easterlin and with the average yearly earnings of male employees in manufacturing—the latter not being wholly independent of the Easterlin estimates.[25] The results prove most useful for comparison within regions, and suggest that weighting these data will give acceptable national averages.[26] Given these state distributions it is possible to weight them to a U.S. distribution not by the LS weights (convenient for survey enumeration)[27] but by the number of non-farm families that the distributions may be reasonably expected to represent. For the count of non-farm families by state we used Census data on the number of married males gainfully employed in non-farm pursuits.[28]

[24] These families—"normal families" in the Commissioner's parlance—have a working husband, wife, no more than 5 children, and no dependent, boarder, lodger or servant. *Op.cit.*, p. 18.

[25] Richard Easterlin, "State Income Estimates," in Everett Lee, et al., *Population Redistribution and Economic Growth United States, 1870–1950*, Vol. 1 (1957), p. 753; 1900 Census, Vol. vii, *Manufactures*, Part 1, p. cxv.

[26] Because of the importance of distributional aspects, an additional check was made by comparing the proportions in the lower income intervals (e.g., incomes under $400) with the state proportions of manufacturing employees engaged in the production of food, tobacco, lumber, and textiles—the typical low wage industries. Again, the results seemed, given the conceptual differences, sufficiently consistent.

[27] *Op.cit.*, p. 15 "In several instances a larger number of family schedules than its due proportion was allowed to a state, and adjoining states . . . were omitted."

[28] 1900 Census, *Occupations*, Table 41, provides for each state data on married males gainfully occupied, by occupation. As indicated below, the number of gainfully occupied married males for the U.S. comes to about 80% of the count for non-farm families, and we

Weighting the state distributions for normal families by these counts gave a preliminary U.S. distribution. This was then adjusted to a final one by allowing for the difference between the average income shown for 11,156 normal families (i.e., those used for state distributions) and the 25,440 families in the entire LS survey.[29]

B

The survey covered only employees on payrolls. Its sample was extensive. But it will not provide unbiased estimates for the income distribution of the non-farm self-employed.[30] As an initial step in developing a distribution for families headed by the self-employed we estimate their number. (Table 3, infra). Estimates for the non-farm self-employed in detailed occupations in 1900 are available.[31] Census data permit us to estimate the proportion of married, widowed, or divorced males in each of these occupations.[32] These proportions were then applied to the estimated number of self-

---

may reasonably assume that their distribution among states is adequate for inferring the distribution of non-farm families among the states.

[29] The LS *Report* (pp. 366, 571) indicates that normal families averaged $99 less income per year than did all survey families. (The husband's income average was almost precisely the same in both normal families and all families. Hence it seems the additional income provided by boarders and lodgers—approximately $50 (pp. 362, 368)—and by working children (over 14 years of age) probably accounted both for the conceptual and arithmetic difference between averages both for normal and all families.) Given a $99 difference, the reported $100 intervals were therefore simply adjusted by a scale factor.

[30] One indication that it does not do so is given by the proportion of families in the sample who reported home ownership—19%—with the average for all non-farm families—36% (LS, *op.cit.*, p. 364). 1900 Census, *Population*, Part II, p. cc.

[31] These underlie the aggregates in the writer's *Manpower in Economic Growth*, p. 516.

[32] The ratios were computed from the 1900 Census, *Occupations*, Table 16.

employed in that occupation, the sum of these detailed estimates, 2,593,000, then constituting the weight for families headed by non-farm self-employed.

Income distributions for individual occupations in each major category of the self-employed were based on occupation data from the LS survey. For example, for the major group of self-employed in construction, the survey income distributions for carpenters, masons, painters, paper hangers, plasterers, and plumbers were weighted together.[33]

By using the earnings distributions for male heads of family we tacitly assume that the income contributed by other members of such families was trivial. The data show that contributions by boarders and lodgers and by working children accounted for most of the $99 in yearly income by which the average survey family exceeded the average for normal families (i.e., those with husband, wife, no boarders or lodgers, under 5 children). We assume that some families of the self-employed were likely to have such additional income (e.g., organ grinders, newspaper salesmen) but that most, being higher income, would have had small contributions from such sources.

Female family heads represent the most difficult, if not most important, problem of estimation. The number of non-farm female family heads in 1900 was 1,559,124.[34] From

[33] Data for individual occupations appear in Table II-B of that study, with the internal survey weights used for weighting. These data are for male head of family earners. For self-employed in trade, we combined the distributions for family heads that were store managers or bookkeepers. (Data for salesmen appear to include too many paper boys, etc.) For hand trades the distributions for barbers, blacksmiths, and bartenders were weighted together; for manufacturing, overseers in cotton mills and foremen in hand trades; for professional service, fortunately only about 10% of the non-farm group, the distributions for survey occupations with substantial proportions of higher income recipients were averaged, namely those for locomotive engineers, conductors, and letter carriers. The result is to imply that about half the self-employed in professional service had incomes in the $1,000 and over group—compared to 6% for urban wage-earner families.

[34] 1900 family data from 1900 Census, *Population*, Part II, p. ccviii.

urban data we estimate that 29.7 percent of these were engaged in the labor force.[35]

Because the BLS survey included almost no families but those with male heads[36] it is necessary to provide an additional distribution for this group. We use the distribution given by the BLS survey for the earnings of the 2,010 heads of families who were employed in domestic and personal service[37] (Table 5, Col. 3). Since the typical female-headed family (one person or broken) would have had virtually no income from other sources, the earnings distributions for such family heads should be reasonably suitable. (This group's distribution is dominated by data for common laborers and janitors, with a significant component for stationary engineers, barbers, policemen, bartenders, waiters, etc.) Summary results appear in Table 4, *in fra.*

III. Other Estimates

In addition to the basic farm and non-farm distributions described above, average incomes in Table 1 were computed. They were derived as follows. For farm families the aggregate income of farm operators was divided by the number of farm operators. The major component of total income, value of products not fed to livestock, and most of the expense items, were taken directly from the Census of Agriculture, using the sources cited above. The aggregate for imputed incomes was computed as the average for each income level (also as estimated above) multiplied by the number of farm operators at that income level.

For non-farm families the mid point in each $100 income interval shown by the BLS survey was used from the $0–99

[35] 1900 Census, *Supplementary Analysis*, pp. 463, 465. Of 775,000 females in cities of 50,000 and over who were widowed or divorced, 29.7% were gainfully occupied.

[36] LS, p. 237. In fact it included only those male heads with wife present. We assume that the income distribution for that group applied to all non-farm employee family heads.

[37] *Ibid.*, p. 264.

interval thru $1,200–1,299. The open end group, $1,300 and over, includes 4 percent of the non-farm families. For that group a fairly arbitrary value of $5,000 was used. It was arrived at as follows. Kuznets' data shows that all income tax returns with incomes over $1,000 in 1917 averaged $4,213.[38] Corresponding figures for 1918 were $4,007; for 1920, $3,621; for 1921, $3,513. Given the trend of price and income increases prior to 1917, we assume that a $5,000 average for the group over $1,300 would serve for 1900. Of course, the use of any average from $3,000 to $10,000 would change the U.S. average income very little.

IV

How do the present estimates relate to other data for 1900? Since there are no prior income distributions for 1900 in common use—one of the reasons for making the present estimates—no direct comparisons can be made.[39] However, two other sources of data should be noted.

The writer has previously estimated a series for average earnings of non-farm employees, which includes a 1900 figure about half that for non-farm families in Table 1.[40] Two conceptual differences account for much of that gap. (1) As Table 5 indicates, the self-employed receive a substantial weight in making up the non-farm average, and have a relatively high average income. The average for wage-earner heads alone that is implicit in Table 5, and therefore in Table 1, is $769. (2) Moreover, the primary source used for estimating family incomes of wage earners in 1900 indicates that wives, children, boarders, etc., con-

[38] Simon Kuznets, *Shares of Upper Income Groups in Income and Savings* (1953), pp. 513, 524.

[39] The reference to "in common use" is merely a cautionary expression of the fact that while no estimates whatever were turned up, scholars will unquestionably discover one or more sometime in the future.

[40] Cf. Lebergott, *Manpower in Economic Growth*, p. 524.

TABLE 1
U.S. FAMILIES BY INCOME: 1900

	Total	Farm	Non-Farm
Number (000)	15,964	6,561	9,403
Percentage Distribution			
Total	100.0	100.0	100.0
$0–199	7.9	18.4	0.6
$200–299	6.3	13.6	1.3
$300–399	5.5	9.8	2.5
$400–499	7.0	8.5	6.0
$500–599	10.4	6.8	12.9
$600–699	12.2	6.8	16.0
$700–799	12.9	5.3	18.0
$800–899	12.3	4.5	17.8
$900–999	6.3	4.5	7.6
$1,000–1,099	5.9	3.8	7.4
$1,100–1,199	4.2	3.8	4.5
$1,200–1,299	1.5	1.5	1.4
$1,300 and over	7.6	12.7	4.0
Average Income	$899	$867	$921

tributed 17 percent of family income.[41] Reducing $769 by 17 percent yields $638 for husband's income. About 30 percent of the 1900 labor force consisted of women and children who, on average, would have earned say 50 percent less than male heads of families. If so, the 1900 earnings average for all earners comparable with $638 would have been $542. That figure is well above $441 for all non-farm employees, the difference probably reflecting an upward bias in the BLS survey results. (For example 37 percent of the families had members in labor organizations although less than 3 percent of the labor force was organized.[42] And 66 percent had life insurance and 31 percent property—extremely high proportions even in much later years.)

[41] LS *Report,* p. 366.
[42] *Report,* p. 505. The proportion of the 1900 labor force organized is estimated in the writer's chapter, "The American Labor Force," in L. Davis et al., *American Economic Growth* (1972), p. 220.

TABLE 2
FARMS, BY FARM INCOME 1900

Value of Product per Farm*	(1) Number of Farms (000)	(2) Average Value of Product	(3) Net Income from Farm Operations	(4) Net Livestock Increase	(5) Net Rental	(6) Labor	(7) Taxes and Interest	(8) Ferti- lizer	(9) Repairs	(10) Ginning
All Farm Average		$ 656	$ 547	$ 14	$ 319	$ 64	$ 35	$10	$ 9	$ 5
$0	53	0	–30	22	202	24	22	2	4	0
$1–49	168	29	18	3	69	4	7	1	2	0
$50–99	306	73	61	3	77	4	7	2	2	0
$100–249	1,248	176	155	4	103	7	10	3	3	2
$250–499	1,603	365	321	7	174	18	17	7	5	4
$500–999	1,379	700	599	14	353	52	38	10	10	5
$1,000–2,499	829	1,451	1,193	28	728	158	85	18	19	6
2,500 and over	154	4,964	3,926	111	1,878	786	226	63	52	22

*Value of product is net of that fed to livestock.

Sources: Cols 1, 2: 1900 Census, *Agriculture*, Vol. 5, Part 1, pp. 230–231.
Cols. 3–10: See text.

TABLE 3

U.S. FAMILIES IN 1900 BY OCCUPATION OF HEAD (000)

	Total	Foreign White	Non-White
(1) Total	15,964	3,857	1,900
(2) Self-employed	8,283	1,450	844
(a) Farm operator	5,690	791	784
(b) Non-farm	2,593	659	60
(3) Employees	7,681	2,407	1,056
(a) Farm	871	88	284
(b) Non-farm	6,810	2,319	772

Sources: 1, 2a: 1900 Census, *Population,* Part 2, pp. ccvii, clviii. Conterminous U.S. These data are for private families.

    2: 2a + 2b

    2b: Non-farm self-employment in 1900 total (*Manpower in Economic Growth,* p. 516) split between family heads and others on the basis of detailed occupation data in underlying estimates (*Ibid.*) and marital status information in 1900 Census, *Occupations,* Tables 16, 19, 20.

    3: 3a + 3b

    3a: Row 2a times relevant ratios of male farm operators married, widowed, or divorced to male farm laborers married, widowed, or divorced. Data for the ratios are from 1900 Census, *Occupations,* pp. 52, 58, 62.

    3b: Row 1 minus [Row 2 + Row 3a].

For 1910 W. I. King made detailed estimates that have appeared repeatedly in later avatars.[43] King gives no description of his methods whatever. And in the gracefully casual way he had of citing sources he lists a variety of titles, some in ways that make them impossible to locate. Among the

[43] W. I. King, *The Wealth and Income of the People of the United States* (1915), pp. 224–226. The National Industrial Conference Board, *Studies in Enterprise and Social Progress* (1939), p. 125, reports a distribution of income and families, with no description whatever of methodology or source. However, a leafing through adjoining chapters turns up several references to King's study, used as a source for other data—suggesting King as a possible source for the NICB table. The numbers are remarkably similar, allowing for interpolation required to give the NICB data by decile. At a later date the NICB data were utilized in Gabriel Kolko, *Wealth and Power in America* (1962), p. 14.

TABLE 4

NON-FARM FAMILIES BY MONEY INCOME AND STATUS: 1900

	All Non-Farm	Male Heads		Female Heads
		Wage Earner	Self-Employed	
Number (000)	9,403	6,310	2,593	500
Percentage Distribution				
Total	100.0%	100.0%	100.0%	100.0%
$0–299	1.9	0.2	0.5	30.5
300–399	2.5	1.3	0.9	25.8
400–499	6.0	5.9	2.2	26.3
500–599	12.9	16.3	4.8	10.9
600–699	16.0	19.9	8.4	5.2
700–799	18.0	20.5	15.7	1.3
800–899	17.8	17.2	22.7	—
900–999	7.6	6.9	10.8	—
1,000–1,099	7.4	6.0	12.2	—
1,100–1,199	4.5	3.2	8.4	—
1,200–1,299	1.4	0.9	3.0	—
1,300 and over	4.0	1.7	10.4	—

few comprehensive and basic sources he cites is the Commissioner's Report, utilized here for 1900. It is not likely that King allowed properly for the distribution of income among farm families. Thus he estimates that only 0.07 percent of families had incomes below $200—in contrast with the present estimate of 6.10 percent. (His figure is quite close to the present estimate for non-farm families.) But in the face of the formidably extensive, detailed, and obviously acceptable data given by the 1900 Census of Agriculture on farmers' receipts and expenditures it is impossible to estimate that so tiny a proportion of U.S. families were in that low income group. Similarly he finds 0.97 percent in the next highest income interval—compared to the present estimate of 8.00 percent for all families and 17.60 percent for farm families. Whatever the quality of the present estimates, it requires only the briefest review of the 1900 Census of Agriculture data to conclude that upward trends in farm prices from 1900 to 1910 could not possibly have wiped out these low incomes as completely as King's estimating procedures (implicitly or explicitly) did.

Spahr estimated the distribution of wealth in New York state in 1892, converted to a U.S. distribution, assumed a 7 percent rate of return on all capital, and made various other undescribed adjustments.[44] From these estimates he inferred that 88 percent of American families had incomes under $1,200–which may be compared with our 92.5 percent figure.[45]

[44] Charles P. Spahr, *An Essay on the Present Distribution of Wealth in the United States* (1896). Spahr's underlying wealth data are challenged by G. K. Holmes, *The Growth of Large Fortunes*. Publications of the American Economic Association, Vol. VIII.

[45] *Ibid.*, p. 128. His distribution provides only one further break, between those from $1,200 to $5,000 and those $5,000 and over.

SERVICE EXPENDITURES SINCE
1900: NEW ESTIMATES

When *La Nouvelle Heloise* first appeared, its success was so great that the booksellers rented rather than sold the book, charging 12 sous an hour for each volume.[1] In an economy whose prices and incomes are such that few people even rent books for a day, this anecdote is a reminder of how thin a line separates goods from services. Goods, no less than services, are purchased primarily for their service value.[2] As that service value becomes available in new goods or services, the line between goods and services will shift. The household production function for cleanliness once required soap, wash boards, and domestic service. With time and technology it began to include commercial laundry services, then home washing machines, and then laundromat services. Other shifts between goods and services are well known: from motion picture admissions (services) to television sets (goods), from patent medicines (goods) to hospitals (services), from public transportation (services) to automobiles (goods).

To assess these shifts within the upward trend of GNP over the 20th century, detailed and reasonably accurate estimates of service expenditures are desirable. At the present time we lack such figures. (The standard Kuznets' series reports annual aggregate services from 1919 on, and 5 year moving averages for 1900ff.)[3] We have more detailed

[1] V.-D. Musset-Pathy, *Histoire de la Vie de J. J. Rousseau* (*Paris*, 1821) Vol. II, p. 361: "Les libraires ne pouvaient souffrir aux demandes de toutes les classes. On louent l'ouvrage a tant par jour, ou par heure. Quand il parut, on exigeait douze sous par volume, en n'accordant que soixantes minutes pour lire."

[2] Service value can, of course, include their Veblenian function of providing evidence of wealth or status.

[3] Simon Kuznets, *Capital in the American Economy* (1961) Appendix Tables R-3, R-9, R-28. John Kendrick, *Productivity Trends*

326

estimates for 1909–1929 based on the work of Martin Gains-brugh and Lough as adapted by Dewhurst, and the very careful estimates of Harold Barger for 1921–1929.[4] None of these detailed estimates is comparable with the official U.S. national income accounts used for the years since 1929. While these series have been developed with much ingenuity, nothing like the endeavor applied to the commodity components of GNP has been lavished on them. Among other things they precede the development of major new statistical resources in the form of historical series developed by Raymond Goldsmith in his *A Study of Saving* and Leo Grebler's *Capital Formation in Real Estate.*

Insofar as aggregate GNP estimates include these earlier series and are used for the analyses of changes in the aggregate production function, trends in productivity, marking off technological "epochs," etc., they tend to suffer from a further limitation: they rely for measures of a major input, labor, on component series that are in no way consistent with the output data, as they should be.[5] One aspect of the present estimates is that they are developed so that there is a much greater consistency between the labor input data and the output data for the service sectors. A further aspect is the detail in which they are developed—something over 50 component series were estimated in developing the service category totals in Table 1 (p. 376). The reason for so doing is somewhat more an interest in the detail, and in

---

in the United States (1961), Table A-1, provides annual GNP estimates that incorporate Kuznets' annual data.

[4] Gainsbrugh's work appeared in William Lough, *High-Level Consumption* (1935), Appendices A and C. J. Frederick Dewhurst, *America's Needs and Resources, A New Survey* (1955), pp. 965ff. Harold Barger, *Outlay and Income in the United States, 1921–1938* (1942), pp. 226–229.

[5] The well-known studies by Kendrick, Knowles, Brown, DeCani, David and van de Klundert, Massell, and many others utilize input measures primarily from Kendrick's estimates. These estimates rely heavily, for services, on preliminary estimates by the writer, later revised in *Manpower in Economic Growth.*

the relating of improved comparability between GNP inputs and GNP output totals, than in the service total per se. It is to be noted, however, that the service totals implicit in the Kuznets GNP figures—on which, of course, Kendrick's and all other GNP estimates basically rest—are of a different character from the other components. For the commodity detail Kuznets develops the estimates with enormous detail, working from detailed production figures, and adding transport and distribution margins with almost equal detail. For consumer services alone, his totals rest almost wholly on the findings of assorted surveys of consumer expenditures.[6]

I

Present Versus Prior Estimates

The contrasts between the present and earlier estimates of services appear in Table 5. Although Kuznets actually provides only 5-year moving average figures for the earlier years, it is clear that the change from 1900, the earliest year, to 1929 is much the same in his series and the present one. Similarly, the changes to 1929 shown by Lough and Barger from the first years in their series (1909 and 1921, respectively) are also much the same as in the present series. That result is reasonably consoling.

When we look at shorter-term movements, however, more obvious contrasts appear. Such comparisons cannot be made before the 1920's, since no prior estimator offered estimates of year-to-year change in services before then. However, as Table 6 reports, the differences in the 1920's are apparent. Most striking is undoubtedly the very marked rises that Kuznets shows from prosperity to recession in 1920–1921, 1923–1924. We show very much more modest gains in both these years. For 1924–1925 and 1925–1926 we also show much more modest changes than does Kuz-

[6] Compare the description in Simon Kuznets, *National Product Since 1869* (1946), Part III.

nets. Barger's changes for the years 1923–1926 are also far smaller than Kuznets', much more like ours. (In 1924–1925 Kuznets' variant III actually shows a sharp decline. Neither our series nor Barger's reports such a drop. In general our series reports smaller year-to-year changes during the 1920's than does Kuznets. Barger's year-to-year changes are also generally smaller. The differences in year-to-year movement between the Kendrick-Kuznets and the present series can be localized:

Direction of Yearly Change— Present Versus Kendrick–Kuznets Estimates

	Same	Different
1900–1919	17	2
1919–1929	6	3

It is obvious that the yearly changes conform closely before 1919, whereas in the decade of the 1920's a sharper degree of inconsistency appears. In turn, the inconsistencies are virtually all associated with business cycle changes. In the early period growth trends prevent 1907–1908 and 1914–1915 declines in the present series, but not in Kendrick-Kuznets. In the 1920's roughly the reverse occurs, with the present estimate reporting declines in the years of cycle downturn, whereas Kuznets shows continued current dollar growth.

The greater volatility of Kuznets' series during the 1920's may arise from the fact that services variant III is derived as a residual by subtracting much larger totals from each other.[7] Hence, although he shows a marked decline in the flow of goods, the computation of services as a residual means that the latter estimate must take up the resultant of various errors and incomparabilities. Since the Kuznets series are uniformly shown as primarily a make-weight in filling out an estimate of gross national product, no particu-

---

[7] *Capital in the American Economy*, p. 489, note 4.

lar problem arises, for they contribute to the solid overall estimate. For separate study, however, our requirements are different. And the changes from 1920–1921 and the others noted above seem less satisfactory than do our direct estimates.

So far as comparison with the Lough estimates is concerned, we show a smaller rate of increase, 1919–1929. That in turn derives from the fact that we show a fairly steady decline in the rate of increase over each biennium from 1919–1921 to 1927–1929—whereas Lough shows no particular trend.

It may be possible to assert that the present estimates are better in a particular instance because, e.g., our judgment of expenditure changes from 1919–1921 suggests a decline in current dollar spending for rent, while other services must have declined and none risen. But for the most part, a judgment on the present series must turn on a comparison of its method of estimate with those of others. Our changes are closest to those shown by Barger, who is fairly specific about his procedures for each component. For some of the earlier estimates no benchmarks whatever were established for component series, so that there is no assurance that the estimate for, say, 1909 is reasonable as compared with the 1929 figures. For some estimates no detail is available, but ratios to a larger expenditure component were used—precluding any market adjustment in which consumers respond to income and relative price changes. And for some components of estimate there is no explanation that can now be gotten as to method of computation.

II

Major Trends, 1900–1970

The greatest changes in the allocation of the consumers' service dollar during the first three-quarters of the 20th century were the following:

Increases: 1900–1970

Hospitals	+5.8%
Telephone	+3.4
Electricity	+3.4
Auto repair	+3.3
Private education	+2.0
Recreation	+1.6

Decreases: 1900–1970

Public transport	−6.6%
Domestic service	−5.8
Housing	−5.2
Care of clothes	−3.2
Funerals	−2.5
Religion, welfare	−2.1

The odd constellation of growth and decline items testifies to no single change in consumer desires, needs, incomes, or velleities. Nor does it testify to omnipotence of advertising, or relative prices. Each of these leading changes has its separate, barely probable, rationale.

Hospitals

The massive increase of consumer spending on hospitals occurred largely after 1940: from 1900 to 1930 the hospital share in the service dollar rose by only 1.1 percent percentage points. The 1940–1970 rise, however, was 4.1 percent points. Several forces were at work.

Hospital Expenditures: 1900–1970

	(1)	(2)	(3)
	Share of Consumers Service Dollar	Number of Midwives (000)	Hospital Expense per Patient Day
1900–1930	+1.1%	+41	+$ 4
1940–1970	+4.1	−46	+ 65

[8] Sources: (1) from Table 1. (2) The 1900 Census, *Occupations*, p. 7, reported under 6 thousand midwives in 1900. Although the 1930 Census provides insufficient detail, an estimate of 47,000 for that date is taken from Louis Reed, *Midwives, Chiropodists and Optometrists*, Abstract of Publication No. 15 of the Committee on the Costs of

Hospital expenditures increased chiefly because of (a) more admissions and (b) higher rates per patient day. (Declining lengths of patient stay tended to offset such increases.)

The number of midwives is a crude indicator of trends in hospital versus home delivery of babies. The rise to 1930 and the decline (to less than 1,000) by 1970 marks this shift.[9] The proportion of all births in hospitals ran something like the following:[10]

1900	5%
1940	51
1960	97
1968	98

In addition to obstetrics, the admission of youngsters for tonsillectomies represented a wide expansion in hospital use.[11]

Medical Care (1932), p. 3; 1960 Census, *Occupation by Industry*, p. 136, reports under 1,000. (3) An average of $1.25 a day for 1900 is estimated from data for selected hospitals in Boston, New York, Philadelphia, and Chicago as presented in John S. Billings and H. M. Hurd, *Hospitals, Dispensaries and Nursing* (1894), p. 125, and 55th Congress 2nd Session, H. R. Report No. 776, *Joint Select Committee . . . Charities and Reformatory Institutions* (1898), Part II, p. 61. For 1970 the average of $70 is from the 1971 *Statistical Abstract*, p. 71 (for non-federal short term). The 1923 level of $3.96 per day is implicit in the U.S. Census, *Hospitals and Dispensaries, 1923*, pp. 9, 19. We arbitrarily take $5 for 1930.

[9] Reed, *op.cit.*, estimates that, around 1930, 15% of births were attended by midwives. Given the data shown below, it would appear that perhaps a third were attended by family and neighbors.

[10] No data are available for 1900. But BLS Bulletin 357, p. 453, shows only 10.7% of all families spending for hospital bills as late as 1918. Since the BLS survey group was relatively high income, and since all other admissions are also included, the proportion of births 18 years earlier could hardly have been much above 5%, if that. For 1940ff. data appear in the 1971 *Statistical Abstract*, pp. 48, 49.

[11] A study of half a million patients discharged in 1960 indicated 71 thousand deliveries, 36 thousand tonsillectomies. No other cause

The increased expense per patient day is notable in column 3 above. Yet, despite increases in wage rates and costs, hospital rates hardly rose at all over the first third of the 20th century—at least by comparison with the rise since 1940. Contributing to the recent rise were dramatic increases in medication, laboratory procedures, X-rays.[12] (To some extent, of course, such intensified procedures helped shorten patient stays, and hence tended to reduce expenditures.)

A second force was undoubtedly the expansion of prepaid medical care—via union agreements, Blue Cross, Medicare, etc. (Indeed a study of hospital admissions surveyed the role of 11 factors that pushed hospital costs up. The single most potent force was the development of such systems.

Telephone

The extension of loquaciousness that the phone made possible is well known:[13]

---

accounted for as much as 10 thousand patients. Cf. American Medical Association, *Report of the Commission on the Cost of Medical Care*, Vol. I (1964), p. 142.

[12] Between 1946 and 1961 drug costs rose nearly fourfold, laboratory costs nearly twofold, while room and board gained by 168%. (AMA, *ibid.*, p. 145.) But the medical procedures differed. For example, in 1961 on the average 30% more different generic drugs were given patients than in 1946, the average number of laboratory procedures more than doubled, and the number of x-ray procedures almost tripled. (*Ibid.*, p. 148.)

[13] 1900, 1932: see text selection below on telephones. 1965: U.S. *Statistical Abstract, 1968, p.* 500. The average local phone bill used for 1970 is that given for 2 person (or larger) families in the BLS *Survey of Consumer Expenditures, 1960–61, Supplement* 3, Part A, p. 144. The proportion of households with phones in 1965 was 81%, and that with phone "service" was 85%. (1968 *Statistical Abstract*, pp. 497, 500.) The 1970 Census, *General Housing Characteristics, U.S. Summary*, HC(1)-A1, pp. 1–16, gives data indicating 86.9% of housing units had phones "available." We add to 81%, then, 86.9% minus 85%.

	Percent of Residences with Telephones	Average Monthly Phone Bill (local)
1900	5%	$16
1932	36	—
1970	83	(6)

Electricity

The proportion of American homes with electricity rose as follows:[14]

1900	3%
1930	68
1940	79
1970	99

And within each home the corollary set of appliances to use electricity is noteworthy. Light in darkness may have been enough for the 3 percent of American families that enjoyed electricity in 1900. By 1970 the extent and variety of electrically driven equipment was striking, if not astounding.[15]

Percent of Households Owning

TV—black and white	77%
TV—color	38
Refrigerator	83
Washing machine	70
Vacuum cleaners	92

Beyond ownership, of course, was use: perhaps 95 percent of households used washing machines in their dwellings even though only 70 percent owned them.[16] The decline

[14] Estimates for 1900 from text, below. Data for 1930 and 1940 from *Historical Statistics*, II, p. 510. The same source shows 98.8% by 1956; we therefore use an arbitrary 99% for 1970.

[15] U.S. Census Bureau, Current Population Reports Series, P-65, No. 33, *Special Report on Household Ownership* . . . p. 8, for all items but vacuum cleaners, the latter from the 1968 *Statistical Abstract*, p. 710.

[16] Use data from the *Abstract, idem.*

in the monthly rate per kilowatt hour, reflecting a great advance in the productivity of the electric power industry, was swamped by the increased usage. (It is, of course, a fair assumption that the declining price induced wider usage—but shifts in demand curves as product after product changed consumer preferences makes it difficult to know that elasticity response.)

Auto Repair

Perhaps the role of the automobile in American life is so obviously central that it may be surprising that the share of the consumers' service dollar did no more than rise from virtually nothing in 1900 to over 3 percent by 1970.[17]

	(1) Passenger Car Registrations (000)	(2) Value of Stock of Cars ($ billions)	(3) Auto Repairs, Parking, etc. ($ millions)
1900	8	*	$8
1970	89,861	$90	8,672

*less than 1 billion.

Private Education

Three separate worlds coexisted under the rubric of private education in 1900: the parochial schools of immigrants newly arrived in the big cities of the Atlantic seaboard, the private colleges for muscular scions of the elite, and the scattering of genteel ladies who taught the fine accomplishments of Czerny and Burne-Jones to reluctant children exposed to the finer things of life. As the virtues inhering in these activities were revalued, and substitute activities

[17] Registrations: *Statistical Abstract, 1971*, p. 534. Includes taxes. Value of stock: The annual sales of new cars, as recorded in the national income accounts, were depreciated at a double declining balance rate of 25%, using the rate adopted by the FRB flow of funds unit. The estimate is for December 31, 1968. Auto repairs: Table 1, infra.

found, their share in their parents' expenditures changed largely.

About 18 percent of all urban pupils (and presumably about the same in expenditures) were in private schools.[18] By 1930 that proportion was cut in half.[19] The earlier proportion represented both the larger role of parochial schools in the big cities, but also (since the proportions were much the same) the role of private schools in smaller cities as the public school system was still developing its reach. By 1970 the consumers' share of elementary and secondary education costs was 5.8 percent.[20] Hence a rough indication of the share of elementary and secondary education paid for by Americans as consumers (rather than as taxpayers) ran

1900	18%
1930	9
1970	6

But because of the great expansion in buildings and facilities construed as necessary for such education, the share of the consumers' dollar rose over the same period, from $7/10$ ths of 1 percent in 1900 to 7.2 percent by 1970. The cries of satisfaction that such an increased commitment of resources produced are either rare or not widely reported.

A similar statement may be made for college education. The share of the consumers' service dollar devoted to educating the young in colleges runs about 15 percent in

[18] Enrollment and other data for 1900 from *Report of the Commissioner of Education . . . 1900–1901*, Vol. 2 (1902), p. 1538, for cities over 8,000 with a count for smaller individual cities made from pp. 1596–1610.

[19] *Biennial Survey of Education, 1928–1930*, Vol. II, p. 11, gives data on expenditures, indicating 9%. No data on attendance are available. By 1932 the national accounts data report $158 millions for private elementary and secondary education, while public expenditures for local education ran to $2,042. OBE, *National Income and Product Accounts of the United States, 1929–1965*, p. 46, and *Historical Statistics of the U.S.*, II, p. 727.

[20] Data from *Survey of Current Business, July* 1971, pp. 24, 30.

1970—compared to about ⅓ of 1 percent in 1900. The expansion of resources devoted to such activities is notable. Neither the parents nor the children give evidence (beyond their financial commitment) of either great or continuing satisfaction with the expenditure. But in this generally competitive market one must assume consumer sovereignty at work, without a clear guide, however, as to whether the parents or the children are in fact the consumers.

The final major rise, for "other education," reflects the battery of instruction in everything from sensitivity testing to tatting. In 1900, of course, the total went overwhelmingly, and in innumerable front parlors, for instruction on the piano and violin. Instruction in driving automobiles and manipulating electric guitars mars the latter decades. (Expanding education and research by foundations accounts for a small portion of the more recent gains.)[21]

THE declines in the share of the service dollar are of two kinds, those which are more obvious and those which are more unexpected. The decline for urban public transportation, in response to the rise of the private automobile, is well known, and accounts for the declining share of public transport. (Yet it is well to note that 1970 employment in public transport was about at 1900 levels.[22]

The overwhelming decline for domestic service is largely a supply phenomenon. Despite the widened use of appli-

---

[21] The national income accounts include foundation expenditures on research and education under this rubric. In 1929 that total came to $79 million, more than tripling—to $281 million—by 1970. Cf. William H. Shaw in *Survey of Current Business* (June 1944), p. 6, and 1971 *Statistical Abstract*, p. 330.

[22] U.S. Bureau of the Census, *Street and Electric Railways*, 1902 (1905), p. 95, indicates that street and interurban railways averaged about 146 thousand employees in 1902. In 1969 the local transit industry averaged 141 thousand employees. (*1971 Statistical Abstract*, p. 543.) There were, in addition, about as many additional employees in school bus and taxicab operation. Cf. for example, U.S. Census, *County Business Patterns*, 1964, pp. 1–13.

ances, the number of domestic servants rose from 1900 to 1930.[23]

	Number of Households (Millions)	Number of Domestics (Millions)	Domestics per 100 Households
1900	15,964	1,800	11.3
1910	20,256	2,090	10.3
1930	29,905	2,270	7.6
1940	34,949	2,300	6.6
1960	53,021	2,489	4.7
1970	63,417	2,115	3.3

The 1900–1910 rise in servants per household was marked, but the flow of immigrants—its major source—was largely stopped after 1914. And the (presumably) increased supply during the depression failed to find any increase in quantity demanded. The absolute decline in domestic servants after 1960, despite rising wage rates and a vigorous market for services of all kinds, points to a supply shift—linked to the rising alternative incomes for domestic servants and, perhaps, the impact of the civil rights changes of the 1960's.

The decline in the share for care of clothing and for the care of souls represent a shift in activities from services purchased by consumers to other modes of production. Thus the trend of the numbers gainfully employed ran[24]

[23] Households: 1900–1940 from *Historical Statistics*, II, p. 16. The (slightly non-comparable) 1970 figure is from the *1971 Statistical Abstract*, p. 38. The number of domestic servants thru 1940 is from *Manpower*, p. 513, with the 1970 figure from the *Survey of Current Business* (July 1971), p. 35.

[24] Clergymen: 1900 Census, *Occupations*, p. 7; David Kaplan and M. Claire Casey, *Occupational Trends in the United States, 1900 to 1950*, p. 10. The 1971 *Statistical Abstract*, p. 42, reports clergymen with charges at varying recent dates, which we round slightly in the light of the 1960 Census count of 200 thousand. Social and welfare workers: 1900. Kaplan and Casey give 114 thousand for this group plus clergymen and we deduct our estimate of clergymen. (The 1910 Census explicitly shows 1 thousand religious and charity workers.) 1930 Census, *Occupations*, p. 576. 1940 Census, *Occupations*, Table 19; 1960 Census, *Occupations*, Table 2, extrapolated by the ratio of social workers in state employment reported there to the number

	Clergymen (000)	Social and Welfare Workers (000)
1900	112	2
1930	149	29
1940	171	70
1970	(220)	130

The steady increase in the share of those concerned with wordly welfare rather than eternal (and wordly) is marked, and clearly reflects changing judgments about the appropriate use of incomes to change individual habits.

The decline in care of clothing reflects a rise in affluence and change in habits—from "repair" to "replace."[25]

	Shoemakers (Not in Factory) (000)	Dressmakers, Milliners and Tailors (000)
1900	67	666
1930	76	373
1940	68	261
1960	36	104

As the cost of labor per unit of output in service rose, while that in factories either declined or rose less, the advantage of repairing old commodities versus buying new ones shifted dramatically. (Undoubtedly part of the differential cost shift was the lack of inflow into such service employ-

---

in state employment in 1967, as reported in the 1971 *Statistical Abstract*, p. 513.

[25] Shoemakers: 1930 and 1940 from Kaplan and Casey, p. 12; 1960 from Table 2, 1960 Census, *Occupations*. For 1900 the Kaplan-Casey estimate transcribes the Census, which is too high. The adjustment is discussed on p. 467 of *Manpower*, and gives a 1900 figure of 67 thousand.

Dressmakers, etc.: 1900 and 1930 data derived as described in *Manpower*, pp. 466–467. 1940: 187 thousand dressmakers and milliners not in factory, from p. 13 Kaplan and Casey, plus 74 thousand male tailors not in factories, from Table 19 of 1940, *Occupational Characteristics*. (The number of female tailors in 1940 was only 17 thousand, and was assumed to be all in factories.)

ment.) About 60 percent of all shoemakers in 1930 were foreign-born, as were tailors.[26] It seems likely that the same factors that led to a rising supply price and declining market for domestic service were at work in these occupations as well.

Another striking decline is that for the share of the consumers' dollar going for funerals. Despite an extensive and hectic literature on the "American Way of Death," these data suggest a different reading. Apparently Americans lavish a smaller portion of their increased incomes on death, and the dead, than their parents did in 1900. There were about 50% more deaths in 1970 than in 1900.[27] Yet the share of the consumers' dollar going for funerals had fallen slightly. The earlier data on the share of the consumers' dollar going for medical care and hospitals—which necessarily does not include a heavy commitment of tax funds for such purposes—suggests Americans are committing more to the retention of life than to the dramatic laying away of those who have left it.

The decline for farm housing is a clear reflection of the urbanization of the U.S., and there is no need to trace the multiplicity of other changes indicated by these series on service expenditures. Those using them for particular analyses will undoubtedly find more meanings and interpretations in them.

III

Methods of Estimate

We outline below estimating procedures used for each component series in Table 1. The size of the item in 1900 (in millions of dollars) appears in parentheses after the heading.

[26] 1930 Census, *Occupations*, pp. 77–78. Under 15% of milliners were. Unfortunately, no later data crossing nativity by occupation are available.

[27] Death rate data for the registration area linked to those for the U.S., using data from *Historical Statistics*, II, pp. 12, 22, 26, 27, and the *1971 Statistical Abstract*, p. 10.

Clothing, Accessories and Jewelry—Services ($1,264)

(1) A benchmark for 1900 is available for all relevant and important industries (but laundries) since the Census of Manufactures in that year covered boot and shoe repairing, dressmaking, custom work and repair of men's clothing, cleaning and dyeing, and watch repairing.[28] For laundries a combination of occupation and manufactures Census data was used. Average sales per person engaged in steam laundries in 1909 can be computed from the Census.[29] This figure was extrapolated to 1900 by the 1900–1909 change in average annual earnings per full-time equivalent employee in personal service.[30] The average was then multiplied by the number of employees of steam laundries and the number of male gainful workers in hand laundries.[31] (Female laundresses not in steam laundries were included in the domestic service group.)

Personal Care Services ($525)

Prior estimates of employment in personal services, underlying published series, multiplied by average full-time earnings in personal service, were used as a payroll index to extrapolate the 1929 OBE benchmark.[32]

[28] 1900 Census, *Manufactures*, Part 1, p. 53.

[29] 1910 Census, *Manufactures*, x, p. 887.

[30] *Manpower*, p. 526, gives the earnings figures used.

[31] 1900 Census, *Occupations*, p. 7. The occupation by nativity data for 1900 indicate that most male launderers not in steam laundries were Chinese, and we assume that none worked in steam laundries or domestic service.

[32] Average earnings form *Manpower*, p. 526. The employment totals for service, shown on pp. 516–518, include series for employment in hand trades, both wage earners and self-employed. As described in *Manpower*, pp. 467–468, these link to decennial benchmarks for the number of barbers, hairdressers, and manicurists. Ratios of all gainful workers in these occupations to total hand trades at each Census date were interpolated, applied to the underlying hand trades employment series to give the required personal care employment series.

Rent

OBE space rent was estimated as the sum of owner and tenant rent.

Owner Net Rent

Space rent was estimated as the sum of (I) net rent and (II) shelter cost.

I. Net rent was the OBE 1929 total[33] extrapolated by Juster's series for imputed return of owners residences.[34]

II. Shelter costs were an extrapolation of the OBE 1929 figure by an owners' cost ratio series multiplied by the value of the stock of non-farm owner occupied housing plus land. The cost series was the sum of the 1929 OBE figures for the following items, each extrapolated by the series noted.

(1) Depreciation—Grebler's estimates for current dollar depreciation of non-farm housing.[35]

(2) Imputed interest on equity—an interest series estimated as the product of annual average interest rates times the value of residential wealth in each year.[36]

(3) Maintenance—Grebler's estimates of expenditures for additions to, and alterations of, housekeeping dwelling units.[37]

---

[33] References to the OBE 1929 total, including expense detail, are to the set of figures in the *Survey of Current Business* for June 1953, pp. 21–22.

[34] F. Thomas Juster, *Household Capital Formation and Financing, 1897–1962* (1966), pp. 136–137, col. 1. Juster took a flat 6% of the value of housing plus land minus outstanding mortgage debt.

[35] Leo Grebler et al., *Capital Formation in Residential Real Estate* (1956), p. 384, col. 1.

[36] The interest rate series is an average of (a) rates in the Bronx, (b) in St. Louis and (c) average bond yield as estimated by Frederick Macaulay. These series appear in Grebler, *op.cit.*, pp. 496–497. The Chicago series was ignored because of its obvious insensitivity. Values of residential wealth from Grebler, *op.cit.*, p. 360, col. 5.

[37] *Ibid.*, pp. 336, 363.

(4) Taxes—an index of local government revenues, most of which, of course, are from taxes on property.[38]

(5) Insurance and miscellaneous costs—the trend of fire losses on dwellings was used as a proxy for the trend of property insurance premia on owner occupied residences.[39]

Tenant Space Rent

Benchmarks for 1900 and 1930 were estimated; an interpolating series was then used to interpolate between the 1900 and the 1930 figure; the resultant series was then used to extrapolate 1929 OBE figure. The 1900 benchmark was derived by taking the average rent paid in each state according to the 1900–1901 cost of living survey by the Commissioner of Labor.[40] The rent averages were based on a sample of 25,440 reporting families. It was assumed that the average for each state was satisfactory, but that the appropriate weights for the U.S. average were the total number of non-farm families in each state. Those counts were derived from data on marital status of the labor force in 1900.[41] The resultant U.S. average rent of $115 was then multiplied by the number of non-farm rented dwellings in 1900.[42]

A review of various data used explicitly and implicitly by W. I. King, and of the Kuznets decadal averages based on field survey data (including portions of the Commissioner's survey) was made to determine whether the 1900 rent average seemed markedly out of line. We concluded that a survey of 25,440 families on their rent was obviously to be preferred to other less comprehensive and direct reports. For rent is an item for which field surveys can do

[38] The revenue index was based on Raymond Goldsmith, *A Study of Saving in the United States* (1955), Vol. 1, p. 1047, Col. 2.

[39] Goldsmith, *ibid.*, p. 669, col. 4.

[40] U.S. Commissioner of Labor, Eighteenth Annual Report, *Cost of Living and Retail Prices of Food* (1904), p. 366.

[41] The number of married males engaged in all pursuits, by state, minus those engaged in agricultural pursuits, was taken from the 1900 Census, *Occupations*, Table 41.

[42] *Historical Statistics*, Vol. 2, p. 395.

reasonably well, particularly in the days before rent included a range of facilities.

The 1930 benchmark was derived from the Census data.[43]

These 1900 and 1929 benchmarks were then interpolated by a rent trend index. That index was computed as the product of (a) the BLS rent index times (b) a series for wealth in rental dwellings (in constant dollars). The rent index was thus applied to the constant dollar stock of rental dwellings, thereby allowing both for an upward drift in the quantum of the real stock as well as in the rental charge per constant unit.[44]

Farm Housing ($913)

The rental value of farm houses is available from the U.S. Department of Agriculture estimates for 1910–1929.[45] A comparable 1900 estimate has been made by Towne and Rasmussen, also of the USDA.[46] Since the basic method of estimates by the USDA assumes that the bulk of imputed value arises in the form of labor costs (original and repairs), we use an average annual earnings series for farm laborers to interpolate between 1900 and 1910.[47]

[43] 1930 Census, *Families*, Vol. VI, p. 39. The Census average for urban dwellings was assumed as most comparable with the Commissioner's average. When multiplied by the count of non-farm dwellings, the result gives aggregate rents as of March 1930. The figure was adopted for 1929 as well on the assumption that the rental values had shifted little by March 1930. In fact, the figure thus derived was within 10% of the OBE space rental figure.

[44] Grebler, p. 360, col. 5, gives current value of residential wealth, from which we deduct Juster's estimates (*op.cit.*, p. 127, col. 1) for the owner occupied component.

The BLS index, from *Historical Statistics*, II: 125, was extrapolated to 1900 by Albert Rees, *Real Wages in Manufacturing* (1961), p. 74.

[45] These data, underlying published USDA income detail, were kindly provided by Dr. Mardy Myers of the USDA Economic Research Service, March 1971.

[46] In Conference on Research in Income and Wealth, *Trends in the American Economy in the Nineteenth Century* (1957), p. 265.

[47] The earnings series is from *Manpower*, p. 525. Its ratio to gross

Other Housing ($249)

This item includes hotels, motels, schools, and institutions. For the pre-1929 period the bulk of expenditure would have been for hotels, and we extrapolate by a series for payrolls in hotels and boarding houses. The estimates of employment and average full-time earnings utilized to estimate payrolls were those underlying the service estimates in *Manpower in Economic Growth*.[48]

Lighting

At the turn of the century America's homes were lit as follows:

American Homes in 1900
by Primary Lighting Source
(millions)

Kerosene and coal oil	14.2
Electricity	0.5
Gas	1.5

Consumers spent some $77 millions for kerosene (according to Shaw's estimate). Virtually all 10 million farm families as well as most city folk used kerosene lamps. About $56 million was spent for gas, about $15 million for electricity. The "gas light era" proves to be a fairly accurate image of only a few cities.

---

farm rentals in 1900 and 1910 was computed, interpolated. The interpolated values were then multiplied by the earnings series. Because estimates of number of farms in this early period are largely linear interpolations, there was no point in allowing for changes in the count of farms, nor in utilizing depreciation figures, which also rest on such interpolations.

[48] Pp. 463–464, 494–496. The earnings estimate was that of the OBE for hotels in 1929, extrapolated by the trend in personal service earnings.

Gas

A 1900 benchmark for consumer expenditure on gas was established from Census of Manufactures data on gas production in the following way. A 1919 figure for domestic consumption (i.e., exclusive of industrial use) is derived by Gould from American Gas Association estimates and the Census of Manufactures.[49] For 1899–1919 total production figures are available, and quite reliable. We extrapolate domestic usage by subtracting industrial from that total. Examination of the fuel consumption data given in the 1914 and 1919 Census indicates that most industrial gas usage was concentrated in certain states where a few industries (e.g., carbon black) were located.[50] By excluding these few states from the U.S. total, therefore, we derive a series that can be used to extrapolate the 1919 domestic usage total back to 1899. When multiplied by the Census data on value per 1,000 cubic feet, the resultant estimates can be used to extrapolate a 1919 benchmark.[51] Similar data from the Census fill out the intervening years.[52]

Domestic users averaged about 29,000 cubic feet of gas consumption in both 1929 and 1919.[53] We estimate 26,500

[49] Jacob M. Gould, *Output and Productivity in the Electric and Gas Utilities, 1899–1942* (1946), p. 84. That figure includes home heating, but the implicit average per consumer of 24,718 cubic feet suggests it is not too high for the families who used gas as their primary illuminant.

[50] 1920 Census, x, p. 718, and viii, pp. 140–141.

[51] 1900 Census, *Manufactures*, Part iv, p. 712, and 1920 Census, *Manufactures*, Vol. x, p. 716. We exclude data for Ohio and Pennsylvania from the U.S. 1899 total to make certain that the figures exclude gas sold to industrial users. (The 1919 table shows such low 1919 totals for West Virginia, Oklahoma, and Louisiana as to imply that industrial consumption was totally excluded—presumably because by 1919 it was produced by the user rather than bought in any volume.)

[52] 1910 Census, *Manufactures*, Vol. x, p. 647.

[53] 1929 Census, *Manufactures*, p. 758. 1919 Census, Vol. x, p. 724. For 1919 we relate the Census figure on number of consumers to

in 1900, when gas heaters and stoves had not been widely introduced. That figure rests on three averages for major cities:[54]

Philadelphia in 1894	26,500 feet
Chicago in 1900	24,750
Cincinnati in 1890	35,130

A figure of 26,500 is also not inconsistent with other data for the industry.[55]

Dividing an average of 26,500 feet per family using gas into the 40.9 billion cubic feet of domestic gas usage estimated above implies that 1,543,000 families used gas in their homes in the Census year 1899–1900, or say 1.6 million in 1900. New York City consumed 27 percent of all gas sold in 1899, while Chicago, Philadelphia, and St. Louis consumed about the same amount.[56] With something like half the U.S. gas consumers in these four cities, that means there were only about ¾ of a million families in all the rest of the U.S. who relied on gas. In 1890 the total number of gas consumers was under 700,000.[57] The number of household consumers was necessarily a smaller number.

Gould's (p. 84) figure on consumption, giving an average of 25 thousand feet.

[54] Data for Chicago computed from the 1900 *Annual Report* of the Peoples Gas Light Company of that city, a copy of which was kindly provided by President McAllister of the company in 1971. Data for the other cities are from Chauncy Depew, *One Hundred Years of American Commerce* (1895), Vol. 1, pp. 296, 297. Since the number of users was relatively small in Cincinnati, we assumed that usage outside the 4 major gas using cities was disproportionately by the well-to-do, leading to such high averages.

[55] Some 5.2 million stoves and heaters were connected in 1914, and 3.6 million in 1909 (1920 Census, x, p. 724). The number of Welsbach mantles in use in 1895 was 1 million, with a forecast of 1.5 million sales for the year ending June 30, 1896 (Depew, *op.cit.*, p. 299).

[56] 1900 Census, *Manufactures*, x, Part IV, p. 713.

[57] 1890 Census of *Manufactures*, Part III, pp. 723–725. The number of consumers was 699,323—including places of business.

Electricity ($616)

The proportion of dwelling units with residential service is estimated as follows:[58]

1907	8
1912	16
1920	35
1930	68

Because of the speed with which electricity was adopted, no mere extrapolation of the 1907 proportion to 1900 was felt to be acceptable. Instead, a 1900 benchmark estimate of 3.1 percent was made on the basis of the 1902–1907–1912 trend in the number of meters.[59] (The 1902 Census of Electrical Industries indicates that "a rough assumption . . . might be made that each meter represented a customer."[60] However, because of the transition away from a period in which numbers of customers paid a flat rate, rather than being metered, we did not use the number of meters as a direct estimate for the number of consumers.)

The consumption of electricity per dwelling unit, for those with service, averaged 324 kwh in 1912.[61] But the

[58] U.S. Census, *Historical Statistics*, ii, p. 510.

[59] In 1907 and 1912 the ratio of (a) dwelling units with residential service to (b) the number of customer's meters came to about 90%. Cf. U.S. Census, *Central Electric Light and Power Stations and Street and Electric Railways . . . 1912* (1915), p. 57, for an estimate of meters. The estimate of families derives from the U.S. Census, *Historical Statistics*, ii, pp. 510, 515. The number thus estimated for families in 1900 with residential service (500,000) proves to be 3.1% of all families—or closely in line with what a simple extrapolation of rates of change would have indicated.

[60] U.S. Census, *Central Electric Light and Power Stations, 1902* (1905), p. 74. The report stipulates "Leaving arc lighting patrons out of consideration." Since the latter were municipalities (street lighting), commercial and industrial establishments, that exclusion is desirable for our purposes.

[61] Census, *Central Electric Power, 1912*, p. 170, provided data based on reports for 30 cities.

rising popularity of electricity as lamp prices and electric rates declined makes it reasonable to assume that 1900 must have been markedly less. We estimate that figure on the basis of the New York City average, running at 213 in 1908, down to 181 in 1912 as smaller consumers came into the market.[62] On the assumption that a smaller consumption level characterized the country as a whole—than NYC—and that between 1900 and 1912 lower rates have increased usage, we adopt a 150 kwh average for dwelling units only (the above figures necessarily include commercial usage) in 1900. At a residential rate of 20¢ per kwh, a typical dwelling unit bill in 1900 would have come to $30.[63]

Water and Refuse Collection ($278)

Benchmarks for 1902 and 1929 were interpolated by the sum of two expenditure series—(a) for water and (b) for refuse collection.

(1) Revenue receipts from earnings of city water systems are available for cities over 30,000 in population for most of the period from 1902 through 1929, and require only minor adjustment.[64] The use of the reported number of cities in each year led to a steady expansion on the total, presumed to be a reasonable reflection of the extension of plumbing usage and water supply in urban areas generally.

[62] *Census . . . 1912*, p. 165.

[63] The 20¢ rate is an extrapolation of the 10.9¢ rate for the 1907 monthly usage of 25 kwh per hour or less by the percentage change in the rates charged all large users of electricity, the latter dropping from 16.2 to 10.5 cents between 1902 and 1917. Data from *Historical Statistics*, ɪɪ, p. 510.

[64] U.S. Bureau of the Census, *Financial Statistics of Cities*, volumes for individual years 1902 through 1929, give data on "receipts from revenues of public service enterprises." The 1921 figure had to be adjusted since it omitted Cleveland, Detroit, Newark, and Baltimore—cities included in both 1919 and 1923. This was done by taking changes for the identical group of cities in the larger-size intervals, ɪ and ɪɪ.

(2) Refuse disposal expenses are provided for the same years in the 1902–1929 period. However an adjustment of the 1911–1919 reported data was necessary to exclude the expenses of street cleaning, included under the general rubric of "refuse disposal" for those years.[65]

(3) Water and refuse totals for the years 1904–1907, 1913–1914, 1920, and 1922 were interpolated from a curve fitted to data for the other years 1902–1929.

(4) The 1929 benchmark was the OBE total. The 1902 benchmark was estimated from the 1902 Census reports on *Statistics of Cities*, which enables us to estimate per-capita expenditures for water, in separate city size groups, as follows:[66]

Cities with Population	Receipts of Municipal Water Works (per cap.)
over 300,000	$2.39
100,000–300,000	2.10
50,000–100,000	2.47
25,000– 50,000	1.88
8,000– 25,000	2.11

For cities and towns under 8,000 we assumed the same $2.11 average as in the 8,000 to 25,000 size group. The resultant aggregate for this group is $11.8 million as compared with $10.0 million for the cities 8,000 to 25,000. This proportion is reasonably confirmed by the fact that total

[65] The ratio of refuse disposal alone to that for disposal plus street cleaning was computed in 1910 and 1923, then interpolated to provide a basis for computing intermediate years. The ratio rose from 30% in 1910 to 43% in 1923.

[66] U.S. Bureau of the Census, Bulletin 20, *Statistics of Cities Having a Population of Over 25,000, 1902 and 1903* (1905), pp. 65–67, 342–347, and Bulletin 45, *Statistics of Cities Having a Population of 8,000 to 25,000: 1902* (1906), Tables 1, 19. The reported Census totals for population in each size group were adjusted to exclude totals for cities not reporting on water receipts, generally because they relied on private systems. (Similar procedures and adjustments were applied to data for expenditures on refuse disposal.)

expenditures for sewers, drainage, and sanitation differed little between these groups.[67]

For rural areas the nearly universal reliance on pumped water as late as 1920 indicates that a zero total for 1902 is reasonable. (Expenditures on pumps, etc., is, of course, not a consumption but an investment expenditure.)

It is to be noted that these data cover expenditures for water by both home owners and tenants, consistent with the present treatment in the national income accounts. It is possible that the figure used as a 1900 benchmark for space rent may include some component covering cost of water. This, however, is uncertain. For example, rents for company housing provided by Pullman's Palace Car company did not include the cost of water, which was charged for separately. The same was true of Lowell tenements offered by the Merrimac Manufacturing Company, but not of mills in New Bedford and in Cumberland Mills, Maine.[68]

The $10 rate charged families by several of these mills (or included in the computation of the rent charge) forms some kind of confirmation of the $2.22 per urban resident estimate we arrive at above: multiplying that by an average family size of 4.6 persons gives an average of $10.21.[69]

Telephones

In estimating telephone expenditures, we begin from the difficult consideration that even as late as 1929 we have no solid expenditure benchmark: both Barger and Lough apply a simple 50–50 ratio as the ratio of consumer to total

[67] Aggregate expenditures for sewers, drainage, and sanitation for each size group appear in U.S. Census, *Wealth, Debt and Taxation— 1902* (1970), pp. 1009, 1013. Errors in the U.S. aggregate derived from estimating the under 8,000 group cannot be large: it accounts for 17% of the aggregate in our estimate.

[68] Eighth Special Report of the Commissioner of Labor, *The Housing of the Working People* (1895), pp. 331, 334, 325, 321.

[69] Average size of private families, from U.S. Census of Population, 1900, Part 2, p. clviii. To judge from the regional averages, an urban average would be much the same.

spending on telephone service.[70] We therefore estimate for benchmark dates the proportion of families with telephones, then estimate the average telephone expenditure for those families.

A

For 1927 and 1932, data on the percent of residences with telephones are available from the Census of Telephones.[71] For 1920 and 1930 the proportion for farm households with phones is reported by the Census of Agriculture, while the 1920 ratio for non-farm households is taken to be that reported by the 1918 BLS expenditure survey.[72]

For 1900 we rely on three categories of data.

(1) The 1902 Census of Telephones reports the number of telephones on rural lines (inclusive of both commercial, mutual and independent rural lines).[73] We take this number to measure the number of farm households with phones in 1902.

(2) A set of 1900 telephone books were sampled to give the proportion of residential to total phones, as indicated by individual phone listings.[74] The proportions ran as

[70] Lough begins from the very relevant fact that 58% of A. T. and T. phones at the end of 1929 were in residences (Lough, *op.cit.*, p. 272). However, the proportion of all telephones, as indicated below, was about 66%.

[71] Census, *Telephones and Telegraphs*, 1932, p. 25, and Census, *Telephones, 1927*, p. 6, and, for number of families, *Historical Statistics*, II, p. 15.

[72] U.S. 15th Census, *Agriculture*, IV, p. 533; BLS Bulletin 357, *Cost of Living in the United States* (1924), p. 455. The BLS figure, undoubtedly too high for wage earners, is reasonable for all urban families.

[73] U.S. Bureau of the Census, *Telephones and Telegraphs*, 1902, p. 24.

[74] The phone books were for listings as of March 1900 (Cincinnati and Buffalo), October 1899 (Chicago), June 1900 (NYC), April 1900 (St. Joseph). The phone books generally indicated after each name the business listing (e.g., "furniture," "saloon," "M.D.") or "residence." Fewer than 5% had no such designation. Judging from the

Buffalo	19.9%
Cincinnati	26.9
Chicago	27.2
Brooklyn	30.3
St. Joseph, Mo.	40.8

The median proportion would seem to be about 30 percent, the rate being somewhat higher in small towns, much lower (8.2 percent) in Manhattan, where the ratio of businesses to residences was relatively high. Moreover, the extent to which any area had telephones would be affected by the density of business, since businessmen, lawyers, and physicians were disproportionately among the first adopters, the returns to them from doing so being so evident and substantial. If one applied the 30 percent rate to the number of non-rural telephones, the number of urban residential phones would run to about 700,000.

(3) A reasonable approximation of urban phones may be indicated by the number of party line phones, net of rural ones.[75] This figure runs to 675,000. We consider the count of party line phones to be an appropriate indicator: the rates charged for regular phones put them out of reach of most non-business consumers. (For example, the charge for residential phones in Chicago was $100 a year in the years prior to 1906, a period when the median urban family income ran to about $600.)[76]

---

fact that a set of those in New York City without such designation were located in business areas, we assumed that these uncategorized names were for lawyers, agents, and other business listings. The sampling was systematic—thus for St. Joseph all names on pages 1, 3, 5, 7, 9, 11, 13, and 15, of the 16-page phone book, were tabulated. The number of entries reviewed ranged from 330 in Cincinnati and 341 in Buffalo, to 1,230 in Manhattan and the Bronx.

[75] The 1902 Census, p. 41, reports 886,152 party line stations, and, on p. 24, 211,221 rural phones, presumably all party line.

[76] *Professor Edward Bemis Report on the Investigation of the Chicago Telephone Company* (1908), p. 72. The 2-party rate was $75; 4-party, $60; and the business flat rate was $175.

For rural family usage of phones in 1900 we take the ratio of phones on rural lines in 1902 to the number of rural families. For urban families we take the encouraging similarity between the 675,000 count of party-line phones in urban areas and the 700,000 total indicated by our sample of phone usage in major cities to warrant the use of the former to measure the number of urban families. The ratio of that number to the number of urban families was then applied to the 1900 Census count of non-farm families.

B

To estimate the average phone bill in 1900 we rely on 1902 data on the average phone bill by type of system.[77]

mutual	$ 1.86
rural-commercial	16.31
urban-commercial	43.84

The above mutual receipts figure fails to measure the average phone bill (even when adjusted for assessments) since the bulk of the phones were located in urban areas. On the other hand, the figure for urban commercial consumers is dominated by business usage. We therefore take the $16.31 figure to be a suitable average for all consumers— which leads to an estimate of $14.4 millions or 20 percent of all phone revenues. As an indication that such an average is in fact not too low, despite the much larger average for urban commercial systems, we may refer to the $16.35 all residential average indicated by the BLS 1918 expenditure survey.[78] Intervening years were estimated by assuming steady growth in the share of consumer to total revenues, applying these proportions to an operating revenue series estimated for all telephone companies.[79]

[77] 1902 Census, pp. 20, 23.
[78] BLS Bulletin 357, p. 454.
[79] Benchmark estimates of revenues for the entire phone industry are given in the quinquennial Censuses of Telephones. These were interpolated by an index of all telephone company revenues. That

The above figures can be summarized as follows:

	Percent of Residences with Telephones			Consumer Expenditures for Telephones (billions)
	All	Farm	Urban	
1900	5%	3%	9%	$ 11
1920	31	39	28	208
1927	42			444
1932	36	34		553

Telegraphs ($13)

An implicit OBE 1929 benchmark was estimated, then extrapolated to 1916 by the operating revenues of the domestic telegraph industry, to 1900 by those of Western Union.[80]

Domestic Service ($1,716)

Prior estimates of employment in domestic service, and average full time equivalent earnings of domestic service were multiplied to give aggregate payrolls for domestic service.[81]

Household Operation—Other ($316)

This category, a hodgepodge of minor items, aggregates to a large enough total to require at least determining several benchmarks. These are briefly described below.

Property insurance. The percent of families purchasing property insurance in 1901 and 1918 is taken from the BLS expenditure surveys for those years, together with the aver-

---

index was computed by using all Bell system revenues (Census, *Historical Statistics* II, p. 481) raised by the ratio, in each year 1900–1920, of all phones to those in the Bell system.

[80] The 1929 OBE benchmark for telephones and telegraph expenditures in 1929, of $569, was split by the telephone/telegraph ratio indicated by earlier OBE estimates for 1929 (*Survey of Current Business*, October 1942) of $15.8 to $559. The data on telegraph revenues are from *Historical Statistics*, II, pp. 483, 485.

[81] These series were taken from the writer's *Manpower in Economic Growth*, pp. 513, 526. Their derivation is described in that volume. This payroll series was then used to extrapolate the OBE 1929 total.

age expenditure per family purchasing. Multiplying the implicit average for all families by the number of U.S. families estimated by the Census gives property insurance premia. The ratio of commissions and other expenses to premia in life insurance was then applied to these figures, with interpolation between the 1901, 1918, and 1929 benchmarks by the trend of life insurance premia.

Moving expense. The average cost per family, as well as the number of families that incurred such costs, was derived from the 1918 expenditure study, and then adjusted to the total number of households. For 1901 the proportion of removals among the 750,000 policy-holders of the Metropolitan Life Insurance Company in 1898 was used, together with the number of families in 1901, and the same $10 per family moving expense as in 1918.

Mark-up on second-hand merchandise. Data are taken from Raymond Goldsmith's *A Study of Saving in the United States*, these being directly comparable with the 1929 OBE estimate in the October 1944 *Survey of Current Business*.

Maintenance for appliances and household furnishings, and miscellaneous household operation services. The benchmark OBE figure is extrapolated to 1901 and 1919 by Goldsmith's estimate of replacement cost depreciation for consumer durables, minus the estimates for passenger cars.

Postage. The 1918 BLS Survey average family expenditure for postage, when divided by the 3¢ first class mail rate for that year, implies 75 equivalent first class letters a year.[82]

The 75 count times the 2¢ rate prevailing in 1901 times the Census estimate of U.S. families gives a 1901 total that is 32 percent of the OBE 1929 total. For interpolation we use the number of postal cards issued, their total in 1901 being 37 percent of the 1929 count.[83] We use postal card data given that (a) the 1901–1929 change is broadly the

[82] BLS Bulletin 357, p. 451. Postal rates from *Historical Statistics*, II, p. 498.

[83] *Historical Statistics*, II, p. 496.

same; (b) changes in intermediate years would be sensitive primarily to consumer influences rather than as, say, first-class mail in general, to variations in business billing practice and use of the mails.

Since the OBE does not now publish the detail for these estimates we use the figures from the 1947 *National Income Supplement,* Table 30, adjusting their sum slightly to the present OBE total for the category "household operation, other."

Medical ($2,202)

Physicians, dentists, other professional ($1,691). Prior estimates for average annual employment of self-employed persons in these professions, and for their average annual earnings, multiplied together gave the aggregate income series used to extrapolate the 1929 OBE benchmark figure.[84]

Examination of the earlier studies by King, Knauth, and others reveals no explicit allowance for this group, while the Lough figures back to 1909 are as hard to assess or understand on the basis of published data. Necessarily, the total service figure in the total national product estimates of Kuznets provides no detail, particularly since the underlying expenditure surveys from which his aggregate figures take their origin give no—or virtually no—itemization of medical expenditures.

In this deplorable demonstration of our ignorance, there is thus little to test the validity of the above estimates. Some partial guides, however, suggest their possible acceptability. One is a fairly direct estimate of average earnings of physicians in 1894–1895 by an obviously knowledgeable contem-

---

[84] The self-employment totals for physicians, dentists, nurses, and midwives are those included in the total for service self-employed shown on p. 516 of *Manpower.* Their derivation is described on pp. 457–461 of that source. The average earnings series is that implicit in Kuznets' estimates for 1919–1929 (*National Income and Its Composition,* pp. 762, 765) extrapolated to 1900 by the trend of average earnings in trade, the description for which appears in *Manpower,* pp. 485–492.

porary.[85] He estimates "the average annual income of a physician in full practice in a large city may be stated as $2,000, and in the smaller towns and in strictly rural districts $1,200." If we tabulate the number of physicians in cities with 50,000 and over population, assume the balance to be in Shrady's second group, and use these as weights, the weighted average for 1900 comes to $1,478.[86] This figure proves to be 29 percent of the 1929 average income for physicians in private practice.[87] This is virtually the same as the 28 percent ratio (for these dates) implicit in the average earnings figures we have used for the medical group.

Hospitals ($403). (1) The 1929 OBE benchmark was extrapolated by a series for hospital patient billings by hospitals. For 1923–1929 the series was that of Rolf Nugent.[88]

(2) The 1904 Census of Benevolent Institutions reports receipts from patients in hospitals that accounted for some 90 percent of hospital facilities. We need therefore only estimate the receipts in the small group of proprietary hospitals to arrive at a U.S. total.

A 1904 benchmark was derived from the 1904 Census as follows. That Census reported the cost of maintenance of such institutions—including patient income, subsidies, deficit—at $28.2 millions, and the number of nurses as 21,844.[89] We take the number of nurses as an indication

---

[85] George F. Shrady, "The Pay of Physicians and Surgeons," *The Forum*, Vol. xviii (September 1894 to February 1895), p. 68.

[86] 1900 Census of Population, *Occupations*, Table 43, provides city data, and Table 2, the U.S. total.

[87] We assume that non-salaried physicians (excluding, as the group does, interns and salaried physicians) would be comparable to "physicians in full practice." The 1929 average for the latter is given in William Weinfield; "Income of Physicians, 1929–49," *Survey of Current Business* (July 1951), p. 11.

[88] Rolf Nugent, *Consumer Credit and Economic Stability* (1939), p. 298.

[89] U.S. Bureau of the Census, *Benevolent Institutions, 1904* (1905), p. 32.

of scale of hospital operations, and compute costs at $1,290 per nurse. For 1898 we can compute the ratio of hospital beds in private hospitals as a proportion of those in benevolent institutions.[90] This proportion, 10.3 percent, times the above count of nurses, yields an estimate of 2,200 nurses in private institutions. Assuming the same $1,290 maintenance cost per nurse then gives a figure of $2.8 millions spent in proprietary hospitals in 1904. We assume this total measures income from patients in those hospitals. Added to the $12.2 million reported income from patients in the benevolent hospitals, it yields a figure of $15 million spent by patients in hospitals in 1904 comparable with the OBE 1929 total of $403 million.

(3) A 1910 benchmark was estimated from the 1910 Census of Benevolent Institutions in a manner similar to that for 1904. The 1898 Polk count of hospital beds indicated 10.3 percent in proprietary hospitals, as noted above, while the 1923 Census of Hospitals yields a corresponding 6 percent rate.[91] We assume a 10 percent rate as appropriate for the pre-war year at 1910, prior to the 1918 influenze epidemic, the impact of World War I, and other major social change. Computing a maintenance cost per nurse in benevolent hospitals as a measure of patient care receipts per nurse in proprietary hospitals yields a total for 1910 of $42 millions.[92]

(4) To interpolate between the above 1904, 1910, and 1923 benchmarks, we utilized an index that measured varia-

[90] R. L. Polk and Co. *Medical and Surgical Register of the United States and Canada,* 5th edition, 1898. A complete tabulation of all hospitals and beds, by nature of hospital ownership, was made for the following states: California, Florida, Georgia, Illinois, Kansas, Michigan, New York, Vermont, Washington, and Wisconsin. These states accounted for about half the hospital beds in 1898.

[91] 1923 data from *Historical Statistics,* ii, p. 36.

[92] U.S. Census Bureau, *Benevolent Institutions, 1910* (1913), pp. 48, 75, 76. Various adjustments were necessary to allow for differences in completeness of hospital reporting from Census table to Census table.

tions in U.S. deaths and the changing average yearly wage of nurses. Deaths indicate variation in aggregate patient load in a period before hospitals were commonly used for obstetrical cases and asepsis and antibiotics had made optional surgery widespread, while the wage variation reflects variations in costs per hospital case.[93]

Health insurance. The 1929 OBE benchmark was extrapolated to 1919 by data on health insurance premia of insurance companies, the life insurance data having indicated that the variation of expense ratios over time was reasonably limited.[94] The resultant 1919 figure for premiums proves virtually identical with an estimate to be derived from the BLS expenditure survey of 1918.[95] For 1910 an estimate can be derived on the basis of an extensive study by the Commissioner of Labor of railroad, union, and other funds that made temporary disability payments to workers, plus a study by I. M. Rubinow.[96] The 1900–1910 change was estimated by the 1900–1910 change in claims paid mutual sick-benefit associations.[97] For intervening years we interpolate by the trend of life insurance premia.

[93] An index of the average yearly wage per full-time nurse was derived from that for personal service, using data from *Manpower*, p. 526. This index was multiplied by an index of deaths—the latter computed as the product of death rates and population counts, using data from *Historical Statistics*, ii, pp. 7, 27. Ratios of the resultant index to total patient care receipts in 1904, 1910, and 1923 were computed, those for intermediate years interpolated and then applied to the index for intermediate years. The 1904 ratio was extrapolated to 1900 as a constant.

[94] Health Insurance Institute, *Source Book of Health Insurance Data*, 1963, p. 38.

[95] BLS Bulletin 357, p. 447, reports accident and health insurance of $3.34 per family, which, given the number of families in 1918, comes to $79 million in that earlier year, compared to the extrapolated total of $90 in 1919.

[96] U.S. Commissioner of Labor, *Workmen's Insurance and Benefit Funds in the United States* (1908), *passim,* and I. M. Rubinow, *Social Insurance* (1913) pp. 292, 294, and 295.

[97] Data from Rubinow, *idem.*

Personal Business ($4,158)

Brokerage ($756). The 1929 benchmark was extrapolated by the sum of Goldsmith's series for brokers' commissions on stocks and on real estate transfers.[98]

Bank service charges ($76). The bulk of this item being accounted for by implicit interest, an extrapolating series was computed as the product of the volume of demand deposits of individuals times the average interest rate on demand deposits.[99]

Expense of life insurance ($874). The 1929 benchmark was extrapolated by the sum of expenses for life insurance companies and for fraternal companies.[100]

Legal services ($402). A payroll series was used to extrapolate the 1929 OBE benchmark, with the number of self-employed in legal services times a series for average earnings of lawyers.[101]

---

[98] Raymond Goldsmith, *A Study of Saving* (1955), Vol. I, pp. 529 (12) and p. 625 (4).

[99] Data from Goldsmith, *op.cit.*, p. 385 (7) and p. 407 (1).

[100] The life insurance expense series is from *Historical Statistics*, II, p. 674. A 1900 ratio of expenses to insurance in force for 136 fraternal societies can be computed from Abb Landis, *Friendly Societies and Fraternal Orders* (n.d.), p. 80. This ratio was applied to a somewhat larger fraternal insurance total from Owen Stalson, *Marketing Life Insurance* (1942), p. 807, to give a $5.8 million benchmark. For other years the same expense ratio times the volume of fraternal insurance in force (Stalson, *ibid.*) was used. Fraternal insurance expenses are 1% of the 1929 total, and no more than 6% in any prior year.

[101] The self-employment series underlies the service estimate in *Manpower*, p. 516, and its derivation described on p. 459. The earnings series is the OBE 1929 average for employees in legal services extrapolated by the earnings series for medical service from p. 527 of *Manpower*. The latter rests on Kuznets' average earnings estimates for curative service, 1919–1928 (pp. 762, 765 of his *National Income and Its Composition*) extrapolated to earlier years by our estimate of the trend in earnings in trade, described on pp. 485–492 of *Manpower*.

Funeral and burial expenses ($607). For 1919–1929 an
extrapolating series was computed as (a) the product of
a series for the number of undertakers times average earnings of undertakers plus (b) a series for the value of monuments, tombs, and caskets. The series for undertakers is
based on the decennial count of the occupation group.[102]
The average earnings per undertaker was taken to equal
the average for all trade entrepreneurs, for a search of the
trade literature revealed little but inconsistent and anecdotal
material. For trade entrepreneurs we estimate a 1900 figure
of $692 from the 1901 Cost of Living Survey, and a 1929
average, from OBE data, of $1,818.[103] The ratio of these
earnings to those of trade employees was computed for
1900 and 1929, the ratios interpolated and multiplied by
the series for earnings of trade employees, to give earnings
of undertakers.[104]

The series for value of caskets, etc., is based on the output
series for monuments, tombs, and caskets as estimated by
Kuznets.[105]

For 1900–1919 benchmark estimates of earnings of undertakers were made for 1900, 1904, 1910, 1914, and 1920 by
the same procedures used for 1919–1929. The value of casket
production for these Census dates is available from Fabricant's estimates.[106] For monuments and tombstones a 1900
figure is given by the Census of Manufactures.[107] The ratio

[102] 1900 Census, *Occupations,* p. 8, 1930 Census, *Occupations,* p. 47,
provide data for the 1900, 1910, 1920, and 1930 totals. A curve fitting
all 4 dates was used to interpolate annually 1920–1929.

[103] The derivation of the 1900 data is discussed in *Manpower,* p.
487. The OBE figure is derived from data in *National Income and
Product, 1929–1965,* pp. 98, 110, 114.

[104] The derivation of the trade employee earning series is given
in *Manpower,* pp. 485–492, with data from p. 526.

[105] *Commodity Flow and Capital Formation* (1938) pp. 146–147
items 6a, 31.

[106] Solomon Fabricant, *Output of Manufacturing Industries* (1940)
p. 623.

[107] 1900 Census, *Manufactures,* vii, p. 317.

of value of production of these items to that of caskets, available for 1900 and 1919, was interpolated, applied to casket values in intermediate Census dates to give figures for monuments.

An approximate benchmark check is given by an estimate of $20 million as the value of goods manufactured for funerals about 1895.[108] If combined with the basic Fabricant data based on Census of Manufactures figures we have used, plus our figures for income of undertakers, the result is within 2 percent of our 1900 estimate for the category.

These benchmark figures were then interpolated as follows. A series for average cost per funeral in each year 1900–1929 was developed based on the average value of industrial life insurance policies.[109] This was multiplied by a series for the number of deaths to give an annual index of burial expenses. Ratios of this index to the benchmark figures for funeral expenditures were computed, interpolated, applied to the index series to give intermediate annual values.

Personal Business–Other

Union dues ($38). A 1929 estimate by William Shaw was extrapolated by the BLS series for union membership,

---

[108] Albert Stevens, in Chauncy Depew, *One Hundred Years of American Commerce* (1895), Vol. 2, p. 652. Stevens then hazards an allowance for "coffins made in remote districts, the profits and work of the undertakers, and the hire of horses and carriages" to infer at least $100 million a year for 1.8 million deaths. The number of deaths and total are both too high, as is the implicit average of $549.

[109] The average value of industrial insurance policies of the Prudential Insurance Company for 1900–1908 appears in John Dryden, *Addresses and Papers on Life Insurance . . . (1909)*, Appendix E; data for all companies 1909–1929 appear in the *Life Insurance Fact Book, 1956*, p. 27. Contemporary reports indicate that these policies typically averaged something like the cost of a funeral.

that series in fact using paid membership in the AF of L as its measure and thereby reflecting more closely changes in dues payments than series on membership per se.[110]

Taking Wolman's independent estimate based on direct reports of membership and the BLS cost of living survey average union dues figures for 1900 and 1918, we arrive at higher figures—by 18 percent and 10 percent respectively. The two figures will differ both because Wolman used different sources, and because the surveys were biassed toward somewhat higher income workers and union members; hence the results are not irreconcilable.[111]

Money order fees ($2). Based on Post Office data.[112]

Classified advertisements ($36). The Shaw 1929 estimate was extrapolated by the dollar volume of advertising.[113] No published information seems to be available on the OBE method of estimate.

Miners expenditures for explosives, etc. ($15). The Shaw 1929 figure was extrapolated by the value of coal production at the mine.[114]

Net purchases from pawnbrokers, second-hand stores ($17). The Population Census reports slightly over 1,000 pawnbrokers in both 1910 and 1920.[115] If we divide the average income per self-employed person in trade in 1929 into the Shaw 1929 estimate, we arrive at an implicit count

[110] The 1929 estimate is from Shaw's "Consumption Expenditures" in *Survey of Current Business* (June 1944), p. 5. The BLS figures are from *Historical Statistics*, II, p. 97. Cf. notes to series D 735, D 737.

[111] Commissioner of Labor, *1901 Survey*, p. 509, and BLS Bulletin 357, p. 448.

[112] The 1901 survey (p. 505) reported 37% of its families with expenditures for union dues—in a year when less than 3% of the labor force was organized. In 1918 the survey reported 31%, when about 12% were organized.

[113] U.S. *Statistical Abstract, 1929*, p. 351.

[114] Shaw, *idem.* Advertising from *Historical Statistics*, II, p. 526 (346). No published information seems to be available on the OBE method of estimate.

[115] *Historical Statistics*, II, p. 350 (15), (16).

of about 1,000 pawnbrokers in 1930 as well.[116] On this basis we take an arbitrary 1,000 brokers in each year throughout the period and multiply by the average earnings of proprietors in trade to get an index for extrapolating the 1929 Shaw estimate.[117]

Employment agency fees ($25). The series used to extrapolate Shaw's 1929 estimate was based on the number of employment office keepers each year times the average income of each.[118] The average income of each was assumed the same as that of all proprietors in trade.[119]

Transportation ($2,562)

Auto repair ($776)

1919. Data on repair costs are given in the Census of Manufactures.[120]

1921, 1923, 1925, 1927. We use the dollar value of finished auto products and accessories to interpolate repairs in these years.[121]

1920, 1922, 1924, 1926, 1928. The ratio of dollar repairs per registered auto in the odd years in the 1919–1929 decade (supra) were interpolated for the even years, the results applied to the registration series give a repair estimate.

1899, 1904, 1909, 1914. The ratio of auto parts and accessories produced as finished goods for auto repairs to the

[113] 1930 Census, *Occupations*, p. 18. The occupation is combined with the much larger group of loan brokers in 1930.

[117] The proprietors' earnings series is derived above in connection with the estimate of funeral expenditures.

[118] Decennial counts from 1930 Census, *Occupations*, p. 18, interpolated. The 1910–1920 and 1920–1930 changes being virtually identical, the 1900–1910 change was assumed to equal the 1910–1920 change.

[119] Cf. its derivation in connection with the estimate of funeral expenditures.

[120] 1920 Census, *Manufactures*, x, pp. 880–881.

[121] Simon Kuznets, *Commodity Flow and Capital Formation* (1938), p. 88. Minor group 27, auto. The ratios of finished materials to repairs were computed for 1919 and 1929, interpolated for these years, and applied to the value of finished auto products.

value of auto repairs was about 37 percent in 1919 and 16 percent in 1929, according to the above data. We assume a steady upward efficiency trend in manufacturing industry, tending to reduce material costs, and a steady upward trend in auto repair labor rates, and extrapolate to a 50 percent ratio for 1900. Interpolated ratios applied to the finished materials output data on those years give us a value of repair figure for each Census of Manufactures year.[122] How do the results compare with the custom work and auto repair figure reported by auto manufacturers in those years? For 1899 the manufacturers reported $74,000—compared with our $80,000 estimate for repairs by manufacturers plus repair shops; for 1904 the manufacturers reported $851,000 compared with our $1,960,000 for all repairs.[123] Given the rapid expansion of repair shops and outside work as the industry developed the figures seem not unreasonable.

Other years. Data for the other pre-war years were then estimated by (a) interpolating the ratio of repairs to auto registrations in the above years, (b) applying the interpolated ratios to the registration series.

Local and intercity transportation ($1,652). Electric railway operating revenues are reported by the Censuses of the industry for 1902, 1907, 1912, 1917, 1922, while King and Kuznets have estimated series for gross income of street railways for the intermediate years 1910–1929.[124] For the intercensal years in the 1900–1910 period, interpolation was by payrolls in street railways, data for which are available from the work of Paul Douglas.[125] The "purchased local

[122] Output of finished auto parts from Kuznets, *idem.*

[123] Manufacturers' data from '1905 Census of Manufactures, p. 270. It is, of course, possible that some of the repairs done by manufacturers classified in the carriage industry were in fact done on autos.

[124] Census data from the *1929 Statistical Abstract*, p. 421. W. I. King, *The National Income and Its Purchasing Power* (1930), p. 95. Simon Kuznets, *National Income and Its Composition, 1919–1938* (1941), p. 659.

[125] Paul Douglas, *Real Wages in the United States, 1890–1926* (1930), pp. 334, 440. In fact the employment estimates were those underlying

transportation" component was thus extrapolated from 1929 to 1900.

Intercity transport expenditures were extrapolated to 1922 by ICC data on railway revenues from passengers, minus an estimate for commutation ticket expenditures, and then back to 1900 by the total passenger revenue series.[126] Because of the lack of data for segregating commutation expenditures prior to 1922, we show only the sum of local and intercity transport expenditures for 1900–1921.

A check on the implicit 1900 total for purchased local transportation was provided as follows. The number of commuters by railroad is reported in the 1890 Census for 151 cities of 10,000 population and over.[127] Dividing by 600 (for a 300-day work year) gives approximately 96 million commuters. We estimate a 20¢ fare for these railroad trips, or a $19 million total for 1890.[128] Adjusting this for the rate of population increase in counties that account for most of the commutation gives a total of $26 million.[129] The total for street railways (extrapolating the 1902 Census total as described above) comes to $181 million. The ratio of the sum of these two components to the corresponding 1929 OBE components, when applied to the OBE 1929 total for the entire purchased local transport group, gives a 1900

---

the transport column in *Manpower*, p. 514, but these had in turn been based on Douglas for this decade.

[126] ICC data on passenger revenues appear in *Historical Statistics*, II, p. 430. We assume that the trend in passenger miles by commutation ticket holders times the average revenue per passenger mile could be used to extrapolate the OBE benchmark in 1929 for that group.

[127] 1890 Census, *Report on the Social Statistics of Cities* (1895), pp. 48–49. We adjust the number of commuters slightly by the ratio of commuters to passengers in cities reporting commuters, by size group.

[128] The 1902 *Census of Street and Electric Railways*, p. 108, gives data suggesting an average trip of 13 miles, while p. 116 gives an average of 1½¢ per mile for interurban railway charges.

[129] Population total for New York, Philadelphia, Chicago, Boston, and the counties adjoining each appear in 1900 Census, *Manufactures*, Vol. VII, Part 1, pp. cclxiv–cclxvi.

figure of $258 millions—virtually identical with the $247 million figure we have used.

Other transport ($134). This category was estimated as the sum of two series. For charges by ferries and bridges, the annual reports of Financial Statistics of Cities for the years 1902 thru 1929 were used.[130] The remaining series, for auto insurance, extrapolates the OBE benchmark by our estimates for the costs of auto repairs, assuming that the trend in repair cost dominated the trend in insurance costs.[131]

A note on comparability. The goal in these estimates has been to extrapolate the OBE official estimates to years prior to 1929. Hence we uniformly adopt the 1929 OBE figure as a benchmark. The 1929 figure for purchased transportation was therefore adopted, although in the process of establishing benchmarks for earlier years we have found reason to doubt its adequacy. The problem appear to arise from reliance on OBE on a May 1942 Office of Defense Transportation survey.[132] That survey indicated about 64 percent of a sample of railroad coach passengers reported their travel to have been for personal reasons. The OBE therefore allocated a round 65 percent of passenger charges to consumers. It seems likely that consumer trips would have been shorter than those of businessmen and salesmen, and the share of passenger charges should therefore have been lower. The 1918 and 1941 BLS consumer expenditures surveys both report data on purchased transport, and both indicate a much lower figure than would derive from the DOT survey. Although consumer field surveys are weak

[130] "Revenue receipts from earnings of public service enterprises—all other enterprises" is the item typically used. Detailed comparisons with data for individual cities—e.g., New York—showed that virtually all this item was for ferries.

[131] Insurance was—in the halcyon days before frequent auto theft—presumably largely for auto repairs and expense of insurance company overhead.

[132] I am indebted to George Jaszi, Director. and to Richard Nelson of the OBE for details on the 1942 benchmark adjustment.

in many respects the role of railway trips in these years would be such as to warrant belief that such relatively notable events would have been reasonably well remembered, and reported. In any event, since it would be out of the question to adjust a single benchmark item in the OBE set we do not do so.

Education ($664)

Higher education ($219). The trend for the expenditures on higher education was estimated from the Office of Education biennial reports on tuition fees paid in private and public institutions of higher education.[133]

Elementary and high schools ($162). A 1900 benchmark for private high school tuition fees is reported by the Commissioner of Education.[134] A similar 1918 benchmark is available.[135]

For elementary schools a 1900 benchmark was computed as the sum of $23.7 million fees in cities of 8,000 population and greater, plus $1.8 million in cities of 4,000 to 8,000.[136]

[133] Data from the *Biennial Survey of Education for 1916–18*, III, *pp.* 683–685; 1918–1920, p. 282; 1920–1922, II, p. 296; 1924, p. 596; 1924–1925, p. 823; 1926–1928, pp. 724, 730; 1928–1930. Vol. 2, p. 372; with intervening years by interpolation.

[134] U.S. Commissioner of Education, *Report, 1900–1901*, Vol. 2, p. 1,942.

[135] *Biennial Survey of Education, 1916–18*, IV, *p.* 365. The $13.7 million reported income from tuition and educational fees was raised to a universe estimate of $20.5 by ratio of total reported working income to the survey's estimated total income for all private high schools.

[136] U.S. Commissioner, *Report, 1900–1901*, Vol. 2, pp. 1,529 and 1,530, reports public-school enrollment and total expendituures in cities of 8,000 and over. An average expenditure per pupil was derived, and applied to the report's count of private and parochial school enrollment. For the cities in the 4,000–8,000 range, a similar calculation was made from data for 473 individual cities from pp. 1,596–1,610, but omitting cities that did not report private school enrollment. The larger city size group spent $23.7 millions, and the smaller only $1.8 million. Hence still smaller cities and villages were assumed at zero.

For 1918 a similar estimate was made.[137]

Given the above benchmarks for 1900, 1918, and the OBE figure for 1929, the intervening years were interpolated by payrolls in private schools, estimated previously.[138]

Education–other ($283). Three component series were estimated, summed to extrapolate the 1929 benchmarks.[139] (1) Commercial school tuition and fees ($62) were extrapolated by the product of the number of teachers in such schools and their average pay.[140] (2) Teachers of music and arts ($139) were assumed to have the same average earnings per year as teachers in private commercial schools, while their number was taken as stable 1910–1930, given the similarity of the decennial Census counts.[141] For

[137] *Biennial Survey, 1916–1918,* Vol. III, p. 148, gives estimated pupils in private elementary schools, and p. 198 average expense per pupil enrolled in state school systems.

[138] The average wage in private schools, and the number of teachers employed, underlie the estimates on pp. 514 and 527 of *Manpower.* The count of teachers was derived from the Biennial Surveys as cited on p. 474 of the same source. Average wages in private schools were derived by extrapolating for 1919–1929 from Kuznets, *op.cit.,* pp. 762, 765. For 1900–1919 these figures were extrapolated by average wages in urban schools, the above data on private schools indicating that most of their employment was in fact in cities of 8,000 population and over. The required employment and payroll totals were taken from the *Biennial Reports* and made as comparable as possible in a memorandum of March 25, 1954, kindly prepared by Emory Foster, Head of the Research and Statistical Service of the U.S. Office of Education.

[139] Three OBE benchmarks were obtained by splitting the $283 OBE total for "Other education" in 1929 by ratios for the more detailed components from Shaw, *Survey of Current Business* (June 1944), Group x.

[140] The count of teachers is taken from the U.S. Office of Education, *Biennial Survey of Education: 1916–18,* IV, p. 389; *1926–28,* p. 426; *1928–30,* II, p. 81. Intervening years not summarized in these volumes, were interpolated. Average pay from *Manpower,* p. 527.

[141] 1910 Census, *Occupations,* p. 430; 1930 Census, *Occupations,* p. 47. We take the number of self-employed music and art teachers as equal to the number of female teachers of music and art, the omission of male music masters balancing the inclusion of female

1900–1910 a similar procedure was used, but the marked 1900–1910 growth in the universe of such teachers was allowed for.[142] (3) Foundation expenditures for education ($82): extrapolated by a series for private benefactions to schools.[143]

Religious and Welfare Activities ($1,196)

Religious activities ($912). Benchmark expenditures for 1916 and 1926 were derived from the Census of Religious Bodies, and from the 1929 OBE figure.[144] For 1906 an expenditure total was derived on the basis of data for ministerial salaries, contributions for domestic and foreign work, and estimated expense of building upkeep.[145]

For the same benchmark dates payrolls in religious bodies were computed from prior estimates.[146] The ratios of payroll

---

music and art teachers in the public schools. A special unpublished Census tabulation (in 1948) of class-of-worker status in the 1910 Census suggests this as a reasonable approximation.

[142] 1900 data from 1910 Census, *Occupations*, p. 54.

[143] U.S. *Biennial Survey* of Education, 1924–1925, p. 562, gives annual data for 1900–1918, while biennial reports on private benefactions to colleges were used for later years from the Surveys for 1924–1925, p. 562; 1926–1928, p. 699; 1928–1930, p. 336; interpolation for inter-survey years.

[144] U.S. Census Bureau, *Religious Bodies, 1916*, (1919), Part I, p. 56, and U.S. Census Bureau, *Religious Bodies: 1926* (1930) Volume I, p. 312. For 1929 the OBE 1951 *National Income Supplement, p.* 196, was used.

[145] The detailed expense data for 1916 (*ibid.*, p. 56) were increased to a 1916 total for all organizations—not merely those reporting expenses. The running expense and "all other" expense totals were extrapolated by the ratio of 1906 to 1916 ministerial salaries. Number of ministers and average salary (*1916*, pp. 66, 72.); the benevolence total by contributions for foreign and domestic work (*1916*, p. 99); and repairs and improvements by the value of church property (*1916*, p. 49).

[146] *Manpower*, p. 527, reports the average earnings series for non-profit service activities used, while the employment series underlies that for services on p. 514. The employment series utilizes Kuznets' religious service employment for 1919–1929 (Kuznets, *National In-*

were then interpolated and applied to the annual payroll estimates to give the final series on expenditures for religious activities.

Welfare ($284).[147] There are something like a dozen separate items under this heading, of which gifts and free services via local agencies account for the great bulk in 1929 according to the OBE.[148]

The 1929 figure was extrapolated to 1924 by a series for 73 community chests plus a series for gifts to the American Red Cross.[149] The 1924 figure was extrapolated to 1920 by data for chest contributions in 13 identical cities.[150]

The 1920 figure was extrapolated to 1913 by a series for benevolences to 11 Protestant denominations plus gifts to the Red Cross during World War I drives.[151] (Data on benevolences to the United Stewardship Council 1924–1930 suggest the same trend as that given by the Community Chest data for the period, and hence we are pre-

---

come and Its Composition, p. 765), with 1900, 1910, 1920 counts from Alba Edwards, *Occupational Trends,* Table 8; interpolations for intercensal years, 1900–1920. The average earnings in non-profit service was an extrapolation to 1919 of the Commerce 1929 figure in non-profit service by Kuznets implicit averages (*op.cit.,* pp. 762, 765), and hence to 1900 by Paul Douglas' series for the average salary of Methodist and Congregational ministers (Paul Douglas, *Real Wages in the United States, 1890–1926* (1930), p. 386.

[147] The 1929 benchmark was taken from the 1951 *National Income Supplement,* p. 196.

[148] A partial itemization appears in *The National Income and Product Accounts of the United States, 1929–1965,* p. 50, n. 25. A letter from John Gorman of the OBE (May 1971) kindly itemized the components under social welfare and relief agencies.

[149] Data for chests in 73 identical cities from Pierce Williams, *Corporate Contributions,* pp. 94, 96. Data for Red Cross gifts from Edward C. Jenkins, *Philanthropy in America . . . 1924–1948* (1950), p. 174.

[150] Williams, *op.cit.,* p. 93.

[151] Data on benevolences from *Yearbook of Philanthropy, 1941–1942,* p. 2. Red Cross data for 1917 and 1918, the only years of massive giving to that agency in this period, were from Pierce Williams, op.cit., p. 49.

pared to assume benevolences for Protestant denominations signal the appropriate changes in the earlier period.)

The period from 1900 to 1913 is taken at a constant level on the basis of the virtual identity of private social welfare agency expenditures in 1904 and 1910. (These agencies provided the bulk of welfare expenditures as late as 1929, and still more so in the period before chests and the Red Cross developed.) Three bits of data support this procedure.

(1) In 1910 donations to benevolent institutions (except hospitals) came to $10.6 million dollars, and in 1904 the cost of maintenance of such institutions (minus public subsidies and pay by inmates) came to $10.2 millions.[152]

(2) The cost of outdoor private relief in 1902 came to $1.3 millions.[153] Since the very active forces of the new charitable organizations had been leading to the steady decline of outdoor relief, with more and more cities dropping such programs in the 1890's and 1900–1914 period, a corresponding estimate for 1910 would undoubtedly be less than the $1.3 million for 1902. Summing contributions to benevolent institutions and to outdoor relief activities, one arrives at essentially the same dollar figures for 1904 and 1910.

(3) A third indicator of stability is in the component of private charitable contributions that appears in the form of depreciation on the value of property used for private charitable activities. The value of private property in benevolent institutions except hospitals in 1910 is available from the Census of that year.[154] We take 2 percent as the rate

---

[152] 1910 *Census of Benevolent Institutions*, p. 74; 1904 *Census of Benevolent Institutions*, p. 23.

[153] Data by city size group on outdoor public relief in 1902 appear in U.S. Bureau of the Census, *Statistics of Cities . . . Over 25,000, 1902 and 1903* (1903), p. 271, and in U.S. Bureau of the Census, *Statistics of Cities . . . 8,000 to 25,000: 1903* (1906), p. 131. The ratio of private to public charities expenditures on outdoor relief in 1897 could be computed for cities under and over 125,000 from data in the *Charities Review* (March 1899), p. 30. Applying these ratios to the public totals for 1902-1903 gave a total of private contributions.

[154] U.S. Census, *Benevolent Institutions, 1910*, pp. 68, 77, provides

of annual depreciation.[155] For 1922 the Federal Trade Commission collected data from about a third of all the institutions reporting value in 1910, and from these data estimated the percent change in value 1910–1922.[156] The result is to give a depreciation aggregate of $9 million in 1910 and of $22 million in 1922, over a span of years in which institutional construction costs had risen by almost 100 percent. We infer that depreciation can have changed by only a few million from 1904 to 1910, when construction costs changed little.[157]

Recreation ($1,696)

The OBE benchmark was extrapolated by prior series for employment in recreation services multiplied by average wage in personal services.[158]

Foreign Travel ($490)

Expenditures by U.S. nations abroad, and by foreign nationals in the U.S., were taken from the official balance of payments estimates, and used to extrapolate the 1929 benchmark.[159]

---

data for separating private from all institutions, and hospitals from others, and for inferring totals from data for institutions reporting.

[155] Raymond Goldsmith, *A Study of Saving in the United States* (1955), Vol. 1, p. 605, estimates a 50 year life for non-profit construction.

[156] U.S. Federal Trade Commission, *National Wealth and Income* (1926), p. 179. Applying these percentage changes to the 1910 values gives a 1922 value estimate. The Commission notes that it did not estimate any increase 1910-1922 in institutions. We follow this, possible, underestimate.

[157] Construction cost indices from Goldsmith, *op.cit.*, p. 609.

[158] Employment data from worksheets underlying pp. 516, 514 of *Manpower*, estimated by procedures described on pp. 464–465; earnings data are from p. 526, estimated by procedures from pp. 494–496.

[159] Data from *Historical Statistics*, II, p. 562 (171), (178).

Expenditures Abroad by U.S. Government Personnel ($21)

Decennial estimates of U.S. population resident abroad are available from the Population Census, and these were interpolated by a series for armed forces on active duty—a series whose substantial movements reflect variations in official U.S. overseas employment.[160] This series was then multiplied by the average annual earnings per nonfarm employee to allow for changes in incomes (and, thereby, of expenditures) of employees stationed abroad.[161]

[160] *Historical Statistics*, II, pp. 7 (6), 736 (763). Estimates of armed forces overseas can be made for the peak years of World War I and II and they confirm this judgment of parallelism.

[161] "Money earnings, when employed" series from *Manpower*, p. 524.

TABLE 1

SERVICES: 1900–1970
CONSUMER EXPENDITURES
(MILLIONS OF DOLLARS)

Year	Grand Total	Care of Clothes Access	Per-sonal Care	HOUSING Total	Non-Farm Owner	Tenant	Farm	Other	HOUSEHOLD OPERATION Total	Gas	Elec-tricity	Water & Refuse Collect.	Phone, Tele-graph	Domestic Service	Other	MEDICAL Total	Physicians, Dentists, Other Prof	Hos-pital	Health Ins
1900	$5,329	$287	$55	$2,160	$1,021	$797	$307	$35	$625	$72	$15	$(50)	$13	$419	$56	$257	$240	$15	$2
1901	5,806	316	60	2,366	1,150	860	319	37	663	86	17	(52)	17	430	61	272	253	17	2
1902	6,008	336	63	2,354	1,079	895	310	40	726	97	20	54	22	476	57	293	273	18	2
1903	6,417	364	68	2,505	1,126	991	345	43	777	109	22	58	26	493	69	317	295	19	3
1904	6,875	381	71	2,755	1,206	1,098	405	46	815	120	24	59	30	514	68	341	317	21	3
1905	7,365	415	78	2,891	1,282	1,190	370	49	844	127	26	63	34	523	71	370	341	25	4
1906	8,129	454	84	3,354	1,604	1,284	413	53	890	134	29	66	38	546	77	393	358	31	4
1907	8,420	483	89	3,417	1,531	1,409	421	56	986	139	34	70	51	613	79	429	382	43	3
1908	8,518	481	89	3,451	1,532	1,435	427	57	1,043	146	39	74	57	645	82	443	403	36	4
1909	8,926	542	100	3,591	1,598	1,494	435	64	1,092	155	45	78	62	661	91	478	432	42	4
1910	9,456	580	105	3,793	1,694	1,585	445	69	1,139	164	56	86	69	682	82	524	458	61	5
1911	9,857	622	113	3,842	1,684	1,621	464	73	1,201	174	66	90	77	695	99	553	486	61	6
1912	10,254	629	114	4,018	1,780	1,666	498	74	1,247	185	79	93	84	709	97	563	495	60	8
1913	10,685	657	119	4,109	1,723	1,791	518	77	1,300	195	89	96	94	723	103	592	515	67	10
1914	11,041	675	122	4,256	1,782	1,865	529	80	1,335	208	102	100	100	719	106	626	545	69	12
1915	11,342	684	123	4,433	1,868	1,918	563	84	1,306	222	110	103	104	657	110	671	577	79	15
1916	12,400	763	137	4,757	2,032	2,018	614	93	1,348	241	118	106	116	648	119	745	624	104	17
1917	13,669	791	152	5,157	2,385	1,998	671	103	1,430	264	129	113	133	667	124	850	701	129	20
1918	15,435	841	174	5,651	2,748	2,045	739	119	1,554	290	157	123	154	695	135	1,061	823	214	24
1919	17,437	946	208	6,480	3,294	2,222	824	140	1,872	341	197	132	187	865	150	1,169	970	165	34

Year																			
1920	20,394	1,074	252	7,818	4,174	2,639	835	170	2,247	389	248	145	220	1,070	175	1,494	1,206	246	42
1921	20,342	1,063	269	7,668	3,671	3,062	769	166	2,385	433	268	163	243	1,092	186	1,637	1,419	190	28
1922	21,198	1,058	289	7,894	3,642	3,323	767	162	2,521	446	288	184	269	1,140	194	1,747	1,493	201	53
1923	22,962	1,062	311	8,806	4,226	3,562	860	168	2,801	463	332	202	292	1,301	211	1,693	1,412	220	61
1924	24,261	1,089	339	9,390	4,490	3,877	854	169	2,990	471	362	216	323	1,393	225	1,772	1,468	239	65
1925	25,895	1,120	371	9,926	4,773	4,106	868	179	3,212	478	420	231	371	1,466	246	1,962	1,618	274	70
1926	26,871	1,155	408	10,471	5,055	4,348	869	199	3,457	521	465	251	418	1,535	267	1,941	1,553	306	82
1927	28,299	1,197	446	10,787	5,259	4,435	878	221	3,683	543	522	261	459	1,607	291	2,110	1,675	329	106
1928	29,103	1,262	496	11,149	5,464	4,564	883	238	3,784	539	561	268	509	1,595	312	2,147	1,673	361	113
1929	30,324	1,264	525	11,530	5,868	4,500	913	249	4,037	542	616	278	569	1,716	316	2,202	1,691	403	108
1930	28,703	1,155	524	11,050	5,552	4,397	865	236	3,882	560	660	296	577	1,483	306	2,134	1,620	404	110
1931	26,023	960	475	10,291	5,101	4,200	775	215	3,515	556	674	296	554	1,146	289	1,915	1,428	395	92
1932	22,202	736	397	9,011	4,416	3,753	664	178	3,047	537	662	278	482	835	253	1,585	1,127	386	72
1933	20,069	637	340	7,907	3,844	3,296	614	153	2,816	495	645	269	436	732	239	1,464	1,031	363	70
1934	20,431	700	383	7,602	3,643	3,158	640	161	3,015	494	671	301	443	850	256	1,572	1,118	369	85
1935	21,266	755	428	7,702	3,646	3,199	683	174	3,170	503	697	311	472	911	276	1,683	1,184	406	93
1936	22,751	836	469	8,011	3,759	3,365	693	194	3,394	516	726	326	511	1,016	298	1,844	1,316	422	106
1937	24,358	921	533	8,533	3,950	3,639	733	211	3,682	528	766	331	542	1,187	328	1,949	1,372	454	123
1938	24,281	902	509	8,936	4,104	3,870	745	217	3,562	528	810	327	542	1,023	337	1,953	1,352	467	134
1939	25,048	916	518	9,139	4,179	3,994	741	225	3,782	538	849	343	576	1,129	347	2,064	1,419	492	153
1940	26,041	993	529	9,446	4,310	4,154	744	238	4,033	573	910	359	615	1,218	358	2,197	1,505	527	165
1941	28,075	1,162	555	10,167	4,706	4,438	767	256	4,251	575	964	368	695	1,237	411	2,346	1,595	555	196
1942	30,801	1,352	626	10,957	5,192	4,692	821	252	4,805	623	1,017	384	825	1,477	479	2,629	1,749	649	231
1943	34,167	1,669	742	11,485	5,588	4,737	879	281	5,228	648	1,045	391	973	1,598	573	2,868	1,837	752	279
1944	37,189	1,816	842	12,049	6,060	4,729	955	305	5,853	667	1,125	407	1,077	1,887	690	3,300	2,139	846	315
1945	39,754	2,004	895	12,479	6,492	4,596	1,052	339	6,424	705	1,194	419	1,189	2,142	775	3,555	2,256	925	374
1946	45,269	2,372	977	13,879	7,343	4,851	1,303	382	6,761	754	1,328	457	1,288	2,120	814	4,508	2,916	1,170	422
1947	49,839	2,606	1,008	15,665	8,428	5,289	1,447	501	7,457	865	1,473	492	1,376	2,348	903	5,184	3,296	1,401	487
1948	54,663	2,727	1,030	17,535	9,679	5,786	1,505	565	8,075	963	1,668	523	1,569	2,363	989	5,924	3,800	1,596	528
1949	57,630	2,707	1,049	19,252	10,902	6,371	1,908	571	8,549	1,038	1,879	548	1,731	2,356	997	6,101	3,836	1,734	531

TABLE 1 (Continued)
SERVICES: 1900–1970
CONSUMER EXPENDITURES
(MILLIONS OF DOLLARS)

Year	Grand Total	Care of Clothes & Access.	Personal Care	HOUSING Total	Non-Farm Owner	Non-Farm Tenant	Farm	Other	HOUSEHOLD OPERATION Total	Gas	Electricity	Water & Refuse Collect.	Phone, Telegraph	Domestic Service	Other	MEDICAL Total	Physicians, Dentists, Other Prof	Hospital	Health Ins.
1950	62,422	2,744	1,084	21,286	12,305	6,910	1,464	607	9,516	1,185	2,138	596	1,942	2,572	1,083	6,583	4,002	1,979	602
1951	67,865	2,862	1,135	23,853	13,980	7,592	1,607	674	10,395	1,345	2,395	640	2,170	2,661	1,184	6,963	4,181	2,171	611
1952	73,395	2,959	1,206	26,476	15,763	8,243	1,736	734	11,132	1,469	2,652	712	2,421	2,614	1,264	7,587	4,477	2,406	704
1953	79,929	3,054	1,293	29,315	17,734	9,022	1,765	794	12,015	1,589	2,932	770	2,683	2,690	1,351	8,409	4,856	2,647	906
1954	85,380	3,076	1,433	31,664	19,534	9,574	1,711	845	12,588	1,800	3,213	824	2,789	2,570	1,382	9,288	5,388	2,878	1,022
1955	91,433	3,149	1,546	33,738	21,178	9,901	1,741	918	14,037	2,027	3,496	906	3,061	3,051	1,496	9,801	5,610	3,135	1,056
1956	98,493	3,282	1,736	36,020	22,959	10,309	1,734	1,018	15,237	2,259	3,802	965	3,341	3,266	1,604	10,537	6,098	3,426	1,013
1957	105,048	3,382	1,912	38,506	24,805	10,772	1,787	1,142	16,188	2,403	4,097	1,030	3,648	3,322	1,688	11,532	6,614	3,775	1,143
1958	112,036	3,365	2,014	41,127	26,809	11,273	1,861	1,184	17,277	2,685	4,381	1,048	3,892	3,503	1,708	12,614	7,282	4,202	1,130
1959	120,278	3,493	2,249	43,654	28,674	11,724	1,957	1,299	18,503	2,901	4,721	1,163	4,188	3,553	1,977	13,745	7,867	4,601	1,277
1960	128,652	3,629	2,354	46,305	30,685	12,220	1,975	1,425	19,951	3,211	5,071	1,291	4,515	3,799	2,064	14,740	8,267	5,096	1,377
1961	135,069	3,773	2,593	48,717	32,493	12,702	2,005	1,517	20,813	3,415	5,340	1,367	4,822	3,733	2,136	15,770	8,631	5,581	1,558
1962	142,960	3,840	2,795	51,950	34,745	13,535	2,072	1,598	22,003	3,644	5,688	1,483	5,101	3,803	2,284	17,095	9,323	6,100	1,672
1963	152,422	4,015	2,890	55,410	37,095	14,435	2,153	1,727	23,119	3,770	5,960	1,596	5,509	3,824	2,460	18,267	9,862	6,751	1,654
1964	163,301	4,294	3,167	59,298	39,337	15,857	2,215	1,889	24,268	3,939	6,294	1,678	5,914	3,908	2,535	20,416	10,912	7,729	1,755
1965	175,472	4,586	3,367	63,509	41,735	17,357	2,300	2,117	25,609	4,075	6,608	1,771	6,423	3,964	2,768	22,149	11,880	8,309	1,960
1966	188,646	4,801	3,525	67,506	44,385	18,479	2,352	2,290	27,096	4,242	7,027	1,873	6,905	4,028	3,021	24,426	12,917	9,294	2,215
1967	203,978	5,146	3,701	71,848	47,057	19,706	2,481	2,604	29,123	4,432	7,496	1,922	7,532	4,477	3,264	27,474	14,309	10,744	2,421
1968	221,334	5,411	3,849	77,311	50,753	21,142	2,586	2,830	31,202	4,613	8,141	2,046	8,178	4,629	3,595	30,194	15,330	12,323	2,541
1969	242,744	5,601	4,032	84,141	54,991	23,203	2,863	3,084	33,758	4,938	8,905	2,246	9,092	4,685	3,892	34,656	17,246	14,640	2,770
1970	262,567	5,693	4,129	90,926	59,585	25,253	2,907	3,181	36,357	5,262	9,824	2,487	9,879	4,830	4,075	38,711	19,295	16,851	2,565

	PERSONAL BUSINESS							TRANSPORTATION					Recreation	EDUCATION				Religious	Welfare	FOREIGN TRAVEL		
Year	Total	Broker-age	Banks	Life Ins	Legal Services	Funeral Exps	Other	Total	Auto Re-pair	Local	Inter-city	Other	Total	Total	Higher	Elem. and Scdy.	Other	Religious Activity	Welfare	Total	+ U.S. Residents	− Foreign Residents
1900	$780	$69	$294	$99	$81	$185	$52	$469	—		$467	$2	$135	$100	$13	$36	$51	$215	$97	$149	$157	$8
1901	892	102	349	109	81	191	60	500	—		498	2	151	110	14	36	60	217	97	162	170	8
1902	950	93	386	120	85	198	68	526	$1		523	2	175	116	15	35	66	219	97	153	162	9
1903	1,011	91	401	134	90	216	79	574	1		571	2	191	128	16	41	71	228	97	157	166	9
1904	1,044	95	391	143	90	243	82	638	2		634	3	207	128	17	41	70	228	97	170	183	13
1905	1,188	126	495	146	94	239	86	705	3		699	3	223	134	18	43	75	229	97	191	209	18
1906	1,254	143	532	139	96	252	92	770	5		761	4	235	140	19	43	78	236	97	222	250	28
1907	1,197	123	483	129	100	268	94	826	7		814	5	248	151	23	43	85	253	97	244	280	36
1908	1,140	114	427	132	102	274	91	838	11		821	6	259	157	26	45	86	256	97	264	304	40
1909	1,193	126	442	145	106	282	92	862	19		836	7	268	162	27	47	88	255	97	286	328	42
1910	1,259	120	474	153	111	303	98	949	26		914	9	285	169	28	50	91	248	97	308	347	39
1911	1,305	108	500	166	116	311	104	1,023	32		980	11	317	181	31	54	96	267	97	336	378	42
1912	1,361	109	533	178	116	315	110	1,087	41		1,034	12	325	186	33	56	97	277	97	350	400	50
1913	1,462	97	617	189	119	323	117	1,154	46		1,094	14	349	204	35	64	105	286	97	356	407	51
1914	1,814	83	662	192	122	334	121	1,205	54		1,135	16	371	218	37	71	110	303	100	316	356	40
1915	1,704	111	771	219	127	348	128	1,198	77		1,103	18	390	225	40	73	112	320	104	184	209	25
1916	2,096	139	1,059	221	137	387	153	1,307	111		1,173	23	428	236	42	72	122	334	110	139	161	22
1917	2,343	138	1,214	248	152	412	179	1,467	161		1,277	29	481	247	43	74	130	353	302	96	131	35
1918	2,740	135	1,398	279	175	552	201	1,689	189		1,465	35	572	258	44	77	137	396	435	64	109	45
1919	3,113	251	1,660	353	206	406	237	1,933	225		1,668	40	686	304	59	83	162	426	196	104	161	57

TABLE 1 (*Continued*)
SERVICES: 1900–1970
CONSUMER EXPENDITURES
(MILLIONS OF DOLLARS)

	PERSONAL BUSINESS							TRANSPORTATION						EDUCATION						FOREIGN TRAVEL		
Year	Total	Broker-age	Banks	Life Ins	Legal Ser-vices	Fu-neral Exps	Other	Total	Auto-Re-pair	Local	Inter-city	Other	Recre-ation Total	Total	Higher	Elem and Scdy	Other	Reli-gious Activ-ity	Wel-fare	Total	U.S. Resi-dents +	Foreign Resi-dents −
1920	3,179	300	1,425	436	255	497	266	2,128	211	1,876		41	852	367	73	95	199	504	298	181	249	68
1921	3,033	276	1,382	431	302	405	237	2,003	173	1,793		37	872	421	91	110	220	553	253	185	262	77
1922	3,141	344	1,358	468	329	415	229	2,082	278	1,045/	707	52	902	459	108	118	233	596	253	256	318	62
1923	3,342	406	1,327	564	314	496	235	2,348	441	1,077	757	73	957	480	123	123	234	640	255	267	340	73
1924	3,455	422	1,403	572	323	502	233	2,409	540	1,081	702	86	1,027	495	137	126	232	703	275	317	396	79
1925	3,762	515	1,459	659	360	530	239	2,531	649	1,097	683	102	1,112	529	152	134	243	762	239	369	454	85
1926	3,644	503	1,300	715	346	543	237	2,598	694	1,125	671	108	1,217	572	166	143	263	802	231	375	487	112
1927	3,952	547	1,465	757	385	551	247	2,558	706	1,120	618	114	1,385	602	186	149	267	836	336	407	523	116
1928	3,935	673	1,235	807	394	592	234	2,539	748	1,104	562	125	1,558	636	206	159	271	872	263	462	586	124
1929	4,158	756	1,278	874	402	607	241	2,562	776	1,117	535	134	1,696	664	219	162	283	912	284	490	632	142
1930	3,704	495	1,141	901	397	547	223	2,233	624	1,053	432	124	1,650	683	242	170	271	1,209		479	611	132
1931	3,311	318	1,017	884	410	480	202	1,886	509	921	335	121	1,533	665	251	185	229	1,125		347	445	98
1932	2,875	224	872	853	348	415	163	1,556	385	786	260	125	1,187	570	226	158	186	973		265	334	69
1933	2,832	340	757	846	334	387	168	1,462	392	720	232	118	1,072	479	203	121	155	872		188	258	70
1934	2,860	195	793	875	359	417	221	1,586	445	761	251	129	1,172	480	210	121	149	870		191	276	85
1935	3,043	213	792	974	371	440	253	1,662	457	790	274	141	1,261	503	224	122	157	862		197	303	100
1936	3,231	263	843	981	383	485	276	1,863	520	845	330	168	1,417	541	237	140	164	899		246	368	122
1937	3,430	243	876	1,025	402	508	376	1,953	543	871	358	181	1,570	594	243	174	177	900		293	433	140
1938	3,265	173	818	1,001	392	484	397	1,862	517	842	338	165	1,513	612	249	192	171	923		244	379	135
1939	3,313	158	817	1,014	407	499	418	2,021	596	878	359	188	1,548	620	259	195	166	938		189	333	144

1940	3,326	131	792	1,029	423	515	436	2,128	647	907	364	210	1,683	632	271	198	163	1,012	67	172	105
1941	3,501	114	852	1,040	450	554	491	2,410	772	978	429	231	1,836	692	278	208	206	1,060	95	189	94
1942	3,599	90	904	1,025	475	577	528	2,721	594	1,294	654	179	2,098	801	300	221	280	1,207	6	128	122
1943	3,968	187	948	1,074	493	643	623	3,424	558	1,646	1,034	186	2,416	936	345	239	352	1,428	3	143	140
1944	4,348	189	1,186	1,106	541	678	648	3,693	695	1,726	1,077	195	2,672	943	375	266	302	1,667	6	175	169
1945	4,656	285	1,325	1,090	590	714	652	4,027	957	1,746	1,107	217	2,979	936	377	299	260	1,735	64	267	203
1946	5,059	325	1,475	1,178	609	736	746	4,958	1,704	1,908	1,021	325	3,686	1,026	448	267	311	1,943	90	450	360
1947	5,426	235	1,474	1,417	668	822	810	5,314	1,961	1,927	975	451	3,773	1,243	585	316	342	1,984	179	597	418
1948	5,950	291	1,638	1,538	765	848	870	5,754	2,194	1,989	1,000	571	3,803	1,387	636	369	382	2,150	328	727	399
1949	6,210	262	1,738	1,598	836	879	897	5,909	2,373	1,951	932	653	3,797	1,507	692	399	416	2,150	399	850	451
1950	6,858	454	1,921	1,755	874	896	958	6,175	2,509	1,934	872	860	3,837	1,618	725	440	453	2,282	439	920	481
1951	7,443	436	2,104	1,911	942	971	1,079	6,748	2,820	1,965	995	968	3,925	1,748	749	501	498	2,437	356	924	568
1952	7,791	375	2,373	1,963	975	1,006	1,099	7,130	2,932	1,990	1,070	1,138	4,053	1,870	779	557	534	2,784	407	1,044	637
1953	8,445	366	2,726	2,105	1,023	1,046	1,179	7,802	3,258	2,008	1,084	1,452	4,197	1,999	820	611	568	2,929	471	1,174	703
1954	9,194	606	2,965	2,212	1,103	1,040	1,268	7,943	3,304	1,938	1,026	1,675	4,382	2,130	871	664	595	3,154	528	1,263	735
1955	10,049	732	3,248	2,428	1,192	1,100	1,349	8,153	3,619	1,933	1,052	1,549	4,738	2,339	948	731	660	3,257	626	1,456	830
1956	10,985	690	3,648	2,795	1,223	1,152	1,477	8,609	3,918	1,971	1,115	1,605	5,132	2,574	1,036	807	731	3,677	704	1,624	920
1957	11,862	682	3,874	3,039	1,378	1,257	1,632	9,014	4,225	1,987	1,167	1,635	5,198	2,853	1,154	905	794	3,860	741	1,738	997
1958	12,768	884	4,074	3,210	1,531	1,328	1,741	9,305	4,387	1,917	1,145	1,856	5,394	3,140	1,282	1,006	852	4,178	854	1,900	1,046
1959	13,872	1,138	4,532	3,212	1,706	1,381	1,903	10,097	4,805	1,971	1,233	2,088	5,839	3,417	1,432	1,105	880	4,434	975	2,113	1,138
1960	14,974	1,035	5,142	3,500	1,754	1,508	2,035	10,781	5,198	2,001	1,308	2,274	6,222	3,718	1,597	1,218	903	4,748	1,230	2,317	1,087
1961	16,021	1,430	5,313	3,688	1,998	1,471	2,121	10,648	4,973	1,953	1,367	2,355	6,561	4,028	1,794	1,331	903	4,926	1,219	2,319	1,100
1962	16,481	1,238	5,420	3,897	2,105	1,575	2,246	11,024	5,200	1,981	1,478	2,365	6,801	4,392	2,018	1,452	922	5,082	1,497	2,556	1,059
1963	18,422	1,421	6,229	4,528	2,245	1,669	2,330	11,427	5,591	1,977	1,468	2,391	7,167	4,736	2,128	1,623	985	5,262	1,707	2,840	1,183
1964	20,055	1,614	6,915	4,865	2,432	1,712	2,517	11,646	5,590	1,988	1,607	2,461	7,609	5,199	2,403	1,733	1,063	5,678	1,670	2,988	1,318
1965	21,879	1,991	7,584	5,178	2,631	1,755	2,740	12,585	6,122	2,017	1,781	2,665	8,004	5,927	2,858	1,816	1,253	5,972	1,885	3,334	1,449
1966	24,287	2,390	8,562	5,619	2,983	1,823	2,910	13,602	6,419	2,099	1,944	3,140	8,452	6,608	3,258	1,923	1,427	6,421	1,922	3,582	1,660
1967	26,182	2,747	9,274	5,942	3,155	1,861	3,203	14,475	6,637	2,216	2,209	3,413	9,030	7,576	3,750	2,067	1,759	6,948	2,475	4,196	1,721
1968	29,532	3,401	10,689	6,583	3,290	2,024	3,545	15,533	7,292	2,266	2,452	3,523	9,686	8,690	4,230	2,285	2,175	7,605	2,321	4,179	1,858
1969	33,277	2,942	13,182	7,476	3,602	2,090	3,985	16,634	7,948	2,386	2,747	3,553	10,416	9,536	4,708	2,444	2,384	8,084	2,609	4,747	2,138
1970	35,314	2,171	14,634	7,948	4,121	2,179	4,261	18,268	8,719	2,505	3,021	4,023	11,166	10,363	5,244	2,625	2,494	8,601	3,039	5,460	2,421

TABLE 2
SERVICES, 1900–1970
(IN BILLIONS OF CURRENT AND 1958 DOLLARS)

	TOTAL SERVICES		HOUSING		OTHER SERVICES	
	Current	*$ '58*	*Current*	*$ '58*	*Current*	*$ '58*
1900	5.329	26.1	2.160	4.7	3.169	21.4
01	5.806	28.0	2.366	5.1	3.440	22.9
02	6.008	28.2	2.354	5.1	3.654	23.1
03	6.417	29.2	2.505	5.1	3.912	24.1
04	6.875	30.4	2.755	5.4	4.120	25.0
05	7.365	32.2	2.891	5.6	4.474	26.6
06	8.129	34.2	3.354	6.4	4.775	27.8
07	8.420	33.6	3.417	6.3	5.003	27.3
08	8.518	33.6	3.451	6.5	5.067	27.1
09	8.926	34.7	3.591	6.9	5.335	27.8
1910	9.456	36.2	3.793	7.2	5.663	29.0
11	9.857	37.2	3.842	7.4	6.015	29.8
12	10.254	38.1	4.018	7.7	6.236	30.4
13	10.685	39.2	4.109	7.7	6.576	31.5
14	11.041	39.9	4.256	8.0	6.785	31.9
15	11.342	40.3	4.433	8.2	6.909	32.1
16	12.400	42.2	4.757	8.7	7.643	33.5
17	13.669	43.7	5.157	9.5	8.512	34.2
18	15.435	45.0	5.651	10.3	9.784	34.7
19	17.437	44.1	6.480	10.9	10.957	33.2
1920	20.394	42.8	7.818	11.2	12.576	31.6
21	20.342	41.6	7.668	9.5	12.674	32.1
22	22.198	43.1	7.894	9.5	13.304	33.6
23	22.962	44.8	8.806	10.4	14.156	34.4
24	24.261	46.0	9.390	10.7	14.871	35.3
25	25.895	48.3	9.926	11.2	15.969	37.1
26	26.871	49.4	10.471	12.0	16.400	37.4
27	28.299	50.8	10.787	12.5	17.512	38.3
28	29.103	51.9	11.149	13.3	17.954	38.6
29	30.324	54.0	11.530	14.1	18.794	39.9
1930	28.703	51.5	11.050	13.9	17.653	37.6
31	26.023	49.4	10.291	13.7	15.732	35.7
32	22.202	45.9	9.011	13.4	13.191	32.5
33	20.069	46.0	7.907	13.5	12.162	32.5
34	20.431	46.1	7.602	13.7	12.829	32.4
35	21.266	47.9	7.702	13.8	13.564	34.1
36	22.751	50.5	8.011	14.1	14.740	36.4
37	24.358	52.0	8.533	14.3	15.825	37.7
38	24.281	50.9	8.936	14.5	15.345	36.4
39	25.048	52.5	9.139	14.9	15.909	37.6

	TOTAL SERVICES		HOUSING		OTHER SERVICES	
	Current	*$ '58*	*Current*	*$ '58*	*Current*	*$ '58*
1940	26.041	54.4	9.446	15.4	16.595	39.0
41	28.075	56.3	10.167	16.2	17.908	40.1
42	30.801	58.5	10.957	17.0	19.844	41.5
43	34.167	61.8	11.485	17.7	22.682	44.1
44	37.189	64.7	12.049	18.4	25.140	46.3
45	39.754	67.7	12.479	18.8	27.275	48.9
46	45.269	72.1	13.879	20.4	31.390	51.7
47	49.839	73.4	15.665	22.3	34.174	51.1
48	54.663	75.8	17.535	23.5	37.128	52.3
49	57.630	77.6	19.252	25.0	38.378	52.6
1950	62.422	81.8	21.286	26.8	41.136	55.0
51	67.865	84.8	23.853	28.8	44.012	56.0
52	73.395	87.8	26.476	30.7	46.919	57.1
53	79.929	91.1	29.315	32.3	50.614	58.8
54	85.380	94.8	31.664	33.9	53.716	60.9
55	91.433	99.3	33.738	35.7	57.695	63.6
56	98.493	104.1	36.020	37.4	62.473	66.7
57	105.048	108.0	38.506	39.3	66.542	68.7
58	112.036	112.0	41.127	41.1	70.909	70.9
59	120.278	116.8	43.654	42.9	76.624	73.9
1960	128.652	121.6	46.305	44.9	82.347	76.7
61	135.069	125.6	48.717	46.6	86.352	78.0
62	142.960	131.1	51.950	49.1	91.010	82.0
63	152.422	137.4	55.410	51.8	97.012	85.6
64	163.301	144.2	59.298	54.8	104.003	89.6
65	175.472	152.5	63.509	58.1	111.963	94.4
66	188.646	159.4	67.506	60.8	121.140	98.6
67	203.978	167.0	71.848	63.5	132.130	103.5
68	221.334	174.4	77.311	66.6	144.023	107.8
69	242.744	182.2	84.141	69.9	158.603	112.3
1970	262.567	187.2	90.926	72.6	171.641	114.6

TABLE 3
SERVICES 1900–1970
PERCENT DISTRIBUTION

Year*	Grand Total	Care of Clothes	Personal Care	HOUSING					HOUSEHOLD OPERATION							MEDICAL			
				Total	Owner	Tenant	Farm	Other	Total	Gas	Elec	Water etc.	Phone	D.S.	Other	Total	MD's+	Hosp	Hlth. Ins
1900	100.00%	5.49%	1.04%	40.03%	18.99%	14.91%	5.47%	0.65%	11.77%	1.49%	0.30%	0.91%	0.30%	7.74%	1.02%	4.80%	4.48%	0.29%	0.04%
1910	100.00	6.18	1.13	39.75	17.62	16.64	4.76	2.73	12.15	1.75	0.59	0.90	0.74	7.22	0.96	5.51	4.87	0.58	0.05
1920	100.00	5.30	1.25	37.76	19.15	13.62	4.17	0.82	11.18	2.00	1.23	0.76	1.12	5.20	0.88	7.39	6.18	1.03	0.18
1930	100.00	3.97	1.79	38.65	19.43	15.40	3.00	0.82	13.44	1.95	2.29	1.02	2.00	5.11	1.07	7.35	5.57	1.41	0.36
1940	100.00	3.88	2.02	36.32	16.67	15.90	2.84	0.91	15.24	2.13	3.44	1.35	2.38	4.53	1.41	8.35	5.71	1.99	0.65
1950	100.00	4.42	1.74	34.27	19.79	11.11	2.38	0.99	15.15	1.90	3.41	0.95	3.11	4.04	1.74	10.46	6.40	3.13	0.93
1960	100.00	2.84	1.87	36.11	23.92	9.54	1.55	1.10	15.43	2.48	3.94	1.00	3.52	2.89	1.61	11.52	6.45	3.98	1.10
1970	100.00	2.17	1.57	34.62	22.69	9.62	1.11	1.21	13.85	2.00	3.75	0.94	3.77	1.84	1.55	14.74	7.35	6.42	0.98
Changes																			
1900 to 1970		−3.32	+.53	−5.41	−3.70	−5.29	−4.36	+.56	+.208	+.51	+.345	+.03	+3.47	−5.90	+.53	+9.94	+2.87	+6.13	+.94

*3 year averages. Centered on given year, except for 1901 and 1970
Source: Table 1.

TABLE 3

SERVICES 1900–1970 (CONTINUED)
(PERCENT DISTRIBUTION)

| | PERSONAL BUSINESS | | | | | | | TRANSPORTATION | | | | |
Year	Total	Broker-age	Banks	Life Ins	Legal	Fu-neral	Other	Total	Auto Rep	Local	Inner-city	Other
1900	15.32%	1.54%	6.01%	1.92%	1.44%	3.35%	1.05%	8.74%	0.01%	8.70%		0 04%
1910	13.30	1.25	5.01	1.64	1.18	3 17	1.04	10.04	0.27	9.67		0.10
1920	16.03	1 42	7 68	2.10	1 31	2 25	1.27	10.42	1.05	9.17		0.20
1930	13.14	1.84	4.04	3.13	1.42	1.92	0.78	7.86	2.24	3.63	1.53	0.45
1940	12.81	0.51	3.11	3.89	1.62	1.98	1.70	8.29	2 55	3.49	1 46	0.79
1950	10.91	0 61	3.07	2 80	1.41	1.46	1.56	10 02	4 10	3.11	1.49	1.32
1960	11.68	0.94	3.90	2.71	1.42	1.14	1.58	8.21	3.90	1.54	1.02	1.75
1970	13 45	−.83	5 59	3.03	1 57	0.83	1.62	6.96	3.33	0 95	1.15	1.53

Changes, 1900–1970

	1.87	−.71	− 51	+1 11	+.13	−2.52	+.57	−1.78	+3.32	−6.60		+1 49

| Recre-ation | EDUCATION | | | | Rel Act | Wel-fare | FOREIGN TRAVEL | | |
	Total	Higher	Ele-mtry	Other			Total	+ U.S	− Frn
2.69%	1.91%	0.25%	0.63%	1.03%	3.80%	1.70%	2.71%	2.86%	0.15%
3.08	1.81	0.30	0.53	0.97	2.73	1.03	3.29	3.73	0 44
4 14	1.88	0.38	0.50	1.00	2 55	1.28	0.81	1.16	0.35
5.74	2.37	0.84	0 61	0 92	4.15		1.55	1.98	0.44
6 40	2.46	1.02	0.76	0.68	3.80		0.44	0.88	0 43
6 15	2.59	1.15	0 71	0 73	3.66		0 64	1.43	0.80
4.85	2 91	1.26	0 95	0.70	3 67		0.89	1.76	0.87
4.25	3 95	2.00	1.00	0.95	3.28		1 16	2 08	0 92

+1.56	+2.04	+1.75	+.37	−.08		−2.22	−1 55	−.78	+ 77

TABLE 4
SERVICE PRICE DEFLATORS
(1958 = 1.000)

	Services except Housing	Housing
1900	.148	.455
01	.150	.465
02	.158	.460
03	.162	.487
04	.165	.513
05	.168	.519
06	.172	.525
07	.183	.546
08	.187	.529
09	.192	.519
10	.195	.529
11	.202	.519
12	.205	.519
13	.209	.535
14	.213	.535
15	.215	.539
16	.228	.546
17	.249	.541
18	.282	.550
19	.330	.596
20	.398	.700
21	.395	.804
22	.396	.828
23	.411	.849
24	.421	.879
25	.430	.883
26	.439	.874
27	.457	.861
28	.465	.840
29	.471	.820
1958	1.000	1.000

TABLE 5

SERVICE EXPENDITURES, 1900–1929
ALTERNATE ESTIMATES

	TOTALS (MILLIONS OF CURRENT DOLLARS)						INDICES (1929 = 100.0)					
	(1)	(2)	(3)	(4)	(5)	(6)	(7)	(8)	(9)	(10)	(11)	(12)
	Present	*Kuznets*					*Present*	*Kuznets*				
	Esti-	*5 year*		*Kendrick*			*Esti-*	*5 year*		*Kendrick*		
Year	*mates*	*Average*	*Var III*	*Kuznets*	*Lough*	*Barger*	*mates*	*Average*	*Var III*	*Kuznets*	*Lough*	*Barger*
1900	$5.0	$4.8		$4.7			17.2	15.6		14.0		
1901	5.5	5.2		5.3			19.0	17.0		15.8		
1902	5.6	5.6		5.6			19.3	18.2		16.6		
1903	6 0	6.1		6.1			20.7	19.7		18.0		
1904	6.5	6.5		6.3			22.4	21.3		18.7		
1905	6.9	7.1		6.9			23.8	23.0		20.3		
1906	7.6	7.4		7.8			26.2	24.2		23.0		
1907	7.9	8.0		8.3			27 2	26.0		24.6		
1908	8.1	8.5		7.9			27.9	27.6		23.3		
1909	8.5	8.9		9.0	9.0		29.3	29.0		26.6	30.7	
1910	9.0	9.3		9.5			31.0	30.4		28.1		
1911	9.4	9.9		9.8			32.4	32.3		28.9		
1912	9.7	10.4		10.6			33.4	33.9		31.3		
1913	10.1	10.9		11.2			34.8	35.5		33.0		
1914	10.4	11 7		11.2	10.1		35.9	38 1		33.2	34.7	
1915	10 6	12.6		11.0			36.6	41.0		32.7		
1916	11.3	13.8		13.1			39.0	45.0		38.8		
1917	12.5	14.8		15.3			43.1	48.2		45.2		
1918	14.0	16.5		17.0			48.3	53.7		50.4		
1919	15.8	18.5	16 3	18 4	15.5		54.5	60 3	48.8	54 5	53.3	
1920	19.0	20.2	20.6	22.4			65.5	65.8	61.7	66.2		
1921	19.0	22.0	24 1	21.6	16.9	19.5	65.5	71.7	72.2	63.9	58.2	71.8
1922	19 8	24.6	23.5	22.9		20 3	68.2	80 1	70.4	67.6		74.8
1923	21.6	25.6	25 5	25.9	19.8	22.3	74.5	83.4	76.3	76 8	67.8	82.0
1924	22.9	26.7	29.2	27.4		23.5	79.0	87.0	87.4	81.2		86.5
1925	24.4	27.9	25 9	27 3	22.8	24.3	84 1	90.9	77.5	80.7	78.2	89.6
1926	25.6	29.1	29.3	29.8		25.2	88.3	94.8	87.7	88.2		92.7
1927	26.8	29.9	29.7	29.6	25.9	25.8	92.4	97.4	88.9	87.7	88.8	95.0
1928	27.9	31.0	31 4	31.5		26.4	96.2	101.0	94.0	93.2		97 1
1929	29.0	30.7	33 4	33.8	29.1	27.2	100.0	100.0	100.0	100.0	100.0	100.0

Sources: Col.1. Present estimates less services of financial intermediaries.

Cols. 2 and 8. Simon Kuznets, *Capital in the American Economy* (1961) Pp 565–566, col 8.

Cols 3 and 9. *Ibid*, P. 502 Col. (5).

Cols 4 and 10. John Kendrick, *Productivity Trends in the United States* (1961).

Table A-11b, col. 1, gives Kuznets' annual consumption totals. To these the ratio of services in consumption were applied using data from Kuznets, *Op. Cit*, p. 561, col 4 and p 565, Col. 8.

Cols. 5 and 11. William H. Lough, *High-Level Consumption* (1935), pp. 239–245 Intangible items.

Cols. 6 and 12. Harold Barger, *Outlay and Income in the United States, 1921–1938* (1942), pp. 228–229.

TABLE 6

Service Expenditures, 1900–1929:
Alternative Estimates of Change

PERCENT CHANGE IN SERVICE ESTIMATES

| Percentage Changes | Present Estimates | Kuznets | | | Barger | Lough |
		5 Year Average	Variant I	Variant III		
Decennial						
1919–1929	83.5%	65.9%	107.3%	104.9%	—	87.8%
Annual						
1920–1921	0.0	8.9	16.8	17.0	—	—
1921–1922	4.2	11.8	−2.5	−2.5	4.2	—
1922–1923	9.1	4.1	8.6	8.5	9.7	—
1923–1924	6.0	4.3	14.5	14.5	5.5	—
1924–1925	6.6	4.5	−11.4	−11.3	3.6	—
1925–1926	4.9	4.3	13.4	13.1	3.4	—
1926–1927	4.7	2.7	1.2	1.4	2.5	—
1927–1928	4.1	3.7	6.0	5.7	2.2	—
1928–1929	3.9	−1.0	7.6	6.4	3.0	—
Biennial						
1919–1921	20.3	18.9	47.4	47.9	—	9.3
1921–1923	13.7	16.4	5.9	5.8	14.3	16.6
1923–1925	13.0	9.0	1.4	1.6	9.2	15.2
1925–1927	9.8	7.2	14.7	14.7	6.0	13.6
1927–1929	8.2	2.7	14.1	12.5	5.3	12.6

Source: Table 5

INDEX

INDEX

LIBRARY OF CONGRESS CATALOGING IN PUBLICATION DATA

Lebergott, Stanley.
  The American economy.

  Includes index.
    1. Income distribution—United States.
  2. Wealth—United States. 3. Poor—United States.
  I. Title.
  HC110.I5L38   339.2′0973   75-4461
  ISBN 0-691-04210-1